Blue State Blues

Blue State Blues

DAVID R. SLAVITT

Wesleyan University Press   MIDDLETOWN, CONNECTICUT

Published by
Wesleyan University Press
Middletown, CT 06459
www.wesleyan.edu/wespress
© 2006 by David R. Slavitt
Printed in the United States of America
5 4 3 2 1

Library of Congress Cataloging-in-Publication Data
Slavitt, David R., 1935–
Blue state blues / David R. Slavitt.
    p.   cm.
Includes bibliographical references.
ISBN -13: 978-0-8195-6806-9 (cloth : alk. paper)
ISBN -10: 0-8195-6806-6 (cloth : alk. paper)
1. Slavitt, David R., 1935– 2. Political candidates—Massachusetts—
Biography. 3. Massachusetts. General Court. House of Representatives
—Elections, 2002. 4. Slavitt, David R., 1935-—Political activity.
5. Massachusetts—Politics and government—1951– 6. Elections—
Massachusetts—History—21st century. 7. Political campaigns—
Massachusetts—History—21st century. I. Title.
F71.22.S58A3 2006
974.4′043092—dc22   2005028914

The author is grateful to the *Boston Globe*, the *Harvard Crimson*, the
Somerville News, the *Jewish Advocate*, the *Somerville Journal*, and the
Cambridge Chronicle for permission to reprint material from their
publications.

For Evan

When a candidate for public office faces the voters he does not face men of sense; he faces a mob of men whose chief distinguishing mark is that they are quite incapable of weighing ideas, or even of comprehending any save the most elemental—men whose whole thinking is done in terms of emotion, and whose dominant emotion is dread of what they cannot understand. So confronted, the candidate must either bark with the pack, or count himself lost. His one aim is to disarm suspicion, to arouse confidence in his orthodoxy, to avoid challenge. If he is a man of convictions, or enthusiasm, or self-respect, it is cruelly hard. . . .

H. L. MENCKEN, *The Baltimore Evening Sun*, July 26, 1920

Part
One

★ ★

It was my son Evan's suggestion. In the spring of 2002, he was running as a Republican for attorney general of Massachusetts. He thought I might run for the legislature and we would be a father-and-son team, both of us standing for office on the same ballot. There are relatively few of these in American politics. We—or, more important, he—might get some added media attention. I called the state Republican Party to ask if anyone was running in my district, and when it turned out that someone was—a young woman from MIT—I thanked them and forgot about it.

As it turned out, Evan was unable to meet the preposterously high requirement of ten thousand signatures one needs to qualify to get onto the ballot for that office. The party ought to have been of more help, but their operatives were running around getting signatures for Kerry Healey, the candidate for lieutenant governor who was Mitt Romney's last-minute choice as a running mate. Evan was the nominee by acclamation of the Republican convention in Lowell, but that didn't count. So he saved himself a great deal of effort and money, and his campaign ended in June rather than November. Tom Reilly, the incumbent, was unbeatable anyway, as Evan knew perfectly well. But because of his wifty idea, my name had been floated, however briefly, and a year later, a young man from the party called me to ask whether I wanted to run as state representative for the Twenty-sixth Middlesex District against Tim Toomey.

Well, why not? My chances of winning were negligible. Toomey is almost a cartoon version of the Irish pol, a graduate of Suffolk University who is a member of both the Cambridge City Council and the state legislature. A Democrat, he is, as an Irish Catholic, more conservative than most Massachusetts voters. He is pro-life and presumably against gay marriage and even same-sex civil unions. He is vulnerable as a "double-dipper," earning $56,000 a year from his city council seat and another $53,000 a year (plus perks) from his state rep job. He is not eloquent or even reliably articulate. He's just Timmy Toomey, who mostly does what he's told (by Speaker Tom Finneran) but is accessible to voters complaining about potholes.

It would be amusing, I thought, to campaign against him, even—or especially—to debate. (I was a member of the Yale Varsity Debating Team.) I am a writer, have published eighty books, and have taught at Columbia, Penn, Princeton, and Bennington. Wouldn't I better represent Cambridge, with all its pretensions, than Toomey?

But Cambridge is anti-intellectual, or, say, anti-Harvard. (I thought, for a while, that I could run as "A Yalie for Cambridge!" but the Twenty-sixth Middlesex includes a swath of Somerville, which messes up the epigram.) Toomey's positions, described on his website, involve a Robin Hood gangsterism, robbing the rich (Harvard and MIT) for the benefit of the undeserving poor. I think that Harvard and MIT are what make Cambridge interesting and important, and without them, we would be just another suburb of Boston, less grungy, maybe, than Everett or Revere, but not at all glorious. Cambridge, and Somerville, too, ought to be represented by someone who can recognize the obvious.

What is involved is strenuous. I shall have to go out and glad-hand people, as my cousin Louis, a New York politico, has taught me to do: you grasp the hand firmly, stand slightly closer than you might normally do, look directly into the eyes of the person you are greeting, and say, almost too fervently, "Hi, I'm David Slavitt. Glad to know you."

★ ★ ★ I bestirred myself and telephoned the National Organization for Women and NARAL Pro-Choice Massachusetts to let them know that I'm pro-choice and planning to run. NOW's political action person wasn't in, but at NARAL, I got through to Melissa Kogut, executive director of the Massachusetts chapter, told her who I am, and tried to persuade her that I'm not a cuckoo and even have a chance, in a presidential election year, of winning. I described myself as a "Schwarzenegger Republican without the groping," a line I'll probably use again.

The conversation left me feeling optimistic—which is dangerous. Friends have told me that I should of course run and that it might be fun, but that I should on no account entertain fantasies of defeating a Democrat here in Cambridge. I promised them—and myself—that I'd remember that and maintain some connection with the real world, but it is impossible, when campaigning, not to try to persuade people from whom one wants money and other kinds of support that one has a chance, and hard not to be persuaded by what one hears oneself saying. Con men first con themselves.

★ ★ ★ What complicates the landscape is the news that Avi Green, who was campaign manager for state senator Jarrett Barrios, may run against Toomey in the Democratic primary. Two years ago, Paul Lachelier of the Green Party, more liberal than Toomey, got more than a third of the vote (3,718, or 37.3 percent, to Toomey's 6,253, or 62.7 percent). From what I hear, the Greens have agreed not to field a candidate in 2004 and to support Avi Green. If Green wins in the primary—which is unlikely– it will be an open seat that he and I will be fighting for. On the other hand, if Toomey wins, it will be after having spent time and money fighting for the nomination, and he may be vulnerable to a candidate more liberal, at least socially, than he is. There must have been times when Quixote thought he might actually beat those windmills.

★ ★ ★ I have a certain literary reputation, but fame is not a perk of poets. My cousin Louis suggested that I write letters to newspapers, although that is a hard way to get "known," and I can't say that I remember the names at the bottom of the letters in today's paper, never mind yesterday's. Or I could try, he said, to get the governor to appoint me to some commission so that I might appear to have had some practical experience. I have asked Evan to make the appropriate inquiries. (He is counsel to the state GOP and knows most of the players.) It crosses my mind that if Governor Romney can't or won't do that much to help out a Republican candidacy, that might be an excuse for me to withdraw. But am I looking for excuses? Am I afraid of this?

Well, of course, I am, a little. I worry that I am not physically strong enough to stand at subway stops and introduce myself to passersby with the required cheerfulness. I have arthritis and back pain (and a handicap-symbol placard for the car). I have fits of depression, not so bad as Churchill's, but not trivial. On the other hand, campaigning will get me out of the house, which is a way to keep gloom at bay.

If the governor were to appoint me to some commission, I should put on a suit and tie and go to the meetings. But I'd lose some of the charm of the amateur. Poets don't generally run for political office. That I am literary and intellectual makes me an amusing choice, a way of protesting the status quo. (The only poet I know who has been a state legislator is William Jay Smith, who served in the Vermont House.)

★ ★ ★ I have a rough draft of a flier to take to the printer. It announces that I am pro-choice and support civil unions. The courts have spoken about abortion and will continue to do so (the ban on "partial-birth abortion" is likely to be overturned because it fails to mention the health of the mother), and the courts will decide about civil unions, which will be the cue for much rabble-rousing and even an attempt to amend the state constitution to define—and protect!—marriage. These same homophobes would restore the laws against buggery, if they could, but the Supreme Court has ruled that that is no longer a crime, so the question now is one about the deprivation of a class of citizens of their civil rights. Political theorists argue that such decisions ought to be left to legislatures, which are most directly connected to the electorate and speak "for the people." The trouble is that these bodies are no longer representative, having rigged the game so that incumbents are almost always re-elected. The public is more liberal, in any event, than their representatives, whose mouths drip mean-spirited pieties as they appeal not to the best but the worst in voters' hearts and minds. Prejudice and bigotry arouse more energy than tolerance and decency any day.

★ ★ ★ The worst part of the abortion discussion is that it is a debate in which both sides have been polarized to prevent people from realizing—or saying publicly—that both sides are right. It is not the business of the government to intrude in a woman's decision about what to do with her body, but neither is it comfortable to contemplate the million pregnancies that are terminated each year (roughly three hundred abortions for every thousand live births). Abortion is a distressing method of birth control, as NOW and NARAL cannot admit. My assumption is that most women who decide to terminate a pregnancy do so only after deep and troubling thought. Any women who are not troubled would be mothers that prompt one to think of Sophocles' dictum about how it is better never to have been born. One can't say such things on the hustings.

What politics lacks in seriousness, it makes up for in . . . reality. There is an engagement with vicissitude that is almost entirely mindless but unimpeachably real. Events of the day as they affect the mood of the electorate have a greater impact on a candidate's prospects than anything he or she may say or do. One exerts the effort and tries to avoid gaffes—which will be difficult for me.

How delighted Toomey and his people would be if they could campaign against a poet who talks about "engagement with vicissitude." And how much more delicious for them if they could make known to the public some of my more eccentric views—as, for example, my doubts about the worth—or, indeed, even the possibility—of universal literacy. Edmund Wilson once told me that this was an experiment that began in the 1870s in the UK and, as he believed, didn't work. The only discernible result was that, in the 1890s, the yellow press was born.

★ ★ ★ I have circulated my draft flier to a few Republican activists in Cambridge—some of whom complain that I am too liberal. They object to my being pro-choice and in favor of civil unions. What are my chances if I cannot even mobilize these Republican dreamers? They ought to be delighted that someone is coming forward willing to do the work of getting the signatures to get my name on the ballot and to run. What I would need in order to win, as a PBS program about JFK made clear, is vast amounts of money—enough to hire three other guys named Tim Toomey to confuse the electorate and divide the vote, as Kennedy did in his first run for congress against Joseph Russo hiring another Joseph Russo and sending out people to get enough signatures to get him onto the ballot. Kennedy got more votes than either Russo but fewer than the two Russos together. The question that keeps arising—and that I fight against—is why bother to run against even one Tim Toomey? The truth is difficult not to acknowledge: anyone good enough to elect to office is too good to run.

★ ★ ★ The Supreme Judicial Court of Massachusetts announced yesterday, November 18, in a four-to-three decision, that it is illegal under the state constitution to ban gay marriages. Seven gay couples had sued the Commonwealth's Department of Public Health for having denied them marriage licenses. Given the United States Supreme Court's decision some months ago decriminalizing homosexual acts, I can't imagine what else they could have done. It is depressing that the decision was so narrow. But it gives me an issue, for there will be homophobes and demagogues who will cynically invoke the "sanctity of marriage," and there will be attempts to amend the state constitution to reverse the decision. This makes someone with my views attractive to the Log Cabin Club (a group of gay Republicans), Gays and Lesbians Against Discrimination (GLAD), Out Somerville, and all the organized gay groups that will not only vote for me but may contribute money. It also puts me in opposition to President Bush and to Governor Romney, whom I heard yesterday say he opposed gay marriage, invoking "three thousand years of recorded history" of marriage as a bond between "a man and a woman."

★ ★ ★ The telephone rang and I had my first political interview, with Deborah Eisner of the *Cambridge Chronicle*, who asked for my views on the SJC decision. I'm a part of the conversation, albeit a minor one, and it is flattering to be consulted.

★ ★ ★ Romney's position is . . . waffling and self-serving. In this morning's *Boston Globe*, Rick Klein discusses the political ramifications of the gay-marriage ruling. Klein has a dry sense of humor. He cites Eric Fehrnstrom, Romney's communication director: "The governor is not a social crusader. He did not run for office to crusade for or against gay rights. . . . But sometimes issues are forced upon you, and they require a response. . . . The governor has taken a consistent, principled position." Whenever a spokesman says his man has a "consistent, principled position," it is only because he obviously doesn't. The only clear principle I can see is that the governor wants very much to get reelected in 2006 and is hoping to keep alive the option of running for the White House. An amendment to ban same-sex marriage would come up for passage in 2006, which is, to say the least, awkward.

★ ★ ★ My flier has a line saying that I am in favor of "excellence in education." It is a line I've seen in the brochures and handouts of city council candidates. (Who is against excellence or, even more refreshing, in favor of mediocrity?) What I mean by it is that public schools should be able to throw out troublemakers and bullies. I would close schools that fail to meet rigorous standards. After the eighth grade, education isn't a right but a privilege, and we waste time and money trying to teach pigs to sing. Fortunately, the shorthand for all those elitist views is opaque and unexceptionable, and with my teaching background, it looks plausible for me to have a position on the subject, however eccentric.

★ ★ ★ I went to a bar in Brighton today with Evan to watch The Game, and during the *longueurs* we talked about my campaign. He thinks that I have a real issue to run with in this gay-marriage decision. His advice is that I should not settle for "civil unions" but go for the full Monty. His view is that Governor Romney, Speaker Finneran, and Representative Toomey have sworn an oath to preserve and protect the constitution of the Commonwealth, and the Supreme Judicial Court has decided what that means. They cannot waffle or drag their heels without violating the oath they took. As Evan put it, "This isn't constitutional law 101; this is politics." I have an issue and should exploit it.

The City of Cambridge, it turns out, has four or five gay city council members, and there has been talk during the past few days of the city's issuing marriage licenses to same-sex couples. It probably won't happen, but their discussion is an interesting gauge of local sentiment. Toomey may have a problem.

Yale advanced the ball by many more yards than Harvard, but the Crimson won, nevertheless. There may be a lesson in it—that luck is so important. Shrewdness and skill are what we emphasize, because we can take credit for them. Character counts—effort, persistence, and all that—but less than we'd like to suppose. Luck is beyond our control, and we're afraid of it, but we would be fools to deny the part it plays in our lives.

★ ★ ★ This morning's paper says that a six-months-long voter registration drive in Somerville got 103 Democrats, 94 independents, 86 Green Party members, and 8 Republicans (and 5 Libertarians). As far as I can tell, there is no GOP organization at all in Somerville. Other than forays to Davis Square to Redbones for barbecue, or McIntyre and Moore, a used bookstore I like, I am rarely in Somerville. I have never even driven through parts of the city that are in my district. I shall have to get up there. When I studied Greek at Harvard's Commission on Extensions, Lowell Edmunds explained how Greek gives an article to the names of kings (except king of Persia, from whom this courtesy is withheld) and important cities. One would say, The Paris, The Rome, The Boston, and probably The Cambridge, but just Somerville.

★ ★ ★ Dismaying news this morning from Iraq, which I cite here with embarrassment, because my campaign assumes the huge success of George W. Bush next year. This morning, two American soldiers were ambushed and killed by a mob of Iraqi teenagers, who shot them, pulled them (still alive) from their vehicle, smashed their heads with concrete blocks, and plundered their bloodied uniforms. Those scenes of a grateful populace presenting flowers to our troops that Rumsfeld and Wolfowitz imagined have not materialized. The Iraqis—or at least some of them—have proved to be an unruly, resentful mob. Never mind Viet Nam and "quagmires," but think of General Burgoyne's reports back to London about Washington's raggedy-ass troops.

I was never happy about the war: nobody was. But I more or less trusted Tom Friedman of the *New York Times*, who thought it could turn out to be a good thing, even without evidence of those WMDs Saddam was supposed to have—but only if we handled the transition well, which we don't seem to be doing. Democracy is not suited to limited warfare: the Hundred Years' War would be difficult for us to manage. Howard Dean has put all his chips on the peacenik position. I have heard him described as a combination of McGovern (antiwar) and Mondale (for higher taxes) and a sure loser, twice over. But McGovern's and Mondale's trouble was that they picked the wrong moments for their campaigns. If Bush goes down, my chances are diminished. Of course, that means I shall have someone to blame. But that will not be much consolation.

★ ★ ★ The poll results published in yesterday's *Globe* are surprising, showing that there is solid support in Massachusetts for the SJC's decision in the Goodrich case: of four hundred state residents, 53 percent oppose any kind of amendment to ban same-sex marriages. Romney, Attorney General Reilly, and, presumably, Speaker Finneran are all out of step. Where the voters and the courts are leading, the leaders will eventually have to follow.

★ ★ ★ There have been a number of e-mails from members of the Cambridge Ward—a nice word that suggests both a political party and a loony bin—about my views on gay marriage. Some conservatives are exercised. My reply yesterday, in part, was this:

> Marriage, until quite recently, was a horrid matter of property rights. Adultery, for instance, is the "adulteration" of the purity of the claim of one's children on one's estate. (The recent New Hampshire court decision about a wife's fooling around with her lesbian lover NOT being adultery because the legitimacy of her children was never in question is a consequence of this sordid and depressing history.) Men used to own their wives and their children. They don't anymore. And that's a good thing. So the tradition these people are invoking is a fantasy.
>
> Of course institutions evolve. Miscegenation used to be a crime. It isn't anymore. Is anyone outraged by that?
>
> No one is forcing anyone to turn gay and get married to a guy. This will affect only a small number of people. And it won't trouble straight men and women at all. —David R. Slavitt

The truth, though, is that I am beginning to be bored by the discussion: it has nothing to do with me. The attorney general's stupid remarks about how the Supreme Judicial Court ought not to be making social policy or deciding important questions like this with a four-to-three decision elicited from Evan the curt response, "That's why I ran against him." *Brown v. Board of Education? Roe v. Wade?* The courts are the only branch of government that can enable these sea changes. Legislatures are too clumsy, too hamstrung, too entrenched, and too beholden.

There is an interesting piece in this morning's *New York Times* by Pam Belluck about how some gays may not be so eager to get married. Some same-sex couples will "tie the knot and cash in with wedding presents from Tiffany and Crate & Barrel, but some will find it difficult to overcome their suspicion and resentment of what is basically a patriarchal institution, while others will feel some loyalty to the outsider status to which lesbians and gays were once relegated." And I admire them for that.

★ ★ ★ Yesterday, I went downtown to help Evan with his move into a larger suite of offices. I am glad he is doing well and was happy to help. His surprise for me was the set of papers I had to sign to open the David Slavitt Committee account. The next step is the public announcement, which involves the preparation of a media kit to send out to the *Globe*, the *Herald*, the *Phoenix*, and the *Cambridge Chronicle* and the *Somerville Journal*. And maybe to Jay Severin, the local conservative talkmeister, and Emily Rooney on *Greater Boston*, a PBS evening talk show that discusses politics.

What Matt St. Hilaire at the party headquarters in Boston tells me I'll need is a head shot, a press release announcing my candidacy and giving biographical information, and my reasons for running on a "push card"—a doorhanger without the hole. This means that a version of the flier has to get printed. My wife, Janet, will shoot a roll of black-and-white film and try for a decent head shot, and then we'll get it. The committee will be spending its first money, which is real. Scary, but exhilarating too.

★ ★ ★ After rather more labor than a page-and-a-half-long document ought to take, I have produced a draft that I've sent out for comments from friends and from my son:

David R. Slavitt for State Representative

FOR IMMEDIATE RELEASE   Contact: David R. Slavitt
January 8, 2004   617 000–0000
SLAVITT ANNOUNCES CANDIDACY:
A REPUBLICAN FOR CAMBRIDGE AND SOMERVILLE!

Poet, novelist, translator, essayist, and teacher David R. Slavitt has announced his candidacy for the 26th Middlesex district seat in the Massachusetts State Legislature. A proud novice in politics, he will be running for the seat presently held by Timothy J. Toomey, a veteran Cambridge pol now in his eighth term as a member of the Cambridge City Council and his seventh term as a state legislator.

Slavitt believes that, as an amateur without any political ambitions whatsoever, he is not beholden to special interests and can show independence and intelligence on Beacon Hill—qualities for which the General Court is not well known.

The thrust of his campaign will be that the two-party system is vital for the health of democratic government and that the tilt in Massachusetts is so severe as to free the legislators from any accountability or responsibility to the electorate.

Describing himself as a "Schwarzenegger Republican without the groping," Slavitt is a fiscal conservative and a social moderate. He is pro-choice, supports same-sex marriages, and, in the best Republican tradition, wants to limit the role of government in our lives. The first and most important order of business, however, is to challenge the Democratic hyper-majority in the General Court and to end the dictatorship of Thomas Finneran, who flaunts his power and flouts the will of the people on such issues as the Clean Elections law and English language immersion. Should he be elected, Slavitt sees his role on Beacon Hill as primarily that of a gadfly and an obstructionist—supporting gubernatorial vetoes, and criticizing the bloated power and the arrogance of the Democrats. If the legislature cannot serve the will of the people, he believes, it ought at least to be more amusing and entertaining—which is exactly what a poet can offer.

The people of Massachusetts view their representatives with a combination of contempt and dismay. And they are frustrated in having no way of removing any of the villains and clowns who have brought the Commonwealth to the brink of financial crisis. In their desperation, the people have elected Republican governors who can at least speak out against the excesses of the majority party. More Republicans—and more vocal Republicans—in the legislature will help meet this vital need for reform.

Slavitt, 68, graduated from Phillips Academy in 1952, earned a BA, Magna Cum Laude, from Yale University (1956), and has an MA from Columbia University (1957). From 1958 to 1965, he worked for *Newsweek*, where he was an associate editor and, for the last two years, the movie critic. Since 1965, he has been a free-lance writer and editor. He has published 29 novels, 17 collections of poetry, and 27 volumes of translations from the Greek, Latin,

Hebrew, Spanish, French, and Portuguese. (His *Re Verse: Essays on Poetry and Poets* and his translation of *The Regrets of Joachim du Bellay* will be published in the spring of this year by Northwestern University Press; his *Poems: New And Selected* will appear from L. S. U. Press in 2005.) He was co-editor of the Johns Hopkins Complete Roman Drama and of the Penn Complete Greek Drama. Slavitt has taught at Temple, Columbia, Penn, Princeton, and Bennington. He has received the award in literature from the American Academy and Institute of Arts and Letters.

He has three children and nine grandchildren, and he and his wife, Janet, live in Cambridge.

Paid for by the David Slavitt Committee

★ ★ ★ An invitation came in this morning from Governor Mitt Romney to a holiday dinner at the Seaport Hotel. It is another sign that this campaign is no mere mental exercise but that my fantasies have slopped over to lists kept by real workers in the party. This is not what we denizens of the imagination expect and is slightly unsettling. It is as if Pushkin had found on the mail tray one morning an invitation to the ball at which he could dance with Olga and Tatiana and sip champagne with Lensky, Onegin, and the rest.

I shall accept, of course.

★ ★ ★ I have received a daunting set of instructions from the party on how to run a campaign. I had thought I needed only 150 signatures on my petition to qualify to get my name on the ballot, but according to their recommendation that number is really 500. Two years ago, working on Evan's campaign, I went through the sordid business of standing out in front of the post office asking whether the passersby were registered in Massachusetts either as Republicans or as independents. I did it often enough so that I was recognized by the one-legged beggar who sits near the Massachusetts Avenue post office steps, sometimes wearing his artificial leg or sometimes, when contributions flag, going so far as to show his stump. And I got to know the homeless people who stand outside the Whole Foods Market on Prospect Street selling *Spare Change*.

Most of the people I accosted, though, were Democrats, or were Green Party, or were from out of state, or were not citizens. Several times I heard in a lovely Irish brogue, "Ah, no, Oi'm an illegal!" Once a fellow clad mostly in leather said that he'd like to sign but "I can't help you, pal. I'm a felon."

What has any of this to do with qualification for public service? Even if I get these signatures, there is the raising of money, an only slightly less demeaning form of begging. The campaign instructions tell me I will need $25,000 to make any kind of plausible run for a seat in the legislature. So far, I have two contributions of $25 each, barely enough for Evan to open the campaign account.

★ ★ ★ There are, in this morning's *Globe*, the results of a poll of the members of the General Court showing which senators and which state representatives would favor or oppose a constitutional amendment banning same-sex unions (marriages or civil unions). I was not surprised to see that 106 of the 200 were holding back to see which way the wind is blowing and how strongly. Speaker Thomas Finneran "has yet to comment on the SJC's ruling," the report noted, "and a spokesman said he may not do so until January, in the weeks immediately preceding the constitutional vote."

Of the 94 senators and representatives who did respond, 60 said they would oppose any bill that would block state recognition of anything other than a heterosexual couple as the "equivalent" of married. Thirty-one respondents said they would back it. Philip Travis of Rehoboth introduced such a bill last year, before the SJC decision. I have no idea who he is, but this is clearly troublesome to him. If gays can get married, and he is married, is he worried that people will think that he is the "equivalent" of gay? Does he feel that the sanctity of his union with his wife is under attack?

As a voter, I suppose I am pleased to read that Timothy J. Toomey, Jr., is opposing such an amendment. My hope, though, is that, torn between his beliefs and those of his constituents, Toomey will come out with some waffled position, for civil unions but against gay marriage. But even that would put him at odds with the letter read out in all the Catholic churches yesterday from the four Massachusetts bishops, who called the same-sex marriage ruling a "national tragedy" and urged Catholics to mobilize against it.

★ ★ ★ There are a relatively small number of lesbians and gays who want to take advantage of the SJC decision and get married, and it is unfortunate that they find themselves the subject of a political debate, which is adversarial, as all debates must be. By its nature, debate toys with issues, exploiting and distorting them so the debater can score points with a judge; serious discussion works in an altogether different way and is a collaborative search for truth without any sordid concern about who wins and who loses.

While I need to emphasize the grandeur of the two-party system, I begin to realize that there are serious intellectual disadvantages in the way this arrangement polarizes issues, exploiting anything that comes to hand for whatever electoral advantage it may offer and preventing compromise, or, rather, sending the business of compromise into closed-door sessions. But in an election, one cannot draw fine distinctions. Karl Rove, Bush's "brain," says that one should watch television reports of campaigns with the sound off. What counts is the size of the crowd, the setting, the quick picture.

The French and Italians have what we Americans think of as laughable coalitions of a great number of parties, which make for unstable governments cobbled together of various factions and splinter groups. This may not be such a bad thing, however. Jefferson would have approved, on the ground that the least government is the best government. Our two-party arrangement was not necessarily what the founding fathers had in mind, and political parties are nowhere mentioned in the Constitution.

I should rather be debating with Toomey about his Robin Hood attitude and his schemes for stealing from the rich (Harvard and MIT, primarily) and giving to the poor of Cambridge, in which he appeals to the worst instincts of the electorate. That this is theft doesn't appear to bother him. (Democrats call it "redistribution of wealth.") What Toomey says in position papers in his campaign for the city council seat is that he wants to tax the big guys, or make them pay more in the way of tax equivalents so that the rest of us can pay less. (This happens anyway, with the Cambridge real estate taxes set at a much higher rate for business than for residential property.) There is also class envy to which Toomey is appealing—many in Cambridge did not go to these schools and resent the presence of these enclaves of privilege. But I cannot say any of that.

★ ★ ★ Toomey, I am reliably informed, is gay. (He is at least what polite people used to call a "confirmed bachelor.") Not that I particularly care, one way or the other, but I do have to find out what his position is on the SJC decision. He is unlikely to march to the bishops' drumbeat, or . . . or is he? He's still pretty much in the closet, although apparently everyone knows (or everyone but me). Barrios is openly gay. And Avi Green, who worked on his campaign and is the other Democrat who'll be fighting Toomey? Is he gay too? Am I the straight candidate?

"Straight talk from Slavitt" is a tempting but unattractive slogan.

When I asked my informant about Toomey, he replied, "Oh, no, he's a loner," which is what neighbors say to television reporters about mass murderers— the obvious clue that more people ought to have noted. For a gay guy to be opposed to a woman's right to choose, though, seems . . . presumptuous?

★ ★ ★ In the end, my only unique position may turn out to be that I object to the ban the legislature left in place when they repealed the blue law against liquor sales on the Sabbath that prevents us in Massachusetts from ordering a Bloody Mary or a mimosa before noon at Sunday brunch. This may be frivolous but is something I believe in.

But there is no real need for any series of articulated positions, except to reassure the Cantabrigian lefties that I am not about to take away their freedoms and impose a police state here. What I have to remember is that I am running to restore two-party government in Massachusetts, which most people think of as a good thing.

I have to learn to stay "on message," a diminishing and vexatious habit in which one learns to avoid or evade difficult or irrelevant questions and hammer home one or two points. Mr. Toomey has his talking points—providing affordable housing for Cambridge (How? Undo the capitalist system and the free market?) and socking it to the rich universities. I have mine—the two-party system and an end to double-dipping. But as Toomey is almost certainly less intelligent than I am, he has the advantage, because his mind is much less likely than mine to skitter off in all directions.

★ ★ ★ I took note this morning of the announcement that Al Gore is endorsing Howard Dean for the Democratic nomination as presidential candidate. Senator Lieberman, in justified anger at his patron's betrayal, pointed out, on the *Today* show, that Dean is "diametrically opposed" to the positions Gore has espoused over the years. Lieberman, of course, in joining Gore on the ticket four years ago, took positions that were no less inconsistent with his own previous views for what was clearly naked expediency.

All the commentators have been remarking on how treacherous Gore's announcement has been, and graceless—not even extending the courtesy of a phone call to Gephardt, who endorsed him in 2000, or Kerry, or even Lieberman, who delayed entering the race until Gore had announced his decision not to run. It is an ugly business.

These are our national leaders, and they seem like young men dazzled and reduced by lust. A primitive part of me that supposes the world to be an elaborate teaching machine takes this as a warning.

★ ★ ★ The governor's "Holiday Dinner" turns out to be a term of art. I checked the invitation when we got home, and, yes, what it says is: "Please join Governor Mitt Romney for a Holiday Dinner," and then gives the time and place. It isn't just "dinner" then, but a "Holiday Dinner," in caps and bold-face—but without any food. Or, no, to be fair, there were hors d'oeuvres, platters of cheeses and crudités, and a table with coffee, hot chocolate, and desserts. But no dinner! To which the governor alluded, saying that the money saved by this maneuver would be put to better use in the campaign.

Ordinarily, I'd resent such treatment, but I did get to meet Romney, shake his hand, and chat for a moment. And along with fifty other potential candidates, I heard his remarks, which were full of boyish charm. He relies perhaps too much on that boyishness, and his hair colorist ought to be rather less aggressive. But his tailoring is good, his posture is terrific, and, so far as I could tell, he is sincere.

He inveighed against the Democrats and their control of the state government. He mentioned his effort to reduce the size of the Alcoholic Beverages Control Commission, which the legislature frustrated because many of the commissioners were relatives of legislators and this was a patronage issue. They restored the commission and put it under the control of the state treasurer (who is, of course, a Democrat).

The governor tried to encourage us, saying that Massachusetts is not so solidly Democratic as is generally supposed. The state voted for Ronald Reagan twice, he said (without mentioning, of course, that Carter and Mondale were the Democrats' candidates). He said that he and the lieutenant governor are going around the state raising money for the election, and have a million and a half dollars in the war chest, and that it wasn't because they are running, but we are. He gave some advice about campaigning, citing President Clinton, who shakes your hand, looks you in the eye, and somehow persuades you for the moment that you are the most important—indeed the only—person in the room! (Is that what he was doing with me ten minutes before? I wondered.)

But he surprised me when he gave us what he thought of as the real reason for running. "You're going to die," he said. "Not right away, of course, but eventually. We all do. And when you look back on your life, you want to have the satisfaction of realizing that . . . you've lived. You've made the effort. You tried to make a difference."

It breaks down a little toward the end, when he gets to the vagueness of that hideous cliché. But in a simplistic way, what he was offering the roomful of practical men and women was nothing less than an existential justification for making the arduous and, as he admitted, sometimes disagreeable effort to run for office.

Romney has a difficult job. With the overwhelming majority of Democrats on Beacon Hill, the difficulties are compounded. It is tough to get anything done. But as he told us, when a *Boston Globe* reporter asked how he managed to deal with defeats on one issue after another, he answered that he just doesn't think about those things. He thinks about what he has accomplished. He thinks about victories—and he listed two or three.

Later on, thinking over what the governor had said, I had the eerie feeling that he had been talking to me in particular, not because he shook hands in any special way but because of that odd remark about how we are all going to die. I was not absolutely the oldest person in the room, but I was up there among the oldest and, presumably, will die sooner rather than later. In that case, I have all the more reason to run, so that, looking back—as I am already doing—I can tell myself that I've done this, too. What impresses me, then, is that, aside from that promise of a dinner, I didn't think I'd been lied to.

★ ★ ★ ★ ★ ★ ★ ★ ★ ★ ★ ★ ★ ★ ★ ★ ★ ★ ★

2

Matt St. Hilaire has read my press release, and his edited version came in this morning. I am surprised not so much by his suggestions for changes as by my realization that these are the kinds of choices that candidates—and politicians—make all the time. He is quite correct in thinking that I'd be better off if I limited myself to a single page. Having worked at *Newsweek* and having read countless press releases, I know how flighty the attention is of reporters. Get in, say it fast, and get out. But do I delete "Schwarzenegger Republican"? And change "amateur" to "outsider?" Sure, why not?

There are perfectly good reasons to resist professional handling. For one, I don't want to wind up like Al Gore, blaming his staff and feeling that, if only he'd "let himself go," he might have won. Or, a fortiori, if I have no expectation of winning and the object is to have fun, then these small concessions to circumspection make no sense whatever.

I can save the Schwarzenegger line for those who interview me, and anyone interested enough to talk with me will find out that "amateur" is a word that leaps inexorably to the hand and tongue. What I should fight about is suggestions that are stupid and indecorous—like Susan Estrich's notion of putting Dukakis in that tank. Or Kerry on the motorcycle on Jay Leno's show. Meanwhile, I have to get another black-and-white photograph, one that shows me in a more smiling aspect.

★ ★ ★ It has nothing to do with the campaign—but it has everything to do with it—that I have a lithotripsy scheduled this Friday. It is not major surgery, but there are risks. The relevance is to the general question of where the line is between public and private. Had we known about John F. Kennedy's Addison's disease, we might not have elected him. (Would Nixon have been better?) We learned about Thomas Eagleton's having been treated for depression and McGovern threw him off the ticket in 1972. But paradoxically it wasn't so much the depression the electorate found troublesome as his having been treated for it. Untreated depression—like Lincoln's or Churchill's—is no impediment.

Presidential candidates are obliged to release their medical records and tax returns and open themselves up to all kinds of scrutiny, the point of which is to enable us to defend ourselves against weakness and knavery. A lithotripsy, however, is not likely to disqualify me. Still, I am thinking about mortality, human frailty, the imperfections of the flesh. The immediate prompting for this is not only next Friday's procedure but this morning's news that Secretary of State Powell is undergoing surgery for prostate cancer. I have an elevated PSA, have a needle biopsy every year, have looked into the options for the treatment of prostate cancer, and know enough to admire Powell and Rudy Giuliani and John Kerry and Yankees manager Joe Torre for their bravery. It is no small thing to perform as they do on the public stage while wearing a diaper.

★ ★ ★ I stopped in yesterday at the office of the Cambridge Elections Commission, which is conveniently located at the end of my block. As a candidate, I get a free a set of diskettes that list all Cambridge voters with their party affiliations and addresses. With these, I can identify the Republicans and independents whom I will hit up for signatures on my petitions, then for money, and then for their votes. It is a huge list, and I shall have to edit it down to those who are in my district and then filter out Democrats and Greens. This is donkeywork, like stuffing envelopes and trudging about from door to door. An incumbent, a Democrat, and a city council member, with a staff and an office on Cambridge Street (across from the Mayflower Live Poultry store), Toomey has enormous advantages in this kind of thing. I tell myself that anyone challenging an incumbent has this uphill battle, but I am not encouraged. Most incumbents get reelected, after all—even without such a disparity between the numbers of registered Democrats and Republicans as we have in Cambridge.

★ ★ ★ The ragtag Cambridge Republican City Committee had a party last night at Ryles Jazz Club on Inman Square. I was there to let them know that I'd filed my papers and was launched on the campaign, and maybe to raise money, because what I get before January 1 doesn't count against next year's limits. It was a depressing group, ranging from presentable down through various ranges of ideological and personal quirkiness.

One woman—a language professor at a local university—was distributing copies of a letter she had written to Michael Capuano, our representative in Congress, urging him to support the Chemical Dependency Treatment Parity Bill that would provide drug and alcohol treatment as a part of health care insurance, which would be not only more humane but also less costly than prison, where drug abusers make up a shockingly high proportion of the inmate population. I am inclined to agree with her, but this is not an issue likely to come before the state legislature and is, anyhow, another hot-button topic that has been thoroughly corrupted by partisan rhetoric. The "War on Drugs" is a signal failure, and we have made no progress since Nancy Reagan's "Just Say No" campaign, which never changed the mind of a junky or kept any youngster from experimenting with drugs. I found myself in the awkward position, then, of agreeing with her, but only nodding and making some noncommittal remark like, "I hear what you're saying." Politics, which should enable such conversations, only distorts and poisons them.

The others? A group of desperadoes, less like a political party than a collection of conspirators. They might as well be monarchists or vegetarians or prohibitionists—except that they are slightly less eccentric and, therefore, less interesting. So why a holiday party? Because it counts as a meeting of the city committee, of which there must be two a year for us to send delegates to the state and national conventions. What they are jockeying for is not electing anyone to the city council or the state legislature. They just want to go to New York City and wear elephant hats!

* * * An e-mail from Deborah Eisner of the *Cambridge Chronicle* arrived yesterday, and she wants to meet. She says there is "another challenger" to Toomey, and I take that as a confirmation of the news I had about Avi Green. If Green beats Toomey in the Democratic primary, then he and I will be fighting for an open seat. As the Democrat, he'd still be the heavy favorite, but I'd run at fifteen to one odds instead of fifty to one. So, at Carberry's, a coffee shop a couple of blocks away, I met with Ms. Eisner and offered to buy her coffee, but she insisted that the paper pay—as if accepting a coffee might compromise her integrity. Much more scrupulous than when I was at *Newsweek*.

We talked for maybe three-quarters of an hour, and I said, I think, the right things. I managed at least to avoid obvious pitfalls, so that, when I talked about the possibility of a debate among the candidates, I mentioned that I'd been a member of the Yale Varsity Debating Team but did not allude to Toomey's having gone to Suffolk. The only trace of my elitism was perhaps in my response to her question about what I could bring to the political life of Cambridge, when I answered that, as a Republican, I'd be "entertaining," which is true but sounds a bit mandarin. But then, I am a mandarin. I also used a version of the Truman Capote line that has always appealed to me about how my wife is the serious person, a hotshot doctor, and that my main job is amusing her and being her "most important fashion accessory." It was a setup for the next line about how I could similarly be an ornament to Cambridge political life. And, having no political ambition, I will be able to say whatever I want and perhaps even serve the Republicans as an attack dog, which is what a minority party needs to do if it can't sustain a gubernatorial veto.

I told her that I have never met Mr. Toomey but that I hear he is a decent fellow. My impression is that he is a typical Irish Catholic Democratic pol, which is why he is pro-life, which is awkward in Cambridge. And that my main difference with him is that he wants to sock it to Harvard and MIT, redistributing wealth, stealing from the rich and giving to the poor, who of course have more votes. Ms. Eisner asked me what I thought of the PILOT program. I had a moment of panic—what in the hell is that?—and then it came to me, the acronym for "Payment in Lieu of Taxes." I told her I thought the universities should make payments for the actual city services they use, like the fire department, but that they were great assets not only to Cambridge and Massachusetts but to the nation and, indeed, the world. And there are other ways in which they contribute to the welfare and prosperity of the community. I mentioned, for example, the groundbreaking last month of Harvard's low-cost housing development in the large tract of land it has bought across the Charles in Allston. Who knows what else I said? I think I sounded reasonably sane and even well informed. But I wasn't taking notes.

I told her when we were done that this had been my first political interview. She said that I'd "done very well," which is encouraging. But we'll see. The piece comes out next week. It won't say that I have announced, because I want the *Globe* and the *Herald* not to be at a disadvantage, but I told her it was okay to write that I was "about to announce," a distinction without a difference. I doubt that the *Globe* and the *Herald* will worry about being scooped by the *Cambridge Chronicle*. And she did call me first.

★ ★ ★ I had a call from Avi Green, a pleasant enough person on the telephone. He said it might be a good idea for us to meet. I couldn't think why, but then I couldn't think why not. And there might be ways in which we can cooperate to defeat Toomey and then fight it out between ourselves for the open seat.

I consulted Evan, of course, and he thought it was a good idea. My differences with Green are ideological and political, with him on the left and me on the right. With Toomey and me, it's more muddled. I said I'd call Green back next week to set up a meeting—if only out of curiosity.

★ ★ ★ Vicissitude. Plot! But that happens. They find Saddam, and Bush's poll numbers soar, while Dean looks not only wrong but, worse, out of date. Never mind the *neiges d'antan*, where are all those old hula hoops?

★ ★ ★ A call from St. Hilaire, to say that Governor Romney wants to contribute to my campaign. Do I have the account set up? Yes, I tell him, and he then says that the governor will send me a check for $250. Wow! He's a millionaire, of course. But it's a nice gesture. More than that, it's one of the first and by far the largest of the contributions I've received. I am grateful and friendly. Or, as they say, much obliged.

★ ★ ★ My generalized worries about the campaign—What's the point? Can I do this? Do I have the stamina? Do I have the psychic resources to cope with the all but inevitable failure?—congealed this morning to a new source of panic. What if Toomey, or Green, goes to the library and looks into my literary career? *The Exhibitionist*, my pseudonymous potboiler of 1967, was widely attacked as a "dirty book," although, perhaps for that reason, it sold four million copies and was on the *New York Times* Bestseller List, for a while as high as number three. Worse than that, among my jeux d'esprit productions, there's an elegant little joke that the poet and small-press publisher Robert Wallace brought out in 1987: *The Cock Book: A Child's First Book of Pornography*. My porn version of Dr. Seuss's *One Fish, Two Fish*, it was a limited edition and is difficult to find. The Widener doesn't even have one. (Yale does, but only because I gave it to them.) As long as I'm worrying, what about *Alice at 80*, my novel about Lewis Carroll's fascination with Alice Liddell as basically a sexual obsession? None of this puts me in the same league with Paris Hilton, but then she is not running for office.

At lunch today, I mentioned some of these worries to Evan, who replied with his characteristically laconic wit. About *The Exhibitionist*, he said, "You defy anyone to infringe your First Amendment rights." "But what about *The Cock Book*?" I asked.

Without a pause, he said, "In Cambridge? There *are* no community standards."

★ ★ ★ Deborah Eisner's piece is out in the *Cambridge Chronicle*. Mostly it's about Green, who is the first challenger Toomey has had to face in a Democratic primary in a decade. She mentions, in the third paragraph, that "the winner of a September primary will face political newcomer Republican David Slavitt." The piece goes on about Green and Toomey, until she gets to me and says:

> Slavitt, 68, of West Street is the author of 26 novels and more than 80 translations. The Republican said he is looking to help balance the two-party system in the state.
>
> "A one-party system is not a great idea. Even if you are a Democrat, there is no accountability if these people keep running unopposed," Slavitt said.
>
> A realist, he said that "it's unlikely, but I think it's possible" for a Republican to win the heavily Democratic seat.

I e-mailed her to thank her and to correct her about the number of books—29 novels, 17 collections of poetry, and 28 volumes of translation. All she had to do was look at the press release I handed her that morning at Carberry's.

★ ★ ★ There is a story in the *Globe* about Romney's check, or, I should say, checks. It isn't quite what I'd supposed. He wasn't sitting around and discussing the political landscape with his advisers and then deciding that, hey, that Slavitt has a shot, you know? I think I'll send him a few bucks. It was more programmatic. According to Raphael Lewis's piece, the Republican leaders decided to pony up "$75,000 to the first 100 legislative candidates who commit to run" against Democrats next fall. "Romney and his wife, Ann, Lieutenant Governor Kerry Healey and her husband, Sean, and Republican Party Chairman Darrell Crate and his wife, Nancy, are each pledging to give at least $125 apiece to GOP legislative candidates, [Dominick] Ianno [executive director of the Massachusetts Republican Party] said yesterday." The story says that the plan is for each of the "wealthy trio of couples" to give three $250 checks to each candidate. That is of course good news. The paragraph that I find most mysterious says: "Democrats have expressed outrage at Romney's pronouncement, saying it was tantamount to an electoral war." They are annoyed—outraged, even!—at having to run against opposing candidates.

★ ★ ★ I met Avi Green for coffee. He's an earnest young man, but not in any way annoying about it. He studied comparative religion at Columbia, then went down to North Carolina to teach at the secondary school level in Winston-Salem, worked on the campaign of Harvey Gantt, the African-American mayor of Charlotte, in his 1990 run against Jesse Helms for the Senate, and then came up to Cambridge to enroll at the JFK School of Government at Harvard. He worked for nonprofit organizations and has been involved in some campaigns—most recently that of Jarrett Barrios, who is now in the state Senate. Green said that if you work for someone, three things can happen. You can win, and he can turn out to be what you'd hoped. Or you can lose, which is less good but tolerable. Or you can win and then find out that the candidate wasn't what you'd hoped. I asked if that had happened with Barrios and, without going into detail, he said yes. And that had driven him to run on his own, where he makes the decisions and where, if he wins, it will be up to him not to be corrupted by the office.

Oddly enough—or perhaps not so oddly—we have a lot in common. He hates Tom Finneran as much as I do. He's running against Finneran and Governor Romney. I'm running against Finneran and in support of Romney, whom I see as the necessary check and balance to the Democrats' power on Beacon Hill. Green said that he doesn't think most Democrats there remember what the ideals of the party are. Their allegiance is simply to power. In that case, I wondered why he doesn't become a Republican.

I told him I'd do anything I could to help him, at least until the primaries. I'd prefer to run against him for an open seat than against Toomey. Indeed, if it came down to that, I'd rather lose to him than to Toomey in a general election. I asked if the Green Party had promised not to field a candidate this year. He told me that they hadn't committed themselves but, apparently, they are as much a ragtag group as the Cambridge Republicans. They don't worry about winning or losing but only about principles. Lofty questions of political philosophy. Power corrupts, but then so does powerlessness.

★ ★ ★ The conviction of Gary Lee Sampson and the jury's recommendation that he be put to death for the two brutal murders he committed are getting headlines, because this would be the first execution for a crime in Massachusetts since 1947. Actually, it wouldn't be in Massachusetts but in the federal prison in Terre Haute, Indiana. But the trial, with its verdict and sentencing recommendation, was in the federal court here, because both murders were connected with a carjacking. Opponents of the death penalty are describing this as an "end run around Massachusetts law," and they are, of course, correct. Romney favors the death penalty and wants to see it restored, particularly in cases like that of Joseph Druce, already serving a life sentence without the possibility of parole, who murdered the pedophile priest John Geoghan in prison in Shirley.

The question I have to think about is whether to declare—in a Cambridge election—that I, too, am in favor of the death penalty. The majesty of the state seems diminished if there are no occasions when "the people" cannot decide that the perpetrators of certain crimes ought not to be allowed to live. Our respect for life is diminished if those who take it can't be punished in some proportionate way—or, in Druce's case, punished at all. That my mother was murdered in 1982 in the house in White Plains in which I grew up may have something to do with my taking this position, but is that a reason to suspect my views or a kind of confirmation?

What does trouble me is that the Sampson case is clearly an intrusion by the United States Department of Justice into the jurisprudence of the Commonwealth of Massachusetts. Of course, if Governor Romney were able get the General Court to change our laws to enable state courts to sentence killers to death, that would obviate the need for such an infringement on what has traditionally been a matter for the states.

I'd guess that, in Cambridge and Somerville, the opposition to the death penalty is fairly strong. If asked, I'll say what my views are, but I ought not to volunteer them.

★ ★ ★ On the other hand, I am surprised to discover something none of the recent newspaper articles have mentioned, which is that in 1982 the voters of Massachusetts approved a constitutional amendment providing for capital punishment, and that in 1984 the Supreme Judicial Court in *Commonwealth v. Colon-Cruz* (who shot a state trooper near Auburn) declared the amendment to be unconstitutional on the ground that the enabling statute provided that the death penalty could be imposed only by a jury and, therefore, put undue pressure on the defendants to plead guilty and, without a jury trial, avoid the death penalty. Rather ingeniously, the SJC found that the statute impermissibly burdened the right against self-incrimination and the right to a jury trial.

It seems to me that these wrinkles could have been ironed out, and given the clear will of the voters as expressed by their ballot on the question, they ought to have been.

★ ★ ★ To write the Romneys a thank-you for their check, I looked in my mother's old *Amy Vanderbilt's Book of Etiquette* to find the proper form of address. I found that three states—New Hampshire, Massachusetts, and South Carolina—have officially adopted the title "Excellency" for their governors. Ms. Vanderbilt suggests that, from within these states, the proper way to address a letter would be to "His Excellency, the Governor of Massachusetts and Mrs. Romney." That may be correct, but I settled for "The Honorable and Mrs. Mitt Romney." Next time I see him, I'll ask which he prefers.

★ ★ ★ On one of the year-end talk shows on television, somebody quoted Benjamin Disraeli, to whom a young man had written asking what he needed to know to go into politics. Disraeli replied that there were only two things that were necessary: to know himself and to know the times. That sounds about right. And I think that, being engaged in this campaign, I understand a little better what the Earl of Beaconsfield meant.

★ ★ ★ I learned today that Dane Baird is running as a Republican in Somerville's other state rep district for the seat currently held by Patricia Jehlen, and that Ms. Jehlen is likely to be challenged in the Democratic primary by Sean O'Donovan, president of the Somerville Board of Aldermen and law partner of Representative Eugene L. O'Flaherty, an ally of Speaker Finneran. So Baird, too, may be running for an open seat.

Baird is also the notional leader of the wraith-like Republican Party in Somerville (it is not well enough organized to send delegates to state or national conventions), and five of the precincts of "my" district are up in Somerville, so I telephoned him and we agreed to meet. It was a rare balmy December day, and I thought I'd go up to the Somerville library and look through back numbers of the *Somerville Journal* to see what issues I'll need to know about next Friday.

The half hour or so I spent in the library was vastly entertaining. Along with the rest of the Boston metropolitan area, Somerville has seen its real estate prices soar, but it is broke, is laying off teachers and policemen, is selling off capital plant, and has been involved for years now in a bizarre wrangle about zoning for Assembly Square—where Ikea and Home Depot wanted to come in and build stores that would have boosted the city's tax revenues by almost $2 million a year. This wonderful piece of real estate that the Mystic View Task Force is trying to protect and keep pristine turns out to be the site of almost weekly heroin busts. And among those who have been busted for selling drugs there is a cop named Alex Capobianco, who was caught selling OxyContin to high school students. (His lawyer claims that the outgoing mayor, Dorothy Kelly Gay, fired him not for the drug selling but because he is a cousin of the new mayor, Joe Curtatone.)

It would be difficult to make this up!

After my session in the library's reference room, I met Baird for coffee. He was prompted to run by his disgust at the corruption and stupidity of politics in Massachusetts in general and in Somerville in particular. And he thinks that Ms. Jehlen is vulnerable, if only because she and Speaker Finneran don't get along. I agreed with him, although Finneran's dislike of her may be her most attractive feature.

We agreed to work together in whatever ways we could.

★ ★ ★ I've been gearing up to send out copies of the press release and the photograph to announce my candidacy. When you are both the candidate and the staff, it is up to you to have prints made of your best picture, create stationery, and learn how to print labels. Handwritten addresses would look amateurish. I discovered capabilities of my computer and printer that I'd never used before. (I learned how to print envelopes only a few months ago!) It turns out that labels are not much more difficult, except that you have to remember which way to put the label sheet into the printer (face down) and keep track of which column and which row you want to print. The *Globe*, the *Herald*, the *Boston Phoenix*, and all the obvious places. . . . You type in each address and indicate where on the sheet you want the printer to put it, and it will do that. I also found a nice schematic GOP elephant on the Web, managed to copy it, reduce it a little, and stick it on the header of my campaign-letter template. I have a sense of accomplishment. And it gives a nice professional look to my thank-you letters.

★ ★ ★ New Year's Day, and I am at my desk, churning out letters to such media figures as Jay Severin and Emily Rooney, hoping that they will have me on their shows. Severin is an arrogant little guy with vast pretensions and a wobbly sense of grammar. There is a commercial he did a year or two ago for some automobile dealership in which he was praising the way they let customers wander about the lot or test-drive cars without salesmen pressuring them. And he said that "you, like I, will appreciate this." I found myself hypnotized whenever the commercial came on and would stop what I was doing and listen for the solecism. He also talks about Ken's Steak House in Framingham and, for a time, praised their "most unique" menu. He calls his audience "the best and brightest," as if listening to his show were a mark of intelligence and good taste. Still, he's a right-winger and might be sympathetic. Emily Rooney, Andy Rooney's daughter, is an earnest woman who hosts *Greater Boston* on WGBH, our PBS station. She's smarter than Severin, speaks in recognizable English, and leaves it to her panelists to be attack dogs so she can seem impartial. She follows the *News Hour* and has a sizable audience—the choice is between her and *Hollywood Squares*.

I'm a writer, and these letters should be easy to do, but there is a different purpose here, an effort not to discover but to persuade and charm. I think of those plodders who believed what their English teachers told them about how "Language is a tool," or "Language is the key that opens the door for you." For this kind of undertaking, that utilitarian characterization is accurate. But for a poet, it is uncomfortable.

★ ★ ★ You don't throw your hat into the ring. What you throw is a pile of envelopes into a mailbox and you hear them hit at the bottom. It's done. The campaign is no longer theoretical but out there for the editors and newsroom functionaries to respond to with enthusiasm or laughter or else simply and balefully to ignore.

Standing there, having emptied my pile of mail into the slot, I felt like a madman. What could I have been thinking? Who am I to put myself forward in this way?

On the other hand, who is Timmy Toomey?

3

★ ★

Joe Curtatone was sworn in yesterday as mayor of Somerville. He announced firings, the sale of twenty-five city-owned cars, and the recall of 115 cell phones that various city officials have been using. Drastic measures, but the city is in desperate straits. The real problem is that expectations have been rising. The statewide repeal of rent control has resulted in a rise in real estate prices in Cambridge, which, in turn, has caused a migration into Somerville of middle-class types who have a sense of entitlement and some expectation that city governments ought to deliver certain basic services—not necessarily schools of any quality (which Cambridge doesn't offer either) but at least trash collection, snow removal, and some minimal effort toward maintaining public safety. (So far as I am able to tell, Representative Toomey has done nothing to relieve these grievous troubles of one of the two cities in his district.)

Meanwhile, here in Cambridge, Michael Sullivan, a pleasant and intelligent fellow whom I've met several times, has been reelected mayor. We don't elect mayors directly. The members of the city council pick one of their own to get the honor, a staff of five, and an extra $25,000 a year in salary. There is now talk—who knows how serious?—about changing the way mayors are elected in Cambridge. This is a system I have never found anywhere else. It turns politics into a junior high school wrangle. But then, it's Cambridge, and that may not be altogether inappropriate.

★ ★ ★ My fund-raising letter to friends and classmates:

Dear NAME TK:

No, it's not a joke. I really am running for the seat in the State Legislature (26th Middlesex) currently held by Tim Toomey. As a Republican! In Somerville and Cambridge!

What's a joke is the lopsided state government, with a minority party so weak that it cannot sustain a gubernatorial veto over the machinations of Tom Finneran and his hordes. These are not even Democrats in any recognizable way, but beyond—or beneath—ideology. They are the Incumbents, are loyal only to incumbency and power, and need to be held accountable and made more responsive to an electorate that feels all but powerless.

The Democrats squealed like scalded pigs at the prospect of Republican opponents in the election in November. They feel a sense of entitlement to the seats they have held so long (and for which, in many instances, they have run unopposed). Bring the power back to the people by supporting a Republican? It is a radical idea!

I invite your support. I am a social moderate, a fiscal conservative, and a grown-up. That I am also a person of some intelligence and culture does not, I think, absolutely disqualify me for office in the State House . . . but that perhaps remains to be seen. Checks, in any amount but not to exceed $500.00, should be made out to The David Slavitt Committee and may be sent to the address above.

It's a presidential election year. New voters will show up at the polls. Who knows? I could even win! Every contribution makes it slightly less unlikely, and even more entertaining.

I thank you and send kind regards,

★ ★ ★ It's probably breezier than the party functionaries would like, but it has to be recognizably from me to these people who know me and whom I'm asking for money. The least they deserve is a little entertainment. And if they decline to contribute to a quixotic enterprise, I shall not hold it against them (or, say, rather, I shall try not to.)

★ ★ ★ But is it so quixotic? At dinner last night, a couple of Cambridge friends—who claim that I may be the only "openly Republican person" they know—report that a friend of theirs on the Globe thinks I have a real chance. My fear is that if I begin to take seriously the possibility of winning, it may corrupt my campaign. (And I wonder why there has been no response to my press release from the Globe, which got several copies.)

So far, thunderous silence. All I am now scheduled for is an appearance next Tuesday on Cambridge Community television, useful at least as a practice session.

★ ★ ★ Speaker Finneran has delivered his attention-grabbing harangue (a week before Governor Romney's January State of the State speech), getting page-one coverage as he laid out his agenda for the new session. His proposals were preschool programs for every child in the state by 2010; an exhortation to the legislature to create "jobs, jobs, and more jobs"; and a plea for more affordable housing in the state. Two and three are lovely but beyond the powers of the state legislature. He could as well have proposed action to improve the weather in the Commonwealth (I'd vote for that: the windchill factor is minus fifteen this morning). What is not frivolous is his proposal of the preschool program, which would cost about $1 billion a year (much of which would come from the federal government), or $700 million a year more than we are now spending.

Who can be against little children? Or education? Or opportunity? Or all those things together? The sad truth is that these programs and the expenditure of these huge sums might do some good, but the problem cannot be solved just by throwing money at it. The preschool through second- or third-grade kids are different from what they were a generation ago. They are violent, have attention deficit disorder, and can't learn, and if they can't sit still and listen to the teacher, the lesson plan is irrelevant.

Waiting for my barber, I looked at a recent issue of *Time*, where there was a piece about the epidemic of violent behavior in kids in these early grades. The experts *Time* consulted said that the children have been watching television, not just casually but for many hours a day, and have the emotional development of two-year-olds in the bodies of six- and seven-year-olds. To give the youngsters of Massachusetts the opportunities that Finneran wants them to have, he'd have to propose legislative limits on the time that kids can watch TV, and if he were serious he would also have to insist that families dine together four or five times a week. His impulses are dictatorial enough; what he lacks is the vision for such recommendations—or, better yet, make them requirements for admission into these expensive state-funded programs.

Paul Weiss, the philosopher, who was my teacher at Yale and my friend, used to say that it is unfair but true that much of education happens in the home and that youngsters who have learned how to have a conversation have an enormous advantage over those who haven't. No amount of attention in well-meaning programs such as Head Start can compensate for the failures of families. It is no mere metaphor that we use when we speak of the "mother tongue." Language is something we learn early, at home, on our mother's knee, as we are talked to, crooned to, and read to. And then at the dinner table, where we learn to participate in conversations that are exciting and entertaining.

I am a senior common room associate of Harvard's Leverett House and eat lunch there once or twice a week. The idea is that the undergraduates should learn from encounters with faculty members and other intellectuals what it is like to be a grown-up and how to incorporate academic learning into the larger context of life experience. The undergraduates are intimidated by the idea of talking and eating. Or they just don't think that this is fun. And the installation of a wi-fi antenna that encourages them to work on computers while shoveling food into their mouths is an admission of defeat. In the library, maybe, or some common room, but not the dining hall!

These Harvard students represent the best of American youth, and their plight is sad. I am therefore cautious about Finneran's proposals. The spending of a billion dollars is, for him, quirky. He's mostly a tightfisted kind of guy. But Scott Greenberger, writing in the *Globe*, suggested that "he may be looking to burnish his legacy with a program that will endure." My own guess is that his ambitious proposals may not be unrelated to the windfall this would provide for the teachers' union, which is both a patron and a client of the Democrats. If Governor Romney is presumptuous enough to field opposition candidates to the members of the General Court, then what Finneran may be looking for is ways to buy votes. A billion is a nice round sum, especially if you can get a good piece of it from the feds. And no one can criticize, because it's for the iddy-bitty children, whom Uncle Tom wants to help.

★ ★ ★ I mentioned my barber, but George Papalimberis, at La Flamme in Harvard Square, deserves more than a passing, nameless reference. He is a good barber. He has cut Governor Weld's hair, and Governor Dukakis's, and, although not recently, Mitt Romney's too. He is a Greek immigrant who has worked hard and sent his son through college and medical school. George has participated in one of those welfare-to-work programs that train people for gainful employment. The trouble, George says, is that you can teach them to sweep the floor, and even to cut hair; what you can't teach them is that they have to show up every day. And if they get fired for absenteeism, all that happens is that they go back on welfare. What George proposes is that there should be a penalty, so that if they don't bother to come in, they don't get put back on the welfare rolls either. What Democrats don't realize is that their social pro-grams are offensive and insulting to working people like George. I am con-vinced, though, that having him as my barber is politically lucky.

★ ★ ★ I turned a page of the *Cambridge Chronicle* and was surprised to see my face under the headline SLAVITT ANNOUNCES CANDIDACY. The story is basically my press release. Or, actually, it is exactly my press release, the only change being that the paper distances itself from me a little by saying that Slavitt wants to "challenge the Democratic hyper-majority in the General Court and to end what he calls the 'dictatorship' of Speaker Thomas Fin-neran." The quotation marks are their only addition.

My hope, of course, is that other papers will pick this up from the *Chronicle*, not that the news is any different from what they had on their desks in my press release. But it looks weightier in print. As I know well, books, too, look different before they are printed. The difficult thing publishers do is imagine a book when all they have in their hands is a collection of manuscript pages. The fact that the newsmongers feed off each other is both depressingly stupid and dismally true. But maybe it will work for me now. The guys at the *Globe* and the *Herald* take the little local papers. This is now a piece of real news that they may feel obliged to report.

★ ★ ★ I am sending out the begging letters, two or three at a time. I find it sufficiently distasteful that I do a couple and then play some solitaire. It will get worse, of course. I'll be out there, face-to-face, handing out my fliers and asking for signatures. It is, in the etymological sense, vulgar, having to do with the people. That democracy is vulgar is not even an observation but a tautology.

I heard some talking head on television this morning allude to George Orwell's remark that repeating the obvious was the job of the few remaining intellectuals. That's almost a koan. And among its meanings is that what is obvious to the intellectuals is not necessarily obvious to everyone else.

★ ★ ★ The temperature these past few days has been in the single digits. Next month, we get the petitions that will get my name on the ballot. I do hope the weather improves. I am not like those Patriots fans sitting there in zero de-grees with their faces freezing, watching the play-off game against the Titans that they could have seen on television. I am lacking in fervor. I think of Yeats's lines about how "The best lack all conviction, while the worst / Are full of passionate intensity." That kind of thinking won't get me contributions or petition signatures, much less the seat in the legislature.

★ ★ ★ Nothing in today's *Globe* about the announcement of my candidacy. I'd thought that in the Sunday paper there might be a paragraph. But no, not a word.

★ ★ ★ Yesterday was the Red Mass at the Cathedral of the Holy Cross, a service devoted to blessing the work of lawyers and judges, and Archbishop O'Malley, who was appointed to replace Cardinal Law after his eminence's disgrace about pederast priests, has issued a high moral call to lawyers to "live your baptismal commitment" and fight to "defend marriage." This is an outrageous intrusion by a religious figure into the life of the community, exactly what anti-Catholic bigots feared when Al Smith was running to be president. No one is forcing Catholic gays to marry or the church to perform or even to sanction such ceremonies. But Catholics do apparently believe in the catholicity of their church and want to extend its teachings universally, which is presumptuous.

I don't suppose that the archbishop's campaign will accomplish anything, but it may embarrass Toomey. His church ought to be pleased with him for his anti-abortion position, which is awkward enough in Cambridge. To require him also to oppose the granting of equal rights to same-sex couples is onerous indeed. He will, I expect, ignore his archbishop, either out of conviction or from fear of being defeated in November.

Later in the day, at Faneuil Hall at a meeting sponsored by Massachusetts Citizens for Life, Speaker Finneran chimed in, criticizing what he called "the judicial tyranny" of the courts. Finneran, who is of course pro-life, said of the judiciary, "It is that unelected branch of government that is far more dangerous than anything the elected branch could do." What he is complaining about is the only branch of government that limits his own tyrannical proclivities.

★ ★ ★ Today is another small milestone. I have an appointment for my first television appearance as a candidate. I am to be interviewed on community television by Roy Bercaw, a guy who seems to be . . . a little nuts. I have no idea how many or how few people watch these programs. I know I need the practice, but he worries me with such bits of e-mailed news as this:

> The issue of one-party Cambridge is one I've been writing and talking about
> for about 8 years. I used to seek support from Harvard administrators in-

cluding Derek Bok, until I realized that they exploit the situation. Do you know that a Harvard institute at the School of Gov't gets a few million each year in US taxpayer funds, to promote two-party democracy in eastern Europe? After I wrote to Bok about this, when I saw him on the street he almost broke into a trot to avoid me.

Harvard, he thinks, is trying to take over Cambridge (trying to build pedestrian tunnels to keep their students from getting run over by aggressive drivers and other such schemes that he finds threatening). But he is, at least nominally, a Republican. Or he calls himself that, meaning that he is a naysayer in politics and in life. The program is half an hour. The hard part will be figuring out how to set up and coordinate the television set, cable box, and VCR so that I can see my performance on tape afterward.

I was on the *Tonight Show* back in Johnny Carson's day. And Bryant Gumbel interviewed me on *Today*. So I ought not to be worried. On the other hand, I didn't do all that well with either of those big-time shows. With Carson, I was promoting one of my Henry Sutton novels, and when I finally got on, he asked me whether it was true that I wrote the Sutton books for the money. I answered that Dr. Johnson had said that no man but a blockhead ever wrote except for money, and Zsa Zsa Gabor, who was on the couch to my right, asked who Dr. Johnson was. I snapped back that he was a dermatologist on West Eighty-sixth Street. Carson was amused, and we had a lively if brief conversation that I do not remember clearly, but I failed to mention my book, and my publisher was furious.

On *Today*, some years later, Bryant Gumbel asked me the questions about *Alice at 80* that were on his clipboard, and the segment went well enough. But after we had finished, I stopped to lend George Brett my ballpoint pen (to autograph a baseball for someone), and from behind me I heard Gumbel asking no one in particular, "Who did he fuck to get himself on the show?"

★ ★ ★ My appearance on CCTV (Cambridge Community Television) was not a catastrophe. I managed to make a tape of the show, which was more than they were able to do, and watched it later in the evening. The show itself is extravagantly amateurish with only one camera aimed at the desk with two seats, so that the whole show is a two-shot. No cameraman. And it didn't start quite on time, which, on that station, doesn't mean much: they just continue with public-service placards and salsa music. But Bercaw was enthusiastic, and I managed an amused tolerance—for the show and for Massachusetts politics, too—and an avuncular charm that is perhaps the best I can do.

I surprised myself only once. Bercaw had been inveighing against the habitual liberalism of Cambridge voters. I suggested that this was perhaps not such a terrible habit and came from a generosity of spirit that was admirable. The trouble, I said, was that the Democrats' idealism, their concern for the little guy and hopes for a better, more equitable society, died decades ago. The Democrats are now merely the party of incumbency. Republicans—Ed Brooke, Bill Weld, Francis Sergeant, Henry Cabot Lodge, Jr., and Mitt Romney—have a gentlemanliness and generosity that is quite different from the Far-Right Republicanism of fly-over country, and is an appealing alternative to Speaker Finneran's program. Here, Republicans are the party of vision.

Do I believe that? It certainly sounds plausible. It is a simplified, or even simplistic, version of Richard Rorty's ideas—in *Achieving Our Country*—about the tradition of the American Left. But simplifications are inherent in the sound-bite business of politics. The roll call of attractive Massachusetts Republicans is, at any rate, something I am likely to use again.

★ ★ ★ I went yesterday to Cambridge Offset Printing to have my doorhangers done. Those are fliers with a cutout at the top so one can hang them on doorknobs. If I go house to house getting signatures, I can hand these to people or leave them on doors of people who aren't at home. When I told the proprietor of the printing shop who I was and what I wanted, he looked at me and at the sample flier I'd made up on the computer. "You're running against Toomey? You know, you could win!" he said. I take some comfort from the fact that he did not dismiss the undertaking altogether.

★ ★ ★ In this morning's *Globe* there are the results of a UMass poll of 401 Massachusetts voters with more promising omens. The electorate's opinion of Speaker Finneran is not good, with 18 percent declaring themselves somewhat unfavorable and 31.4 percent very unfavorable (16 percent had no opinion and 6.2 percent had never heard of him). About Governor Romney's campaign to elect more Republicans in the Senate to keep his vetoes from being overridden, 43.9 percent thought that was very important, and 15.7 percent thought it was somewhat important. (The chances of enough state representatives getting into office to sustain vetoes are nil, which was why the poll focused on the Senate.) What it means, I think, is that the basic thrust of my campaign is correct and that by attacking Finneran and appealing to the need for two parties, I have my best chance of persuading those who are, at least by habit, Democrats, not to mention the independents.

★ ★ ★ I had lunch today at the Harvard Faculty Club with Ethridge King, a Republican who ran for city council last year. It was the first time he'd been there, having been only recently hired away from Boston University by the Radcliffe development office. He told me a couple of mildly intimidating things. First, I'll need eventually to open a campaign office, probably in August or September, where workers can address envelopes and do the stuff they have to do without crowding us out of the apartment. And, second, my door-to-door work, to which I had not been looking forward with any enthusiasm, was more complicated than just knocking at the doors and being charming for a couple of minutes. After the "contact," you have to send a postcard saying how nice it was to meet him or her. Preferably, this should be handwritten. And then a couple of mailings. Jarrett Barrios is apparently the master of this kind of thing; it is how he defeated Anthony Galluccio when they were both trying for the Democratic nomination for the state Senate seat. Ethridge says he learned the trick about the thank-you card from Barrios.

More work. And more printing.

Meanwhile, I am starting to comb through the electronic files I got from the election commission in Cambridge. (Somerville is also getting me a set of these, and they will be ready next week.) I exercise a find maneuver and go through the voter rolls looking for street names, and then copy names of Republicans or uncommitteds into a new file. This way, there will be a list of prospects already arranged geographically.

But, good Lord, it's tedious.

★ ★ ★ I was invited to the Parker House Omni last night for a Romney rally to show support for his State of the State address. Fifty or sixty Republicans were there, and they had a cash bar, cheese and veggie platters, and, this time, an actual dinner of sorts—two kinds of pasta. I skipped the food, wandered around the room introducing myself, and then, when the address came on the big-screen TV, sat with the rest and applauded at the applause lines. One feels slightly stupid applauding a television image, but we were supposed to be showing support, and what else was there to do?

The speech was pretty good. At the minimum, there was nothing embarrassing, nothing I can't run on. And Romney made a series of proposals about education, his "Legacy of Learning" program, about which my only criticism would be of the dismaying alliteration. The most interesting idea was that students who place in the top 25 percent in their scores on the MCAS tests (Massachusetts Comprehensive Assessment System) will have their tuition waived at any UMass. campus or any Massachusetts community college. And those in the top 10 percent will have student fees waived, too.

This is designed to keep bright students in the state for their higher education. It also puts greater pressure on students—and on teachers, too—to get good results on the MCAS. These tests, which are awkwardly named (probably because the MCAT initials had been taken by the Medical College Admission Tests), are controversial because one can think of them as "elitist," which is politically incorrect. That elitism is inherent in competitive education—and in life—is an embarrassing truth no one mentions anymore.

Romney announced that he also wants to give principals the authority to hire and fire, which makes sense (and, of course, also sticks it to the teachers' unions), and to spend $5 million on grants for discipline programs to take "chronically disruptive" kids out of the classroom and put them elsewhere. Further, he wants to "jump-start" construction on one hundred new or renovated schools. All of this seems sound to me, and it gives some content to the "excellence in education" bullet on my flier. Now, if I'm asked what that means, I can refer to the governor's proposals.

After he finished the speech at the State House, the governor and lieutenant governor came over to the Parker House to talk to us and thank us for our support. I thought he was referring to our coming out in terrible weather, but when I read the next morning's paper I learned that this had been a $250-a-plate affair and that, having gone without having been asked to pay, I was, at least notionally, further in debt to the party.

The governor was in good spirits, happy to be at a gathering where he could count on more than 15 percent of the audience to applaud at appropriate places. He referred almost proudly to the boos he'd had in the State House from some of the Democrats when he had spoken of the Massachusetts Turnpike Authority with its bizarre plans to have an expensive party in one of the Big Dig tunnels or the batty idea of its chairman about putting up a monorail on the center strip of the turnpike. And he used one phrase that was so mannerist that I cannot even remember the sentence. It was, apparently, his version of Governor Schwarzenegger's "Hasta la vista, baby," but perhaps even more macho because it made no sense whatever and might even have been a delicate venture into parody. I have not read, at any rate, any references to Governor Romney's prior use of the peculiar locution that means, I assume, the same thing: "Adios Nabisco!"

★ ★ ★ A check for three hundred dollars came in from one of my Yale classmates. I'm deeply grateful, of course, but I realize that there are a number of schnorring letters I've sent out, and I think of those friends and classmates who have not replied. Perhaps some of them will. And the rest? Will I learn not to resent it or take it personally? These are the difficult lessons of being a grown-up that I have never had, not having been in business, where such rebuffs are normal. I know what rejection is, of course, as any writer does. But this is different. And yet I must acquire the ability to take courage from the contributions of a few and not worry about the unresponsiveness of the rest. What will help here, as it has helped in my writing career, is the knack we all have of forgetting. After a little time has elapsed, it is only the deepest cuts that we remember.

★ ★ ★ The talking heads this morning were full of analysis of tomorrow's Iowa caucuses, in which the polling suggests that Edwards and Kerry have come up, and that Dean has been declining, while Gephardt is holding steady. It looks to be a four-way race (Lieberman is not participating). And organization is key. One needs not so much to win (although it will be a setback for Dean if he disappoints the high expectations that have been set for him) as to place among the top three.

As if it were some kind of a game.

As, of course, it is.

★ ★ ★ And, of course, the talking heads were all wrong. Kerry wins big, and Edwards shows strong. Dean comes in a lame third and does himself a lot of harm by showing his frustration and anger. Gephardt does so badly that he drops out.

It's frightening in that (a) the reasons for Dean's poor showing seem to be almost unknowable; (b) Iowa was supposed to be "retail" politics, but the expenditure of large sums of money is what helped Kerry and Edwards; and (c) there is no way for me to guess what I'd have done differently from Dean. That he let his "anger" and "arrogance" show is perfectly understandable, at least to me. I am older than he is and even less tolerant of rudeness and foolishness, which one encounters a lot in indiscriminate encounters with the public and the press.

★ ★ ★ For the past several days, the papers and the television news programs have been celebrating—no other word will do—Dean's speech to his supporters in Iowa. Clearly, he was trying to encourage them, and himself, by a moment of Huey Long extravagance, but the constraints of political decorum these days are such that there is no place left for . . . fun? Self-parody? A momentary riff?

I hardly think Dr. Dean is a lunatic or a demagogue. He was beaten in Iowa, came in a poor third, and wanted to reenergize the youngsters who were at least as disappointed as he was himself. His speech was cruelly distorted by the technology so that his shirtsleeved, tub-thumping rhetorical extravagance, which might not have seemed at all strange at a distance of forty or fifty feet and in the company of hundreds of shouting supporters, looked weird indeed to the close-up lenses of television cameras, where he seemed out of scale and out of control. I have since heard that Mara Liason, of NPR, who was there in the room, didn't find it at all frightening or even remarkable.

But the television shows have been replaying that clip scores, hundreds of times. The late-night comedians have been making their jokes about it. And the pundits, who are on television and ought to understand its distortions, have been asking whether this is the man we want to have in the White House with his finger on the nuclear button.

It is frightening to me because I can imagine myself in just such an extravagant moment, although it is not likely that any lapse of mine would draw such a glare of press attention. Platitudes, pieties, mealymouthed misrepresentations of reality, sentimentality . . . these are everywhere and go unremarked, and are more dangerous to our culture and political life than Dean's brief riff. In the new *Granta*, Paul Fussell takes exception to Colin Powell's frequent locution about the "community of nations," which implies a civility that is not merely fictive but a misrepresentation of what Powell and the administration believe to be the truth. Fussell's disquiet strikes me as more serious than any of these silly and easy reactions to Dean's speech.

★ ★ ★ The polls show an erosion of Dean's support in New Hampshire, and, of course, this causes further erosion because, as the analysts iterate endlessly, the voters are looking for "electability," so that any decline in a candidate's numbers immediately becomes a reason for further decline. Of course, it is the president's election to lose. What Kerry, Edwards, Dean, Lieberman, and Clark are fighting about is which of them might stand to benefit if Bush were somehow to implode and destroy himself. In other words, they are all fighting to be me in a contest with Bush's Toomey.

I find this only mildly amusing.

★ ★ ★ I took the day off and did absolutely nothing in the way of campaigning. Instead, I wrote a poem with which I am well pleased. All my life, my practice has been to suspend almost any other kind of activity if a poem has presented itself to me. And now that it is done and I am satisfied with it, I return to political chores, writing thank-you letters to contributors and arranging interviews. It is . . . a descent. And an imposture.

Whom am I trying to fool?

★ ★ ★ One of my prep school and college classmates sent me a check with my solicitation letter, on which he wrote at the top: "As Havel took Czechoslovakia, so Slavitt, Middlesex County? Good luck." Further down on the page, where I describe myself, as "a social moderate, a fiscal conservative, and a grown-up," and say that "I am also a person of some intelligence and culture," my classmate has circled "social moderate," "fiscal conservative," "intelligence," and "culture," and checked all these. He has also circled "grown-up," but above that he has a question mark.

I agree with him. I have said, and perhaps written, my doubts about whether there are, actually, any such creatures as grown-ups. And this is one of the stresses of political life. The first masquerade a candidate must attempt is that he or she is a responsible, serious, deliberative, grown-up kind of person in whom voters can put their trust.

There are such people, I imagine, but my suspicion is that their maturity is only a function of their lack of self-knowledge or candor.

★ ★ ★ Kerry wins in New Hampshire, with Dean a poorish second, trailing by fifteen points. Will Kerry go on to be the nominee? Will Michael Dukakis's lieutenant governor do better than his chief did? He's a Massachusetts liberal and can't do well in the big red middle of the country, or in the south either. But he'd be likely to carry his home state. And Bush's coattails, on which I am relying, would be considerably shortened in Cambridge and Somerville if Kerry were at the top of the Democratic ticket.

One caucus and one primary in a small state, and it's all over?

The printer delivered my doorhangers today, and they cheered me up. A little.

★ ★ ★ Dean has fired Joe Trippi, his campaign manager, and replaced him with Roy Neel, who was an aide to Al Gore and was deputy chief of staff to President Clinton. Neel has been an important Washington lobbyist for the past several years. So much for Dean's plausibility as an "outsider" who will go down to Washington to clean up the mess. He has also asked his staff to defer their salaries for a couple of weeks.

If he were an honest man, he'd just quit. This is embarrassing, even more than his appearance reciting the Top Ten list on the David Letterman show.

★ ★ ★ I didn't watch the candidates' debate in South Carolina last night. These are not debates, and, unless one of the participants makes a fool of himself or loses his temper, they seem to have no effect on the voting. Even if they did, South Carolina is likely to vote for Bush in the general election and has only a few delegates at the Democratic National Convention. (So why am I worrying about debating Toomey here in Cambridge?)

★ ★ ★ What I did watch this week was the city council meeting at which our city leaders discussed the new library, which has been in the works since 1992 and was originally budgeted for something like $30 million. But now we are hit for an extra $31.5 million for open space (sinking some of the adjacent high school below ground level to preserve the lawn!) and for making it a "green building." The building will have to survive for centuries for the energy savings to amortize the extra initial investment. There are other stupid objections (how can people object to a library?). One councilwoman who wanted the new library built in Central Square complains, still, about transportation access, even though there are two bus routes that go right by it. It is foolish and self-indulgent! I think of Mrs. John Kluge's remark at a University of Virginia trustees' meeting when she complained that "it's very expensive to be rich."

Part of the trouble with Cambridge is that its finances are relatively healthy and the city can afford to indulge absurdities like this. The present plan is to have the ribbon-cutting ceremony, at which our stalwart city councillors can show up and pose for photographs and take credit for their great accomplishment, in 2007.

★ ★ ★ I went up to Somerville to join Dane Baird and his workers (workers? I don't have any!) to distribute slips of paper inviting Republicans and voters without a declared affiliation to a party on February 10 at Toast Lounge in Union Square. This will be a fund-raiser and an organizational meeting in a bar, which happens, actually, to be in my district. And I am hoping that I will have the petitions by then and that I will be able to pick up some Somerville signatures. And maybe even a few campaign volunteers. I went door-to-door with a young man named Jim, a college chum of Baird's (Boston College), on Medford Street, a semigrungy street that goes through Winter Hill. This is a district where even the two of us might not have felt altogether safe had we been doing this after dark. There are drug deals and turf wars, and there is a "Winter Hill Gang," about which I do not know much and don't care to know much more.

We were giving out little slips of red paper with a Cupid and an invitation to "make Somerville Your Valentine" and to support Dane Baird, who has the solution to Somerville's problems. If he does indeed have the solution to the city's terrible problems, he should be not merely a state rep but the philosopher king. But he does have energy and optimism. And a campaign manager! He is better organized than I am, I thought, as he handed out street assignments listing each unenrolled and each Republican voter, arranged by house numbers—which is an enormous job, as I have been discovering.

Jim and I walked along Medford Street, starting with 252, which is subsidized housing for the elderly and the infirm and has twenty-one unaffiliated voters. A rich treasure of them, we thought. But it turned out to be a disappointment. We buzzed the first name on our list, and the occupant buzzed us into the lobby. We could then go from door to door and offer our little red party invitations . . . to the aged, the infirm, the blind, halt, and demented. A man in the elevator in a less than clean white undershirt over an enormous potbelly told us we had no right to be in the building (I believe that, actually, having been admitted, we are allowed to distribute political materials: we are in a different category from door-to-door salesmen). I asked him whether he was a registered voter. And he answered, belligerently, that he was not political. "They're all thieves!"

It was not an opportune moment for a reasonable discussion. Jim and I decided just to leave a pile of the invitations on the lobby table and hope that none of the residents would show up at the Toast Lounge.

Then up and down the street, in bitter cold weather. We determined that the voter rolls supplied by the Somerville Board of Elections might have been accurate at the last election, but the turnover among residents is such that the names on many of the mailboxes are different. There is a substantial transient population that is not much involved in local politics and, therefore, not much empowered. Cambridge and Somerville are run mostly by the people who have been here for a long time, who put up with the transients the way Cape Codders put up with the summer people. (They hold their town meetings in February, when none of the summer people can show up.) After two hours of this, Jim and I drove back to drop off the street list (we'd stricken out the names that no longer appeared on mailboxes or doorbells) and called it a day. I felt terrible for Dane, who has got such an uphill fight, and for myself, because I am even less well prepared than he is.

★ ★ ★ I am spending a lot of time going through the voter rolls trolling for Republican and independent voters and then arranging them by street addresses so that when I go out to canvass, I will know which doors to knock on to get my signatures—or at least leave my hangers. These doorhangers, I have calculated, cost me twenty-five cents apiece. I wonder whether I might do better with a billboard. But that, a friend advises me, might seem pushy in Cambridge. It would also be beyond the means of my as yet very modest budget.

I am hoping that when I have my signatures, the media (other than the local weeklies) will begin to take some notice. The announcement of my candidacy has been greeted by the kind of silence I ought to have learned to tolerate from my experiences with the publication of books of poetry. And, for that matter, some novels.

Not that I have ever managed really to accept that, either.

★ ★ ★ I stopped in at the Cambridge Board of Elections to drop off my request for an absentee ballot for the primary (on March 2). The Republican primary is not likely to be a nail-biter, but there are votes to cast for members of the Republican City Committee. I asked when the nomination papers would be available and was surprised to learn that they were there and I could have a stack of them. I was given a form to sign, and there was the name Timothy J. Toomey, Jr., already inscribed. Was he informed by some sympathetic elections board worker? Or is he just astonishingly efficient?

I have an extra week to get my signatures, which is helpful.

I e-mailed Avi Green to alert him and advise him to pick up the papers and get cracking. And I made a preliminary foray onto Maple Avenue, a nearby street where I'd arranged the voters by house numbers. I spent about an hour in the late afternoon getting cold and tired, but not very many signatures. Very many? I got . . . three!

This house-to-house method is inefficient and depressing. It might work better in the evenings, when more people are at home (except that it's dark then, and people are less eager to open their doors to strangers). Or maybe on the weekends I'd have better luck. But there must be a more effective way to do this. It is very discouraging. I went to bed last night aching from the exertion. And woke up before five, worrying about getting the required number of names. Toomey, of course, has his loyal helpers. I need help too.

★ ★ ★ The supermarket parking lot was less catastrophic, although hardly easy. I picked a Star Market over near the Somerville line, one that draws from eastern Cambridge and southern and eastern Somerville—my district. A Brooks Pharmacy and an Office Depot are also there, as well as a couple of storage warehouses. It looks like a piece of New Jersey that one can find almost anywhere in America. The CambridgeSide Galleria is much prettier and more upscale, but that is neither relevant nor helpful, because it draws customers from farther away, and many of them would be from outside my precincts. Also, at the Galleria, I would have to get permission. Here, at least outside, I am permitted to approach passersby. I cannot solicit signatures inside, but the manager of the Star Market has told me that I can come into the store, or its foyer, to get warm, which is a real help.

I ask anyone coming toward the entrance if he or she is registered to vote in Cambridge or Somerville. Maybe half are unregistered, some because they don't believe in politics and politicians, and others because they are not yet citizens. Some, mysteriously, respond, "Not right now," or "Not at the moment," which is curious. Are they felons? More than a few of them don't even speak English, and I am reminded how this is still the country of hope and opportunity.

I then ask if they are independent or Republican, and of those who are registered, most turn out to be Democrats. Some are defiant about it. Others understand what I'm doing and are sympathetic or regretful, or they even express their dissatisfaction with the Democratic Party or, once or twice, with Toomey himself.

I do get a few names on the petition sheet, some of which, I am pretty sure, will pass muster at the Board of Elections and the office of the secretary of state. It is better than yesterday, but it is still slow, tough work. I have until April 27, and if I work at it like a maniac, plodding along, smiling like a fool even when my legs begin to ache, and feeling utterly ridiculous, I can make the quota. But it is by no means a sure bet that I will succeed.

If it weren't for the money that friends have sent me, I should acknowledge that this is too strenuous, is folly, and that, like Joe Lieberman—who conceded last night—I should recognize when enough is enough.

Of course, I also have this book to resort to, which is familiar and respectable. It distances me a little from that cold and tired beggar in the supermarket parking lot with the clipboard and ballpoint pen who is not myself but only a character who has, for the moment, materialized from this text.

The Supreme Judicial Court handed down their advisory opinion this week and held—correctly, I think—that same-sex marriages under any other name would be inherently unequal. The right for gays and lesbians to marry, and call it marriage, is, in the court's view, guaranteed by the constitution of the Commonwealth.

There was outrage from the Far Right and much demagoguery about defending the "sanctity" of marriage. It is hardly worth pointing out that the civil government is not in the sanctity business. The Menendez brothers, convicted murderers of their parents, could get marriage licenses from the state of California. Elizabeth Taylor could get seven or eight of them. Television "reality show" contestants who have never met can marry.

This vehemence against the SJC opinion is homophobia and ignorance dressed up as the defense of virtue, and there is much noise about amending the state constitution so as to restrict the definition of "marriage" to the union between one man and one woman. As Congressman Barney Frank pointed out, the people who were criticizing Vermont's civil union law when it was passed are now embracing the idea of civil unions. No heterosexual marriages in Vermont have been threatened or diminished in the past few years. It will take at least two years to go through the cumbersome process of amending the state constitution, and by then the fuss will have died down, if only because of the public's attention deficit disorder.

Governor Romney, in a piece he wrote for the *Wall Street Journal*, criticized the courts and said that he wants the voters to have their say, which sounds good, except that the voters would probably not endorse most of the Bill of Rights if it were put to them in a referendum. The courts are the only branch of government that has both the power and the freedom to exercise leadership, striking down laws prohibiting miscegenation or school segregation—as the public would surely not have done.

★ ★ ★ My interest in this is mostly theoretical, but I need to establish my position as a supporter of same-sex marriage if only to keep gays and lesbians from contributing to Toomey's campaign in order to fight off the challenge of a gay-bashing Republican. If their organizations know that both the candidates for the Twenty-sixth Middlesex seat are in favor of same-sex marriage, then they will put their money elsewhere.

Mostly to establish my credentials, then, I went to the State House to participate in a lobbying day that MassEquality was putting on in anticipation of the constitutional convention that comes up next week. I do think it is unfair that the partner of a dying homosexual cannot visit in an ICU or a nursing home, or that partners cannot qualify for state-funded home care, or are charged higher co-pays and deductibles on medical insurance. But I also wanted to make myself known to the members of this quite active coalition as a friend and supporter. I was also interested in the process, never having lobbied before.

This was the big surprise of the two or three hours I spent in the State House—that the doors of the senators and representatives are open, and that anyone can knock and go in to talk, if not to the elected official then at least to an aide. And I was pleased and relieved to discover that these aides—or at least the ones I met—are intelligent and civilized.

I identified myself as a state rep candidate, but the others trudging up and down the ornate corridors of the fussy building were simply constituents, and nobody reported any difficulty about getting in to talk to the officials. If, by some preposterous and unlikely circumstances, I were to win, it might not be so terrible having an office there and listening to people's problems, even if there was not much I could do to solve them.

★ ★ ★ Weeks have elapsed since the piece about me ran in the *Cambridge Chronicle*, and I had thought there was no effect at all, but out of the blue I had a phone call from a young man who had read the article and wants to work on my campaign. I warned him that what I was doing now was unglamorous grunt work, going door-to-door and getting signatures for my nomination papers, but he was willing to do that. And I agreed to meet him for coffee and give him a nomination sheet to try to fill up.

He is in his late twenties and seems bright enough. He works in computer technology and had interesting things to say about the collapse of the Dean campaign—mostly that the size of rallies organized in conventional ways are a reliable sign of much wider support, but that gatherings of people from meet-ups and other Web devices cannot accurately predict a wider enthusiasm. What we saw was all there was. In effect, it was another dot-com bubble that grew, glistened temptingly, and popped.

I gave André—that is his name—a clipboard, a couple of sheets of nomination papers, and a list of names and addresses of independents and Republicans on Fayette street, and watched him as he went to work, picking his way along icy sidewalks to get names. I went back to Maple Street to try houses where I'd left doorhangers on my first pass.

I had better success than he did, but his appearance and his investment of an hour and a half in this drudgery was, in itself, enormously encouraging. I began to think that maybe I could do this. On the other hand, it has been almost a week since I got the forms from the Election Commission, and I have yet to return one completed sheet of 22 names. I need at least ten of these sheets to get 150 certified voters to qualify me.

★ ★ ★ Things are looking up. Evan came over to help, to pay me back for my having been out there in front of the post office accosting passersby to get signatures for him a couple of years ago. Even though I need only 150 signatures, they have to live in the district, so it's mostly the house-to-house slog. He went out to Amory Street, and I did another foray on Fayette. It was bitter cold, but we did well and now have a full sheet and most of a second. And I am off to have lunch today with Fred Baker, who ran King's campaign for city council last year. He has offered to do a sheet or two for me.

★ ★ ★ Fred has also agreed to be my committee chairman, which is good news. He has lived in Cambridge all his life, knows all the Republicans, and knows the process. That Ethridge did not do well was hardly Fred's fault. Ethridge was changing jobs and had a new baby. I, on the other hand, will be unimpeded. As Fred said, in the summertime it will begin to be strenuous as I appear at picnics and festivals, giving speeches or just shaking hands—if I can collect the signatures to get to that part of the campaign.

★ ★ ★ My fear is that all this attention to same-sex marriage, which does not affect very many people, will allow the General Court (i.e., Senate and House) to sneak through more sinister amendments to the state constitution, one of which would double the terms of state senators and state representatives. These churls find it troublesome to have to run for office, even unopposed. Another amendment would raise the number of signatures needed to get an initiative petition onto the ballot. They hardly need that one. Initiative referenda that have passed—the Clean Elections Law, or the restoration of capital punishment, for instance—Finneran and his lackeys blandly ignore or, worse, work strenuously to frustrate and nullify. Finally, there is an amendment that would provide for the election of judges, taking that function away from the governor (who can sometimes be a Republican) and bringing it back into the Democrats' control. It is also a gesture of retribution, I am persuaded, for the SJC's decision about same-sex marriages: judges who were elected would be less likely to assert or protect the rights of minorities in the face of any strong sentiments of the majority.

★ ★ ★ I hate apartment houses. One can't get signatures there for nomination papers. The No Soliciting signs don't actually apply—I am not soliciting but doing political canvassing, a protected kind of speech. I have to get invited into the building, which means trying to persuade a tenant to buzz me in—and the intercoms turn their voices, and presumably mine, too, into Donald Duck noises. What I shall have to do, I am afraid, is look up the telephone numbers of the tenants, telephone them, and try to make appointments to come over and have them sign my papers. Very tedious!

The collection of signatures is not, in itself, an unreasonable requirement. But the number of signatures is relevant. For statewide offices—governor, lieutenant governor, and attorney general—the necessary number is ten thousand, which is burdensome, indeed. This is easier for incumbents and Democrats than for challengers and Republicans. The incumbents are not stupid and have not settled on these numbers accidentally.

★ ★ ★ I watched some of the televised debate of the combined session of the legislature. One could get a sense of the discussion and of the participants, and the level of argument was a little higher than I had expected, and rather more civil. But Speaker Finneran behaved badly, taking advantage of Senate president Robert Travaglini's invitation to address the meeting of the combined bodies—a courtesy, really, from one presiding officer to another—to offer a surprise amendment that would have barred gay marriage while permitting (although not requiring) legislation that would authorize civil unions. Gay rights activists said that if Finneran's proposal passed, he and Governor Romney would then work together to block civil union legislation. Travaglini, who usually works closely with Finneran, opposed the amendment, and it was defeated, but only by the slenderest margin, 100 to 98. Evan called to make sure that I was watching. What he likes most is the parliamentary maneuvering. He is a *Robert's Rules of Order* kind of guy. If I am elected, I shall have to learn some of that.

★ ★ ★ I picked up my stickers from the printer. They look terrific! And as I learned at another candidate's party, you can put one on a luggage tag and hang the luggage tag around your neck as a quasi-official badge, which is reassuring to people you stop in the streets for signatures and also can be used at parties to identify the campaign workers.

I have a thousand of them. Many, I fear, will end up as souvenirs, along with the doorhangers and the signs.

★ ★ ★ The governor is behaving badly. He is thinking of issuing an executive order, which would be overturned by the court in maybe ten minutes, to prevent the city and town clerks from issuing licenses for same-sex marriages on May 17 when the SJC decision takes effect. Is he cynically placating the White House and the Right? Or does he believe in what he is doing, which would be a violation of his oath to support and maintain the Massachusetts constitution and also an act of bigotry that, as a Mormon, he might want to be more careful about? His diplomatic characterization of the Constitutional Convention—"It reflects the democratic process," is what he said—doesn't reassure me. So did the election of Adolph Hitler.

As I lay in bed with my coffee and the papers, I tried to imagine some peculiar scenario in which I criticize the governor, the party then disowns me, and I withdraw my candidacy. If that could happen right away, I'd be spared having to go out and get ninety more people to sign my goddamn papers.

Janet offered to go out for an hour or two this afternoon and help. I told her I wasn't sure I wanted her to do that. She asked why not, and I told her—surprising myself—that I didn't want to send my wife out into the streets to beg, which is what it feels like.

"It's not begging," she said.

I told her that she hadn't done it, and I have, and that's what it feels like.

★ ★ ★ Wide awake at 2:15 AM, I found myself wondering what got me into this. If I get the damned signatures, I shall have to slog on until November, and my chances of winning are impossibly remote. Kerry will carry Cambridge and Somerville by a huge margin. Toomey will coast into office on Kerry's coattails and sheer inertia. I shall have knocked myself out, spent time and money, and will have nothing to show for it. Romney's weird reason for running—that we're all going to die—is also good a reason for not running. We have only so much time left, and it is stupid to waste it in projects that cannot possibly succeed. Politics is supposed to be the art of the possible. Why have I not recognized this or taken it into account?

★ ★ ★ I was downtown yesterday and had lunch with Evan, to whom I confided at least some of my worries. His response was to ask me whether I was having fun.

In a bizarre way, I guess I am. It is like ice fishing or duck hunting. You're cold and you are out there on the ice or hip deep in cold water at some ungodly hour, wondering what could be wrong with the fish and the poultry available in food stores. But in an irrational way, mostly having to do with the pretense of living closer to nature and demonstrating survival skills, yes, you are proud of yourself and, with just enough evidence to sustain the illusion, you are enjoying yourself. The great game of power, prestige, and influence? It starts here, in some shabby parking lot in a marginal mall, accosting strangers and asking them if they are registered to vote.

★ ★ ★ The Democrats, this morning's paper informs us, are trying to work out a way to keep Governor Romney from appointing someone—presumably a Republican—to fill Kerry's Senate seat in the event that he gets elected to the White House. What the Democrats want is to keep the seat vacant for sixty days and then hold a special election. William Straus, the representative from Mattapoisett and House chairman of the Joint Committee on Election Laws, is reported to have insisted that he was not being partisan, which must have been a difficult line for him to deliver with a straight face. Secretary of State William Galvin, a Democrat, is cautious about the idea, pointing out that this plan would deprive Massachusetts of a senator for two months and that the special election would cost a million dollars or so. The Democrats would have to pass a law changing the process, and the governor would, of course, veto this, and the House and Senate would then have to override the veto, which they can do quite easily these days.

This is why they need people like me up there. Just to show up and vote no.

★ ★ ★ I had a meeting yesterday with Bradley Jones, the minority leader in the state legislature. He is meeting with Republican candidates, and he had invited me and John Nunnari, an architect and city planner who is a candidate from Southie, to meet with him. There was no particular agenda, but he wanted to be helpful and answer any questions we had. What struck me most was that there is a kind of institutional pride he takes even as the minority leader, which means that he loses most of the time. He is a chunky fellow with his hair *en brosse* and a Dickensian clerky look to him. I'd worn a black suit for the occasion, as had Nunnari.

The minority leader has a reasonably grand suite with an inner office that features a conference table at one end, a couch and several easy chairs in the middle, opposite a fireplace with its ornate Victorian mantel, and then, near the window, his work area with the desk and bookcases. I was not taking notes, which can distort the encounter. It is better, sometimes, to let the filter of memory sort out what it interesting: what remains the next day is what the meeting was about.

What I remember most vividly is his feeling about the legislature. He is a man who has worked his way up, starting out as a selectman and then running for the legislature, where he was elected in 1994, became assistant minority leader in 2001, and then the minority leader in 2003. He is proud of this progress and enjoys the collegiality of the place, the way senior members—even Republicans—have more clout and respect than incoming members of the majority party. He likes the technical aspects of political campaigning as well as of legislation, and said several times that we had to figure out how many votes were in our districts, how many votes the winner got last time, and how to get 51 percent of the votes that would be cast in November.

New members cannot introduce legislation. It is set up that way, not inadvertently—nothing is inadvertent in the way things happen in the State House, where everyone spends a great deal of energy figuring the angles. Bills, Jones explained, have to be introduced in December, and new members are sworn in in January. Obviously, there is no way to introduce a bill before you are sworn in. So for the first year, you just sit there and listen, and maybe speak once or twice. Which is fine with me.

On an impulse, I asked how much the job pays. It is $53,000 (committee chairmen get more), plus an aide one gets to hire. There is an excellent health plan, which is free. And one gets a parking space in the garage! (Janet usually has the car; we live only three T stops away from the Park Street station, and I wondered whether I could rent my space to someone else—but this did not seem the moment to ask about that.)

5

★ ★

I have finally seen Tim Toomey, on TV at least. A comic character out of Jackie Gleason's barroom skits, he was present at a city council meeting and spoke, although not particularly cogently, criticizing some of the other council members and suggesting that they were out of line, talking about what Cambridge properties the Boston Archdiocese might sell and what parishes they might be forced to close. The members of the council, quite properly, wanted to explore uses of these sizable tracts of land in one of the most densely populated cities in America. Toomey mouthed pieties about how these were parishes where people had been baptized and married and buried, and it was distasteful to be speculating about what churches might close.

That the church has—literally—fucked up and finds itself having to pay out huge sums of money to the victims of pederast priests is certainly not the fault of the citizens of Cambridge or the members of the city council. And the councillors would be derelict in their duties if they were not in discussion with the archdiocese about what tracts of real estate might come onto the market. (Land values are high here, and if the Church closes a Cambridge church, they will get more money selling it than they would from selling one in Malden or Everett.) But Toomey saw an opening for a moment of sanctity and high-mindedness, and he took it.

It will be humiliating to lose to such a walking cliché.

★ ★ ★ I turned in another sheet of signatures yesterday and got a sheet back, with disappointing results. Only twelve names out of the twenty-two were good. That is the risk of soliciting in front of the Star Market or the Cambridge Street Post Office.

But I have sixty-two validated names, plus whatever is valid on yesterday's page.

★ ★ ★ March 2 was Super Tuesday, and Kerry's triumphs have made him the Democrats' undisputed candidate for next November, which is what everyone had come to expect. He will almost certainly carry Massachusetts, and Bush's coattails will be even shorter. Still, my guess is that the presidential election may bring out more voters and could attract recent Cambridge settlers to show up at the polls, which would be good for me. I find myself wondering whether Governor Dean and Senator Edwards do not at least in some part enjoy this awakening from the enchantment of their campaigns, their release from the peculiar and unnatural focusing of effort and attention on a long-odds quest. Theirs is the same kind of adjustment that a writer must make each time he completes a book and must reacclimatize himself to the quotidian existence of ordinary people. It is not a coming down but, on the contrary, a return to real-ism, to health.

The collapse of my campaign beckons in that way. I could of course give in to this blandishment by working just a little less hard so that I fail to get the req-uisite number of signatures, but I would feel guilty about that. I owe it to those who have given me money not to abandon the fantasy so easily and so early.

I picked up another sheet of signatures this morning from the Board of Elections. There were seventeen names that passed muster. (The others were Democrats or did not live in the district.) This brings me to seventy-nine.

★ ★ ★ I also had an interview this morning, with Amy Speer, the director of appointments for the governor's office. This was the result of my cousin Louis's suggestion about getting the governor to appoint me to some commission or other. Nothing controversial. I don't want to have anything to do with Fisher-ies, say. But . . . Weights and Measures? Maintaining the sixteen-ounce pound?

Actually, having looked at my CV, they thought I'd be of some use on some body that overlooks education. Which would not be so terrible. The only diffi-culty is that I have very unpopular views about education. I am not convinced that there is a need for college training for most jobs, and I think that, below the second-tier schools, all that a college degree means to employers is that the ap-plicant, having endured four years of boring tasks in which he or she was not in-terested or talented, will probably endure thirty years of boring employment. My own plan—which I was careful not to mention—would be to give every American a master's degree at the age of eight and then let the employers train whoever shows talent and willingness to put in the time. The effect on education would be splendid. Most schools would close, and those that remained open would be serving a small group who are interested in learning for its own sake.

What we did talk about was the governor's proposal for the Adams Scholarships, the reward for performing well on the MCAS tests. There has been criticism that this is skewed to favor the students in richer communities with better schools. . . . To which the first answer would have to be . . . Duh! I told Ms. Speer that one could very well take the opposite view—that the youngster from Belmont High School who does well is likely to go to Dartmouth, while the kid from Dorchester who, despite the odds, scores in the top quarter or top 10 percent, is likely to take advantage of the Adams program, which could be decisive in enabling him or her, with a part-time job, to go to UMass/Boston or Bunker Hill Community College. Those are the people one would want most to help because, for them, that help makes the greatest difference. She did not register agreement or approval, but I don't think I sounded like a loony.

But if I did? I am content. Better a sincere loony than a mealymouthed conformist, saying only the right things.

The one thing Ms. Speer said that I found disturbing was that the campuses of UMass (and perhaps the junior colleges and the teachers colleges as well) do not get to keep the money that comes into their coffers from tuitions and fees. It all goes into the general fund, and then each of these entities comes, hat in hand, to request funding for the next academic year. It is a system designed to keep power on Beacon Hill even if it discourages frugality or, for that matter, encourages the spending of every nickel the administrators can get their hands on, so they can ask for more in the following year.

★ ★ ★ Do I want an appointment to a board of governors or trustees, or overseers, of any public college in Massachusetts? I have never been to any of these institutions, but I know what they are like, having once given a reading at SUNY Cortland, a desperate place in New York State. It used to be a teachers college—like Fitchburg, Framingham, and others here in Massachusetts—and once did a decent enough job, back before women's liberation. But the bright women now go to law school and medical school and into business, so that the pool of applicants for teachers colleges is shallower than it used to be, and there is a hangdog quality to these places. Even worse than being second rate is knowing that you are, which is enormously depressing. The town of Cortland is also economically depressing, so that most of the houses look as though they could use a coat of paint. The soul shrivels in such places. The only thing that ever happened in Cortland was the murder Theodore Dreiser wrote about in *An American Tragedy.* They talked about that with a certain dismal pride, because it was better than nothing at all.

So what would I do to Fall River and Fitchburg and all those other places, assuming that they are like SUNY Cortland? As I said to Ms. Speer, the students are not there voluntarily, and therefore our obligation to them is all the greater. Schools that are compulsory and that don't teach are worse than prisons; they are like Soviet mental hospitals, which were jails, masquerading as therapeutic institutions.

I believe all this and would be banging my head against some very solid walls.

★ ★ ★ The morning paper has lovely news—that Common Cause is asking the U.S. Attorney's office to investigate House Speaker Thomas M. Finneran, who almost certainly lied under oath in a U.S. district court when the state legislature's 2001 redistricting plan was challenged. Pamela Wilmot, Common Cause executive director, said at a press conference yesterday that "perjury by a public official cannot and will not be tolerated. . . . The citizens of this Commonwealth expect and deserve their public officials will tell the truth when they are under oath."

There is no blue dress with stains from Finneran's bodily fluids, but that would be asking too much.

★ ★ ★ Assuming that I get onto the ballot and that I begin to attract enough attention to be worrisome, Toomey, or one of his associates, may think of Googling me or looking me up on Lexis to find whatever might be embarrassing. It would not be difficult. I tried it and found myself in an article from the *Ottawa Citizen* of last April:

HEADLINE: Universities are reaping what the cult of self-esteem has sown
BYLINE: Naomi Lakritz
CALGARY—Don't place the blame for grade inflation entirely on universities. It's just that the chickens have come home to roost. . . .

The universities are reaping what the cult of self-esteem has sown. These are the kids whose soccer coaches made sure they all received trophies and medals, just for participating.

They're the ones teachers said would suffer if they were made to learn the rules of grammar and spelling, because insisting on standards would stifle their creativity and self-expression and do their egos irreparable damage. Far better for standards to go down than for a kid's self-esteem to suffer from realizing he hadn't lived up to them and needed to work harder.

David Slavitt, a teacher of writing at the University of Pennsylvania, sums up this mentality quite nicely in his contribution to the book, *Dumbing Down*:

Essays on the Strip-Mining of American Culture. "Now, so that everyone may feel good, the students are lumped together, the bright and the normal and the 'special.' . . . And a teacher who gives a student a less-desirable grade is, in this Doonesbury world, guilty of discrimination," Slavitt writes. He calls the grade-inflation mindset "the new tactfulness," and his tongue-in-cheek solution is to give everyone a PhD at age eight. That way, only the real scholars would go on to university and intellectual standards could be re-established.

It goes on from there, but without further reference to me.

I am pleased to be cited, but I think of the whoops of glee in Toomey's office. Or another possibility is that the governor's office could do this kind of search and make the same discovery, which would take me out of the running as an education appointee.

There is no place for satirists in contemporary political life. Worse yet, the extravagances are such that there is no need, either.

★ ★ ★ It now seems that, however badly I do, I shall not finish last in this race. I read in today's *Cambridge Chronicle* of a new candidate, Helder "Sonny" Peixoto, who sent out press releases announcing his bid for the twenty-sixth Middlesex District on the same day as he pleaded guilty to charges of vehicular homicide in Malden. A former MBTA officer, he was sentenced to five years of probation, a ten-year loss of license, and a hundred hours of community service. (Does running for state rep count as community service?)

"In his release," Deborah Eisner writes, "Peixoto pointed to crime and traffic in East Cambridge as two main issues. 'Eastern Cambridge and eastern Somerville cannot afford to lose a State Representative office to the special interest groups. That is why I am announcing my candidacy for the office of State Representative as a INDEPENDENT [sic],' the release reads."

The last paragraph of the story is less amusing. Apparently Toomey has accused Peixoto of harassment, "alleging that Peixoto left threatening voicemails on the state rep's home answering machine." Toomey seems to have been worried enough to take these charges to court, where they were dismissed last January. I wonder if Peixoto is sane enough—or threatening enough, as he wanders the streets—to get 150 signatures.

★ ★ ★ There was another meeting of the Constitutional Convention, and this time they managed to get the compromise "leadership amendment" Travaglini and Finneran cobbled together to pass three readings, which sets it up for a final vote on March 29. (If it passes then, the next Constitutional Convention has to approve it for it to get on the ballot in 2006.) The Far Right voted for it because it preserves the word "marriage" to describe the union of a man and a woman; the Left liked it because it establishes civil unions for same-sex couples with "entirely the same benefits, protections, rights, and responsibilities" as come with marriage. So, better this than nothing. But there was also a lot of parliamentary play. Some of those who are sympathetic to same-sex marriages supported this amendment to get the proposal to that last step where it can no longer be amended so that they can vote it down, and then there would be no amendment at all.

I listened to some of the debate on television, but it was less fun than in the earlier session. Everything that can be said was said the first time. This was just a display of rhetoric while people in the corridors horse-traded and wheedled and bullied for votes, while demonstrators outside prayed (those were the homophobe crazies) or, in the gay and lesbian contingent, sang the national anthem (but never beyond the first stanza).

Sadly, I see that the governor's spokespeople are talking about legal moves he might make to ask the SJC to stay its decision until 2006 to see what happens in the amendment process. I doubt that he will be successful. Meanwhile, the Log Cabin Club of Massachusetts is complaining that he promised them in the campaign two years ago that he would not crusade against gay rights.

★ ★ ★ My minimalist notion of what I would do if, against all odds, I were elected and had to show up to serve in the legislature has been dented a little. I read in this morning's paper that there was a gathering of Jewish activists at the State House, urging the lawmakers to support programs for seniors, immigrants, the homeless, the disabled, and the uninsured—as a part of an annual Jewish Community Advocacy Day. What particularly caught my attention was that Senate president Travaglini was applauded when he alluded to the legislature's override of Governor Romney's veto of a budget measure to reimburse nursing homes for providing kosher food to observant Jews. "It's part of the dignity that people deserve," Travaglini said. "It's a responsibility of a caring, strong government to provide that. It's automatic."

Well, it may or may not be automatic, but it strikes me as remarkably dim, politically, for Romney to have made an issue of the extra costs for providing kosher food in nursing homes. This could not have been a big money item, and it looks mean for the governor to have done such a thing. I wonder if that was all there was to it, and whether there was something else in the measure he felt impelled to veto. But allowing for the possibility that this was the way he chose to save a few dollars, I cannot imagine myself voting to sustain his veto. So much for my party loyalty.

★ ★ ★ I am about to go out for more signatures, but this time with an observer from the *Harvard Crimson*. I've managed to interest the Harvard student paper in the quirkiness of my campaign, and Jonathan Abel, their political editor, came up with the bright idea of having a reporter watch me as I accost people and collect signatures. It is good journalistic thinking and could well make for a lively piece. It is not likely to be an altogether flattering portrayal, but if it is truthful, it could win me at least a certain sympathy. These sordid confrontations with reality are exotic to Harvard students, the kind of thing they don't know and only rarely imagine, which is why the paper's readers may find this interesting. Much of the purpose of going to places like Harvard and Yale is to obviate the need for such vulgar encounters.

★ ★ ★ I met the reporter—Michael Mendel Grynbaum—at the *Crimson* office on Plympton Street. It turns out that he is a member of Leverett, where I am a senior common room associate, and I think we got on well. He laughed a lot, took many notes, and came along with me to the Twin Cities Plaza to watch me get signers. I did well enough in that department so that it was not a disgraceful outing, actually finishing another page, which, in theory, puts me up at around 120 names. There was a young woman, a pre-med sophomore named Ann something, who took photographs of me, suitably attired in sneakers, black jeans, and a black leather jacket with my Slavitt sticker on display. And Grynbaum and I spent a little more than two hours together. It is impossible to know what kind of piece will emerge from this, but it felt comfortable. I'm not so much looking to reach voters with this as I am trying to assemble a set of clippings to show other editors, as well as radio and TV hosts. For that, the *Crimson* could be useful.

★ ★ ★ The weather has relented, and although the morning was gray and dank, there was a front that passed through so that, by early afternoon, we had bright sun and temperatures up in the fifties. It was pleasant to be outside, even at the Antonioniesque Twin Cities Plaza. It was also satisfying to realize that I am likely to succeed in my quest for signers. Assuming that my net of approved names holds steady at around 70 percent, I got maybe seven good names in a couple of hours. At three and a half or four names an hour, 150 names works out to thirty-seven hours of disagreeable effort. "Nah, I don't vote!" one of my prospects snarled at me, grimacing. "They're all a bunch of crooks."

★ ★ ★ A quirky piece in the *Globe* this week by Yvonne Abraham about Thomas Finneran demonstrates with wonderful authority what I have been supposing all along—that he is not well liked, that even on his own turf and in his own district he is a paradoxical figure. She mentions the fact that in the 2002 election Finneran got 60 percent of the vote . . . and was running unopposed. It is a manifestation of strenuous dislike that 40 percent of the voters showed up and cast blank votes. I checked in the *Massachusetts Election Statistics* book, and it's true. Indeed, there are a couple of precincts in which Finneran just barely squeaked past Blank. In Ward Seventeen, Precinct Eleven, for instance, he got 127 votes to Blank's 104. *Barely better than nobody* is a strange device to display on one's banner.

With these paltry numbers, with a total vote count of 7,616 in Boston and a small patch of Milton, Mr. Finneran imagines himself to be the most powerful man in the state, and somehow gets a considerable number of people to agree with him.

★ ★ ★ I got a questionnaire from Clean Water Action, an environmentalist group that wanted to know my positions on a number of ecological issues. I sent it along to Evan, who knows much more about these things than I do and whom I trust. We talked yesterday, in the Twin Cities Plaza parking lot. He was standing out there in raw weather, a good son getting signatures for his father. And it was a nice break for him to come and sit with me in the car for a while. He said that it was a very long list and that he was working on it. Mostly, I'd be taking positions that they'll like, he told me, but there was one question that might give me trouble, about genetically modified foods:

8. GENETIC ALTERED FOODS. Genetically engineered ingredients are now in 60% of processed foods on grocery store shelves. The federal government, however, has conducted no long-term safety tests on these foods before they entered the food supply and the environment. Both the FDA and USDA currently allow the corporations developing the genetically engineered crops to conduct all pre-market safety testing, and while the USDA does review some of this data, the FDA still has a voluntary consultation process for new genetically engineered foods entering the market. Many of these corporate studies contain "confidential business information" making it next

to impossible for independent researchers to test the findings of the biotechnology corporations. Thus, there is much information still missing regarding the health and environmental effects of commercial sale and environmental release of these foods. In addition poll after poll show that an overwhelming majority of people want genetically engineered food labeled—primarily so they can avoid them. In June 2001 an ABC News poll found that 93% want labels and of those polled 52% believe genetically engineered foods are unsafe.

A) Would you support legislation calling for a moratorium on the commercial sale and environmental release of these crops until independent testing can be conducted to determine their safety for both human health and the environment? (either federal legislation or state legislation)

_____Yes _____ No Explain/Comment:

B) Would you support legislation to require mandatory labeling of genetically engineered foods to give the public the right to know what they are eating?

_____Yes _____ No Explain/Comment:

The trouble, as Evan explained, is that genetically engineered foods require less pesticides, which is what they've been engineered for, and therefore they produce less toxic runoff and make for cleaner water. They also have higher yields, which means that they feed more people more cheaply and are good for our exports and for the poor and hungry all over the earth. These ought to be values the Clean Water Action people embrace, but basically they are Luddites and are also reflexively against corporations, which is an unfortunate legacy from their leftist student days.

It was this kind of stupidity that I suspected, and that was why I asked Evan to look at it for me. He told me years ago that the recycling of newsprint is a bad idea, that the bleach they have to use to get rid of the ink on the newspapers is more harmful to the environment than if we just burned the damned papers in a smoky bonfire. But it makes people feel good and lets them think they are doing something for Mother Earth.

★ ★ ★ Evan and I tallied up the approved signatures we have so far, and we're very nearly at 150. We still have another 30 or so to get to keep Toomey from even thinking about challenging any of my names. (If I turned in 155 and he could get 6 of them knocked off, that would keep me off the ballot and he could run unopposed—again—assuming that he gets by Avi Green in the primary.)

I ought to feel good about having succeeded in this first phase of the campaign. As Evan says, this is the boring part, and from here on it gets more interesting. Still, this was the doable part, tedious but comprehensible, and the rest of it is difficult for me to imagine and, more important, unlikely to be successful. I have to keep in mind the dismal truth that a Republican can't win in this district.

So, instead of feeling festive and triumphant, I am mostly depressed.

6

★ ★ ★ ★ ★ ★ ★ ★ ★ ★ ★ ★ ★ ★ ★ ★ ★ ★ ★

The Constitutional Convention passed the amendment yesterday defining marriage as the union of one man and one woman, enabling civil unions between same-sex couples, and satisfying no one. In the political process, ideas get muddied, differing factions struggle, and in the end there is a messy compromise that reflects, if it doesn't actually exaggerate, society's imperfections. What passed was the Travaglini-Lees amendment, which legislators viewed as "highly undesirable" but "preferable to the possibility that nothing would be sent to the state ballot for voters to weigh in on."

The legislators wanted to refer it to the voters, not out of respect for the wisdom of the electorate but only to get rid of a hot-potato issue. The governor, after the vote, announced that he would ask the Supreme Judicial Court to delay the imposition of its decision until the amendment process has played itself out (in 2006). This could "avoid confusion," as the governor said. What does one do, after all, about the couples who get married between May 17, when the SJC decision takes effect, and the end of 2006, when there could be an amendment that would deny the legitimacy of same-sex marriages? Romney is trying to look like the champion of traditional marriage in spite of the Constitutional Convention (which he manipulated to pass the amendment).

I have no idea what will happen, of course. My hope is that the same-sex marriages we will almost certainly see in six weeks will seem less and less threatening over the course of the next couple of years. The religious Right will still object, and the homophobes will continue to make noise, but the great muddled middle will behave as they always do in the short-attention-span theater of political life. It won't be so big a deal in a year (when the Constitutional Convention has to pass the amendment a second time) or two (when it could come to the ballot). It will be an issue in the election this November—but not in Cambridge. Pink politically and mauve sexually, this city will consider support for same-sex marriage a prerequisite for public office.

★ ★ ★ Satire is not a genre to which the present era is hospitable. The news reports—and the words and actions of public figures—are so bizarre as to defy exaggeration. The squabbling between the governor and the attorney general continues, and the position Attorney General Reilly took in a news conference yesterday is, as they used to say on *Laugh-In*, "Unbelievable!" He has decided to invoke a 1913 Massachusetts law that prevents people from out of state from marrying in the Commonwealth if they are not eligible for marriage in their own states. This was a piece of racism of which citizens of Massachusetts ought to be ashamed, for it was clearly a way of enforcing the South's antimiscegenation laws here without having to use the word. The law ought to have been repealed, but even to do that would be to advert to the disgraceful behavior of those who enacted the legislation in the first place.

★ ★ ★ Meanwhile, Mike Barnicle, a local columnist and talk-show personality, is in trouble for using the word "Mandingo," referring to former Maine senator and secretary of defense William Cohen and his wife Janet Langhart, who is black; he has been forced by the radio station to issue a public apology. Reilly is smarter than Barnicle, however, and he knows that racism in Boston is alive and well and that homophobia is thriving. He also knows how to appeal to racists and homophobes without looking like an utter goon. So, if he can threaten to use this old law to keep the queers from getting married here, he gets points from the Church and right-wingers whether he is successful or not. This takes the curse off his defiance of the governor, whom he has refused to represent in the Supreme Judicial Court when Romney requests a two-and-a-half-year stay on the Court's order legitimating same-sex marriages. He can say no to the governor without appearing too friendly toward gays. His cleverness only makes him more odious.

★ ★ ★ I met yesterday afternoon with Ken Sanchez, president of the Massachusetts chapter of the Log Cabin Republicans, who are having a hell of a time with Bush in Washington and Romney here in Massachusetts. I can't expect much help from the GLAD people, who will be devoting their energy and money to defeating antigay candidates. Toomey voted against the amendment, and so he is not a target. But the Log Cabin people are Republicans, and their aim is both to defeat the amendment and also to promote their views within the party, so I look attractive to them. We had a good meeting, I thought. Mr. Sanchez is a young man from New York who went to Fordham and Boston College Law School (where Reilly went, too). He is a bright, articulate fellow with a sense of humor, which is helpful for people in awkward situations. He is going to have me meet the Log Cabin board, and their endorsement is likely. There may be some money I can get from them, or volunteer work, or some coffees and networking. This is what I am likely to be doing during the next seven months—campaigning.

★ ★ ★ I had a disappointing yield from the recent set of ballot petitions. Evidently, a number of unenrolled voters decided to come out and vote in the Democratic primary for Kerry (whose victory was a foregone conclusion) and didn't realize that this changed them from Unenrolled to Democrat. So some of the sheets had fewer names than I usually get. Still, we're up to 143 valid signatures, plus one sheet being checked in Somerville.

★ ★ ★ Just as I had decided that it could not get any sillier, Paul Loscocco, a Republican of Holliston, comes up with the batty idea, reported in this morning's paper, that the state should get out of the marriage business entirely. He suggests that we do what the French do, separating the civil and religious aspects of marriage, and issue licenses only for civil unions for heterosexual as well as homosexual couples. "Unions" would be the business of the state, and "marriages" would be up to the religious institutions. This would solve the separate-but-equal problem. The Catholic Church is against it, the gays are against it, and there is no enthusiasm for it in the state senate. But then, Republicans have learned to adjust to not having their ideas immediately adopted, even the zany ones.

★ ★ ★ It rained for much of the past week, hard enough to cause flooding in some areas. And it is supposed to snow on Sunday, although they don't expect much accumulation in Boston and Cambridge. But it is April, and our patience for snow is exhausted, just as my patience for accosting strangers is wearing thin. I was out for a couple of hours this morning, and the Twin Cities Plaza is yielding less than it did. The regulars know me and have either signed or have indicated—by blank stares, by shaking their heads, or by that incredibly annoying "I'm all set"—that they can't or won't sign. One or two expressed encouragement and said that it was a good thing to be running, and a few signed the paper on my clipboard, but I've moved on mentally, and the prospect of another eight or ten hours of this is daunting. I am sick of people who think *Republican* is a dirty word and, even though they are unenrolled, won't sign their names to help get me on the ballot. I explain that it doesn't commit them to vote for me, but they just can't do it. When I was cold and my legs started to hurt, I went up to the Target in Somerville to try there, where there's a bench I can sit on, but with no better success.

Then, as long as I was at Target, I went inside to buy Janet a new umbrella, the storms of last week having destroyed her old one. At least I accomplished something.

★ ★ ★ The phone rang this morning, waking me up, a woman from the Somerville Election Commission returning my call of Friday afternoon. They close at twelve thirty on Fridays to compensate for staying open on Thursday evenings. I had called on Friday to ask whether that last sheet I had left with them was done and how many validated names it had produced. This morning the answer was two. Two? Out of twenty-two?

What with the signatures I got this weekend and with those that Fred Baker has for me, I'm still probably up there at 150, but this news from Somerville is dismal. It has nothing to do with how I was going about the job. It was just bad luck. And as a writer, I ought to know about such things. A manuscript pleases an editor or doesn't. A publishing company is cutting back and an editor who likes your work gets fired. There are things that happen that are beyond your control, as I ought to understand after all these years in a game as tough as politics. But a callus in one place doesn't protect you from a bruise in another.

★ ★ ★ Deb Eisner (Deb, or Deborah, but *not* Debbie, she insists) of the *Cambridge Chronicle* called, asking for my views about the latest redistricting plans, about which I knew nothing whatever. So she e-mailed me the two plans, one by the legislature and one by the plaintiffs in the SJC redistricting case. The plaintiffs' plan actually changes the boundaries of the Twenty-sixth Middlesex District in which I am a candidate. I would lose one precinct up in Somerville and I would gain a precinct in Cambridge—Ward Three, Precinct Three—which is close to where I live. I'd pick this up from the Eighth Suffolk District. There would not be a great deal of difference in the racial and ethnic composition of the district that I can see. I would get one or two housing projects where there are blacks and Hispanics, but the part of Somerville I'd lose is hardly silk-stocking. The reason for the adjustment would be a domino effect from the redrawing of the lines down in Mattapan, where Finneran was protecting his safe seat.

I consulted with Evan, and his view is that Finneran is a bigot and a liar, and that if he hadn't dragged his feet on this, there wouldn't be the need, at this late date, to redraw districts so that candidates have to scramble to make sure that their signatures are still valid and that their signers haven't been disqualified by revisions in the map. (The deadline for turning in the signatures would be extended from April 27 to May 11, but I would not be happy to have this agony protracted.) I was not quite so vehement when I spoke with Ms. Eisner. I referred to the Common Cause press conference in which Pamela Wilmot accused Finneran of perjury, and I asked whether, when a perjurer denies that he is a bigot, we are required to believe him.

It is not as though this is the first time that Mr. Finneran has dicked around with redistricting to accomplish his private and less than admirable purposes. In 2001, Finneran redrew the lines of the districts in Lowell and Salem so that U.S. Representatives Martin Meehan of Lowell and John Tierney of Salem had to run against each other in 2002. Both Meehan and Tierney are Democrats, and it was weird for a Democratic legislature to be doing a thing like this to people in their own party. Finneran claimed that he thought Meehan was going to be running for governor. (The idea of telephoning the representative never occurred to him!) Some cynics suggested that Finneran was punishing Meehan for his support of the Clean Elections Law that Finneran disliked.

It was a minor part of that exercise that the Cambridge state rep districts were redrawn so that Jarrett Barrios's district, traditionally black or Latino, disappeared. Barrios was too liberal for Finneran, was Latino, and was gay, so that one can only guess about Finneran's attitude toward him, but he came out of it well, running instead for the state senate and defeating former Cambridge mayor Anthony Galluccio.

★ ★ ★ The *Somerville News* piece is out:

A poet in politics
by Reem Abu-Libdeh

In David R. Slavitt's office, across the wall from an old etching of Alexander Pope, and diagonal from the computer where he is surely working on either his 17th book of poetry, or 30th novel, hangs a small wooden plaque with a complex ambigram of sorts. An ambigram being a word or words that can be read in more than one way, or from different vantage points.

If you look at the word one way, you see "David." Or maybe you see "Slavitt." It all depends on what you're thinking about when you look at it.

In the next several months, residents of the 26th Middlesex district will decide if they see a state representative when they look at this 69-year-old poet, translator, novelist and playwright. Is Slavitt a political newcomer who can give the district, and the state legislature, a breath of fresh air, or just another Republican candidate who faces no chance against twelve-year incumbent Timothy J. Toomey, Jr.?

"I'm running on the theory that a two-party system would run better with two parties," said Slavitt, who describes himself as a "socially liberal Republican."

The most important order of business, Slavitt said, is challenging the "Democratic hyper-majority" in the general courts and ending the "dictatorship of Speaker Thomas Finneran, who flaunts his power and flouts the will of the people."

"We're very glad to have David running," said Matt St. Hilaire, acting political director for the Massachusetts Republican Party. "We'd love to have him on Beacon Hill to support this reform agenda.

"[Slavitt] is someone who has no connections to special interest groups and can take a fresh look at things. He has not been involved in local politics and can take a different approach. And his life experiences are certainly going to add to that," said St. Hilaire.

Slavitt's life experiences have yielded 29 novels, 17 collections of poetry, and 28 volumes of translations from Greek, Latin, Hebrew, Spanish, French, and Portuguese. While he may be a political novice, Slavitt's a familiar face in the literary world.

Slavitt, a native of White Plains, N.Y., said his roots in Massachusetts go back to the fifties when he was a student at Andover, and his ties to Cambridge go back to the seventies. He spent 20 years in Philadelphia, teaching at the University of Pennsylvania, University of Maryland, and Temple University, and returned to Cambridge in 2000 when his wife Janet was hired as the director of Palliative Care and Symptom Management at Dana-Farber/Brigham and Women's Cancer Center.

For Slavitt, his political inexperience, on the local and state levels, makes him a stronger candidate. "As an outsider without any political ambitions whatsoever, I am not beholden to special interests and can show independence and intelligence on Beacon Hill—qualities for which the General Court is not well-known," said Slavitt.

"The thing about the Democratic Party in Massachusetts is that it's supposed to be the party of concern for the underdog, the party of hope, the party of inclusion. And it's not. It's the party of incumbency. It's not very welcoming to ethnic groups other than, say, Irish and Italians.

"Republicans, of whom the Massachusetts electorate is worried because they don't want bible-belt, hard right, Ashcroft-like Republicans, are people like Lodge and Weld and Romney. They are the guys who have a kind of large, generous, friendly, understandable notion of what public service should be and how government should work. And there aren't even enough of them in the state house to maintain gubernatorial vetoes," he said.

His main job, Slavitt said, would be voting to sustain gubernatorial vetoes and doing what he can for constituents who come by with problems.

Slavitt, who describes himself as a "fiscal conservative and social moderate," is pro-choice and supports same-sex marriage. "I am more of a libertarian Republican. I want to get the government off of my back, out of the bedroom, and no prayer in school," he said.

Slavitt almost ran for state rep in 2002 when his son, Evan, a lawyer and general counsel to the Massachusetts Republican Party, was running for attorney general.

"At the point where [Evan] was going on and getting the signatures and making the speeches and raising money, he said, 'You know, I had a wacko idea last night. Why don't you run for state rep? We'd be a father-son team and could get some media coverage.' So I called up the party and said, 'Is anybody running for the 26th Middlesex?' And they said, 'Well, yes.' But, two years later they called me."

Once Evan's campaign was over in 2002, he told Slavitt that he might like running on his own since he enjoyed working on Evan's campaign and was "somewhat energized about the one-party problem the state faces."

"When the party was recruiting candidates for this cycle, I encouraged him to volunteer," Evan said.

Slavitt's campaign got underway last fall when St. Hilaire asked him if he would consider running for state rep.

"This year, the governor and lieutenant governor and the party are making a concerted effort to put more Republicans in the state house and to redress, to some degree, this preposterous imbalance. So they called me and I thought, 'You know, I've been a flicker picker at Newsweek, I'm a poet and a novelist and a journalist. I'm never going to have a chance like this again. This is a nutty thing to do.

"So I thought about it and I went to a dinner where the governor spoke and he was trying to convince people on the fence who weren't decided yet and he said, 'When you look back on your life you want to say you took your shot, you did your thing.' And I said, 'You know, that's exactly what I was thinking.' It would be kind of fun. I mean, I get to meet him and hang out with decent people, some of them are villains and knaves, and some of them are quite interesting. And I have the time. I can afford to do it. And I thought, 'Why not?' As the governor said, I'll take a shot. I'll see what happens."

The chances are slim, Slavitt said, but not non-existent that he could win. "I brought the proof of the campaign door hangers into the printer, old wizened guy, does a lot of political work for both parties, [and he] looks at me, looks at the thing, looks at me again and says, 'You're running against Tim Toomey? You could win.'"

One hundred and fifty signatures are required to get on the ballot for state representative. To date, Slavitt has collected 155 signatures, and his goal is to collect 180 to avoid any potential problems with unqualified signatures. The sheets are due May 25 at the office of the secretary of the Commonwealth, William Galvin.

★ ★ ★ Nice enough, and it is useful for the press file that I will be sending to other media after the signatures are turned in. Reporters believe what they read in the papers, even though they, of all people, ought to know better.

My comments to Deborah Eisner about resitricting didn't get into the *Cambridge Chronicle*, but that is just as well. I can insult Mr. Finneran later in a better venue. What the article told me that I hadn't known was that the Three-Three Precinct, if it is added to the Twenty-sixth Middlesex District, probably helps Avi Green in his primary fight with Toomey.

At the Somerville Board of Elections yesterday, I saw that Green had more than two hundred signatures—and that was just Somerville, which is a small part of the district: he almost certainly has more in Cambridge. I felt a pang of jealousy, and a frisson of inadequacy, and then I realized that he is approaching people who are mostly registered as Democrats, so he can get qualified signers much more easily than I. I looked at his website (mine is yet to go up, although I have a friend who is working on it) and read some of his press clippings. There was a piece about Green in the *Globe* last December that said that he had already raised "about $20,000." I have raised . . . about $2,000.

These are reminders that I will almost certainly lose in November. I know that, but most of the time I manage a kind of denial.

★ ★ ★ I had a particularly disagreeable couple of hours at the Twin Cities Plaza today. I got very few signers—only a half dozen or so in all that time—and the people were particularly hostile, refusing to look at me or respond, even when I smiled and wished them good morning before asking if they were registered voters. A number of them walked by as if I weren't audible or visible. Others were vehement in their denials, as if I had asked them whether they gambled, or went to prostitutes. "Are you registered to vote in Cambridge or Somerville?" I would ask, and the reply would be almost apoplectic: "Certainly not!" Or, I would get a grudging and skeptical "Yes," but then, when I asked the follow-up question, "As a Republican or Unenrolled?" they would get nasty.

It is a horrid, hateful business, and I found myself wondering if it might possibly be doing me any good in some mysterious, spiritual way. The Jesuits train their novices by having them do menial chores. My parents used to tell me that it was good for me to have stupid summer jobs, and that I would learn what work was. (Mostly what I learned was that I wanted never to do it—which I have been lucky enough to arrange, most of my life.) Even to entertain such ideas, though, is worrisome. Am I becoming sentimental, looking on the bright side of a subject that does not have one?

One way or another, it will be over in nineteen days. And then I can get on to the real business of the campaign, going down to a more or less ignominious defeat to Green, who is bright but a kid, or Toomey, a sinkhole of mealy-mouthed piety.

★ ★ ★ Last night, at the Central Square branch of the Cambridge Public Library, there was an organizational meeting of the Cambridge Republican City Committee and the ward committees. I had been dreading this, because of the last Cambridge Republican function I attended, back at Christmas. But last night, there were around twenty-five people, some of whom had been out gathering signatures for me. Their harvest was not rich, but a dozen names from people we know are Republicans or Unenrolled and who live in the district are hardly negligible. That's hours out at the Twin City Plaza.

Fred Baker was elected city chairman, which he deserves. What puny strength the city committee has will be available to me as we get into the networking and the public appearances during the summer and fall.

After the organizational part of the meeting, Fred invited me to say a few words to introduce myself, which I did. I talked mostly about the need to restore two-party government to Massachusetts. I didn't say anything about my education—a mention of Yale can sound uppity, even among Republicans— or about my social and political views. Almost certainly, many of those in the room were opposed to same-sex marriage (or afraid of it), or were pro-life. Or they wanted prayer in public schools. These are all divisive issues and have nothing to do with the business of a state rep, so I just attacked Mr. Finneran and Tim Toomey his henchman. It went well, I think.

After me, Bob Ferencsik, a candidate for the state Senate, spoke. He graduated from the Naval Academy in 1978, which means he is roughly Evan's age. And then Kevin Cuddleback, a state rep candidate from northern Cambridge, Belmont, and a little piece of Arlington, talked for a few minutes. Romney carried Belmont comfortably, and that is in Cuddleback's district. So he has hope or at least is saying so.

I was elected as treasurer of the Sixth Ward committee, having been promised that there would be no money for me to handle. But the office must be filled in order to conform to the regulations. I forget who the ward chairman is. (Fred Baker knows this.) This is my first elective office, I think, except for the presidency of the Student Organization of the Temple Israel Hebrew School in White Plains in 1947–48.

★ ★ ★ The state Republican Party is offering a hundred bucks as a campaign contribution to any candidate who gets his or her signatures turned in by April 22. In a sense, it is pathetic. It is also a recognition that this is arduous and time-consuming, and they want to congratulate us. I have to hand in photocopies of 250 raw signatures with a note from the town clerks or election commissions that they have been turned in, or, alternatively, a receipt from the secretary of state's office proving that they have been given 150 certified signatures. I ought to be able to do that.

★ ★ ★ The Cambridge Election Commission is busy with Michael Capuano's signatures. He is a candidate for the U.S. House of Representatives and needs, I think, three thousand names, and it will take the people in the election commission office a few days to work through his sheets before they get to mine. So it will be Thursday before I am able to take my certified names over to the secretary of state's office, and the receipt to the party office.

Meanwhile, the campaign is about to begin. I had a call this afternoon from Reem Abu-Libdeh of the *Somerville News*. The paper will be hosting a candidates' forum at the Mt. Vernon Restaurant in Somerville on May twelfth. Tim Toomey, Avi Green, and I will appear, make statements, and answer questions for an hour or so. That's what I'd been hoping for months ago when I imagined running for office. It should be fun.

I also had an e-mail from Fred Baker reminding me that next Monday is Patriots' Day and that there is a celebration on the Cambridge Common, and I ought to go there and work the crowd. That will be rather less fun, I think, and Toomey is a part of the program. But I have to show up.

Is it a school holiday? Perhaps I can take my grandchildren. That'd be entertaining for them, and it would look good for me to be seen with grandchildren. Is it cynical even to have thought of such a thing? Maybe, but I'll ask them anyway.

★ ★ ★ I sent out a news item this morning to the *Cambridge Chronicle* and the *Somerville News:*

4/15/04
Slavitt Files Signatures with Secretary of State's Office
The David Slavitt Committee announced today that Mr. Slavitt filed 176 signatures with the elections office of the Secretary of State of the Commonwealth of Massachusetts yesterday, which qualify him to appear on the ballot in the Republican primary in September (where he is unopposed) and on ballot of the general election in November. He is running for the office of State Representative in the 26th Middlesex district and will face the winner of the Democratic Primary fight between incumbent Timothy J. Toomey and challenger Avi Green.

Mr. Slavitt is a poet, novelist, and translator whose English version of *The Regrets of Joachim du Bellay* will be published in July by Northwestern University Press. He said that he is happy to have qualified for the ballot, that the experience of soliciting signatures was "interesting," but that "on the other hand, I'm not sorry that it is over and that I can now get to the real business of campaigning. The conversation can now begin."

I wonder how many will get the joke. The reference is to the Dudley Moore routine in *Beyond the Fringe* about going down into the coal mine to dig coal, and he says that the first lump of coal was "very interesting," and the second lump was "interesting," and then his "interest began to wane," so that he was looking forward to tea break. And at tea break, he asks his mates whether they are familiar with the works of Marcel Proust, and, oddly, none of them is. So he tells them about how Proust dipped his biscuit into his tea and his whole life came back before his eyes. And one of his mates tries it, and he remembers the first day he came down into the mine, and how the first lump of coal was "interesting. . . ."

Cruel, but funny.

★ ★ ★ Turning in the papers was, in fact, slightly more dramatic than the press release suggests. I had heard at the Somerville Elections Commission that they had been told that Galvin, the secretary of state, might not be accepting signatures from candidates in districts that could be changed by the decision of the courts and that, in these districts, the candidates might have to start from the beginning and go through the entire process again. To be sure of what I'd heard, I figured I could call the secretary of state's office and ask if they were accepting nomination papers.

On the way back from Somerville—where my sheet of 22 names had only 3 that were valid—I stopped at the Cambridge Election Commission, down the block from where I live, and found that the papers I'd left with them were now ready, and that I now had a total of 176 validated names. The secretary of state's elections office told me that they were accepting nomination papers, and I decided not to take any further risks but to run down there at once. They asked if I had my receipt from the Ethics Commission for having filed my financial disclosure forms. What? No one had ever mentioned this part of the process to me. Had I filed such a form? Had Evan?

The Ethics Commission office was down on the sixth floor, which, in the John W. McCormack Building, means that you go down to the first floor and then up on the local elevator to six. It was a quarter to four, and all these ethicist bureaucrats were gone, leaving one woman to take care of the office and answer the phones. (The door was locked because she was alone, even though there are security people down in the lobby.) She let me in, looked my name up in the files, found nothing, and gave me a copy of the form—an eight-page questionnaire with eighteen pages of instructions. One has to list all stocks and bonds, mortgages, honoraria, business ownerships, gifts, trusts, forgiven debts, and other such information. It was too complicated to sit there and write out. So I took some forms and went back down to the first floor and then, in the other bank of elevators, back up to seventeen, where the elections people gave me a receipt indicating I was not yet on the ballot because the ethics receipt was missing.

So I still have to do that. But they took the names. I do not have to begin again and collect 150-plus more signatures. I just fill out the form, get the receipt, turn it in, and then the press release comes true.

★ ★ ★ The financial disclosure information was not all that difficult to assemble. It was April 15, after all, and I had my income tax forms to consult, all beautifully organized by our accountant. But getting the information to the Ethics Commission was not easy. There is a website, but it was not clear how to sign in. One had to e-mail them to get a password, and then it was unclear where to go on the site to use the password. Phone calls—they give a number that one can call for help—always resulted in a busy signal or, almost as bad, a machine on which one could leave a message. I gave up after a couple of hours, filled out the form by hand, photocopied it (one needs to submit three copies!), and then took the T back to Park Street. I walked up the hill to Ashburton Place, got through security and into the elevator. But the car wasn't working. The door would close and then open again. Five, six, seven times. We got out and waited for another car.

An omen, like tripping as you leave your house on a trip?

But, no, it went well enough from there on. On the sixth floor, I turned in my financial forms, got my receipt, went back down to one and then up to seventeen, where I presented the ethics receipt and got a new receipt from the election people with the "On ballot" box checked. It was done. I was a candidate!

Now, of course, what I need is a miracle.

Part Two

7

Tomorrow, my first day of electioneering, is Patriots' Day. Across the river they will be running the Boston Marathon, but here in Cambridge we have a reenactment of William Dawes's ride. Dawes was the one Longfellow didn't write about. Someone dressed like him will come cantering on a horse to the Cambridge Common to announce to Mayor Sullivan that the British are coming. It is a big gathering, and Fred says I should show up, shake hands with anyone willing to listen, introduce myself, and try to make my presence and candidacy known. This is not natural to me, but if it is intimidating it is also exciting. I will go up to people, tell them that I'm David Slavitt and I'm running for state rep, and be engaging. If the imposture is good enough, I may persuade myself.

★ ★ ★ It was a pitiable ceremony with more people on the platform or in uniform in front of it than in the audience. Partly, this is because Patriots' Day is a kind of pre–Memorial Day occasion and Cambridge is very antiwar. There were salutes with rifles and, from the Massachusetts Bicentennial Battery, a cannon, and there were wreaths laid at General Washington's monument and then General Kosciusko's and General Pulaski's. The president of the Gold Star Wives of America spoke about how we should feel grateful to those who have served and are serving in the armed forces and especially those who have given their lives for their country. But only a few parents came with kids to let them see the man dressed up as General Dawes ride up on a handsome horse. I was delighted to hear him recite an 1896 poem by Helen F. Moore—not great but great fun, and ours, like a local cheese. It is a parody of Longfellow's, and after complaining that "Poets have never sung my praise. / Nobody crowned my brow with bays," it concludes:

HISTORY rings with his silvery name;
Closed to me are the portals of fame.
Had he been Dawes and I Revere,
No one had heard of him, I fear.
No one has heard of me because
He was Revere and I was Dawes.

After the rider dismounted, Mayor Sullivan greeted him and gave him a message to take on to the mayor of Arlington. Up on the platform, behind Sullivan, were several of the city councillors, including Toomey. It crossed my mind to introduce myself to him after the ceremonies, but then I thought that I'd as soon wait until next month and the candidates' forum. Why blemish his afternoon? Why blemish my own?

★ ★ ★ The papers today are full of Finneran—and of the previous Speaker, one Charlie Flaherty, who was convicted of bribery and tax evasion and for whom prominent Democrats put on a fund-raiser to pay his $50,000 fine. Speaking at that event were Senators Kennedy and Kerry. Flaherty never served a day in jail and didn't even have to pay the fine, because the pols bailed him out. Finneran, one columnist suggests, went to law school and ought to have known better than to lie under oath to federal judges.

★ ★ ★ We assume that representative democracy is a good thing, but the Democratic Party in Massachusetts is less a confederation of people sympathetic to the plight of the underdog and the working man than a cynical merger of ethnics that stick together no matter what. Flaherty and Finneran? They may be crooks but they are not the Brahmins, whom the Irish and Italians still resent for affronts to their immigrant grandparents. But voters don't want the truth; they want to be flattered and made to feel good. They are like an idiot king who amuses himself while his nobles carry on the business of government and grand larceny. To tell the monarch the truth is risky, for he is unlikely to welcome news that he is being cheated and has colluded by his stupidity and indolence.

★ ★ ★ I began the business of fund-raising, going through reports of various websites, the Federal Election Commission's and that of the Massachusetts Office of Campaign and Political Finance, picking out Cambridge residents who donated to Romney or Bush, and phoning them. If I'm persuasive, they let me mail them a letter with a copy of the *Somerville News* piece. It's a terrible job, but I get to sit at my desk and drink coffee. There are worse tasks, as I learned on the pavement of the Twin Cities Plaza.

★ ★ ★ I had a call from the Bush/Cheney campaign that was a lesson in how to ask for money. The young man first inquired, on a scale of one to five, how important it was to me for President Bush to be reelected this year. Only after I'd answered did he go into his pitch. I could ask people how important the two-party system is to them, with the checks and balances of a robust opposition, and only then go into my request for money. It is devious and in a way unattractive. I have had a sheltered life and never had to do these unpleasant things much of the economy is based on. I am, for all my assertiveness, shy in some situations. This foray into politics may cure that.

★ ★ ★ I found myself wide awake at three in the morning. And one of the subjects that flittered across my mind was the debate in Somerville in three weeks. I shall be on a platform with Toomey and Avi Green. I want to be pleasant, charming, slightly condescending perhaps, but unimpeachably polite. The way to do that is to be soft-spoken but armed with lots of incriminating information. Is Toomey as much a Finneran henchman as I have been saying? What if he denies it? So this morning, I fooled around with the computer, looking up things and doing some calculations. Toomey voted with Finneran 97.8 percent of the time in 2003 (418 of 427 votes) and 97.8 percent of the time from 1997 to 2003. Meanwhile, Pat Jehlen, Somerville's other state rep and a Democrat, voted with Finneran 81.8 percent of the time—which wasn't enough, because she is on his enemies list. I also learned that there are only 23 Republicans in the legislature. We'd need 54 to sustain a veto (a third of 160). My chances of getting elected are slim; the chances of 30 other Republicans beating incumbent opponents are nil. The party perhaps plans to narrow the gap over several election cycles. In Massachusetts? It is unlikely.

★ ★ ★ It is the last signature-gathering weekend. I have my receipt from the secretary of state's office and am on the ballot, but for a lot of other candidates the deadline is next Tuesday. Dane Baird, who is running in Somerville against Pat Jehlen, has 132 names and needs 18 more, so he has a strenuous weekend. He told me his most disheartening moment was getting back a sheet with zero valid names. What could I say in consolation? At least the Somerville Election Board people were sympathetic and helpful. Another candidate reported turning in a sheet on which her own signature was deemed invalid because it was "illegible." She can, of course, sign again and resubmit, but it is dismaying. And it's what you get when the clerks are less than friendly. I am glad all this is behind me. I won't gloat, because I know that I have only set myself up for a larger disappointment later on. But it is nice to be doing something else this weekend.

★ ★ ★ There was a piece in the *Cambridge Chronicle* about Avi Green challenging Toomey to a series of five debates, and a cartoon showing Green and Toomey in a boxing ring. I thought I ought to be included in these events and I e-mailed Green:

> Dear Avi,
>
> I like the cartoon in the Chronicle!
>
> May I participate in these debates? It'd be a more realistic offering to the electorate, and there are differences between us. I am against rent control, and in favor of the death penalty. So the range of viewpoints and positions would be greater.
>
> We'll talk further after our meeting on the 12th of May.
>
> Best, David

And then Toomey:

> Dear Representative Toomey,
>
> I look forward to meeting you on the 12th of May at the Somerville News candidates' evening.
>
> I've written to Avi Green suggesting that these debates—to which you have generously agreed in principle—ought to be three-way encounters. This would give the voters a wider range of choices and positions. Unlike you and Avi, I am in favor of the death penalty and opposed to rent control.
>
> Let us discuss what seems reasonable and fair after the May 12th event.
>
> Sincerely, David R. Slavitt

To this, the representative answered:

> David:
>
> In response to your email concerning debates, I have no problem with your participation in all debates. Since Avi and I agree on most issues, without you the 5 debates could become tedious affairs. Tim

It may not be effusive but it's civil. As I shall try to be, too. After all, I'm not attacking him so much as Finneran, who won't be there. Of course, Evan points out that my presence on the platform is entirely to Toomey's advantage. It puts me on the right and Green on the left, and leaves him the high ground of the centrist position, which is what works in politics. Still, it is exposure, without which I cannot get very far.

★ ★ ★ Romney's spokesperson announced yesterday that the governor is going to enforce the 1913 antimiscegenation law. This will exclude most out-of-state same-sex couples from the legally married status currently available to Massachusetts residents and is a more sweeping interpretation than that of Attorney General Reilly, who thought it applies only to the thirty-eight states that have passed definition-of-marriage acts. Romney believes that the 1913 law applies to residents of all the other states and has written to all the governors and attorneys general asking them if he is wrong in his belief. It is an unpleasant maneuver, reviving an old bigotry and applying it to a new situation. But it makes Romney look as though he is on Bush's side and validates his national credentials. Or it is a deep-seated belief Romney holds and is acting on. That only seems worse.

★ ★ ★ I have thought up a way of alienating everyone in the audience at the candidates' forum. All I would have to do is begin my four- or five-minute talk by saying that there are three things that citizens of Massachusetts have in common, commitments to the Boston Red Sox, the Catholic Church, and the Democratic Party, even though all of these institutions are in a state of catastrophic disrepair. The Red Sox do well enough each summer to break our hearts. The Church is closing parishes, shutting down schools, selling off property, and trying to pay off enormous settlements for the crimes of its pederast priests. And the Democratic Party is a never-ending story of corruption, greed, petty bickering, and blithe disregard of the voters' interests.

★ ★ ★ One of the great rewards of this campaign is my ability to appreciate the dexterity of Evan's appearance last night on Emily Rooney's *Greater Boston*. She had a segment about that 1913 law and Romney's declaration that he will see that it is observed. As a favor to her and to the Republican Party, Evan appeared to defend him. On the other side was James Roosevelt, grandson of FDR and counsel to the state Democratic Party. (Evan is counsel to the Republicans.) My son's enthusiasm for the law is no greater than mine, but this did not inconvenience him much. On the contrary, it was a constraint that added grace to the performance, if one knew how to listen.

In the setup, Lawrence Tribe opined (he always opines!) that the right to marry whomever one chooses is fundamental and cannot be limited to residents. But in the discussion, Evan said that (a) the governor is merely enforcing the law and doing so impartially, his office having announced that justices of the peace who refuse to marry same-sex couples who *are* residents will be required to resign; and (b) if the legislature wants to repeal the 1913 law, they can, and that Speaker Finneran and Senate president Travaglini have had plenty of notice. He was wry, amused, amusing, almost playful. At no time did he say that what the governor is doing is a good thing, but he defused the issue and shifted the blame. There was not much for Roosevelt to say, except that it is a terrible law and embarrassing for the governor to be enforcing it. (My father would have loved seeing his grandson and FDR's debating on television.)

It is one of the joys in life to admire the achievements of a child, and I was like a young person at a recital whose fumbling efforts at the piano enable him better to understand the brilliance of the virtuoso on the stage. I shall have to get up on the stage, myself, in a couple of weeks, and Evan will be in the audience. I hope I do half as well.

★ ★ ★ The piece in the *Crimson* came out this morning:

For Local Writer, Literature Leads to Politics
By Michael M. Grynbaum
Crimson Staff Writer

"A sense of humor is fatal in politics," David R. Slavitt says dryly, in his usual cynical tone. This November, he'd like to prove that maxim wrong.

It's a dreary day, and Slavitt is en route to Somerville to collect signatures. Poet, author, critic, and translator, Slavitt hopes to tack yet another title onto his resume: politician. After collecting his 150th signature last week, he is now the only Republican challenger to Democratic State Representative Timothy J. Toomey, who represents parts of Cambridge and Somerville.

But shoe-leather campaigning hasn't been easy for the 69-year-old member of the Leverett Senior Common Room.

"It's a humiliating experience," Slavitt says of the signature-gathering. "I see myself doing stuff that the entire purpose of a Harvard degree is to defend against."

On a chilly spring day, Slavitt stands in front of the Star Market at Somerville's Twin Cities Plaza, a slowly sinking strip mall. A closed Mars Music store sits entombed at one end of the lot, its windows revealing a dark and empty interior. Drab storefronts advertise a Fleet Bank, Dunkin' Donuts and SuperCuts. Shoppers carry grocery bags to their cars.

The writer-cum-candidate, sporting white sneakers, a black leather jacket and a baseball cap, accosts customers. "Excuse me sir, are you registered to vote in Somerville or Cambridge?"

He receives a near-endless parade of nasty looks and blank stares in response. The apathy of the U.S. voter is present in the Plaza this afternoon, and Slavitt is bearing the brunt of it.

Nevertheless, he pursues the passersby, limping after those who ignore his initial pleas. Slavitt is insistent, but not pushy. Many of the women he speaks to seem charmed by his one-liners and flattery. By the end of the afternoon, he has amassed his signature quota for the day.

Slavitt has chutzpah, and he surely needs it. The political task at hand is not a simple one—Slavitt is looking to uproot a six-term incumbent who is also a Cambridge city councilor. It doesn't help that he's running as a Republican, in a town that leans so far to the left some have dubbed it "The People's Republic."

"The idea of a Republican primary in Cambridge sounds Dadaist," Slavitt admits. But, he says, in politics one never knows.

"[Toomey] could be hit by a bus," he says. "An enormous bird could pick him up and take him to a . . . cliff in the Arabian nights. You don't know. As God said to the guy who prayed for the lottery, be fair—buy a ticket."

PORTRAIT OF THE POET

Slavitt is a combination of pomposity and sardonicism, a man who is smart, talented, funny—and knows it. He was raised in the affluent suburbs of Westchester, N.Y., the son of a prominent Manhattan lawyer. In his teens he shipped off to Phillips Academy in Andover, Mass., matriculating at Yale College in 1952.

As a Jewish student who attended elite Northeastern schools in the heyday of the Protestant Establishment, Slavitt faced prejudice growing up. When he applied for admission to Choate, a school representative calmly informed his parents that the year's "Hebrew quota" had already been reached. Slavitt, a middle-schooler at the time, was in the room.

He remembers being angry, but now laughs at the irony he has lived to see.

"Are there any Ivies with non-Jewish presidents?" Slavitt jokes.

He excelled as a Bulldog, publishing his poetry in top-notch publications like the Yale Review and the Chicago Review. "I was a phenom," Slavitt says happily.

After being named a Scholar of the House—a senior-year honors program that allowed the blossoming writer to waive his fourth-year classes—Slavitt graduated magna cum laude with a degree in English.

"There's a certain kind of self-starting person who doesn't need courses," he says. He recalls "hanging around" a lot during his senior year, mostly spending time at Yale's exclusive literary society, the Elizabethan Club.

After picking up a Master's degree from Columbia, Slavitt moved into the professional world. In 1958, he was hired as a film critic for Newsweek—or, as he describes it, a "flicker picker."

"It's every English major's dumb idea," Slavitt says. "I can always go to New York and review books and novels for Time or Newsweek."

It wasn't, of course, as simple as that. Slavitt's father was friends with a top official at the magazine, and helped his son procure an interview.

"You're the third most important reviewer in the world just because of your position," Slavitt says, recalling his experience as a critic.

But it was never his intention to make a career of thumbs-up, thumbs-down. Slavitt said he commuted to film screenings on the same train as Bosley Crowther, The New York Times' now-legendary longtime critic and also a Westchester resident.

"I thought, how humiliating," Slavitt said. "This man is a living joke and doesn't understand it." He recalls attending Frankie Avalon movies and being disgusted by the profession.

"I also found I could get [a film] a terrible review in the Times if I could sit in [Crowther's] favorite chair" at the theater, he laughs.

Slavitt left Newsweek in 1965, set on a career as a writer. He has since produced a prolific collection of over 80 works, ranging from poetry to novels to Latin translations.

"MY LIFE IS MY HOBBY"

In 2002, Slavitt's son Evan launched an unsuccessful bid for Massachusetts attorney general. The younger Slavitt was unable to attain the 10,000 signatures needed to earn a spot on the ballot, but he encouraged his father to take a stab at the political process.

"Why don't you run for state rep?" Slavitt remembers his son asking him. "You only need 150 signatures."

At times, Slavitt sounds like he is pursuing political office on a whim.

"My life is my hobby," he says. "I've never [run for office] before. I'm 69 years old. The chances of my taking up snowboarding are remote. But this is an interesting new thing I can do."

Later on, he waxes patriotic.

"It seems to me to be the unselfish thing to do," he says. "I owe it to a country that's been very good to me."

A socially liberal conservative, Slavitt is pro-choice and supports same-sex marriage. He stands by his Republican affiliation, however.

"Santa Claus is a Democrat, God is a Republican," he quips. The Democrats "make people dependent on the government. The system works best when it's left to itself."

There are literary concerns, too.

"The best writers are really quite conservative," Slavitt says. "Hemingway, Faulkner. . . . The lefty crazies in college manage to teach these books without ever letting you know that they're right-wing."

Indeed, Slavitt is not happy with the current state of American academia.

"They want diversity, they want everybody to be represented," he says. "They've thrown out Dryden and put in Morrison."

And to Slavitt, the faculty assignments at these institutions are just as flawed as the curricula.

"You can't have a non-Asian-American teaching Asian Studies; you can't have a non-black teaching black studies. You can hardly have a straight guy teaching Auden, Whitman, or James Merrill," he says, lamenting what he believes are current university hiring practices.

DON'T TALK TOOMEY

Slavitt's dislike of the opposition is anything but equivocal.

He accuses his opponent ("Teeny Tiny Timmy Toomey, as I try not to call him") of taking orders from Thomas M. Finneran, the Democratic speaker of the house.

"There is so much animus against Toomey," he says. "He's not the sharpest knife in the drawer."

"Tim Toomey is sort of like a Robin Hood guy. He wants to steal from the rich and give to the poor," Slavitt says. "He is not in favor of PILOT [Payment In Lieu Of Taxes] and he wants Harvard to take in vastly more money than it does and he wants to give it to his constituency. Without Harvard or MIT, Cambridge basically is Everett or Somerville. It's a great national ornament and it should be protected."

Toomey is also being challenged by a fellow Democrat, Avi Green, a local political consultant who, like Slavitt, is launching his first campaign.

"Mr. Slavitt is running as he says—to bring a two-party system to the district," says Josh Sugarman, Green's campaign manager. "The Green campaign supports that completely and respects his desire to do so."

Slavitt himself says it is too early to gauge Green's chances in the election.

It is questionable, however, whether Slavitt's own political career will be taking off anytime soon.

Slavitt is well-respected, says local political pundit Robert Winters, who edits the Cambridge Civic Journal. "Not that he stands a chance in hell of winning in a place like Cambridge," Winters adds.

Toomey himself expressed ambivalence towards his challenger. "I haven't had the fortune to meet him yet," Toomey says. But, he adds, "every election is a challenge."

I let Mr. Grynbaum know that I approved. He got the spirit right. And the space was terrific.

★ ★ ★ There is a party tonight on Otis Street for the Bush-Cheney campaign, to which I'm told I must go—to meet Republicans, shake hands, and perhaps hand out doorhangers and contribution envelopes for my campaign. Most people have their private purposes and ambitions, and they go out in the evenings with their eyes focused on the main chance. To meet X or renew a connection with Y, to sell him aluminum siding or life insurance? It happens all the time, but mostly I have not needed to do this.

One could say that it is about time! Or regret that such a long stretch of good luck has come to an end. Francis Ponge says somewhere that one of the good things about being king is that you never have to touch a doorknob. My life has not been quite so protected as that, but given the relative scale of things, I come fairly close.

I am also apprehensive about my meeting next week with the editors of the *Somerville News*. Should I familiarize myself with the issues of life in Somerville? Or ought I to be more candid, admit ignorance, let them know that there is almost nothing first-term representatives can do, but make it clear that I am sympathetic to business, from which employment and taxes come—and let it go at that?

★ ★ ★ The party at Lorene Leiter's was not so bad as I'd feared. There were twenty or so people, and I got there in time for the main event, a short talk by Vice President Cheney that we watched live on a computer hookup. The scheme was to have 2,004 of these parties all round the country to drum up financial support and recruit volunteers. The Massachusetts piece of this endeavor is irrelevant, because the Bush-Cheney campaign has written off the state—heavily Democratic and with Kerry a native son—but they go through the motions.

I didn't feel as though my private agenda was different from everyone else's or shameful. This was a political evening. I handed out contribution envelopes and people took them cheerfully. It was like a pickup bar where everyone was hoping to be hit on. I didn't hand out doorhangers: some were pro-life evangelicals who would have been put off by my large-type proclamation of my pro-choice position. This is an awkward split among Republicans and, as a minority party here in Massachusetts, the libertarians and the evangelicals have to contrive a way of getting along with each other or Finneran will continue with his hypermajority forever (or at least until he is convicted of something and another beady-eyed clone comes along to stand at the Speaker's desk).

★ ★ ★ A newspaper article says that the state GOP has announced that 133 Republicans have qualified to run for state legislative office (in 130 districts). This number includes 25 incumbents and is the most we've had since 1990. In the last four election cycles, the party has fielded fewer than 80 candidates. Putting their spin on this news, Jane Lane, director of communications for the Massachusetts Democrats, said, "We have reason to doubt those figures at this point. There is always a chance that any of these candidates could not have the required number of signatures. What we know is, they have been actively recruiting. They have been dialing for candidates. We have heard that for the past several months, they are literally dialing through the directory asking people to run against Democratic incumbents." I did get such a phone call, but they knew who I was. Still, I wonder how many people will believe that I was just lucky—or unlucky.

★ ★ ★ I went this morning to a caucus in Boston to pick delegates to the Republican National Convention in New York. It's not a desirable job. To be a delegate costs you $2,500, and you get no say about the platform or the candidates (Bush and Cheney, of course) and must sit there, wave signs, and look interested. Eye candy, as they call it.

Still, a roomful of Republicans is worth showing up for, or so Fred says. I drove across the BU Bridge to the MATCH School (an acronym for the Media and Technology Charter High School) to sit with perhaps thirty stalwarts and vote for the recommended slate of three delegates and three alternates. During the proceedings, Shawn Jenkins, the chair, introduced me and allowed me to say a few words.

I did my number about the numbers—how there are twenty-three Republicans in the legislature and we need fifty-four to sustain a veto. And I figured out a way of using my subversive Red Sox thought, closing with the suggestion that Bostonians seem to be committed to the Red Sox and the Democratic Party, and if there is nothing I can do about the baseball team, there is hope for change in the political standings.

It went over well enough, and a couple of people asked me for my card and made noises about having me come to speak. On the other hand, one elderly guy, a grizzled old pol about my age, came up to me afterward to suggest that it might be counterproductive to refer to the Democrats on Beacon Hill as "a gang of thugs" as I had done.

I told him he was probably right. (Is he?) It's a learning experience. I could figure out other, less blunt ways to allude to the arrogant irresponsibility of Finneran and his minions.

★ ★ ★ I have been sketching out what I can say next week, at that candidate's forum:

> The first principle of representative government is that the elected representatives hold office and derive their power from the consent of the governed. The lopsidedness of our politics here in Massachusetts has made the Democratic Party invulnerable to recall or challenge, and their dominance has made them lazy and arrogant. They assume that they hold office by right and for life. This is an unhealthy situation for them and a catastrophe for the Commonwealth. It has corrupted the Democratic Party, drained them of the idealism that made them attractive in the first place, and turned them into a party of privilege and incumbency. For too long, they have been running without serious opposition, and often without any opposition at all. And even this seems distasteful to them. In the constitutional conven-

tion we had recently, while the question of same-sex marriages was getting all the attention, there was another proposition put forward—that the two-year term of the representatives should be extended to four.

This is the body that is supposed to be closest to the electorate, and they object to having to come before us every two years to have their powers renewed. Even when we have referenda—such as those on Clean Elections or capital punishment, or the roll-back of the tax rate to 5%—they contrive to ignore the will of the voters if it does not coincide with the preferences of Speaker Thomas Finneran and his excessively well disciplined colleagues. Whatever your views on these particular questions, you must have noticed the general overweening arrogance of that man. When I was out getting signatures, I met a great number of people who refused to listen to me, not because I am a Republican but because they were disgusted by all politicians of all parties. "They are all crooks," was a phrase I heard over and over again.

Well, they are not all crooks. Mr. Toomey is not a crook. But Charlie Flaherty, the previous speaker, is a convicted felon. And three federal judges said that the testimony of Speaker Finneran was incredible, so that the U.S. Attorney is investigating him as a possible perjurer. This is the 26th Middlesex District. You cannot vote against Speaker Finneran. But you can vote to restrain him. You can vote to have an independent voice representing you on Beacon Hill. There are presently 23 Republicans in the State Legislature of 160 members. We need 54 in order to sustain a gubernatorial veto.

The hard part, of course, will be the questions. What also worries me is the kind of lapse older people experience and that, at the keyboard, I can just wait out. Earlier, searching my mind for the name of Francis Ponge, what I came up with was Sponde—a French Renaissance poet whose work I have translated. And to get from Sponde to Ponge was laborious. Ponge knew Max Jacob and Picasso. I looked up Jacob and found an anthology with the work of both men. But I won't be able to do that in a bar in Somerville.

★ ★ ★ Evan tells me that I have to have talking points, little anecdotes or zingers I can use when fielding questions. And my cousin Lou had a couple of shrewd suggestions. Almost certainly, someone will ask me whether I am going to support Bush, because among Democrats he is loathed with the fervor that Republicans felt about Clinton, and that Democrats felt about Nixon. What Lou said, looking with clear distaste at the Bush/Cheney '04 bumper sticker on the kitchen counter, was that I should get as far away from the subject as fast as possible, and one way to do that would be to say that, yes, I support the president (don't name him!) even though I have differences with him on certain issues. He is pro-life, for example, and I am pro-choice. I could even say that I should not be upset if people were to split their ticket, voting for Kerry for president and me for state rep. This way, I could deflect some of the rage the questioner hoped to tap into and I might even manage to associate Toomey with Bush on the pro-life issue.

Lou's other idea is that I can say that I shall try to get on the Education Committee of the legislature, where I can help improve the quality of education in the Commonwealth. Whether I actually get on that committee or not, I can honestly say that I will try, which then allows me to talk about the governor's idea for the Adams Scholarships. I want to have some positive suggestions to make, some affirmative program other than attacks on Representative Toomey.

There will almost certainly be an opportunity for brief closing remarks:

> The truth of the matter is that an individual legislator can't do much over there. The speaker and a few of his cronies have all the power, and they work on bills behind closed doors and then come out and present complicated pieces of legislation that the members barely have time to read, let alone question or discuss. It is a dysfunctional system, and party discipline keeps even well-intentioned Democrats from challenging decisions they might disagree with or that their constituents might find distasteful or wasteful or wrong. But that doesn't mean that your vote doesn't matter. You can vote to reform the system, and you can vote to restore representative government, the two-party system, and something resembling the checks and balances that the founding fathers in Massachusetts and in Philadelphia proposed as a way of limiting the power of officials who otherwise might ignore our wishes and seize control of the machinery and the money of government. You can vote for the other party, which is to say Republican. If that bothers the hell out of you, you can split your ticket, if that's what you want to do, and vote for Kerry for President—he's likely to win in Massachusetts anyway— and then, for state rep, for me or, over in the next district, for Dane Baird. With 54 votes out of 160, we would be on our way to a level playing field.

> Mr. Green and Mr. Toomey have similar views on many subjects. Indeed, all three of us agree, I think, more often than we disagree. But they are both Democrats and they would be subject to Speaker Finneran's leadership and party discipline. I'm not, and I wouldn't be. That's what I urge you to keep in mind!

I can almost hear the peals of applause, while the balloons fall from the ceiling, the band plays something by Sousa, and Toomey and Green slink out into the drizzle and fog.

★ ★ ★ An e-mail from Fred Baker drags me back to the drearier terrain of real life:

EVENT TONIGHT (Toomey will be there):

At Paine Park, corner of Amory and St Mary's road. 7 PM.

This is a 'Paine Park Neighborhood Meeting' — you might have got a flyer about it. If you have a fax I can fax you the flyer.

Agenda for the neighborhood meeting is:

* Meet neighbors, old and new

* Help plan the annual block party

* Discuss park and neighborhood issues with Councilor/Rep. Tim Toomey.

* Brainstorm future activities

The park is about three blocks from my house. I probably ought to go. Will I be horning in? Of course! That is what running for office against an incumbent amounts to.

★ ★ ★ I spent an hour or so this afternoon with Alderman William White, Jr., a Somerville Republican. He is a Somerville boy who went to Harvard and Georgetown Law, clerked for a judge in Washington during the Carter administration, and, from that experience, was converted to Republicanism. What I needed to know from him was what kinds of questions I'd get from the editorial board of the *Somerville News*.

There are issues I knew about and issues I'd never heard of, for all my conscientious reading of the local papers. I knew that gangs were a problem in Somerville but was unaware that they are now sophisticated operations with pagers and cell phones and that the problem in Somerville is keeping out gang members from East Boston, Chelsea, and Revere. There is an effort to put through some antigang legislation, which would require a home-rule petition that the legislature would have to pass, allowing the aldermen to enact a municipal ordinance permitting police to order known gang members to disperse and arrest them if they failed do so. Who could object to that? The Far Left worries that cops could use this as a way to harass Latinos.

Apparently, these gang members are not difficult to identify. The Salvadoran MS-13 gang wears bright blue bandanas, and the Haitian H-Block sports black quilted jackets. But even as ethnics, they are no more entitled to break the laws than anyone else or to refuse a legitimate police order. If I'm asked about this, I'll let them know that I'm in favor at least of the home-rule petition. How the ordinance is drafted and how it is enforced are beyond my powers to control.

I did a miniversion of my remarks for next week's delegates' forum, and White was sufficiently pleased to say that he might very well come to hear me.

★ ★ ★ I went to that meeting of the Paine Park Neighborhood Association at the park on the corner of Amory and St. Mary streets. St. Mary Street is a couple of blocks long, a minicommunity, and its park is a place where kids play, young men shoot basketballs, and mothers sit and watch their toddlers. The purpose of the meeting was to discuss the new four-kilovolt transformer NSTAR has put up on the sidewalk that is supposed to replace the three barrel transformers up on a pole about ten feet away. The street-level transformer, about five feet wide and five feet high, is in a big metal box with warning signs about its high voltage. It is near the swings. The Paine Park neighbors are worried about their children and the long-term effects of exposure to the radiation from a transformer so close to where they play. (Some of the youngsters even climb up on the transformer and sit on it, especially in cool weather, because the top is warm.) So there was a meeting, and Councillor/Rep Toomey was scheduled to come with the city electrician and a man from NSTAR. At Fred's suggestion, I showed up to listen. And to meet Toomey, at last.

He is a decent, hardworking guy. He was wearing brown slacks (or the pants to a suit?), a white shirt, and a tie. It was chilly to be in shirtsleeves, but he didn't seem to mind the temperature, and with admirable patience listened to the residents' questions and the answers, some of them satisfactory and some of them fairly silly, from the city electrician and the NSTAR guy. Apparently, NSTAR has some sort of facility about a hundred yards away, just around the corner on Prospect Street and with a parking lot on the back, on Amory, and they could have put the transformer there, instead of next to a park where kids play. But nobody thought of that when they were doing the planning.

There were questions about burying it, which is expensive and dangerous, because buried transformers can get flooded and then they blow up. Or shielded, somehow? That is difficult to do, and the radiation falls off dramatically as you get just a few feet from the transformer. And so on, and so on.

All of this was mildly interesting for the first few minutes, and then thrillingly boring (unless you live on the block), but Mr. Toomey's attention was unflagging. He was there to help if he could, or at least to listen and let the people know that someone in government cared and was paying attention. It is difficult to knock that!

And he was very pleasant to me. I introduced myself, and we shook hands. He even wished me the best of luck, which was extravagantly polite, or perhaps a sign that, as a Republican, I am so unthreatening to him that he can afford to be gracious. He does not speak well and is inclined to mumble. But he listens well. I spent much of the time trying to figure out whether he is as dim as he seems or uses that to beguile and disarm adversaries. He is, after all, a successful politician, having been elected and reelected to both offices many times.

But that success could be because he comes out and spends his evenings doing stuff like this, listening to half an hour of palaver by about fifteen men and women about their transformer. And then, as we adjourned to the community room of a nearby apartment house, paying just as close attention to the next item on the agenda, which was that two or three kids with motorized minibikes race early on Sunday mornings and the motors make noise (the point, after all, is to sound like a Harley!). They also go the wrong way on the one-way street, and they zip through the stop sign, and they do this without helmets, and. . . . And what can be done?

I figured out right away that if the problem is that dangerous, all we have to do is wait until one of the kids gets killed and then the racing will stop and the noise will abate. But one can't say that. Toomey's more measured reply was to talk about a home-rule petition working its way through the legislature that has passed his Public Safety Committee, is ready for its third reading, and will then go to the Senate. If it passes there, the City of Cambridge (where he is on the city council) can pass ordinances controlling the use of minibikes. How long will this take? It is hard to imagine anything before, say, November. This is, essentially, my solution, but in more politic terms.

I mentioned that I had seen the kids (establishing that I, too, am a neighbor) and was concerned that they were not wearing helmets. Helmets, Toomey told us, are required for riding on any kind of bike up to the age of twelve. (After twelve, you can kill yourself?)

There is a noise abatement officer, but one has to make an appointment for her to come and measure decibels, and it is hard to tell when the children will be playing. There are the cops, but it won't improve community relations for neighbors to call the cops on one another's children. It was decided that a member of the association should speak to the parents involved, expressing the concern about the children's safety. Sure! Fine! That's going to fix it. As Mr. Toomey remarked, "I can't understand a parent who would buy a child one of these things." I am glad I have decided not to attack him personally. Finneran is easier to hate. Attacking Toomey would be unsportsmanlike—like shooting a moose.

8

★ ★ ★ ★ ★ ★ ★ ★ ★ ★ ★ ★ ★ ★ ★ ★ ★ ★ ★ ★

In the latest *Somerville News*, there is a piece about Avi Green's meeting last week with their editorial board. He is, apparently, exactly the kind of leftist moon child I took him to be. About the Somerville gang problem, he suggested: "Crime, particularly the rise in teen gang activity, can be solved by fully funding youth programs."

The gang problem isn't just teenagers but thugs in their twenties who are, as White pointed out, armed with pagers, cell phones, and not infrequently machetes and guns. From a small collection of petty criminals MS-13 has grown to be a notorious nationwide gang, implicated in countless murders, rapes, beatings, and drive-by shootings, and involved in dealing drugs, smuggling illegal immigrants, trafficking weapons, prostitution, extortion, and kidnapping. To this threat to public safety in Somerville, Avi Green intends to respond with fully funded youth programs? He is not stupid but blinded by leftist beliefs. Democrats always look to money and niceness as the solution to all ills, even though what we need is tough laws and well-trained policemen.

Reem Abu-Libdeh's e-mail to me describing what to expect of these sessions when I show up there in a couple of days was rather more forthcoming. She said:

We have a contributors meeting every Friday morning from 8 to 9 a.m. The first half-hour is Neil (the editor) talking, and the second half hour is always a guest who's connected to Somerville somehow talking about what he's doing, and/or a kind of Q&A. [U.S. Representative Michael] Capuano came to speak a few weeks ago and he was a riot (but maybe not in a good way) and [former attorney general] Scott Harshbarger came two weeks ago, he was pretty interesting. But poor, poor Avi Green. He was our speaker last week and showed up at 9 a.m. (when the meeting ends) looking completely frazzled and nervous. Our editor kind of ripped him apart with his line of questioning. (He asked Avi Green who he would vote for between you and Toomey considering that on social aspects you're much more liberal than Toomey. Avi paused for a moment and then said, "Well, I would never go over the Democratic party. I'd vote for Toomey, of course."My editor, a pretty staunch conservative, especially on social issues, was so unimpressed—we all were, I think.) Anyhow, one of our reporters will write up the meeting and all that was said for the following issue. And we'll have coffee and donut holes.

In any event, I no longer feel bound to keep in confidence Green's revelation to me some months ago about his parting of the ways with state senator Jarrett Barrios. He virtually said as much to the *News* editors. They all knew he'd worked in Barrios's campaign, and the only way the remark made any sense was to infer that Barrios had somehow disappointed Green, failed to show his gratitude, or more probably, given Green's leanings, flunked some ideological test. Given the choice between the two of them, if I were voting in the Democratic primary, I'm afraid I'd now vote for Toomey.

★ ★ ★ The *News* editorial board meeting went well enough so that Doug Holder, the arts editor, e-mailed me that same morning to invite me onto his community cable TV show, *Writer to Writer*. The editor, Neil McCabe, I had already met. He had come down with Reem Abu-Libdeh to take the pictures for their piece about me. He spent about half an hour talking to the young writers and photographers about the next issue and spoke about the different kinds of photographs, from long establishing shots to tight close-ups, what they were for, how to compose and crop them, and their use in layout and design. It was all clear and very professional and I rather liked it. It was like being back at *Newsweek*. I had come a little early, so as not to make Green's mistake, and I sat drinking coffee from the Dunkin' Donuts "Box o' Joe" and indulging in a donut hole.

Then, after McCabe introduced me, I did a rather more relaxed version of the remarks I had prepared for the delegates' forum. I also talked about what an auspicious time I thought it was for Somerville. The extension of the MBTA Red Line to Davis Square some years back has given an undeniable vitality and prosperity to that part of the city, and the extension of the Green Line to Union Square will do much the same for central and eastern parts of the city. The Assembly Mall development looks at last to be happening. The sale of the old armory on Highland Avenue to a developer who wants to turn it into a series of artists' studios and lofts is an exciting prospect. Somerville is close enough to Boston, and yet it has its own character, an ethnic diversity, and a range of amenities that could make it a wonderful place. All that is required is restraint on the part of politicians, who should get out of the way and allow progress to happen. Free enterprise requires freedom. Public safety has to be maintained, of course, but that ought to be possible.

There were only a few questions, and for only one of these was I unprepared. I had been talking about Toomey's unfriendliness toward Harvard and MIT, and one of the younger writers asked about the high cost of student housing in Brighton, Cambridge, and Somerville. What could be done about that? Falling back on fundamental principles, I said it was a matter of supply and demand and that the housing stock in greater Boston needs to be increased. The only way to do that is not by more regulation but less. And I told them about a meeting of the Cambridge City Council I had seen on community TV a couple of nights before and the recitation of Kafkaesque regulations about what kinds of trees could be cut down, and how many four-inch trees you needed to plant to make up for cutting down an eight-inch tree, and the differences between "historic" trees and city-owned trees and trees on private plots of different sizes. They're trees. They're nice. They grow in the ground and birds nest in them. But there are people who also need to nest somewhere, and if entrepreneurs can't see their way to investing in residential real estate, then the prices are going to stay high or go even higher.

There was a question from Doug Holder I could not have expected: "What are the benefits of your being a writer that might apply in the political world?" I replied that Confucius said that for the reform of government the first requirement is that the language must be purified, and I asked who can do that better than a poet? Then, invoking another, less exotic writer, I said that Hemingway somewhere describes a writer's most important piece of equipment as a built-in, foolproof, portable shit detector. And in politics that could be either a great asset or as great a liability.

Holder asked me, a little later on, whether, if the politics thing didn't work out, I had ever considered a career as a stand-up comic. (Actually, the thought has crossed my mind from time to time, or used to, but the life is too strenuous and unpleasant. There are few careers that are worse than that of poet, but stand-up comic is one of them.)

The best moment, for me, came when I was explaining why I was running. I didn't want to sound too pompous—"I owe it to my country to give something back" isn't really me. But neither did I want to sound frivolous or light-weight. What I believe in is knowledge, which comes from experience. And I assume that other people can understand this and share the impulse. So, in along with the narrative explanation about Evan's suggestion a couple of years ago and my inquiry to the party, I said that it was something I'd never done before, and that that's the way to learn. And then, in a lovely moment of inspiration, a comparison came floating into my mind and I said that it was like the moment in Wagner when Siegfried understands the meanings of songs the birds are singing. Even dipping a toe into the political waters allows me to read newspapers differently, to wonder about motives, ambitions, and enmities of the players. We'll see, next week, when the piece comes out, whether it really went as well as I thought it did.

Actually, we learned sooner than that. Janet and I went to the party the *News* had that evening at Toast. The men were in jackets and ties and the women were in skirts and blouses or dresses, which is to say that, for Somerville, this was dressy. And important people were there, like Toomey, who was, again, pleasant and friendly. He asked me how it was going and whether I was enjoying myself. I told him that it was very interesting and that I was learning a lot. And then, without thinking, I started to do the bit about Siegfried understanding the bird-songs. I realized, of course, that Toomey was not absolutely the ideal audience for this kind of comparison. Not that he is a moron, but he seems not to be a man of aggressively high culture. There was no way to extricate myself and I said that I was now understanding newspapers the way Siegfried came to understand the birds, but it was his well-learned patience that produced the nods more probably than any comprehension, let alone recognition, of the aptness of the trope.

We met Bill White, who arrived as we were leaving, and I thanked him for his help that made me sound a lot better informed and smarter than I might otherwise have appeared. Mayor Joe Curtatone was supposed to show up, but as it was getting late I told a couple of his aides who were there that I admired what he was doing, asked them to convey my respects, and said that there would surely be other occasions when he and I could meet. Avi Green was not there, which was odd. (It is possible that he was otherwise engaged, but I wonder if he is really trying hard.)

At any rate, Janet overheard Neil McCabe, the *News* editor, talking about my appearance at the editorial board that morning. His adjective was "awesome."

★ ★ ★ The pictures of torture—or, as Secretary Rumsfeld would prefer to call it, "abuse"—are dismaying, and I worry that the disgust most Americans feel may give Kerry a boost in November. Neither the secretary nor the president would have authorized such behavior, but their eagerness to find weapons of mass destruction would have resulted in the application of "manipulative interrogation" techniques, which is the euphemism we have for conduct close to torture. Janet thinks the lack of training of the reservists wasn't what produced the scenes we have seen in the papers and on TV, but it might well have brought about the revelations of the behavior, the photographs and videotapes. Better-trained guards, hardened to such cruelty, would have been able to keep it to themselves.

This news from Iraq is disheartening, and I find it difficult to concentrate on my absurd campaign. I will be practicing my introductory remarks today. And I wrote a letter to the editor at the *Globe*. There is a front-page article about charter schools—and I am duty bound at least to read these things now. Senator Robert Antonioni opposes the moratorium on charter schools (as does Governor Romney), while Senator Warren Tolman supports it. He admits that "charter schools are doing good work. But he worries that the idea of charters as laboratories for education reform has been lost and that they are now hurting existing schools financially. 'I don't think these good ideas are being incorporated into other schools,' Tolman said. 'I really worry we're creating a two-tier school system." His complaint is that while the charters are better; the public schools are not taking advantage of their innovations or learning from their good results It was too easy a shot not to take:

> Senator Warren Tolman is correct in his belief that charter schools ought to be "laboratories for education reform," but his complaint that the "good ideas" of these schools are not "being incorporated into other schools," strikes me as bizarre. If charter schools are demonstrating ways to improve and provide a better education to our youngsters, how can he blame *them* if the conventional public schools fail to take advantage of their innovations or to adopt their better practices? The fault, rather, is with those public schools that refuse, themselves, to learn and are not very good at teaching.

> David R. Slavitt

Even though the *Globe* has never printed a letter of mine, it was a way of beguiling myself into the idea that I was doing something. I just don't have the heart today to make fund-raising calls or to go out and start my door-to-door campaigning.

★ ★ ★ The website is up at www.davidslavitt.com and looks terrific! Now I have to get it cross referenced and listed in places where people can find it. I may have inexpensive pens made up with the website address printed on them. And if there are any more fliers or labels or other such paraphernalia, the web address will of course appear prominently. The CV goes on forever, and people are sometimes impressed by it. My response—not merely a modest conceit— is that it is probably somewhat shameful to have published that many books and to be as obscure as I am.

★ ★ ★ A packet came in to me from the Massachusetts Nurses Association, addressing me as "Dear Candidate for the General Court," which I am, and asking for my support for House Bill 1282: An Act Ensuring Quality Patient Care and Safe RN Staffing. Well, who is against quality patient care or safe RN staffing? I glanced at it, felt inadequate, gave it to Janet, and asked her to run it by someone over at the Brigham who actually knows about this. Janet did, and Nancy Kruger sent me an e-mail explaining why the bill is not such a great idea. I was able to reply to the Nurses Association with the following:

Thank you for your letter and the information about House Bill 1282.

I am worried that the proposed legislation seems too rigid and that there are no distinctions made between very sick patients and those who are less sick, or between experienced RNs and those who have just been certified. Obviously, we are all in agreement that the nurses who are outrageously overworked cannot give the best care to their patients, but I am not altogether persuaded that doctors or hospital administrators are unaware of this, or that legislation is the best way to correct the situation.

There are not now enough nurses or enough people in the pipeline. The problem is real. But the solution this legislation proposes lacks nuance. It would put more nurses into OB, for instance, where the patients are not so sick, and that would tax other wards where the critical care needs are greater. I don't see any cost analysis in this. And we are working in the real world. There are only so many nurses out there, and this bill might get hospitals into a bidding war that would be ruinous for them, for patients, and for the Commonwealth at large.

I'd welcome your thoughts about these matters and whatever clarification or reassurance you can provide.

David R. Slavitt
Candidate for State Rep. — 26th Middlesex District

This is not what they want to hear. For all the façade of professionalism, what they are is a union, and they want to put it to management. So they will resent my questions. The fact that my response is the correct one won't win me points with them.

★ ★ ★ An irksome moment. I had asked to be put on the e-mail list for the Paine Park Neighborhood Association, and when I got their report of the meeting that Toomey and I had attended, I thought it would be informative if I directed their attention to my new website. I wasn't bludgeoning or soliciting, but just letting them know who I am and that the site is up and available. What I said was:

> It was a great pleasure to meet you all. I shall be following with great interest and concern the developments as we address the transformer question and the scooter problem.
>
> I invite you all to take a look at my website which is just up:
> www.davidslavitt.com
>
> Kind regards,
>
> David R. Slavitt

To this relatively innocuous message, I received the following reply:

> Hi David,
>
> You asked to be on the list as a friend of the group since you don't live in the immediate Paine Park neighborhood which is Amory, Inman (btwn Broadway & Hampshire), St. Mary Rd. and the odd side of Prospect. The description of the group is as "a very informal group that distributes information of neighborhood interest, and plans & runs events . . . PPN is open to everyone who lives in the neighborhood. There are no dues or membership requirements, and there is no political affiliation."
>
> The list is primarily a list of people who work actively on behalf of the neighborhood in the ways described above. At the May 4 meeting (unless you left early) we discussed the use of the PPNeighbors e-mail list and reaffirmed that its use is limited: to people's individual concerns, e.g. "lost cat," and to neighborhood events and news. We specifically excluded its use to solicit support for organizations, political or other, however worthy the cause. Many of the Paine Park Neighbors are very deeply involved in political and

other organizations for which we want to gain support. However, we contact only people with whom we have personal connections and we do not use the PPNeighbors e-mail list to solicit support. When you get the summary of the meeting (in an e-mail later today) you'll see this topic listed and can follow the policy in the future.

Thanks,

Marie

Well, as Steve Martin used to say, excu-u-u-u-se me! I wasn't soliciting support but directing attention to an informative site, neighborhood "news," as a matter of fact. Political speech is constitutionally protected and is different from soliciting. If Toomey was there, it was political. The terms of his deal were clear enough—I'll listen to you about the transformer and the noisy scooters, and you'll vote for me in November.

Not that there is any advantage in my arguing with them. I said, simply, that I hadn't known this and begged pardon for having violated the rules. But it wasn't me. I sent a message to Fred Baker, whose idea it had been for me to go there in the first place. His response was sympathetic and reassuring, although woeful:

Some people . . . I tell ya.

The toughest neighborhood for me to get acceptance in when I ran for School Committee in '01 was MY OWN. And that's the very neighborhood you're referring to.

Lots of aging flower children there, politically correct to the core. One person even COMPLAINED when I sent her a birthday card. Considered it an insult and that I was 'spying' on her by getting her age off the voter list.

Now you begin to see the troubles one encounters in a place like this. PEOPLE!

★ ★ ★ I went to the mayor's MIT senior citizens' picnic. There are two of these events each year, this MIT version and, later on in the summer, the one in Harvard Yard. There is a free lunch—fried chicken, corn, and mashed potatoes—and "entertainment," which is the gospel group of the Cambridge Rindge and Latin School (not bad, but much too loud), the Cambridge Senior Chorus (terrible, and also grotesque as they sang "Enjoy Yourself, It's Later Than You Think" to these old people), and some union musicians' band. There were welcoming speeches by the mayor and a representative of the president of MIT. Members of the city council were working the room, going up and down the aisles (seven rows of six large tables each, which was forty-two ten-seat tables, most of which were full). I saw the indefatigable Toomey trudging along, saying hello, shaking hands, registering his presence, and most of the others were there, too. Then the city council sang "You Are My Sunshine" and "Let Me Call You Sweetheart," and they were no worse than the Rindge and Latin gospel singers and better than the senior chorus.

I had been going from table to table also, and my job was harder than that of the city council people, because I had to ask who was from eastern Cambridge, where my district is. And then I had to identify myself as a Republican. Some seniors didn't want to talk politics. Others wanted to too much. One woman asked me where I stood on gay marriage, and when I said I was in favor of it, the woman beside her got up and walked away.

It wasn't all terrible. I handed out some doorhangers, and some people seemed receptive. The efficiency of the enterprise is what is attractive. One can greet many more people this way than by going door-to-door, which is what I shall have to begin doing soon. And for the city councillors, all they had to do was say hello and smile and shake any hand that was extended to them. They weren't worried about issues. It was all name and face recognition. When the election comes, people will remember: *Ah, yes, Decker*, or *Sullivan*, or *Reeves*, or *Toomey. I met him (or her) at that picnic.*

"Picnic" is a misleading name. It was indoors, in the MIT hockey rink, which was safer than outdoors because no one can predict the weather. But it was relentlessly grim. I was there as a matter of right, as a Cambridge resident over sixty. But getting old is no picnic. The organizers don't want to exclude anyone, so the level of entertainment and discourse is lowered to what one might expect in grammar school. There were also lots of people from nursing homes, and their caretakers spoke to them with that clarity and emphasis one uses to communicate with four-year-olds. And then there was all that bad singing with the random punctuation of whining feedback from the loudspeakers. (Many of us were able to turn off our hearing aids, but even that was inadequate.)

Watching Toomey, I realized that this bothers him rather less. He may even enjoy it. But then, he is the incumbent and I am the challenger, which is only a step away from saying that he is the authentic pol and I am the impostor.

★ ★ ★ At the debate in Somerville, I'm told I did okay. It is difficult for a participant to judge, but it felt all right. My only mistake was my comment that

Toomey had voted for the redistricting plan that the courts had rejected—it turned out that he hadn't, and he corrected me. But my other complaints about the Democrats' hypermajority, and about some of Toomey's other votes (as on the restoration of the Alcoholic Beverages Control Commission and its transfer to the supervision of the treasurer), were unanswerable.

Both Toomey and Green knew what they were doing. They each had a "stand-out" in front of the restaurant, which is to say that their supporters were out there with signs, looking . . . numerous and enthusiastic. I have to get some signs made and find people who will stand out, hold them, and wave them at passersby.

The opening remarks went well enough. It was reassuring to discover that I can still perform, almost as well as I used to nearly fifty years ago when I was a Yale debater. After these three set speeches—we'd drawn lots for position, and I was in the middle—the moderator, Elio LoRusso, asked each of us a question the *Somerville News* people had told us about ahead of time. The question I got was: "Governor Romney has proposed a new raft of tax cuts in Massachusetts. Given the huge amount of budget cuts which the City of Somerville will be facing, do you support further cuts in state taxes?"

I answered: "I'd have to see the specifics, of course, but I can give you three general remarks that will explain to you where I stand on these issues. First of all, revenues have been running this year half a billion dollars ahead of projections. What Governor Romney has proposed is to give back to taxpayers slightly less than half of that. That seems to me a perfectly reasonable idea. Two, in 2000, there was a referendum where the voters expressed their will. This is merely amusing to Speaker Finneran, but the intention was that taxes should be rolled back, and what the governor is proposing is to roll back from 5.3 percent to 5 percent, which seems to me not Draconian, and not nuts, and it's what the voters asked for. So I think it's a good thing. Finally, Somerville's problems are Somerville's problems. That is to say that there are tough times now, but I think they will be getting better. What bothers me is the idea that all of these cities and towns in the Commonwealth go every year with their hats in their hands to the legislature to ask for more porridge—and it's a way of keeping the power in Speaker Finneran's hands. Once the economy of Somerville improves, and once the economy of the Commonwealth improves, as these tax cuts are calculated to have happen, you won't need to do that, and we'll all be better off."

Both Green and Toomey, being Democrats, were against any tax cuts, of course. I would set their remarks down, but they were not sufficiently interesting for me to transcribe from the tape recording Evan made for me. Toomey actually wants to raise taxes. And Green was particularly annoying, naming a number of schools in Somerville that are run down and need renovations. This was supposed to show that he knew Somerville and was in touch with their problems and cared—I certainly couldn't have named five schools in Somerville—but it was beside the point because vast amounts of money are going to be spent on education, not from kindheartedness but as a result of a court decision requiring special grants for the equalization of funding for education throughout the Commonwealth. But there was no opportunity to rebut a rebuttal.

Green's question was what to do about the gangs in Somerville, and he was against the home-rule petition, worried about the constitutionality of any antigang ordinance that the Somerville aldermen might pass, and concerned about the costs of defending such an ordinance in the courts. Toomey, who is a Democrat but not a nut, was in favor of the enabling legislation, and said that as long as it was narrowly drawn and had to do only with known gang members, he would support that effort, "absolutely."

Because of my coffee with Alderman White, I knew about these gangs, had Googled them and learned even more, and was able to comment with some energy: "I agree with Representative Toomey. The gang problem in Somerville is very bad, and it is relatively easy to identify the gang members. The Salvadoran MS-13 gang wears bright blue bandanas. They're probably the ones under the bandanas. They have pagers, they have phones, and they have machetes and guns and are into serious stuff. And while Avi Green's worldview is that we need more education and social work, 'Officer Krupke, we're no good.' There's also a Haitian gang, and they wear quilted black jackets—not too hard for even the most casually trained cop to figure out, 'Aha! Possibly a gang member!' As far as I understand it, the legislation is drafted so as to enable the officer to order them to disperse, which seems to me not at all constitutionally worrisome."

There were a couple of questions about the revival of the eastern part of Somerville, and I said it would happen when the T stops came in, and that it had already begun to happen. This renaissance, I said, is "like a spark, and the Democrats want to water it—with more regulation and taxes than are good for it. All they have to do is stand back and let it happen, and it will." At one point, after Avi Green had said for maybe the fourth time that he wanted to increase the taxes on corporations, I called him a neosocialist and alluded to the obvious truth that everyone seems to have learned except a few people in Massachusetts and in Berkeley, California, that socialism doesn't work and produces poverty and tyranny, and that free enterprise is what built this country.

My concluding remarks were extemporized. I had already used much of what I'd planned for my closing, so I had to wing it. "I was moved," I said, "by Tim Toomey's account of his family and their union connections. I was myself the unit chairman at *Newsweek* of the Newspaper Guild, and I saw close up and from the inside what happened when the drivers and the printers decided that they wanted more money and they didn't like the way they were being treated, and what they did was ruin and wreck the *New York Mirror* and put it out of business. Now this did not help them; it didn't help the owners; and it didn't help the readers. And I realized that there have to be other models. There have to be ways in which people can be persuaded to get on. The adversarial relationship, the attitude that corporations are bad and the working guy is good is not helpful. You got the forty-hour week, and you got all the benefits, except that the jobs are going to Guatemala and Sri Lanka and China. That's not a good outcome. What you need is people who understand what Calvin Coolidge, a good Republican, once said—that the business of America is business. And the way you're going to make Somerville prosperous, and the way you're going to make the Commonwealth of Massachusetts prosperous, is to have a congenial and welcoming environment for business, which is a good thing. I have been watching with some disgust the politics of Massachusetts ever since I came up here to go to school in 1950. It occurs to me that, as Mitt Romney said, you're not getting any younger, and if you're going to do something about it, you ought to take your shot and do it. And I figured that, you know, he's right. He's a Mormon, but he's an existentialist Mormon, and you don't see a lot of these."

That got a laugh, so I figured it was a good moment to stop.

The *Somerville News* people said, afterward, that I'd "nailed it," but we'll see what their piece says when it runs in the paper.

★ ★ ★ Last night, at the state party headquarters on Merrimac Street, I went to a training session in how to use the Campaign Portal, which is an expensive, interactive website for candidates and their staffs. It is full of information about voters in each candidate's district, by precinct and ward and street, by age or gender, by registration. It also has information about our opponents, their voting records, and whatever news stories have appeared about them in the papers. It lets the party monitor how I'm doing and how many voters I've managed to attract. And it will be useful later on when I have precinct captains and workers getting out the vote on Election Day. In my district, for example, there are 21,083 registered voters, of whom 13,575 are likely to show up at the polls. And of these 5,361 are either Republican or Unenrolled.

Those would have been grim numbers two years ago, but in a presidential year there will be first-time voters. And it may also be true that the Unenrolled figure is lower than it should be because the numbers are so up to date. A good many people might have participated in the Democratic primary to vote for Kerry (although he already had the nomination locked up by the time our primary was held). Still, if an unenrolled voter cast a vote in the Democratic primary and did not thereafter change back to "Unenrolled," he or she would now be automatically listed as a Democrat.

I can use the database to generate either door-to-door or phone lists. It is an expensive toy. The party paid a lot to get the information, organize it, and put it on this elaborate system. Do the Democrats have this? (Do they need it?)

★ ★ ★ We had dinner last night with a high-powered doc from the Brigham and his wife, and naturally enough my candidacy came up among the subjects of conversation. He was amused that I am running as a Republican and apparently sympathetic as I told him why I was running (to try to loosen the Democratic stranglehold on our state's politics). At the end of the evening, though, he said, in a friendly and jocular way, that this was maybe the first time he had knowingly had dinner with a Republican.

I managed a smile and told him that some of us actually have reasonable table manners, but it is a depressing business. He is not a knee-jerk liberal, knows enough to understand the constraints of legislative answers to problems—like the nursing shortage, for example—that are not conveniently addressed by such clumsy machinery. His commitment to the Democrats is inherited. Jews are Democrats, right? But we had talked about the impossibility of finding good rye bread in Boston, how there is maybe a reasonable deli in Waban, and how when he was in training here, there were great delis along Blue Hill Avenue. I pointed out what I'd learned from a PBS documentary about Jews in Boston, that the Irish and the Italians had manipulated the lending policies of the local banks so that when the blacks were coming into town, they couldn't move into the Irish or Italian neighborhoods but went to Blue Hill Avenue where the Jews were, because they didn't have the clout to keep them out. And then the Jews moved to the West End (around Scollay Square and along Cambridge Street) and then were displaced when that turned into Government Center and a fiefdom of Mass. General. The Democrats, in other words, have not treated us well. The Republicans are the other party. To continue to hold Republicans in fear or contempt out of sheer prejudice is not reasonable or smart—and this guy and his wife are unquestionably smart.

It is a depressing political landscape. Rightly or wrongly, Iraq has become a huge liability. The recent revelations of the torture of prisoners there is a catastrophic embarrassment. But worse than any of that, as far as I can see, is the reaction of Janet's medical colleague, a kind of recoiling from the word "Republican."

★ ★ ★ Civilization seems not to have come to an end, even though the City of Cambridge began issuing marriage licenses at midnight last night. Janet and I went down to City Hall, a familiar walk of a couple of blocks. It's the way I go to the post office or the T stop. But there were crowds on the streets, same-sex couples or groups, going to the lawn of our gaudy Italianate City Hall to watch as the applicants lined up to get a number, be admitted to the party inside, have cake and nonalcoholic champagne, and then, at the stroke of midnight, have their numbers called to get their license applications.

We hung around for a half hour. Janet was slightly weepy for these people—many of them middle-aged couples who had until now been denied the right to do this. Janet sees them at the hospital and has watched some of the outrages, as the relatives of one member of the couple exclude the other, whom they hate for having seduced their son or daughter into a perverse, deviant lifestyle, and ignore the dying patient's wishes just to assert their power. (He wanted to be cremated? We'll have him buried!)

It was a gentle mob, one that the *Globe* reporters described as something between a Mardi Gras and Earth Day gathering, with only a few homophobes or religious nuts across the street on the post office side of Mass Avenue in what the authorities tactfully called the "first amendment area," holding up nasty signs about how "God Hates Fags." Janet thought it felt like her undergraduate days at Berkeley, when they demonstrated all the time to end the war, save the earth, and improve the human condition one way or another. I talked to a few of the people in the crowd, introducing myself when it seemed appropriate and explaining that I was a candidate for state rep, a Republican in favor of same-sex marriage, and sometimes even handing out doorhangers. One couple, a young man and young woman with a baby in one of those papoose-like arrangements, carried a two-person sign saying that they were straight, were married, and glad that their daughter could grow up in this new world. They had come all the way from Lowell to do this, to demonstrate and to be able someday to tell their daughter that she had been there.

I suppose I could have spent more time working the crowd and handing out my doorhangers and contribution envelopes, but it just seemed too crass.

It was enough, I decided, that like the Lowell family I could say that I'd been there.

★ ★ ★ Another trip to Cambridge Offset Printing, this time for bookmarks to hand out as I go door-to-door and signs for supporters' windows and for campaign workers to hold up at the next debate or at stand-outs, if only to demonstrate that my organization is not so weak as to be unable to do this. The proprietor, Dick Geraigery, advised that if I don't have a whole lot of volunteers, I should not be too ambitious. Don't send two workers with signs to four places, but send all eight to one place. The point is to look robust and numerous.

The bookmarks will be like the doorhangers, except that they will not mention Tim Toomey (why give the other guy any name recognition?) and will specify that I'm running in Cambridge and Somerville in the Twenty-sixth Middlesex District, and will have the website address. I had thought it might be fun to have a smaller version of the hole so as to resemble a doorhanger, but Geraigery dissuaded me. If I didn't punch the hole, he explained, I'd have more room for the copy and it would look less crowded. The minimum order for the heavyweight weatherproof signs is 250, and at $3 a sign, that's $750. Miraculously, the campaign can afford that and the bookmarks, too.

★ ★ ★ Late afternoon and early evening has become a difficult time. This is when I do my telephoning to try to reach supporters, contributors, and volunteers. I am calling people whom the Campaign Portal lists as Republicans in my district, except that many of them have moved (or have given up their telephone service). I get some reasonable receptions from people who are glad to be called by a Republican. But I also get the Far Right loonies who want to know how I stand on gun control or, more pointedly, gay marriage. Just a few moments ago I answered that question, saying to the man I'd called that same-sex marriage didn't bother me, and that my wife had seen very painful scenes at the Brigham, when one partner was dying and the other. . . . Click! Hum! The man had hung up on me. Do I want people like that to have guns, too? Will he go out and shoot poofters and bushwhackers in the name of an angry deity that has ordered him to cleanse Sodom, Gomorrah, and Cambridge?

Enough! I'll make more of these phone calls when I'm in a better frame of mind.

★ ★ ★ Mitt, meanwhile, continues his positioning. The morning headline in the *Globe* reads "Romney eyes order on licenses," and the page-one story goes on to report that he is seeking an injunction against the town clerks of Worcester, Springfield, Provincetown, and Somerville who have announced that they will issue marriage licenses to out-of-state same-sex couples. Romney's spokesman said that the governor is not seeking criminal penalties against the clerks—fines of from one hundred dollars to five hundred dollars, or up to a year in jail, or both. (But the mention of such penalties amounts to a threat.) All the governor wants is an injunction. Then, if the clerks refuse to obey the courts, the judges can jail the clerks for contempt, leaving the governor's hands clean. Romney's office has demanded copies of all marriage license applications issued this week in those municipalities, presumably for use in the request for the injunction. On the other hand, my understanding is that here in Cambridge and next door in Watertown, clerks have not been strenuous in their scrutiny of the application forms' information about residence, but those four municipalities have proclaimed their defiance and all but invited the executive branch's response.

The legislature is no less entertaining. Senator Barrios and Senator Stanley Rosenberg have introduced an amendment to the budget bill that would repeal the 1913 law, but Speaker Finneran doesn't want to impede any of Governor Romney's foolish exertions, so he is going to block the amendment. His sanctimonious reasoning is that this is too important to be rushed through in an amendment and that the members of the house deserve the chance to debate the question.

In a related story, I read that the FBI has vacuumed the Speaker's computers looking for evidence that Finneran was lying to that panel of federal judges when he said he hadn't the vaguest idea what the redistricting plan might be—even though he handpicked the committee that drew up the plan and the committee lawyer, Lawrence DiCara, its "principle functionary," was Finneran's boyhood friend.

We could be a banana republic, if we had bananas.

★ ★ ★ The *Somerville News* report of the debate is online:

Toomey, rivals spar over taxes, gangs, storefronts
by Nicholas Pinto-Wong

The three candidates for state representative for the 26th Middlesex district took part in a candidates' debate organized by the Somerville News on May 12 at the Mount Vernon Restaurant.

Representative Timothy J. Toomey Jr., D-Somerville, who has held the seat since 1992, is being challenged for the Democratic nomination by Avi Green, a former teacher and political consultant. The winner of the Democratic Primary on September 12 will face the Republican candidate, David R. Slavitt, in the general election.

As the hour of the debate drew near, supporters of each of the three campaigns assembled on the sidewalk outside the restaurant to brandish signs and support their candidates as they arrived.

Inside, the candidates made their final preparations and discussed the format of the debate with the moderator, Elio LoRusso, the owner of Somerville Ornamental Ironworks and a former candidate for Alderman-at-large.

After welcoming the audience and introducing the candidates, LoRusso invited the candidates to make opening remarks.

In his opening statement, Toomey stressed his lifelong commitment to district. "I was born and raised in our community. Most of you know me well," he said.

Toomey also sought to distinguish his campaign from those of his opponents. "For me, representing the people of Somerville and Cambridge is not merely an extension of a political consulting career or academic exercise, but rather a commitment to the community," he said.

In his opening statement, Slavitt presented himself as a counterbalance to the dominance of the Democratic Party in Massachusetts. "The lopsidedness of our politics here in Massachusetts has made the Democratic Party invulnerable to recall or challenge. Their dominance has made them lazy and arrogant," he said.

"They assume that they know better than we do and that they hold office by right and for life. This is unhealthy for them and catastrophic for the Commonwealth. It has corrupted the Democratic Party and drained it of the idealism that once made it attractive," he said.

Slavitt said that while he considers Toomey to be a decent man, he is hog-tied by his adherence to the Democratic line. "In 2003 Timmy Toomey voted with Tommy Finneran 97.8 percent of the time. This is the 26th Middlesex district. You can't vote against Speaker Finneran. But you can vote to restrain him. You can vote to have an independent voice on Beacon Hill," Slavitt said.

Green used his opening remarks to introduce himself and demonstrate his connections to the district. "When I talk to my friends in East Somerville, what I keep hearing from them is that it is time for a change," he said.

After the opening remarks, LoRusso asked each candidate a prepared question about the challenges facing Somerville. He then read questions submitted by the audience.

The candidates' answers to the audience questions threw their political philosophies into sharp contrast. Toomey emphasized his commitment to constituent services, while Green stressed his conviction that large corporations must be made to carry more of the tax burden in East Somerville and East Cambridge.

Slavitt derided Green's philosophy as "socialist."

"Throughout history, socialism has inevitably led to two things: poverty and tyranny," Slavitt said.

All three candidates agreed on the importance of expanding public transportation in Somerville and bringing the Green Line to Union Square.

The candidates disagreed, however, on the anti-gang proposal that was passed the next day by the Board of Aldermen. Toomey and Slavitt both said they supported the home-rule petition, which allows city police to arrest crowds of known gang members if they refuse to disperse.

Green said he would not support such a petition because he does not believe it would be effective in combating gang activity. The way to fight the rise of gangs in the district is to secure more funding for education, after school programs, and community infrastructure, he said.

At the end of the debate, the candidates, their supporters, and members of the audience lingered at the Mount Vernon to discuss the event.

"I was pleased with how it all went," Slavitt said.

★ ★ ★ I have my first endorsement, from the Log Cabin Republicans of Massachusetts. The meeting of the executive committee was upstairs at Dedo's (a dedo is a friendly gargoyle) in Bay Village. Half a dozen brave gays who feel betrayed by their president and governor and assaulted by the evangelicals' takeover of the party are doing what they can to exploit the opportunity the courts have afforded them. (There are 200 members of the Massachusetts chapter, but of these 180 are in arrears with their dues.)

They asked me to say a few words and I told them who I was, what my position was on same-sex marriage, and why I believe that it's none of the government's business to interfere in our private lives. They endorsed me unanimously without even going through the bother of sending me a questionnaire. What this means is that if there are any Log Cabin Republicans in my district, I may pick up a few volunteers. I may get some money out of them. And some attention, too. They've asked me to march with them in the Gay Pride parade on June 12. Fortunately, I'll have signs by then. And if I can find a few volunteers to march with me, so that we don't look too puny and pathetic, I'll have some exposure. (My pitch to possible marchers? If you're gay, fine; and if you're straight, this is a way of demonstrating how confident you are in your sexuality.)

★ ★ ★ Along with the description of the debate, the *Somerville News* has an account of my meeting with the editorial board:

Slavitt stands for G.O.P.
by Franklin W. Liu

The Republican candidate for state representative for the 26th Middlesex district spoke at the contributors meeting of the Somerville News May 7. I'm running on the platform that a two-party system would run better with two parties," said David R. Slavitt, 69, a self-described libertarian Republican. "The imbalance, politically, in Massachusetts is so severe that not only is it not good for the Republican Party, it's not good for the Democrats. The Democrats have, for so long, been accustomed to being beyond recall, beyond responsibility, beyond any kind of connection to the voters who put them there, that they have become arrogant, lazy, and self-confident. And they ignore the will of the electorate and the will of the people," said Slavitt.

"The notion of checks and balances was not just some wacko idea that Mr. Adams had, and the founding fathers of Philadelphia shared. It's a vital part of the democratic process, and we don't have it here. I just don't see it. What we need is Republicans," he said.

Slavitt said the main focus of his campaign is not that he is running against twelve-year incumbent Rep. Timothy J. Toomey, Jr. "Everyone says that Toomey is a very earnest, decent fellow. But he is limited and constrained because he is a Democrat. Over the last four years, Toomey has voted with [House Speaker Thomas M.] Finneran 97.8 percent of the time. That seems to be less rebellious and independent-minded than I'd like.

"Toomey is not a crook. But Toomey basically works for a crook. And it would be political suicide for Toomey to stand up and say 'no' in thunder. But I can do that," Slavitt said.

"It seems to me the main thing we have to do, politically, in Massachusetts is get rid of Thomas Finneran. And that involves having more Republicans on Beacon Hill. There are 160 members in the state legislature. There are presently 23 Republicans. If we had 54 we could sustain a gubernatorial veto," he said.

Slavitt, who grew up in White Plains, N.Y., is a prolific and successful writer. He has published 29 novels, 17 collections of poetry, and 28 translations from Greek, Latin, Hebrew, Spanish, French and Portuguese. He has lectured at the University of Pennsylvania, Princeton, University of Maryland, and Temple University, among many others.

"Confucius said, 'For the good governance of the country, the first thing we have to do is purify the language.' That's what poets do. When people stand up at Beacon Hill and spout offensive nonsense, the first person who's going to notice this is a poet.

"And if I may speak crudely and quote Ernest Hemingway, the most important equipment that a writer has is a portable, built-in, fool-proof sh-t detector. I have that."

Slavitt said that Somerville is on the verge of change for the better, but that the city must take more measures to ensure its progress.

"What happened in Davis Square is going to happen in eastern Somerville. There is the beginning of a kind of new dawn here in Somerville.

"It's very close to Boston, but it has its own character. It has a lot of ethnic diversity. It doesn't have Cambridge's attitude. And, wonderful things will happen here. But they will not happen if you cannot walk safely in the streets after the sun goes down," he said.

Slavitt said he would support the city's gang ordinance, which passed in the Board of Aldermen May 13.

"This is not Deadwood. This is a city in Massachusetts, and I would very, very strongly support a home-rule petition in the legislature that allowed the Somerville aldermen to pass the law that [Alderman-at-Large Bill] White wants to pass, giving police the power to disperse congregations of known gang members. And if they don't immediately disperse on the lawful order of the cops, then arrest them," Slavitt said.

"What we need is not social workers, education and doughnut holes. We need guys with guns. And we need it to take back the city and allow the city to prosper and grow," he said.

"It's like that moment in the spring when the leaves are not yet on the trees, but it looks blurry. And you know that in four days, it will be spring. And Somerville is kind of like that, except it's already happened here in Davis Square, and it will happen in much of the rest of the community. And you should be delighting in this, reveling in this. This is a good place to be."

It is the kind of attention I had been counting on, a way of converting my literary stature and getting some political traction out of it. That it has not happened with the major papers—the *Globe* and the *Herald* or any of the radio or television talk shows—is depressing but not actually surprising. And the *Somerville News* may help rouse the slumbering beasts across the river.

The *News* is by no means contemptible. It is read in precincts in my district.

No organization! Not even a ghost of a party in Somerville! I asked Alderman White whom he could recommend, and his reply was not encouraging:

> David:
>
> You probably have a greater chance of meeting a Yeti than locating Republican volunteers in Wards 1 and 2. There is no current Republican organization in Somerville and there really hasn't been an effective one in my political memory, which goes back to 1973. During the course of the last 10 years, a Republican City Committee has periodically existed, usually with fewer than 10 active members. During this period, I do not believe that Ward 1 was ever organized and I am not sure about Ward 2. The Romney campaign would probably be your best bet to locate potential volunteers and donors in Somerville. Ian Bayne was the last Republican organizer who tried to recruit members, without much success. Ian moved out of the City and I don't have his address. Good luck. Bill White

The state party has nothing to offer. So I am reduced to calling the people on the Campaign Portal list. Many numbers are wrong. Some are right but the person is dead. Or just out of the hospital, or eighty-five years old. These are not potential precinct workers.

★ ★ ★ A postcard came in to Janet today from Toomey's organization. Janet is "Unenrolled," and almost certainly Toomey has sent such cards to every Democrat and Unenrolled voter in the district. Green has him worried enough to exert himself. The postcard is well done, with Toomey's name in bright green (Irish, in case you'd missed it) on a pale blue background, with the identification as state representative and the claim that he is "working hard for us."

On the verso, it says, "Tim Toomey knows the citizens of Somerville and Cambridge deserve and demand effective, energetic leadership. Tim's public record is clear—time and again he delivers the results we need." There are headlines from the *Somerville Journal*, the *Boston Herald*, and the *Cambridge Chronicle* praising him for his noncontroversial exertions such as his "leadership on combating drunk driving." The one from the *Chronicle* calls him "Cambridge's own Robin Hood," which is a phrase he used at the Mt. Vernon Restaurant debate.

★ ★ ★ Tomorrow I go to the Park Plaza Hotel for Mitt's Reform slate rollout—133 GOP candidates for the Senate and House. It's a press event, but there will be a thirty-second session with each candidate during which we get our pictures taken with the governor. These will be distributed digitally for our press releases and on websites and mailings. After the photographs have been taken, we go into a ballroom to pose on risers behind a curtain until the governor pulls a cord and a curtain drops to reveal this array of challengers to the Democrats' hegemony. In other words, we'll be herded about like cattle, photographed, and dismissed. The governor will be the center of attention.

★ ★ ★ The rollout was as I'd feared, but different: one learns as a novelist that life is what one can't predict. Brad Jones, minority leader of the House, and Brian Lees, minority leader of the Senate, were in the herd too, even if they had reserved places. They had to stand and wait with the rest of us behind the curtain. And for Romney and Kerry Healy, it was an hour and a half of stupid smiling, handshaking, and posing. I had my thirty seconds with the governor at a desk in front of a fireplace. The photographer told me to put my left hand on the desk and cover the taped X and look at the X in the circle on the paper the governor was either explaining to me or consulting me about. Once for me, but 130 times for him. We had a very brief conversation. "What's the lapel pin?" he asked. "Harvard?" "No, it's Trumbull College at Yale. I'm a fellow." "Couldn't have been farther off then, could I?" I didn't say there were lots of farther-off places—like Brigham Young University.

When the photographer was done, we shook hands and I was escorted out and through a kitchen (to avoid the reporters and cameramen) onto the risers. Through the kitchen? Is that how to treat us? But I thought of Bobby Kennedy leaving the ballroom through the Roosevelt Hotel kitchen in Los Angeles. One mustn't complain.

Twenty minutes of standing there on the risers—although I took advantage of my age and white hair to sit down for most of it. Then Mitt thanks us for our selflessness in running for office. Selfless? It is a monomaniacal assertion of self! But it could benefit the Commonwealth and is tedious and strenuous, so maybe one can call it selfless.

Then the curtain comes down, there is music, and there are a couple of small explosions and metallic confetti fills the air. For us? For the jaded reporters? There are no members of the public here, no vulgar consumers to be caught up in the manufactured excitement. It is like stand-outs, something they do because not to would seem rude.

The party had picked out nine of us to present to the press—mostly women and ethnics, to show how diverse we are and appeal to the news people and their editors. Afterward, we went out to the ballroom, where the lieutenant governor greeted us. Her job is to stand behind the governor and look enthusiastic. I told her I was Evan's father, and she brightened, which was interesting as the official smile turned, for a moment, real.

★ ★ ★ That evening, we were all invited to a reception in our honor with Romney, Healey, and special guest Ed Gillespie, chairman of the Republican National Committee. "Reception" is almost as honorific as that holiday "dinner" at the Seaport Hotel. The same tray of crudités and cheese and crackers, and a cash bar. And for those who weren't candidates, this was fifty bucks a head! More speeches, of course, with the lieutenant governor introducing the governor, and then Mitt introducing Gillespie, and all of them talking about the revival of the party. They'd brought the big banner with them to the Parker Omni House: "'R' stands for Reform." Not quite catchy enough, I think.

What made it tolerable was that Evan came over to join Janet and me, and people came up to us to say hello to him, meet me, and say nice things to me about him.

There were reports of the rollout on the evening news shows, but I missed them because we'd been at the reception. The big story in the next day's paper was Archbishop O'Malley's announcement of which parishes would close— sixty-five of them, no less. That pushed our group picture back to the City and Region section. I'd been standing just to the left of Greer Swiston, an attractive Chinese-American they'd picked for a ten-second spot. She is in the *Globe* photograph, but I'm out of frame.

Raphael Lewis was not exactly blown away by the event, which he described as "highly choreographed" and "replete with a thumping pop music soundtrack, a velvet curtain, strobe lights, and confetti bombs." He called it "glitzy." He reminded readers that only 15 percent of voters in Massachusetts are registered as Republicans, while more than 40 percent are Democrats. And he quoted Philip W. Johnson, the Democrats' chairman, as saying that only "about nine races are truly competitive." If you figure that the nineteen Republican incumbents all get reelected and you add nine to that, you get twenty-eight—a gain of five seats. The word I heard from one fellow candidate is that the party hopes that about a quarter of us will succeed, in which case there'd be thirty-three.

★ ★ ★ One benefit from the rollout exercises was the press release offered on the Campaign Portal. I took it, adjusted the underlined material so that it was personalized for my campaign, and sent it out to the *Cambridge Chronicle* and the *Somerville News*. It is boilerplate, of course, but not bad, as far as boilerplate goes:

Slavitt Joins Governor Romney, Other Legislative Candidates at Official "Reform Team" Kickoff

Candidate for State Representative files paperwork to meet May 25th deadline to run for office

State Representative Candidate David R. Slavitt joined Governor Mitt Romney, Lt. Governor Kerry Healey, Mass GOP Chairman Darrell Crate and over 100 other legislative "Reform Team" candidates to officially kick off the 2004 campaign season at a press conference in downtown Boston. Slavitt filed paper work to run as a candidate for the Twenty-sixth Middlesex Representative District, which includes parts of Cambridge and Somerville.

"I am honored to be a part of this historic campaign to reform Beacon Hill," said Slavitt. "Governor Romney was elected to end Beacon Hill politics-as-usual, but his reforms have not received their due support in the Legislature. The voters want reform and as a State Representative, I will make sure we put the public's interests ahead of the special interests."

"This is the year to finally bring change to Beacon Hill," said Governor Romney. "It is heartening to see so many distinguished citizens step up and run for public office. These candidates are our neighbors and our friends who want nothing more than to bring reform to state government. We owe them our support and good wishes."

"What impresses me most is the quality of this group of candidates," said Lt. Governor Healey. "We have individuals from all walks of life, doctors, lawyers, teachers, health care professionals, recent college graduates, retirees and stay-at-home parents who have decided to put aside their personal lives and make a commitment to public service."

The Massachusetts Republican Party announced that 131 candidates have met the ballot requirements to seek legislative office this year, a nearly 70% increase over the previous election cycle and the most legislative candidates for the GOP since 1990. Party Chairman Darrell Crate credited Governor Romney and Lt. Governor Healey for their strong leadership and push to enact reform as the main reasons for the surge in candidates.

"This administration has offered so many reasonable reform ideas, including the Mass Turnpike–Highway Department merger, court consolidation, school building assistance reform, pension reform and construction reform," said Crate. "We should be able to save hundreds of millions of dollars in wasteful spending if we just had more Representatives like David Slavitt in office to support these proposals."

★ ★ ★ Tomorrow, I pick up my bookmarks and signs, and the campaign begins in earnest. I shall be trudging from house to house, giving out these bookmarks, getting to know my neighbors, and, more to the point, getting them to recognize my name. "Oh, him!" is the basis for most decisions at the polls. Even with the Campaign Portal's list-making capabilities, this will be strenuous. The end is five months off, and I shall be glad to see it come whether it brings victory or defeat. I could be out there ringing bells today, but I don't have my bookmarks yet, and Janet isn't feeling well. Those are excuses. The real reason is that it's just too dismal to plunge into it on a nice day like this. (That it's a nice day is, in itself, an accusation, of course, but I refuse to be shamed into action.)

Even Toomey must take a day off sometimes.

★ ★ ★ I went up to Malden to spend a little time with Evan and ask him what he thought my basic attitude ought to be about this campaign. After all, if it is really hopeless and if defeat is inevitable, then there is no point in my knocking myself out. All I ought to do is what is entertaining—the debates and such events—and I could avoid some of the donkeywork, the money raising and the door-to-door trudging. Shrewdly, he limited himself to smaller, more manageable issues. He said that I ought not to worry much about the party's fund-raising goals, because in my district, there are constraints on how I could spend the money. I can't do much paid advertising, because Boston media outlets are so expensive. There aren't any efficient, cheap thousand-watt stations, and the cost of those with fifty thousand watts is prohibitive. What I should do is look up Toomey's expenditures of two years ago and see what money he spent and where. These are matters of public record after all. What I am doing, Evan thinks, is running a "guerrilla campaign," and in his view it has been going reasonably well. I am getting free media attention, or, as they call it in the game, "earned" attention. And while he didn't address my larger questions directly, he left me thinking that these answers would emerge, not so much from any intellectual exercise as from experience. I will find a balance between overreaching and underperforming that will be more a function of character than anything else. We don't get to decide about such things but only discover them.

★ ★ ★ Two drastically different events yesterday. The first was a revival meeting in Portuguese, a "Celebrando a Vida," at the Comunidade Cristã Apostólica in Somerville. Dave Funnell, a candidate for state rep in the Eighteenth Worcester District, had told me about this and suggested that it would be a good place to meet conservatives. Because Somerville has so few Republicans, it seemed a good idea. Even if I lose, if I leave some sort of skeletal party organization in Somerville, I shall have accomplished something.

I've never been to a revival meeting. My familiarity with services of Christian worship pretty much ended with my graduation from Andover, where attendance at Cochran Chapel was compulsory. This was different, as I could tell, even before the service began. People were extraordinarily friendly, coming up to wish me a good morning, and, in several instances, adding, "God bless you!" Well, okay, it's a worship service, and this is a devout group. Or maybe Brazilians are just outgoing people.

In a big barny room over a Dunkin' Donuts, with tables at the back and a not bad breakfast, Bispo (Bishop) Thomas Walker welcomed me. His parents had been missionaries in Brazil, which was how he learned Portuguese. He wore jeans and a sport jacket, and I asked how he liked to be addressed. He said "Thomas" would be fine.

I arrived at 9:30 in the morning. There were a couple of other candidates, a Democrat running for sheriff of Middlesex County and Nicolas Sanchez, a Republican running for state rep in the Sixth Middlesex District. Dr. Sanchez (he is a professor at Holy Cross) was carrying a Bible. By ten, Dave Funnell and his wife showed up, and they had a Bible also. Mrs. Funnell told me it was a new one: they wear them out. We sat together and had coffee and muffins and fruit, and he referred to a verse in Leviticus (18:3): "You shall not do what is done in the land of Egypt where you lived, nor are you to do what is done in the land of Canaan where I am bringing you; you shall not walk in their statutes." With a smile, he asked what we thought this warning not to follow in the ways of the Egyptians meant. (Not to build pyramids? I wondered.) What it means, he said, what Maimonides said it means, was that we should not follow their customs in which men marry men and women marry women. Ah, the same-sex marriage business! I was unaware of any such Egyptian custom, but I was not going to argue with him. These matters are obviously beyond rational discussion. That I am pro-choice and in favor of same-sex marriage did not seem necessary to bring up just then.

I was relieved that the service now started, and there was singing (Christian pop in Portuguese), testifying, and much calling and response. It was more enthusiastic than anything I am used to, with people shouting "Hallelujah" and waving their arms. One burly guy in a red T-shirt was kneeling, Arab-style, his head on the floor, and weeping. The service was very loud as if God were hard of hearing, and long. It began a little after ten, and by noon I was calculating whether I shouldn't bail out or, having already invested two and a half hours, wait another few minutes. How much longer could this go on?

The star turn was the sermon by Pastor Cristiano Neto, a fervent exhortation to accept God's direction in our lives. The heart of the talk was a parable about a grand bamboo tree that stood in the gateway of the king's beautiful garden and with the help of the zephyrs (a word I could pick up even from Portuguese) would bow to the king to greet him when he visited the garden. But then one day, the king said to the bamboo that he had a use for it, and the bamboo was delighted. But the king said that he would have to cut down the bamboo. The bamboo was not happy but agreed. The king cut the bamboo, and then lopped off its branches and then cut them in half lengthwise. And then he took the branches from the beautiful garden out to the dry wilderness and laid them on the barren ground, fastening the halved sections together to make a pipe that could bring water from the river to irrigate the dry land and make it fruitful to feed the subjects of the kingdom. The message was that like the bamboo we should accept the decisions of our king, rejoice that he has use for us, and have faith in his just purposes. Good Lord!

After the sermon, there were announcements. One young man got up to say that he had been bewitched but through prayer had managed to lift the witch's spell and resume his normal life. (Salem has witches, not Somerville!) Then it was my turn, and I got up wondering what I could say. Dave Funnell came up with me to translate. I told them that I was running for state rep in Somerville and Cambridge and that we needed more Republicans to restore democracy on Beacon Hill. But that seemed rather dry. So I said I had been moved by the parable about the bamboo but I had another—about a poor man who prayed to the Lord with passion and fervor that he might win the lottery. He needed the money to feed and clothe his children, and day and night he prayed to the Lord, O let me win the lottery. Finally the Lord answered, "I hear you. And I will grant you your prayer. But you have to do your part. Be reasonable. Help me. Buy a ticket!"

It's a dumb joke that came out of the recesses of my mind where jokes lurk, but it worked well enough. "And you must do your part," I said, with more vigor than I generally display, although not waving my hands or shouting. "Help me. Vote in November. Buy a ticket!" It seemed to go over well enough. I lit out, got into my car, and drove away, wondering whether I should be worried about the commandment from Leviticus as I endorsed the Egyptians' customs. I also wondered how many of those Brazilians were citizens, how many vote, and how many of the voters are in my district.

Four hours? I'd probably have done better going door-to-door, ringing bells.

⋆ ⋆ ⋆ That evening, there was a Townhall Meetup, a get-together arranged on the Internet (www.townhall.meetup.com) modeled on Governor Dean's organizational strategies and sponsored by the American Heritage Foundation. I went back to the Park Plaza, the site of Romney's rollout, and at M. J. O'Connor's, an Irish pub that is part of the hotel, found a dozen conservatives looking for ways to further the cause. They were delighted that I was running and volunteered to work with me, show up at stand-outs, come to events like the debate, and hold coffees where I can meet their neighbors. They are, many of them, far to the right, and hold different views from mine on same-sex marriages and abortion rights, but they were sophisticated enough to understand that someone who agreed with them on these issues would not have a prayer of winning in Cambridge and Somerville. We'll see what comes of it.

⋆ ⋆ ⋆ I have the signs and will have to find people willing to put them up in their windows or on their fences. They look terrific. The bookmarks have the text off center on one side, so the printer is redoing them. When I have them in hand, I will be out of excuses about not ringing doorbells. It should be easier than signature gathering. All I have to do is get people to listen for a few moments. They don't have to do anything. If they are receptive, I enter their inclination on the Campaign Portal database and make sure that on Election Day or just before, a campaign worker calls them—assuming that I have campaign workers. But after the meetup that begins to look possible.

It would not be disgraceful to lose, not as a Republican in this district. If I run a respectable race, it is possible that I could get some lagniappe from the governor's office. A job in higher education might be more attractive than listening to Finneran and his coconspirators for two years. But I am not doing it for that. Oddly enough, this is the Zen of politics: my only hope of winning is never to allow myself to think that I can win; and the only honorable way to accept some gubernatorial appointment is not to have wanted it enough to run in a hopeless campaign.

★ ★ ★ The page-one story in the *Globe* this morning, just under the lead piece about the resignation of George Tennant as director of the CIA, was about Governor Romney's proposals to increase state aid to Massachusetts cities and towns and provide them with money for roads, parks, health care, and education. His supplemental budget includes $254 million for construction projects, $100 million for cities and towns, and $83 million for health care and education programs (including $19 million for adult basic education, $11 million for substance abuse treatment, and $10 million for MCAS tutoring). He is also proposing a tax cut. Who can be against any of that?

The Democrats can be, and are. Senate president Travaglini is reported to have said, "This is not the time to act rashly," and Speaker Finneran, several days ago, warned against an "orgy" of tax cuts. These men don't want the governor to look good, doing what they should have done on their own. And, as another story in the City and Region section of the paper makes clear, they are enraged about Romney's proposal for a bailout of Springfield, which is financially embarrassed and to which he offers $52 million, the catch being that he wants to help them solve their problems, as they cannot do by themselves. The governor's plan creates a fiscal oversight board that can suspend municipal labor contracts and unilaterally cut the city budget. (It's not abstruse: if you can't raise revenues, you cut costs!) Labor leaders see this as "union busting," because it threatens the sweetheart deals Springfield has been making with the municipal unions over the years. That is in large part what got the city into the present mess in which its bonds have been downgraded to the "junk" category. Democrats are accustomed to operate in this cozy manner, taxing us excessively and using the money to buy union votes. The unions are those "special interests" to which Romney keeps referring, without ever using the hot-button word: turnpike toll takers have been getting six-figure incomes (admittedly working overtime, but they did badly on their SATs). The Springfield mess is something to throw in the faces of Toomey and Green at our debate later this month.

★ ★ ★ Among the sound bites from Ronald Reagan's speeches that have been floating through the ether as the television networks note his death, one struck me as useful for my own modest purposes. He said that the question before the voters was not so much one of left and right as of up and down. Who are the servants and who are the masters? In what he called the "evil empire," the people take orders from the government, while in a democracy the government takes its orders from the people. This is not far from what I have been saying, but it has that snap Reagan was famous for.

★ ★ ★ I am to appear this afternoon on Doug Holder's *Writer to Writer*, a community TV production that appears on the Somerville station. Holder is on the *Somerville News* staff and has been friendly, so this interview is hardly threatening, but I have been thinking about it and feeling some apprehension. I was wide awake at five in the morning, considering what I might say. It ought to be an ideal venue, a way of combining at least for that occasion my literary and political selves, but I find myself wondering whether there is any such combination that makes sense. Is there any connection beyond the fungibility of celebrity? Norman Mailer for mayor of New York? Gore Vidal for representative from Dutchess County? They would have been catastrophic, more likely than not, if they'd been elected—and Gore actually came close. Yeats was a senator in Ireland, but he believed in pernes and gyres and phases of the moon, and while this may be fun to read, I am not sure that I'd want a person like that voting on legislation that could affect my life.

There have been, of course, some eminent writers who were men of public affairs. Chaucer and Milton come immediately to mind. And when, in the thirty-year peace between the first and second Peloponnesian Wars, Pericles decided to firm up the empire by moderating the amount of the tribute the client states had to pay Athens, he appointed Sophocles as one of the members of the board, either trusting the tragedian's wisdom or putting to use his considerable prestige. (Or very probably, both.) But I will seem impossibly erudite if I try to allude to this.

★ ★ ★ Evan called last night, and I asked whether I need to buy sticks—to staple the signs to for the Gay Pride parade on Saturday and at other such events. Yes, he said. Get some laths. So I went to Home Depot, got seven eight-foot laths, had them cut into thirty-two-inch lengths, and lugged them home, along with a staple gun and a box of staples. It will be arts-and-crafts time for Janet and me either tomorrow night or Friday. Janet wondered why I couldn't get volunteers to do this. I'll be grateful if any volunteers actually show up to march and carry the damned signs.

★ ★ ★ An irksome e-mail from the state Republican Party:

Candidates,

As you know we have been pushing all legislative candidates to work on developing a Finance Plan. I have sent out a couple emails with a Finance Plan template we developed to help you with this process. In order for us to be able to help you with your campaign it is essential that we see a Finance Plan. Without knowing what you are planning to spend money on throughout the campaign and without knowing how you plan to raise the funds needed to carry out your plan we can not provide you assistance.

A successful campaign cannot be run without a plan. I have attached a Finance Plan template as well as a Sample Finance Plan for a State Rep. race. I know each of you has a lot going on with your campaigns but the Finance Plan is critical. **We are setting a deadline of Friday, June 18th for you to turn in a completed Finance Plan to the State Party. Please send your plan to my email address—msthilaire@massgop.com.**

Matt

So if we don't have the plan in by the eighteenth, which is a week from tomorrow, what are they going to do? Not help me any more? They need me as much as I need them.

With the e-mail are a couple of attachments, one with a sample financial plan and one that is a template for the plan we are supposed to submit. These are intimidating, with large budgets and hefty expenditures quite different from the campaign I am running. I may buy an ad in the *Somerville News* and one in the *Cambridge Chronicle* and *Somerville Journal* (these are Townline newspapers, owned by the *Boston Herald*, which is owned by Rupert Murdoch). But those won't be that pricey. The big expenditures, so far, have been with the printer. These signs at three dollars apiece (250 is the minimum order) represent a substantial investment for my "guerrilla campaign."

Still, I've forwarded Matt's e-mail to Evan, and we'll figure out, over the weekend, how to respond.

★ ★ ★ The *Writer to Writer* appearance was more literary than was good for me, but I didn't have much control over it. Doug Holder asked me a series of questions he had before him in an old-fashioned schoolboy's notebook. He had done enough reading to be reasonably well informed. And when he asked me to explain my distrust of literary criticism and my preference for "remarks," there was nothing for me to do except reply—pointing out that one of the rare books of literary criticism I could think of was Barbara Herrnstein Smith's *Poetic Closure*, which considers the endings of poems and their range of literary strategies and how various poets have used them and with what effect. But the entire book, sensible as it is, doesn't seem any more useful to a practicing poet than Robert Frost's remark "No surprise for the writer, no surprise for the reader," which is an invaluable aperçu, particularly if one considers it alongside one of his other famous dicta about how a poem "begins in delight and ends in wisdom." While this literary chat was quite comfortable, I felt that it was self-indulgent as I spoke as briefly as I could about how we begin by playing with a cadence or a metaphor or sometimes a phrase that has popped into our heads but, because we've read many poems before and can see, much too quickly, various ways the poem might go, it is the constraints of form—rhyme, meter, or whatever—that drive us to improvisations and, sometimes, force us to something better and truer than what we might have written without such pressure. This is what I believe and is important to me, but all the time there was an awareness of its irrelevance to the campaign. I'd managed to put the entire audience in the position into which I'd forced Toomey with that metaphor about Siegfried and the birdsongs. Or I was back in elementary school with classmates making fun of my use of some low-frequency word.

Even if this was unlikely to get me many votes among the largely working-class neighborhoods of Somerville, I did think to bring along one of my Slavitt signs and with a thumbtack put it up on the wall behind us, so that it was in frame the whole time.

Holder and I were talking when, in medias res, our faces appeared on the monitor, and we realized we were on the air. We were still talking away when, half an hour later, the monitor showed something entirely other, which was our cue that the program had ended. That kind of amateurishness is apparently endemic to community television, but so far I haven't had much welcome among the more professional outlets. I begin even to develop a fondness for these homemade programs, which the networks might think of imitating because, in their clumsiness, these local shows appear to be more authentic and believable. Holder will send me a videotape, and he recorded the conversation on an audiotape recorder. He will be transcribing the interview and eventually posting it on his blog.

✶ ✶ ✶ The *Cambridge Chronicle* did not see fit to run the press release about Governor Romney's rollout of his 130 candidates and his endorsement of me. But there is an article headlined "Nurses Group Endorses Toomey" that I found annoying:

> The Massachusetts Nurses Association, which represents more than 22,000 registered nurses and health-care professionals in Massachusetts, announced its endorsement and support for Timothy Toomey, Democratic [sic] for re-election as state representative of the 26th Middlesex District, which includes precincts in both Cambridge and Somerville.
>
> "The MNA is behind Timothy Toomey because he is committed to improving our health care system and to addressing the core fundamental problems of recruitment and retention in nursing," said Karen Higgins, MNA president. "He clearly understands the vital role nurses play in delivering safe, high-quality patient care. He has shown great support for efforts to improve registered nurse staffing levels and to create conditions that will allow nurses to deliver the care their patients deserve. We look forward to working with Tim in improving health care for all residents of the commonwealth."

He filled out the same questionnaire as I did, but his answers were more acceptable. He never met a union demand he didn't like. I sent an e-mail to the *Chronicle:*

> Your "In Brief" item (June 10) about the endorsement by the Massachusetts Nurses Association of Representative Tim Toomey ought perhaps to have been a longer and better considered article. Mr. Toomey's gut instincts are always that unions are right and management is wrong, workers are good and employers are bad. In the real world life is often more complicated. The legislation for which the MNA is lobbying, and which Mr. Toomey apparently supports (I got the same questionnaire from the MNA), is a further level of regulation that ties the hands of intelligent and hard-working hospital administrators who are doing their best with a nursing shortage that cannot be remedied by legislative fiat. This proposed bill makes no distinction between experienced nurses and those on whose credentials the ink is barely dry. It does not acknowledge that nurses on an obstetrical floor can

take care of more patients than, say, on a burn unit. Everyone—nurses, doctors, administrators, and patients—wants better nursing care. This legislation will make things worse, and I suspect that Mr. Toomey knows this, but he also knows that his support is from unions and there is almost nothing they can do that he won't agree to or applaud. In this larger context, then, their endorsement of his candidacy looks considerably less attractive.

David R. Slavitt
Republican Candidate for State Rep. (26th Middlesex District)

★ ★ ★ I did a couple of hours of canvassing yesterday, starting with a nearby street that I'd done a few months ago on my quest for signatures. The weather was perfect, and I had my bookmarks and doorhangers in a bag. Also stickers and contribution envelopes. In another, slightly larger bag, I had a few yard signs. And, of course, I had my list generated from the Campaign Portal, which turns out to be less accurate than one would like. On Fayette Street, there were fifty-four names of Republicans and voters who were registered but not enrolled in a party. What was disappointing was that, of those names, nineteen turned out to be wrong. When I complained to the party headquarters, their answer was that in Cambridge people move a lot—as if it were Cambridge's fault, or mine. Still, I left eight doorhangers and got seven people to say that they'd vote for me in November, maybe five of whom I think actually might do so.

Oddly enough, a letter came in on that same day from Jody Dow, vice chair of Northeast Region of the Republican National Committee, telling me that door-to-door campaigning is "the most cost effective way to make voter contact" and offering a sheet of Helpful Hints. With some skepticism, I looked at the list. After all, what's the hard part of this? But there was one useful suggestion that I hadn't thought of. "Make sure you write 'Sorry I missed you' on the hand cards the night before visiting the neighborhoods. You don't want to waste time while you are door knocking."

It isn't just the time, although that adds up. But if you write the little messages the night before, seated comfortably at a desk or table, the handwriting is legible.

★ ★ ★ According to a story on page one of the City & Region section of today's *Globe*, Senator Kennedy has issued "a personal appeal" to Speaker Finneran and Senate president Travaglini to take up the stalled bill that would create a special election process to replace Senator Kerry in the event that he should be elected to the presidency and his seat should therefore become vacant. As it now stands, Governor Romney could name an interim appointee, who would presumably be a Republican. What interests me is that both Finneran and Travaglini were "concerned about the potential backlash to what Republicans charge would be a blatant partisan power grab." But it isn't the blatant partisan power grab that worries them or even the backlash; it's the blame for so nasty a maneuver. Now that the blame can be passed on to Kennedy himself, who, as he demonstrated at Chappaquiddick, is beyond praise and blame, they will of course go ahead and hold hearings next Tuesday. The bill will go through and get vetoed, and they'll override the veto. And the citizens of the Commonwealth will be disgusted but not surprised and, as always, absolutely powerless to do anything about it.

This is, all by itself, a reason to vote for Bush.

★ ★ ★ At the Gay Pride parade yesterday, a hundred thousand people lined the route, some of them dressed—or cross-dressed—as outrageously as possible in sexy getups with high heels, some looking more or less normal but with T-shirts with equal signs or proclaiming "Justly Married." It was a long wait—the Log Cabin people had told me to show up at ten, and I figured ten thirty would be time enough. The parade didn't actually get going until after twelve thirty, and then it was, for me anyway, a longish walk. Evan and Janet walked with me, and Lorene Leiter. Fred Baker had a high school reunion to go to. But we were there, showed up, fulfilled the promise I'd made to the Log Cabin Republicans. And maybe even got noticed. There was a moment near the end, when we were walking along Boylston Street and I was very tired, that a guy on a motorcycle came up behind us. It wasn't clear whether he was expressing support for Gay Pride or gay rights or was just trying to sell the motorcycle, which had a For Sale sign on it. I was so beat I thought of maybe buying the bike. But then he offered me a ride. His girlfriend was walking along beside him and let me borrow her helmet. So I got on behind him and with one hand held onto his shoulder and with the other brandished my Slavitt sign.

I'd never been on a motorcycle before. It was fun but, after ten minutes, painful. The seat is narrow and uncomfortable, and one's butt starts to hurt, which was why the girlfriend was walking alongside. The good thing, though, is that a friend of Ken Sanchez, the president of the Log Cabin Republicans, had a camera and took a couple of pictures of me on the bike, and if they look like anything, they'll be just odd enough for me to send to the papers. The point is not only to be there but to have been there, so that one can send out a press release to that effect. And with the picture, the press release is likelier to get used.

That is not, perhaps, the level of political discourse I had in mind when I decided to run, but if Kerry can ride a bike onto Jay Leno's set, I can pose on the back of one looking sporty. The music, in any event, was good. We were behind a float for Ramrod, a gay nightclub, with very buff guys dancing to thunderous rock on loud loudspeakers.

Walking along in our group just behind that float, I held my sign high with one hand and, with the other, waved. Now and then Janet would remind me to smile, which was not so easy, given that my hip and my legs were hurting and we had a long way yet to go. I told her I felt like the queen. She pointed out that, no, they were the queens; I was the straight guy. For a couple of seconds my smile turned real.

★ ★ ★ During the march, Evan told me that what I should do with Matt St. Hilaire's e-mail demand for a financial plan was to invent something. Just make it up. So, having telephoned him on Thursday afternoon when he was away from his desk and not having heard back, I sent him an e-mail this morning that was stern but not quite hostile:

Dear Matt,

We have only a sketchy plan. It's a guerilla campaign, as Evan points out. We are in such an expensive district with out-of-sight prices on media buys that we can be competitive with Toomey for rather little. He's not going to buy space in the Globe or Herald or time on the major radio and TV stations. He didn't two years ago (we looked) and won't this time around. So we have, paradoxically, a modest but realistic budget of $15 to $20 K, of which we've raised, so far, about a quarter. We have some fundraiser coffees planned for later this month and for September, and we'll be laying on more of these as we see how the first one goes and refine our methods. We also have a mailing that will be going out within the next week or so to Fred Baker's Cambridge GOP people. And some donors have promised money during the summer. I'm not, I think, in terrible shape. (It is also true that Toomey and Green are fighting each other with some real energy and money, and the main thrust of my effort will come after the primary when I know who my opponent is.)

The Campaign Portal is only moderately helpful. On a typical day, I go to a street with 50 names on it (Republican and Unenrolled) and 19 have moved. Or I go to a project on Harvard Street where the Portal does not list names by apartment number and where the residents don't have names on the doors. So there's no way to know whose bell I'm ringing, or, sometimes, whom I've persuaded to vote for me. And not a prayer of coming back to enter this in the data base, which takes a lot of time and energy and produces nothing for me (although it gives you something to look at).

Finally, I'm troubled by the last sentence of your first paragraph below. "Without knowing what you are planning to spend money on throughout the campaign and without knowing how you plan to raise the funds needed to carry out your plan we can not provide you assistance." Does that mean "can not" or "will not" and is this a kind of threat?

You want to know what's going on? Call me. Or at least return my calls when I call you.

Best,
David

★ ★ ★ There is a young man named Shawn Jenkins whom I've met a couple of times and who is running for sheriff of Suffolk County (which is, basically, Boston), and in yesterday's *Globe*, I read—woefully belatedly, it turns out— that he turned in a thousand signatures, some of which have been challenged. As the counsel for the Massachusetts GOP, Evan represented him—he hadn't mentioned this to me. But when I referred to the piece in the paper, he explained what had happened. Jenkins farmed out the signature gathering to a firm that does this, and they turned in all the names at once at the end. Their guesses about yields had been too high, and some of the sheets had only two or three valid names. So Jenkins's petition had exactly the requisite thousand names. And on challenge, two of these turned out to be wrong: one signer wasn't registered and another was a Democrat. This happened last Wednesday, some days ago, which makes the *Globe* look rather languid. Unless Evan can find a couple of names that ought to have been allowed, Jenkins is out.

Hearing this, I felt a pang of envy.

★ ★ ★ A draft of my opening remarks for the second debate in a couple of weeks:

Here we are again. I thank you for coming and I salute you for your interest in public affairs and the governance of the commonwealth.

I'm a poet, a novelist, a critic, and I have been a teacher—at such places as Columbia, Penn, and Princeton. I am the Republican, which means that I am the long-shot. But as I was thinking about what to say tonight—I found myself wondering what questions I'd put to Representative Toomey if I were sitting out there. And I realized that, at least in that small way, I am already representing you. Which is what a writer learns to do. What does the reader— or in this case, the voter—want to know?

There are questions I asked last time, to which Mr. Toomey did not respond, perhaps because the format didn't allow it, or possibly because there aren't any sensible answers. "Why do you vote 97.8% of the time with Speaker Finneran?" is such a question. A more important and more embarrassing question would be why should Speaker Finneran, with 7,600 votes in Mattapan, have more power on Beacon Hill than Governor Romney, who got more than a million votes throughout the commonwealth? Senate President Travaglini and Speaker Finneran are not presiding over a General Court but are operating a protection racket, and what they are protecting is the Democratic Party, which is accustomed to power, hates being accountable in any way to the electorate, and ignores referenda in which we, the voters, express our wishes about the death penalty or the Clean Elections Law or Total Immersion in the schools, or the tax roll-back. How many pot-holes can you fix, how many scooter regulations can you enact, how many constituent services can you perform that will put a decent face on the arrogance and the irresponsibility of your party and its contempt for the voters of Massachusetts?

And I have one final question. In the last debate, Mr. Toomey compared himself with Robin Hood. Sounds good, right? Steal from the rich (by which he means Harvard and MIT) and give to the poor, by which he means the working men and women of East Cambridge. He's proud of this and he claims it in his mailings! But what does it mean? Does Representative Toomey run around in green tights in the woods with merry men? No! Is he fighting for us against the oppressive sheriff of Nottingham? Of course not! He is the Sheriff of Nottingham. He is the government! There is no bad King John on the throne. This is the standard operating procedure of the Democrats in Massachusetts. Tax everybody, and tell the voters "We're doing it for you!" Steal from the taxpayers and give to the guys with whom the Democrats have been cozy for decades, the special interests, which is to say mostly the unions. And in Representative Toomey's case, I suspect that it isn't just shrewd politics, but also maybe a little envy. Who are these high-toned Harvard guys with their twenty billion dollars? Isn't it fun to think how an Irish kid from east of the tracks who went to Suffolk can make the lives of the Harvard guys and the MIT guys hell?

But Representative Toomey knows better than this. He is a decent man, and his brother, I believe, is a priest, and he knows in his soul that he is not Robin Hood and that stealing is wrong. And he knows, too, that envy is no admirable thing. He shouldn't give in to it, himself, and he should not appeal to it in us!

I'm David Slavitt. I want to be your representative. I can speak up and say out loud what you've been muttering under your breath for years.

My chances are only infinitesimally improved from what they were before I wrote that—but it does have a nice ring to it!

★ ★

10

A decent note from Matt St. Hilaire at the state party headquarters:

Thanks David,

I know that you have to devise a creative plan in your district and it sounds like you are in good shape at this point. Fundraising is a difficult task but if you are able to put together several small dollar events you can both meet voters and raise some money at the same time. As you mentioned, going to the "air waves" is probably not the best way to spend your resources and you should hold off on spending until after the Primary.

I understand your frustration with the portal. Your district probably has more people moving in and out of it than most. As long as you are door knocking and identifying your support, you are in good shape.

I was not threatening you and I apologize if it came across that way. My point in writing that paragraph is that we cannot provide you with advice and help if we don't know what's going on with your campaign. We have 131 candidates running and cannot possibly know what each campaign is up to on a daily basis. We are trying to give you an idea of what it is we would like to know about your race so that when the time comes we can make informed decisions about how our resources will be spent. Things like the Portal and the Finance Plan are ways for us to understand your plan and campaigns progress.

Matt

I replied in a mollified and mollifying way, of course. But it remains true that our interests do not coincide. With 130 candidates to back (that odd 131st will be out after the primary in September) and with limited resources, they have to be as picky as a down-on-his-luck horseplayer about which ones to put money on—or supply with interns. There are some campaigns that have been given high school kids to do some of the donkeywork. Mostly these kids are from comfortable Republican suburbs, and I can understand that few of them would want to commute from Andover or Weston into Cambridge to work for me, which may be why I didn't get one. Or it could be that the party is not yet persuaded that my efforts have any hope of success. That could change, of course, and, later on, if I begin to get attention from the media, the party could take heart about my prospects and actually enhance them by throwing me some support. Meanwhile, that Campaign Portal of theirs is a two-edged sword, providing me with some help as I make up walking lists of various streets in Cambridge and Somerville but also requiring me to record these encounters in such a way as to allow the party workers to track my activities. Such observation is never altogether comfortable.

★ ★ ★ I went last night to a reception for Lieutenant Governor Healey and former governor of New Jersey Christine Todd Whitman. As a candidate, I got in free and was allowed to bring a guest, so I asked Lorene Leiter to come with me, as a way of recognizing her efforts in holding the fund-raiser coffee for me next week. She works at MIT doing experiments on schizophrenic mice. I learned all this as we were driving up I-93, a terrible place to be during rush hour.

The reception was up in Wakefield at the Sheraton Colonial. The hors d'oeuvres were slightly better than usual. There was a cash bar (two glasses of white wine were ten bucks). I recognized some of my fellow candidates, and we chatted a bit. Then at seven, Darrell Crate came out, thanked us for coming, and introduced Kerry Healey, who repeated what she'd said to the press earlier in the day when she had called on Kerry to resign from the Senate the way Bob Dole did when he was a candidate. She was pretty good, citing impressive numbers about how Senator Kerry has missed 87 percent of the votes in the Senate and hasn't been doing his job. The lieutenant governor is the Bush-Cheney campaign cochair in Massachusetts. She is also on any short list of names among which Romney would pick if he could make an interim appointment to fill Kerry's vacant seat.

Then Healey introduced Christine Todd Whitman, who gave a graceful speech about public service, congratulating all of us who were running and urging everyone else in the room to support us. I wasn't taking notes but I remember that she echoed Healey's criticism of Kerry, mentioning that her husband (or was it one of her husband's friends?) had been at school with young John Kerry, and it was clear at the age of thirteen that he wanted to be president. She let that sink in for a moment. Then she said that the worrisome thing about such a desire in a thirteen-year-old was that he had no idea why he wanted to be president or what he wanted to do for the country; he just wanted the office. And that, she said, was still clearly the case with him.

After her prepared remarks she took a few questions (spontaneous or prearranged, it was impossible to tell). Someone asked about the place of women in the Republican Party, and her instantaneous response was quite clever. She invited all the women candidates to come up and join her on the platform. It was an impressive array, with fifteen or twenty women standing behind her. A great photo op, and cameras were clicking and flashes were flashing. (This was why I wondered if it had been planned beforehand. But it doesn't matter. If it was on the spur of the moment, it was brilliant. And if someone scripted it ahead of time, it was hardly less so.) A big round of applause!

Someone then asked her about the Environmental Protection Agency and what had happened to her there, and she welcomed the question and was gracious and poised. She has been asked this before, of course. She was not in the Bush inner circle, I think, and my guess is that she either misread signals or never got any signals in the first place, so that, not surprisingly, she eventually put a foot wrong somewhere. But she didn't allude to any of that. She merely praised Bush for his refusal to join the extremists at either end of the spectrum, those who think that the environment must be protected everywhere and at all costs and those who want no restrictions at all on what business and industry may do to the environment. She was so upbeat that it was only a few minutes later that we realized that she hadn't ever quite answered the question. Which means that she won.

After her speech, she and the lieutenant governor and their entourage darted out a side door. Lorene and I left. She said she enjoyed the event, but I wasn't sorry Janet had missed it.

★ ★ ★ Not surprisingly, there are a couple of challenges to the position Governor Romney and Attorney General Reilly have taken about that 1913 law prohibiting the marriage in Massachusetts of parties "residing and intending to continue to reside in another jurisdiction if such marriage would be void if contracted in such other jurisdiction." Gay and Lesbian Advocates and Defenders, which brought the *Goodridge* suit that legalized same-sex marriages, have one action in the Suffolk Superior Court, and in a parallel suit clerks from a dozen cities and towns will ask the court to allow them to grant licenses to residents of other states, even though General Reilly has ordered some of them to cease and desist. Both Somerville and Cambridge are parties to this action. According to the *Globe*, Romney's spokeswoman referred questions about the suits to Reilly's office, where the spokesman declined comment. The Senate voted to repeal the law as a part of the budget bill, but that provision was left out of the reconciled measure the legislature agreed to this week.

★ ★ ★ Evan's e-mailed comments on the draft of my opening remarks for the June 30 debate:

> I would leave out the personal attack on Toomey near the end—the envy bit. Not needed. The point is made. Also that will eliminate the need to praise him. Instead, I would devote the last bit to you—fresh voice for Cambridge and Somerville—a new and skeptical attitude toward business as usual. Show the Institutional party that they have no right to their seats, they have to earn them every two years from the voters and they have not done so.

What he wants me to delete is:

> And in Representative Toomey's case, I suspect that it isn't just shrewd politics, but also maybe a little envy. Who are these high-toned Harvard guys with their twenty billion dollars? Isn't it fun to think how an Irish kid from east of the tracks who went to Suffolk can make the lives of the Harvard guys and the MIT guys hell?
>
> But Representative Toomey knows better than this. He is a decent man, and his brother, I believe, is a priest, and he knows in his soul that he is not Robin Hood and that stealing is wrong. And he knows, too, that envy is no admirable thing. He shouldn't give in to it, himself, and he should not appeal to it in us!

He's probably right. Janet agrees with him and doesn't want me to mention Suffolk. So I'll probably accede to their judgment and let *capital froideur* prevail. What I can say is:

> Representative Toomey knows in his heart that stealing is wrong, but he has been on Beacon Hill for too long and has lost his way. What Cambridge and Somerville need is a voice in that wilderness, someone whose moral compass is still operational. The institutional party does not have a lifetime ten-

ancy of those seats, which are ours to give or withhold. Your representatives have to earn re-election, and Tim Toomey has not done that. Vote for me! I'm a liberal Republican, pro-choice and in favor of same-sex marriages. Insofar as possible, I want to keep government out of our hair. And I will speak up for you and say out loud what you have been muttering under your breath now for years.

Less fun, but less vicious. I don't want to seem mean-spirited. I guess.

★ ★ ★ An interesting bit of information came across my computer screen yesterday, and I realize that it may be significant, even though the *Globe* and the *Times* and the other media have failed to take notice of it. This was the election of Chief Justice Margaret Marshall of the Supreme Judicial Court, the author of the *Goodridge* decision, to the Corporation of Yale University. The Yale alumni are hardly a radical group, and if we think highly of her judgment and want her as one of the leaders of our university, that kind of election is an endorsement not only of her courage—which even her opponents would have to concede—but of her wisdom. It is not just a straw in the wind but a large piece of lumber, which means that the acceptance of same-sex marriages is inevitable. I have no idea how Bush or Kerry voted, but Yale alumni are spread all over the country and tend to be in positions of power and authority. And they voted for her.

★ ★ ★ The *Somerville News* ran the press release about Romney's endorsement, and the photo of Mitt and me. And on the same day, the *Cambridge Chronicle* ran my letter about the Massachusetts Nurses Association's endorsement of Toomey. Of course, there were, on the Politics page, photographs of Toomey giving some award, and of Avi Green planting flowers and participating in the "Cleaning Day at the East End House." I have to get that picture of me on the motorcycle and send it out. I have to have more photographs of such staged events. These are better, I'm afraid, and grabbier than letters to the editor, the text of which few people read.

★ ★ ★ Fred Baker sent me a draft of his fund-raising letter, which looks fine, I think:

Dear KOMING,

Too often we as Republicans have set forth to vote on Election Day only to find the usual ballot filled with unopposed incumbent Democrats. This year, in the 26th Middlesex House district, we have a candidate willing to put in the necessary time and effort to challenge incumbent Tim Toomey and become an outstanding State Representative committed to changing and reducing Massachusetts government.

The ballot is often the last refuge for enacting legislation aimed at improving life in the Bay State. Yet the list of initiative petitions and referenda Massachusetts' voters have approved, later to be watered down, phased in or thrown out completely by the pretentious solons "working" on our behalf on Beacon Hill is substantial. The will of voters has been made clear on such issues as capital punishment, rent control abolition, bilingual education abolition, the income tax rollback, term limits, and the charitable giving tax credit. And **all of the above** have been weakened or cancelled outright by the state legislature after having passed—often with substantial majorities—by the voters on notable Election Days of years past.

David Slavitt, as a State Representative, will always respect the will of Massachusetts' voters, as there is no clearer indication of their intent than ballot results on crucial issues.

And David Slavitt has the courage to face the Finneran juggernaut on Beacon Hill. In a climate where a Rep. can make the Enemies List when voting as *infrequently* as 81% of the time with the Speaker's wishes, David Slavitt is determined to defend tirelessly the need for economic and social freedom on behalf of those burdened by the income tax, sales tax, property tax, automobile excise tax, tolls, fines, fees, rules and regulations that perpetuate the difficult living and business environment known as the Commonwealth of Massachusetts.

Economically conservative and socially moderate, David Slavitt is an accomplished author with over 80 publications. His fascinating background includes a stint as a Newsweek writer and film critic, appearances on The Tonight Show with Johnny Carson, and numerous university appointments. A resident of West Street, David lives with his wife Janet and is the father of former Massachusetts Attorney General aspirant Evan Slavitt.

I encourage all Cambridge and Somerville Republicans to seize this opportunity to promote what has, sadly, become a rarity in recent years in this area: a candidate for State Representative who can fearlessly challenge a long-time incumbent on the issues. There are three primary areas in which you can help

David's objective of gaining a seat on Beacon Hill. The first is by giving him your vote in the November 2nd election. A vote, as I've always said, is worth 10 if not 100 yard signs and just as many bumper stickers and buttons. Secondly, your time as a campaign volunteer would be appreciated as we have an almost insurmountable mountain of work to finish in procuring a Rep. seat that's been long unchallenged by Republicans. The work is varied and we can make use of whatever special talents you may have time to share, regardless of whether or not you actually live in the 26th Middlesex House district.

Lastly, money is—like it or not—the life-blood of any political campaign. Successful candidates frequently amass revenue totaling six figures. Incumbents are almost always able to out-raise the challengers for campaign donations in municipal, state and national elections. With Tim Toomey's substantial combined earnings from City Council and State Rep. contributions looming heavily, it is of special urgency that we raise the largest amount possible to run a campaign that will have any chance of producing a victory. While I certainly wouldn't ask anyone to donate beyond their means, I do ask that you give as generously as possible: we're up against a very difficult task, as many of you know from involvement in prior campaigns. Your donations help ensure a credible and respectable campaign able to deliver its message to people effectively. We thank you in advance for anything you contribute, be it in effort, money or both.

With sincere gratitude,

Fred Baker

Chairman of the Cambridge Republican City Committee
Former Cambridge School Committee candidate (2001)
Campaign Manager for David Slavitt for State Representative

★ ★ ★ I went to have coffee—well, okay, a mocha slide—at a coffeehouse in Inman Square to meet Bill Hees, who is a member of the Libertarian Party, or the shreddy remnant of it. They don't have any meetings or any organization. They do, however, have a mailing list, and I figured that if I could get hold of that and get it to Fred, we'd have more people to send the letter to. But Libertarians are like any other splinter group, powerless but persnickety. There is, indeed, a mailing list, but the state chairman has it, and he has to approve its use. Hees is trying to get that approval for me, but it was impossible for him to say what the decision would be.

The orthodox libertarians are 100 percent against gun control and think that the Constitution guarantees any citizen the right to own as many grenade launchers as he or she can afford. They believe that unless a government function is specified in the Constitution, the federal government ought not to be doing it, so that they are at least in theory opposed to the Centers for Disease Control or the National Institutes of Health. But the coffeehouse was only two blocks away, and the mocha slide was good. If it was a waste of time and calories, it was not unpleasant.

I gave Hees a bookmark and a contributor's envelope, although I doubt that an out-of-work computer programmer will prove to be a major benefactor.

★ ★ ★ I took the weekend off. Janet and I went to New York to see a play and have dinner. I felt for a couple of days as though I were a normal person. I was not tempted to go up to strangers on the street, hold out my hand, and say that I was running for office, nor did I feel at all remiss about not doing such awful things. The Met in the morning, the Stage for lunch, and then Stoppard in the afternoon. What could be better?

The trouble is that after the weekend, Monday comes around again, and I'm back home facing the great Demos, which I must try to rouse from its torpor to get it to vote for me. That this is unlikely to happen has almost nothing to do with the effort I must put forth, and it crosses my mind that my avoidance of team sports may have left me unprepared for these existentialist ventures. It must be clear to members of a team when, in the late stages of a game, the score is so lopsided that it doesn't make sense to keep trying and stay focused, not for victory's sake anymore but now only for that of honor.

What I learned as a poet and novelist is quite the opposite lesson. If a poem or a novel is not going well, the sensible thing is generally to give it up and find a project that is better suited to my interests or talents or temperament. And if I'd been shrewder, I might have thrown in the towel on that entire enterprise and become . . . a lawyer?

Well, no. Perhaps not. So perhaps I, too, am a kind of existentialist. Or loony.

★ ★ ★ It is a lovely day, the first full day of summer, and the weather is too good for me to make excuses, so I was out, not trudging door-to-door with these almost useless lists, but working, as I much prefer to do, at wholesale. I thought I might go up and down Cambridge Street and get some of the merchants and restaurateurs to put signs in their windows. I was reasonably successful around Inman Square, where convenience stores, fish stores, hardware stores, and such places were sometimes receptive. I placed a half dozen signs. The trick is to find a business where they are just hanging on, not too spiffy in respect to their windows, but not so shabby that it looks bad for my name to be in any way associated with their decline and fall. I did well enough so that I thought it would be amusing to venture farther east to Toomey's office and get some signs up on that block.

Tim Toomey now has two offices, one on the corner of Seventh Street and a new one just before the railroad tracks near Cardinal Medeiros Avenue. No business on that block was welcoming. There were a couple of bakeries I tried, but this was a decision for the owner (one would be in at six in the evening, another would be in tomorrow). An insurance and travel agency across the street considered my proposition for maybe ten seconds and then said, "No, I can see it would be funny, but Tim's a friend. He isn't around as often as I'd like, but I wouldn't want to risk the friendship, even so." Sal's Flowers—not a thriving enterprise—was as hostile as anyplace I visited. I introduced myself as the Republican, and got a horselaugh from the geezer behind the counter. "Not in a million years!" was the answer to my question about a sign in his window.

I'd been out for a little more than an hour, and it was warm. It was time to pack it in. I put a couple of Slavitt stickers up on the streetlight stanchion outside Toomey's new office. They won't last long, but they'll let him know that a Slavitt supporter was there.

★ ★ ★ Governor Romney is going down to Washington this morning to testify at a hearing of the Senate Judiciary Committee in support of a federal constitutional amendment banning gay marriage. This is depressing. He zips down for a ten-minute turn before the committee, then flies back to do whatever he does in the afternoon, and then, this evening, hosts the reception for Arkansas governor Mike Huckabee at the Westin. Former governors Weld and Swift will be there, and the big givers from the Key Club (at one thousand dollars a plate), and Republican candidates (at one hundred dollars a plate), including Janet and me. That I will not have a chance to make some remark to Romney about his activities earlier in the day is something of a relief. The *Globe* quotes Don Stewart, communications director for U.S. Senator John Cornyn, one of the committee members, as saying that "the will of the people of Massachusetts and the Legislature was changed by a court, and the problem has become a federal problem now because of that." Stewart's explanation of Romney's appearance is that he has become "a direct symbol of elected representatives being overruled by the courts, and he can speak directly to how that has affected his state and his constituency."

My first question is what would an "indirect symbol" be? And my second is about Governor Faubus, Huckabee's predecessor, who was also an elected representative and was overruled by the courts. These appeals to the people and their will and wisdom risk demagoguery. The people are often wrong, which is why this is not a democracy but a representative republic. Hamilton was right to worry about mob rule.

Maybe I should rethink my attacks on Finneran, whose contempt for the popular will is not so different from my own. Or, if I continue criticizing him for ignoring referenda, I might cut Governor Romney some slack for his similar specious appeal.

★ ★ ★ Joan Vennochi's *Globe* column is more enlightening about Governor Romney's testimony in Washington this morning. Apparently, some senior Republican senators—including Ted Stevens of Alaska and John Warner of Virginia—were reluctant to have these hearings and bring the matter to a vote, but Rick Santorum of Pennsylvania pressed the issue, to force Senator Kerry to vote on a controversial question before the Democratic National Convention here in Boston. Kerry's position is ambiguous, as most of his positions are—against gay marriage, in favor of civil unions, but against an amendment to the federal Constitution to limit or define the rights of the states to legislate on this issue. Romney and his people must know all this, but it wouldn't bother the governor at all to put the Massachusetts junior senator in an awkward position while getting a little national attention for himself. (All that talk about the will of the people? Window dressing. Persiflage and rhodomontade.)

★ ★ ★ Another questionnaire came in today's mail, this one pure fun, from the Massachusetts Citizens for Life, Inc. It is a delight not to have to worry about what I'm saying. The choice here, of course, was only whether to ignore the form (in which case they'd print my name and indicate "no response," which means I'm agin 'em) or let them know where I stand. With nothing to lose, it was a cheerful thing to tick off no, no, no, no to all their questions. Do I believe that the law should protect the right to life of each human being from conception to natural death? Of course not! Would I vote for a law that makes the unborn child a second victim when a crime is committed against a pregnant woman? No (but I'd be tempted if that crime carried the death penalty). Would I vote to ban Embryonic Stem Cell research? No (and let's win one for the Gipper). Would I vote to prohibit *all cloning* (italics theirs) including "so-called 'therapeutic cloning' which creates human embryos for experimentation and destruction? No, sir, no ma'am.

So I'm a zero on their scale, and proud of it.

They enclose a Business Reply Mail envelope, but with a message printed over the picture of a fat little baby saying, "Your stamp on this envelope will be an extra offering for the unborn. Thank you!" and with a representation of a rose. I'm a nice guy and won't tape the envelope to a brick so that they have to pay many dollars in postage.

★ ★ ★ The Huckabee dinner was, in at least two ways, a success. The state Republican committee raised $350,000, which is a lot of money. And there was an actual meal that was served, which was a refreshing change. Janet and I were at a table with Deborah Jones, a glitzy blonde who is running for the Senate, and with Winifred Gray, who isn't running for anything but is a friend of the Romneys' and used to do dressage with Ann Romney. The speeches were more or less predictable. Darrell Crate introduced Lieutenant Governor Healey, who introduced Mitt, who introduced Mike Huckabee, the main attraction. Crate was brief and did the chores, recognizing people in the room who needed to be recognized—former governor Weld stood up, as did members of the state committee and then, of course, we candidates. Kerry Healey was entertaining and modest about her fifteen minutes of fame (from having called for Kerry's resignation from the Senate). Mitt was quite good, talking about the American character and venturing for uplift. ("He's running for national office," Janet whispered. "As Jeb Bush's vice president?" I asked her.)

Then Huckabee got up and told lame jokes, among which were interspersed reflections on the condition of the Republican Party in Arkansas—almost as parlous as here in Massachusetts. He is a graduate of Ouachita Baptist University at Arkadelphia and for a couple of years attended the Southwestern Baptist Theological Seminary in Fort Worth, Texas. He is only the fourth Republican governor of Arkansas since Reconstruction, and he does a fairly good Clinton imitation. (He, too, is from Hope.) But it was not an impressive performance. The last five minutes were devoted to an account of a visit he and his family made to Israel. (He's a Baptist minister and evangelical enough to have an unhealthy interest in Israel.) He took his eleven-year-old daughter, Sarah, to Yad Vashem, where she saw all the photographs and exhibits. He had been worried that it might be too strong, too depressing, too upsetting for a child that young. At the end of the tour, there is a book where visitors can sign their names and make comments, and little Miss Huckabee took her father's pen, inscribed her name and address, and, in the comment space in her schoolgirl's hand, demonstrated her understanding of what she had seen, writing, "Why didn't anyone do something?"

The point was that when there is a one-party system as in Arkansas or Massachusetts, it is our moral responsibility to "do something." But there is a big difference between Democrats and Nazis. Malapropos, I thought, and maladroit.

★ ★ ★ The reports in this morning's papers of Governor Romney's appearance yesterday before the Judiciary Committee are entertaining. Apparently, he did not have a good time down there. Senator Russell Feingold asked him how he could support the Massachusetts amendment, which allows for civil unions, as well as the federal amendment, which does not. Romney backed and filled and declared he was for letting the people decide. And Feingold followed up asking if Romney thought the federal amendment would nullify the Massachusetts amendment. Romney's reply was: "Uh . . . I . . . well . . . the challenge of that question I have is, if this amendment were to say that Massachusetts and the voters of Massachusetts could not provide any benefits whatsoever to same-sex couples, then I would oppose it." "That's exactly what it does," Feingold told him.

His trouble is that he is neither stupid nor unprincipled. He wants to be reasonable, recognizes the bigotry in the blanket opposition to same-sex civil unions, and is disinclined to hurt anyone. Lacking killer instincts, he dislikes using this emotional issue to stir up the populace to his own advantage. A lesser man could look better.

He had an easier time at the reception at the Heritage Foundation, where he was introduced by Ed Meese and could talk to welcoming conservatives. Although Meese praised him for his "leadership on the marriage issue," it is impossible to say where he is leading. In any event, nobody is likely to follow him. There are reportedly forty votes in the Senate against the federal amendment, which means that a filibuster would block it. And in Massachusetts, the push-me-pull-you amendment to the state constitution (anti–gay marriage, pro–civil union) is hardly likely to get approved by the voters.

★ ★ ★ Lorene gave a coffee for me yesterday evening, or at any rate tried to. There were cookies, nuts, potato chips, sodas, beer, coffee . . . everything but people. She'd been a little diffident about inviting all the Republicans in her precinct, worrying that there would be too many for the apartment. So the turnout was Fred Baker, my chairman, Lorene, and me. And a guy in his late fifties or early sixties who shows up at a lot of these Republican things and is barely distinguishable from your upper-level street person.

It was like one of those scenes in tear-jerking movies with the hostess and the elaborate party fixings and no guests. We hung around for an hour and tried to console her or distract her, but it felt terrible, as though it were really the social occasion it had been pretending to be, and she had been stiffed by actual friends. I woke up this morning with the gloom still hanging over me and a conviction that this was a preview of the election night "party" when I will have to call Toomey, concede, and congratulate him.

★ ★ ★ An e-mail came in from the Progressive Democrats of Somerville and Cambridge, who are sponsoring the debate next Wednesday. They have given the three of us and Councillor Reeves an advance look at the questions they will put to us:

1. All three candidates have said they would vote against a Constitutional Amendment defining marriage at next year's Constitutional Convention. We'd like to explore why for each of you: Are you against majority rule on this issue? Or simply pro-same-sex marriage? Or some other basis?

We'll all agree, so it will just be an occasion to perform. I know what my position is and what the rationale is. The fillip at the end is simple enough. I just talk about the limits of majority rule and the protection of minorities that the founding fathers wrote into the constitutions of the Commonwealth and of the federal government.

2. Your opinion on the Community Path extension from Davis Square to Lechmere, and potentially through North Point to the Esplanade? Particularly your opinion on access from East Somerville to the Lechmere T station or other public transportation improvements resulting from these projects? Your opinions on alternative and public transportation in general, and its priority with regards to automobile transportation?

Who can be against walking and biking, especially when obesity has become pandemic in the society? I've e-mailed Bill White to find out whether there is any opposition and, if so, what their reasons are. But I expect we'll all agree about this, too.

3. Would you vote to keep Tom Finneran as speaker? Would you support a term limit on the speakership? If next year's vote is a repeat of the previous vote between Tom Finneran, Byron Rushing, and Brad Jones, for whom would you vote?

I found out who Rushing is—a black, liberal representative who, with Brad Jones, the Republican leader, attempted to reform the rules of the House by which Finneran keeps a tight control over what bills come up, bottling legislation he dislikes and manipulating the timing of roll-call votes. That Toomey voted on all five votes with Finneran and against Rushing is shameful, and great for me. According to the Common Cause website, where I found much of this information, there were eighteen localities that passed ballot questions instructing their representatives not to vote for Finneran as Speaker two years ago. He is loathed. And there is no way Toomey can defend him.

4. The federal Assault Weapons Ban is set to expire on Sept. 13 of this year. What would you do in the Massachusetts legislature to implement the ban at the state level if the federal ban expires?

We'll all agree on this. I'm different from Green and Toomey in that I support the right of citizens to bear arms, but I don't see the need for assault weapons. I'm still chafing from my encounter with those libertarian gun nuts.

5. Do you think there's a fair way to implement the death penalty in Massachusetts? What impact do you think the federal execution of Massachusetts resident Gary Sampson, who may be executed in MA or NH, might have on this issue?

I have as much "respect for life" as Mr. Toomey does or Mr. Green, but my respect is for the lives of the victims. As a matter of fact, I don't worry excessively about the occasional mistake or the execution of the innocent. As forensics improve, these errors are likely to happen less frequently, and when such an error does happen and someone is executed by mistake, he is a sacrifice to the majesty of the state and its power to protect its citizens. We accept with equanimity the deaths of thousands of citizens each year as the cost of our freedom to travel at high speeds in cars. The freedom to walk the streets or sleep in safety in our beds at night is no less important, and I can tolerate an occasional miscarriage of justice for civil order. The perfect ought not to be the enemy of the good. (I won't say any of this, though. I am trying to win the votes of a Cambridge audience.)

6. The Massachusetts Democratic Issues Convention passed the Accountability Amendment in June 2003 and the Democratic State Committee
   agreed to implement it as the Platform Support Card by Sept. 1 2004 (info
   at www.MassScorecard.org), comparing key legislative votes to the Democratic Party Platform. Will you instruct the Massachusetts Democratic
   Party to implement the Platform Support Card with your voting record
   (or would-be voting record) in time for this September's primary? Do you
   support the Massachusetts Democratic Party publishing your votes (or
   would-be votes) on the Internet, with a comparison to the Democratic
   Party Platform?

I don't care what they do. Why don't they come clean and publish Finneran's
appointment calendar? He doesn't take orders from the platform or the party;
he gives them. And the Progressive Democrats' attempts to restrain him are
hopeless. If they want to control him, they should put fifty-four Republicans
in the legislature. These are plans to bell the cat, and the mice ought to figure
out that what they need is a big dog.

7. What policies and programs do you support to preserve and increase
   affordable housing in Cambridge and Somerville?

Oh, yawn! Do I have a position on this? I guess. You lift some of the bizarre
landlord-tenant regulations and allow owners to evict badasses and lunatics,
and you'd have a revival of rooming houses, which would be a way of solving
the homelessness problem. It would be cheaper to put those people in rooming houses than motel units, and they could have some sense of having not just
housing but a home.

I suppose I could tell the story of the terrible tailor who makes the suit for
the customer, and it doesn't fit well at all. One sleeve is longer than the other,
and the jacket doesn't hang right, and the pants are similarly deformed, and
the tailor has the customer lower one arm, and twist his body a little to the left,
and raise one shoulder, and jut out one hip. And then when he's out on the
street, in this bizarre contortion, someone sees him and says to his compan-
ion, "What a wonderful tailor to make a suit that fits a cripple like that!" The
laws and regulations and restrictions on property owners are such that the entire society is deformed by the interference of government.

It is better than any of Mike Huckabee's stories, but whether I tell it or not
will depend on how the evening has been going.

★ ★ ★ Another disagreeable e-mail exchange. From Greer Swiston:

Hello, Reform Team!

Long time no hear . . . I know everyone has been so busy with campaigning . . . that is really good! Great to be seeing lots of people at events.

First of all . . . is Steven Leahy still out there? I met him in Chatham . . . but I've noticed he's awfully quiet and hasn't uttered a peep. Anyone have an update on him?

I just sent out over 3000 mailings using the addresses gotten from the campaign portal.The last 1800+ were sent using first class postage and as a result, I am getting deluged with the return mail. I've not got a final count yet, but we're coming in close to over 10% returned . . . does this sound right? I know that the data in the portal is 9 months old and we've just got to expect some bad data . . . I'm just curious what percentage is reasonable to expect and what people are doing about it.

I had sent mailing out to several 100 households using addresses gotten from City Hall and had less than 5% returned. But then:

1) My town does an annual census
2) That data is now getting to be 6 months old now too . . . should I be getting a new list?

There are, of course, two things to consider.

1) Waste of money sending things to bad addresses
This can be solved easily, I think, in that Simard Printing (one of the recommended vendors provided by the State Committee) uses software that cleans any mailing list of bad addresses. They are updated weekly (?) I think? This will make sure you don't waste your material or your stamp, but it still means households that won't get hit.

2) Missing people
Of course getting 100% of the people isn't realistic . . . but missing what percentage of people is reasonable given that you're already aware that a percentage of those who actually get your mailing just throws it away any way. Anyone else have thoughts and experience to share?

Greer

From me, back to everyone on the list:

The Campaign Portal is worse than useless. It is absurdly out of date. Of a page of, say, 50 names, almost thirty are moved, dead, or have had the phone numbers disconnected. The walking tours are similarly inaccurate and out of date. You can waste your time on the portal lists or you can waste your time ringing bells of people who are Democrats: the second is probably better because some of them can be converted, persuaded, or redeemed.

I complained about this to Matt, and his attitude was that it was Cambridge's fault for having a population that moves around a lot.

The lists from the election commissioners (which you can get for free) are much more up to date, but it is even more tedious to comb out Republicans and Unenrolled by streets from their disks. (If I had a volunteer, he or she could be doing that for me, but I don't.)

I am ignoring the Portal as being a) a waste of my time and b) a way the party headquarters can keep tabs on me.

From Alex Dunn at the state party, to me and all the other candidates as well:

David,

Just want to clear up some points with you about the campaign portal.

—The list on the portal is already from the election commissioners. The list is about 12 months old so we are posting an updated list we got June 3rd.
—The only reason we want to, as you put it "keep tabs on you" is to help you win, but help can only be given if you want it.

I will remove you today from the portal so you no longer have to waste your time.

Alex Dunn

And then from me back:

Don't remove me. The June 3rd update may help some of these difficulties that we have been having. We should have been told in advance how out-of-date the data base was. Greer's campaign would have been saved a good deal of money.

Leave me on the portal. I am not obliged to use it but I am willing to try it again from time to time, and it may have its uses down the road.
Thanks

They actually did take me off, and I couldn't get access. I called back and spoke to Juan Jacome, the IT guy, who said it was an "administrative decision" and I'd have to speak with Dunn. He transferred me, and I said I was sorry if I'd been peremptory but we should have been told that an update was in process. Mollification back and forth, and he's putting me back on the portal.

★ ★ ★ This morning, I saw several e-mails chiding me for my lack of team spirit. I did have one telephone call yesterday from one of the candidates who was sympathetic and warned me not to expect too much from the state party. This was nice of him but also cautious, because he didn't do this in a way that would allow the other candidates and the party functionaries to know about it. I should have been less naïve, anyway. The party, two years ago, was woefully inadequate in their help for Evan in his attempt to get those ten thousand signatures he needed to get onto the ballot to run for attorney general.

★ ★ ★ Fred Baker tells me that it is absolutely essential for me to have tchotchkes to hand out at picnics and large events. Pens, or jar openers, or dopey things like that. So I looked through a couple of catalogues and decided on flyswatters. "Crush Finneran" crossed my mind as a possible text. Or "Swat Finneran"? Or, leaving him out of it:

David R. Slavitt for State Rep.
REPUBLICAN SWAT TEAM
26th Middlesex / Cambridge & Somerville

which says it without naming him. Five hundred of them, in assorted colors, with black printing, for $225 plus shipping. (Couldn't I just buy the votes for fifty cents apiece?)

★ ★ ★ I spent an hour or so with Fred, Lorene, Peter Sheinfeld, and Ben Hunter yesterday morning folding papers, stuffing envelopes, and affixing stamps for our small mailing—to Fred's list of the hundred likeliest Republican givers in Cambridge. It was a pleasant enough effort. We had some discussion about whether or not to put stamps on the return envelopes. Fred thought it would look cheap not to put the stamps on. I thought it was perhaps extravagant and also unnecessary. If these givers were going to send fifty or a hundred dollars or more, would they begrudge us the thirty-seven cents?

In the end, we decided that, for this mailing, we'd put the stamps on. And then, if there is another, more general mailing to all the Republicans in Cambridge, we'll leave them off. Later in the morning, a solicitation came in to Janet (registered as Unenrolled) from Toomey's campaign. Their return envelope did not have a stamp on it. It did, however, have places to check, inviting people to indicate that they might be willing to:

_____Phone voters		_____Put up a house sign
_____Office work		_____Visibilities
_____Go door to door		_____Host a Fundraiser
_____Drop literature		_____Work election day

("Visibilities" is his word for stand-outs, I assume.) I saved the envelope and will include a list like that on the next printing of my envelopes. Thank you, Tim.

★ ★ ★ The *Globe* has finally noticed me. In the City Weekly section, there is an item about the debate on Wednesday:

Now there are 3

Meet the three candidates running for state representative in Cambridge and Somerville, the 26th Middlesex District, at a forum 7 p.m. Wednesday in East Cambridge. Two are challenging Democratic incumbent Timothy Toomey, who is also a City Councilor: Democrat Avi Green, a local political consultant, and Republican David Slavitt, a writer and former film critic. The event at Filarmonica Santo Antonio Centro Cultural on 575 Cambridge St. will be moderated by City Councilor Kenneth E. Reeves. The Democratic Primary is Sept. 14; the general election Nov. 2.

And what I hear is that they're going to send someone to cover it, which is encouraging.

★ ★ ★ Senator Kerry is not going to address the U.S. Conference of Mayors that Mayor Menino is holding here in Boston. Kerry is high-minded and steadfast and has canceled, refusing to cross a picket line. Menino is not pleased. A woeful mush-mouth, he said, "Everyone makes their own political decisions," and if the grammar is catastrophic, the meaning is clear enough. He also pointed out that the reason there are no negotiations with the firemen's union is that their lawyers are on vacation until July 4. As far as the policemen's union is concerned, he has offered a raise of 11.9 percent over four years; the union wants 16 to 18 percent; and the mayor has proposed that they go to binding arbitration, which the union refuses to do. These are "informational" picket lines but are designed to embarrass the city government in general and Menino in particular. The real threat, of course, is that if there are no contracts by the time the Democratic National Convention begins next month, the unions can repeat and intensify this humiliation for the mayor. For Kerry to behave this way and betray a fellow Democrat is less a matter of principle than of opportunism (he needs the union votes and the unions' campaign workers). Or, putting it more clearly, cowardice (he is afraid of losing their support). I love it.

★ ★ ★ I went out to do more door-to-door campaigning, but I realized that even though it was a Sunday, there were lots of small businesses open in Somerville—bakeries, convenience stores, clothing stores, and liquor stores— where I could try to place signs. I worked a part of eastern Somerville I hadn't tried before. I got five or six signs up into windows on streets with a good deal of traffic, which is the important thing. Toomey has name recognition already, having run so many times for both offices. The name says a lot—a fine broth of a boyo!—and he's got signs all over, most of which, I assume, have been put there by campaign workers. I'm doing mine myself, so far.

It is, as I keep realizing, hopeless, but people tell me that they have seen the signs. And Fred Baker has congratulated me. "How do you get them to put signs in their windows?" "I asked them!" I told him. And that's what I have to do, one sign at a time.

Half a dozen is not at all bad for a Sunday afternoon's work.

★ ★ ★ On the parade ground at the Coast Guard Academy where we were waiting to see my grandson march in with the other swabs and get sworn in to the Coast Guard, Evan and I spoke for a moment about Senator Kerry's disinclination to cross the picket line. Evan thought it was foolish, because the decision leaves him vulnerable for the rest of the campaign. Any union can throw up a picket line anywhere and disrupt his speaking schedule or embarrass local officials. This wasn't even a strike, Evan pointed out. Cops are not allowed to strike. This was informational. If Kerry had been smart, he'd have taken a brochure and said something about hoping that the matter could be resolved soon.

So Mitt Romney addressed the conference of mayors. Mayor Menino, in this morning's *Globe*, is reported as saying that Romney was not a "substitute" for Kerry, but the ovation he got from the mayors suggests that they understood otherwise.

On the other hand, the policemen's union is now so grateful to Kerry that they have promised not to picket the Democrats' convention here next month, and that story made the front page of the paper. But as Evan speculated yesterday, there are other unions elsewhere that may not feel so obligated to him or be able to resist the temptation to create nuisances by which they can get attention for themselves.

★ ★ ★ We went to the Mid-Cambridge Neighborhood Association ice-cream social last night in Joan Lorentz Park, down the street from us near the library. It was an opportunity to glad-hand and pass out bookmarks, and Fred Baker had said I ought to go. So Janet and I trekked down there. Green was there, but Toomey, oddly, was not. Avi, Janet said, is rather awkward about meeting people. I have to force myself to some of this and am not altogether comfortable walking up to strangers to announce my name and the fact that I'm running for the state legislature, but I play the role plausibly enough, or so she says. Avi's discomfort, with which I feel some sympathy, is more evident. People were wearing name tags that gave the street they lived on, and that told me which of them were in my district. It was less hit-or-miss than the MIT picnic.

The reactions I got varied from dyed-in-the-wool Democrats who recoiled from "Republican" to those who would listen and even agree with my criticisms of Finneran. It was gratifying to hear from several of them that they were planning to come to the debate, and a few even said that they had heard I'd done well at the one in Somerville.

★ ★ ★ My researches on the Web have turned up the news that Toomey voted *for* the death penalty as late as 1999, and I'm wondering whether I can refer to the still, small voice in the night that changed his mind and that perhaps sounds just a little like the voice of Speaker Finneran. (I could probably get away with that, but I ought not to say that it also sounds like Archbishop O'Malley's, even though the Church has made conformity of candidates to approved doctrine an issue this year by threatening to withhold communion from the likes of Senator Kerry. It would be "impolitic" to make such an allusion.)

★ ★ ★ I sent a press release to the *Cambridge Chronicle*. Along with a photo of my grandson Isaac and me, there was the caption:

Cadet Isaac Slavitt, of Malden, Mass., was sworn in at the United States Coast Guard Academy in New London, Connecticut on Monday, June 28. He is shown here on the parade ground immediately following the ceremony with his grandfather, David R. Slavitt, of West Street, Cambridge, the Republican Candidate for State Representative in the 26th Middlesex District.

Shameless to do this? Perhaps, but not worse than many of the other things I find myself doing these days.

★ ★ ★ Our envelopes are starting to come back. A check yesterday for ten dollars. A check today for fifty, and another envelope with a pair of five-dollar bills. And one from that street person at Lorene's party with a single dollar bill taped to a note saying that family circumstances prevented him from sending more. It is an enormous nuisance to free a dollar bill that has been Scotch-taped to a letter.

★ ★ ★ The debate went well, Evan and Janet thought. There were somewhere between 125 and 150 people in the hall, and there were reporters from the *Somerville News*, the *Cambridge Chronicle*, and Michael Jonas from the *Globe*. There was a videotaping crew, and this, too, will play on Cambridge and Somerville community television. It felt so good that I have to remember the chances of my winning the election remain very slim.

Ken Reeves, the city councilman and former mayor of Cambridge, was introduced as the "first openly gay black mayor of any city in America." He is a colleague and a friend of Toomey's but was mostly fair and reasonable, except that a couple of times he forgot, as we went around the table answering his questions or those that had been submitted from the audience, that Avi Green was there. Avi had to demand to be recognized so that he, too, could give his response. I don't think it was calculated or deliberate. It's just that Green has so little to say. He still talks about "energy" and bringing "change" but is fuzzy on actualities. At one point, answering a question about affordable housing, he suggested that a part of the solution would be to extend the Green Line to Union Square in Somerville. I then asked if he was out of his mind. The T stop would *raise* real estate prices, as the Red Line stop in Davis Square raised prices there.

Evan's take was that Green and I were getting to Toomey, and my Robin Hood routine—which I saved for my closing remarks—goaded him into an extravagant riff, a revelation of what he really believes, and it was such a parody that I can use it next time we debate. After I finished, Toomey closed out the evening. (This was the only advantage that Ken Reeves was able to contrive for his colleague, but then someone had to go last.) What he said was:

Mr. Slavitt might be a little bit entertaining with his remarks, but do not be fooled by what he just said. The fact is that there is a key difference between the Democratic Party and the Republican Party. Would I take from the rich to give to the poor? Absolutely! It's no laughing matter. There are poor people in our community, right now, throughout the city. And if the Republicans were in control, there would be no social programs, there would be no public education, no health care for all. That's the difference between Republicans and Democrats, and don't you ever, ever forget that. Don't forget who the true friends of the working class of Massachusetts are. It's the Democratic Party. And I will not stand and allow a Republican to come in and say that they know what's best for the working-class people. Forget it! It will never happen. With Republicans, the working-class people would no longer be in existence.

There was an energy in this, some real fervor that Representative Toomey had not hitherto displayed. He was, for the moment, an enraged bull that the picadors had been working over, but Evan is right about his extravagance and its vulnerability. Toomey can't be seriously suggesting that Republicans would end all social programs and public education, bring back the seven-day workweek and the twenty-two-hour day, and cancel Christmas. The paradox of American politics is that there are more poor people than rich and that, therefore, the Democrats ought to have an advantage if they are the party of the Untermenschen. The government—overwhelmingly Democrats—makes a few gestures in the way of meals and taxicab vouchers for seniors and with these lagniappes, which the taxpayers have provided, buys the gratitude and loyalty of voters. All the Republicans can appeal to is their sense of fairness and their hopes. What voter does not imagine that he might rise someday to the top? Toomey's expectation (and his experience) is that his supporters will vote their empty pocketbooks and their resentment of those who have been luckier or more successful than they.

In the next debate, I will zotz him again and see what other over-the-top fulminations I can provoke. The three of us may meet once more before the primary in September. And then Fred Baker will be sponsoring a two-man debate after the primary election between the Democratic winner—presumably Toomey—and me.

★ ★

11

Finneran is refusing to allow debate on legislation the Senate passed that would make the morning-after contraception pill more easily available to rape victims. Finneran is a Catholic (well, of course!) and pro-life (well, of course!), and the fact that fifty-six representatives have presented a petition demanding action on the bill is just flattering to his sense of power. I cannot criticize the Church on this, even though they have mounted a lobbying campaign and an editorial in The Pilot, the official newspaper of the archdiocese, says that the bill "will oblige Catholic hospitals to cooperate with the evil of abortion." Nobody is forcing Catholic rape victims to have abortions or take a morning-after pill. But for those who want it, the pill should be available.

Shawn Feddeman, Mitt Romney's spokeswoman, "declined to comment on the governor's position on the bill." Presumably, the governor shares Finneran's views about birth control and the morning-after pill, even for rape victims.

★ ★ ★ I woke up early Sunday morning, eager to see what the Globe had to say about the Twenty-sixth Middlesex debate, and . . . not a word. We got squeezed out by the rowdy behavior of Councillor and Vice Mayor Marjorie Decker, who turned the meeting of the Cambridge City Council into a sideshow in a dispute with Mayor Sullivan that he ended by adjourning it. This worse-than-usual behavior made news and bumped the debate. I am also annoyed with the Republican Party. Alex Dunn said he was restoring my access to the Campaign Portal, but either he didn't do it, or he tried and failed. In any case, I found out late Thursday that I couldn't get to the site and called Friday, but the office was closed for the long July Fourth weekend. Whatever benefit the portal offered was lost for four days. I'd hoped to recruit campaign workers in Somerville and perhaps raise some money. One tries not leap to the conclusion that *everything* is going badly. But sometimes it feels that way.

★ ★ ★ Fred had a Fourth of July picnic yesterday afternoon for the Republican City Committee of Cambridge. There were too many people to accommodate in his backyard, so he held it in the park on Broadway, which meant that we couldn't grill hot dogs or hamburgers (no fires are allowed) or have beer. Still, it was a pleasant get-together, and the feeling was less hangdog than at some of the other Republican functions I've been to in Cambridge. It was a comfortable couple of hours, and for a change the discrepancy between my candidacy and my recognizable self was somewhat reduced.

Later in the evening we went to some friends in Brookline for a barbecue and, after dinner, to watch the fireworks on television. The fireworks were okay, but the music was just dreadful, cheap bubblegum pop, which the pyrotechnics didn't need. I found myself wondering how you can vulgarize fireworks. And I winced in distress when Harry Smith offered commentary and interviews with other onlookers on the esplanade—because that is what television has persuaded itself is necessary. I am not too refined to enjoy colorful explosions up in the sky, but my distress at the way the program's producers framed them made me realize that I am not one of "the people." I certainly would not have camped out all day for a good view, am not a fan of the Boston Pops, and am not "representative"—although that is the office for which I am running.

★ ★ ★ I did a poetry reading at the Out of the Blue Gallery yesterday evening. I'd been hustling readings as a way of getting my name out there, finding places where, in exchange for my reading poems, I could hand out bookmarks and solicit votes. This turns out not to be such a good idea. The reading was part of the Stone Soup series run by Roland Perrault, a well-meaning but disorganized soul. He was dismayed when I showed up. He thought it was supposed to be the twelfth. No, I said, it was in my organizer and I'd checked his e-mail message. The fifth. What to do? An open reading was scheduled from eight to nine, and then the featured reader at nine. This was a young man in a T-shirt and an already prominent paunch whose name was "Rat." I looked around the room and saw fugitives from a neurology ward, a couple of grossly obese young people compared to whom fat Rat was almost svelte, a number of men and women who had been experimenting with time machines and were "beat" in the style of the sixties in terms of tonsure and haberdashery, and, here and there, a scattering of normal-looking people whose only obvious fault was that, for the chance of reading their own work, they were willing to sit through wretched poetry in a room where the walls were covered by bad art. Amateur poetry is as painful as amateur dentistry, but less fun to watch. I decided I did not want to have this hanging over me for another week. I would go on at nine thirty, if Rat could finish up by then. Each of us would have half an hour. (The reading—or anyway two hours of it—is taped and plays on Cambridge Community TV.) Roland and Rat both agreed. Janet and I went back home to watch *Antique Roadshow*. We got back at nine. I could miss the open reading, but if Rat was featured and he and I were, at least notionally, sharing the lectern and the evening, it was the least I could do in the way of civility. But I was misguided. He was as bad as any of the open-mike poets (one of whom was "Cat," his brother), but more profane and obscene. He took a nine-year-old's delight in shouting dirty words. But the quality of his poetry was unimportant. What was outrageous was that he went on past nine thirty. Ten minutes later, I let him know that his time was up. He resented this and insisted on two more poems, because, as he said, he was about to move to Florida. He took a further ten minutes spewing vernacular expressions for "vagina," and then he, his dumpy girlfriend, and his brother left with their claque, so that the audience of eighteen was reduced to a dozen. I read four poems and passed out some bookmarks. One of the presentable members of the audience handed my bookmark back because he "could never vote Republican." In politics, the public has an unimpeachable authority; in art, numbers don't count, or count against you, art being naturally aristocratic.

★ ★ ★ An encouraging phone call this afternoon from Michael Jonas of the *Globe*. The fact that there wasn't a story in last Sunday's paper is not fatal and may even work to my advantage. Jonas saw and heard me, was impressed enough to follow up, and seems to be doing a piece about me. A very good interview, it lasted for forty minutes. I was up for it, don't think I said anything stupid or dangerous, and was funny but not too funny. I have benefited from my practice with the *Somerville News* and the *Cambridge Chronicle*. It is weird for someone like me to be running for office, and it makes a legitimate story.

★ ★ ★ I have been unsuccessful in my efforts to get back onto the Campaign Portal. I called again yesterday (Tuesday) and spoke with Juan, the IT guy, who said that he'd work on it. And this morning I still can't log on. St. Hilaire doesn't answer his phone, nor does Alex Dunn, nor does Tim O'Brien, the man who runs things there. And the receptionist was snippy when I expressed my dissatisfaction. It is not big enough—yet—to take to the lieutenant governor. But that option crosses my mind. My fallback position is that if it isn't settled today, I can call the party counsel—Evan—and have him work it out. He has clout there. What I need the portal for is to make walking lists and to find contacts in those large apartment houses near the Museum of Science where I can get in, talk to rich Republicans, and ask for support and money. I can try to place more signs in store windows today, but these people at state party headquarters are supposed to be helping us and aren't.

★ ★ ★ An afternoon of small but satisfactory achievements. I had asked Lydia of Lydia's Photography to put a sign in her window on Prospect Street where there's a heavy volume of traffic, and she had grilled me about my "positions"—on same-sex marriage, on the right to choose, on rent control, and God knows what else. I thought I had passed muster and managed not to offend her, but the sign kept not being there, and I wondered if she might have been toying with me, or brushing me off. But this afternoon, on my way to Somerville, I saw it, all by itself in a window that is otherwise covered by a curtain, so that my sign stands out and is easily visible to drivers going by.

Then in Somerville, I got a sign in Mongo's Tattoo Madness, a breathtaking place for a Republican sign and excellent for visibility. It is at the circle where Washington Avenue crosses McGrath Highway, and the traffic lights allow drivers and passengers a long time to contemplate Mongo's name and my own, and their lovely dissonance.

Finally, on Pearl Street, I saw Angie's Place, a convenience store where both Green and Toomey had signs. Admiring their catholicity, I went in with mine. "Sure, sure," the young man said, "if you can find a place for it, go ahead." It is jolly for all of us to be there together. I told the manager that whoever won would be grateful to him. "Exactly!" he said, and we shook hands.

★ ★ ★ My problems with the Campaign Portal seem to be solved. I called again this morning (Thursday) and got through, only to find that Juan had e-mailed my user name and password but had mailed them to the wrong address, leaving out my middle initial. That reduces but does not entirely extinguish the warmth of my annoyance. (Don't these people return phone calls? Should a candidate have to spend two days to get through to someone to find this out?) More to the point is the fact that I was toying last night with the idea of quitting, of just chucking it. They aren't supporting me? I don't need this!

It was like fantasies of leaving one's spouse, when a husband or a wife first toys with the notion of divorce. The pretext is unimportant except insofar as it has revealed the underlying flaw, hitherto unsuspected. I do have reservations about this enterprise, and if the writing of the journal weren't sustaining me, the campaign would be in worse trouble. Why would I otherwise consider four more months of strenuousness that will lead, in November, either to a loss to Toomey or a victory that will condemn me to two years in the State House, where not very bright men and women discuss issues in which I am not interested and make deals I have no power to prevent or even influence?

But I am now back on the Campaign Portal and can generate lists for door-to-door excursions and telephone sessions. Hip deep in the big muddy, I slog on.

★ ★ ★ A piquant e-mail from Fred Baker asks:

> Are you sending better than the 23 cent postcard to the larger donors? Certain candidates of the past have been HIGHLY criticized for their 'manner' of thanking donors. Carla Howell [the Libertarian Party candidate for Governor in 2002] highest on that list: give $100 and get a cheap form-generated postcard with no personal handwriting or even a signature. Cheap! And people remembered . . .

To which I replied:

> No, I'm not sending postcards to donors over $25.00. They get actual letters. I've sent very few postcards. Susan [Fred's girlfriend, who sent $15.00] got one, but then I wasn't trying to impress her. (And it was handwritten, rather than typed, so it's actually worth more if she wants to sell it to an autograph dealer.) Cheers, David

★ ★ ★ The new issues of the *Cambridge Chronicle* and the *Somerville News* are out, and neither has the picture I sent of Isaac and me at the swearing-in ceremony of the Coast Guard Academy. I am relieved, never having felt right about exploiting his undertaking for my irrelevant political purposes. And yet the picture and the caption, had they appeared, would not have diminished his efforts or his commitment by a jot or tittle.

★ ★ ★ I had a "heads-up," as he called it, from Michael Jonas of the *Globe* to let me know ahead of time that his piece in next Sunday's paper would be mostly about Green and Toomey, whose primary is much sooner than the general election in which I'm running. I am mentioned, but the piece concentrates on them. It was gentlemanly of Jonas to make such a call, and he did say that he was planning on doing a piece about me, either after the September primary or, perhaps, even sooner, because my candidacy was, in itself, interesting. I was disappointed but grateful for his thoughtfulness.

★ ★ ★ More sign placements. On Washington Street near McGrath Highway and Mongo's, I went into Mike's Barber Shop. Mike had several Joe Curtatone for Mayor posters in his window and one for Elio LoRusso, and I told him that that election has been over for a while. Mike knew and was a little resentful, because apparently a pipe had burst across the street from his shop, and his car, legally parked, was towed away so the crew could make the repair, and he had to pay the towing fee. He called Mayor Curtatone, who, he figured, owed him a favor, but Curtatone never took his call. I said that was disgraceful and suggested that he might show his displeasure by taking the Curtatone signs down and putting up mine. This seemed reasonable to him, and I've now got two signs in his window, facing a street where lots of traffic flows every day.

Across the street, there is a pet-grooming place, "The Dog House," that Peter Patalano owns. I asked him if I could put up a sign. He said he didn't do political signs because he doesn't want to alienate any customers. I thanked him and told him I was the Republican running against either Toomey or Green. He brightened a bit and said he was a Republican too, but he was still reluctant. I thanked him again for his time and was about to leave when he asked me if I had a moment. Sure. "What's your position on gun control?" I told him I didn't see why ordinary citizens needed grenade launchers but I believed the right to bear arms was clear, and people who want weapons for self-defense or hunting or target shooting ought not to be prevented from owning them.

"Let me give you a piece of advice," he said in the friendliest way. "Don't call them 'weapons.' Say 'firearms.' It sounds better. Soldiers have weapons. Citizens have firearms." It turns out he is a licensed dealer and a firearms instructor.

I thanked him for the advice. And he said, "You know, I think I'll make an exception for you. Let me have a sign. I'll put it up."

★ ★ ★ The *Cambridge Chronicle* does have a piece, after all, reporting the debate:

Toomey, Green, Slavitt face off at forum

By Chris Helms/ Chronicle Staff

Thursday, July 8, 2004

More than 120 people packed the parquet-floored ballroom at the Filarmonica Santo Antonio Cultural Center for a lively debate between hopefuls in the race for Democrat Tim Toomey's State House seat.

Toomey, fellow Democrat Avi Green and Republican David Slavitt took questions from the audience and moderator Ken Reeves during the one and a half hour session last Wednesday.

Reeves congratulated the audience for their civic spirit.

"We never see this many people at the debates. So give yourselves a hand," said Reeves, a Cambridge city councilor and former mayor.

Sponsors of the East Cambridge event said e-mail contact and door-to-door publicity helped fill the hall, but that high interest in the 26th Middlesex race was the main factor.

"It's a contested race. You don't see too many of those," said Eric Weltman of the Progressive Democrats of Cambridge. Progressive Democrats of Somerville also sponsored the debate.

Below are excerpts from the night. The primary between Toomey and Green takes place Sept. 14 with the winner facing Slavitt in the Nov. 2 general election.

What new idea would you bring to the Legislature about affordable housing so that more people of working income could remain in Cambridge and Somerville?

Green: We need new energy to make more of Boston accessible. You could bring down the cost of transportation by bringing the Green Line to Union Square. It would make that area much more accessible for people to live, including people close to Inman Square who could then easily walk to the T to get to work. A major factor in whether they can afford a home is whether or not they have to afford a car.

Slavitt: Avi's idea of taking the Green Line to Union Square will raise the prices around Union Square dramatically, just as happened in Davis Square. It's the law of unintended consequences.

Toomey: We have to work with people who want to provide housing to provide some tax breaks. It's the middle-income tenants who have very little or no programs to help them stay in the city. Cambridge and, recently, Somerville are becoming cities of the haves and the have-nots.

What are your opinions on alternative and public transportation in general?

Toomey: My colleagues and I were able to put $260 million into the 2004 transportation bill for the extension of the Green Line into Somerville. [As regards the bus link from Lechmere Station to North Station during construction] I put in the state budget an amendment that there be no fares charged on that bus until it gets to North Station.

Green: Access to Lechmere today is only an issue because of Tim Toomey's silence on the issue of transportation in Somerville over the past 12 years. Somerville residents should have a Green Line stop of their own. In the last year and a half I helped start a community group called STEP, the Somerville Transportation Partnership.

Slavitt: As Tim Toomey pointed out at our last debate, the temporary station at Lechmere has been the temporary station for 80 years. It requires leadership like that provided by (Governor) Mitt Romney who can hold these people up to scorn and ridicule for sitting on their hands for so long.

Which Democrat was wrong about crossing the picket line at the National Conference of Mayors, Mayor Thomas Menino or Sen. John Kerry?
[Kerry canceled his speech to the mayors in order not to cross the Police Patrol Officers Union picket line.]

Toomey: I respect the decision of Senator Kerry not to cross the picket line. I come from a very strong union family. If it wasn't for the unions, the Republicans would still have us working 20 hours a day, seven days a week.

Slavitt: Kerry was wrong. It's the taxpayers money (Menino) is trying to preserve. It was not a strike, but an informational picket. It was a demonstration not only of cowardice but also of dopiness, which you get a lot of from Kerry. Now any union anywhere in the country can hold him for ransom anytime between now and the election.

Green: I think Mayor Menino was wrong to let it get the negotiations this point and John Kerry was right to stand up for the working people who are involved in this debate. The reasons that Boston's negotiations have gone on so long is that the city's finances have been decimated by cuts to state aid. Those have come down from (House Speaker) Tom Finneran and Mitt Romney, who are the true enemies and the true problems in this situation.

Are you for or against giving citizens the right to choose charter schools for their children?

Green: We need to drive innovation and choice within the public schools. I don't think that charter schools are the answer. I would support the moratorium bill that would prevent there from being any more charter schools while the state is in a fiscal crisis and while the funding formula is unfair.

Slavitt: I am opposed to the moratorium. I think that a parent has a right to choose. Rich people can already do that. If you happen not to have a lot of money, why should you be penalized by the teachers' union? We spend lavish amounts of money on public education in Cambridge and the quality of it is terrible because the principals can't fire people and they can't promote people on merit.

Toomey: I support the charter school concept. I played a role, along with many other legislators, in convincing Speaker Finneran to move forward with the moratorium on charter schools. The funding formula has to be changed. That is what we did in the budget the governor just vetoed.

How would you solve the problem of charter school funding?

Slavitt: I think that they should all be funded. As Mao said, "Let a thousand flowers bloom." The more competition among schools for the kids and for their parents' support, the better those schools are likely to be.

Toomey: Fair funding is the key to funding the charter schools issue. I support a one cent increase in the sales tax to go exclusively to public education so that all public education needs will be met.

Green: You can either fund a few of them, or all of them or none of them. I would take one look at the Lincoln Park School and say it's not time to open new schools, it's time to fix the ones that we have. Sales taxes are a regressive way to do it. The way to do it is to create a progressive income tax in this state.

Should the state interfere with a woman's right to choose an abortion?

Toomey: I believe in a consistent theory of life. I oppose the death penalty and I am pro-life. My focus at the State House has been to increase family planning funds to prevent unplanned pregnancies and to prevent abortions.

Slavitt: I'm a libertarian. I want to keep the government out of my bedroom. I want to keep the government out of doctors' consulting rooms. It's none of their business. I think a woman's right to choose is a fundamental right that has been asserted by the Supreme Court.

Green: The decision needs to be made by a woman in consultation with her family, her clergy if she so chooses, and her doctor. We are now five seats away from having a pro-choice State House. This is an important difference and can make a difference when you choose who your next representative is.

What are your closing statements?

Green: Conservatives believe that you're better off alone. Progressives believe we are better off together. I'm proud to be the progressive Democrat in this race.

Slavitt: In the last debate, Representative Toomey called himself the Robin Hood of Cambridge and I thought he couldn't mean that. Sounds good, right? Steal from the rich, by which he means Harvard and MIT and the corporations, and give to the poor, by which he means the working men and women of East Cambridge. He's proud of this. Does he run around in green tights in the woods with his Merry Men? I don't think so.

The standard operating procedure of these guys is to tax everybody to the eyeballs and say they're doing it for you then give it to the special interests, which is to say, the unions. Representative Toomey knows that stealing is wrong but he has been on Beacon Hill too long and has lost his way. I haven't.

Toomey: Mr. Slavitt might be a little bit entertaining. But the fact is there's a key difference between the Democratic and Republic parties. Do not be fooled by what he just said. Would I take from the rich to give to the poor? Absolutely. It's no laughing matter. Don't forget who true friends of the working class people of Massachusetts are, it's the Democrats.

As far as my Democratic opponent, he can have all his $500 fundraisers in Brookline and Arlington and Brattle Street and distort my record and call me a conservative Democrat, but that is not true. I'm as progressive as anybody else.

★ ★ ★ I spent a couple of hours over in East Cambridge on Cambridge Street, where the entire area is Toomescent with his green signs. I am not able to match him, but I thought I could establish a presence. Korean and Chinese nail salons, pizza joints, hamburger and sub shops, beauty parlors, and one electrical supply place all agreed. Also the Lechmere Rug Company on Third, which is a way of getting from Cambridge Street to the McGrath Highway. Lots of cars go by, and the fellow there waved his hand and said, "Sure."

There were some turndowns, of course, mostly from people who wanted to stay neutral, or from proprietors of businesses where the landlord has to give permission for any signs. There was one pizza place that had a Toomey sign in the window, but thinking of Angie's place in Somerville, I thought I'd give it a shot, and I went in and asked. "Go ahead," the guy behind the counter told me. Toomey's sign was in a corner window, below the line where the glass is tinted, so it was not easy to see. I put mine above his, where the glass is clear and the colors are vivid. It stands out beautifully.

★ ★ ★ One of those group e-mails to the candidates came in this morning, this one about websites, and the sender gave five examples of good ones, one of which was mine. This is nice to hear. It is also reassuring to know that there are candidates still working on getting a website up. I read reports of barbecues or other such events and worry that my campaign is not active enough. But then there are bits of evidence that others are behind in other ways. It is also a delight to have my flyswatters, which arrived yesterday afternoon, in bright green, deep blue, garish orange, and Day-Glo pink. They will be souvenirs. One of them will go to the Beinecke Library at Yale, where my papers are stored. It is just a big box full of . . . plastic flyswatters! But the zaniness of it speaks to me. And I am happy to have a life in which a carton full of such objects can be a part.

★ ★ ★ A questionnaire from the Massachusetts Chapter of the National Federation of Independent Business also arrived yesterday and is intimidating. Some of the questions are so arcane that I can't imagine what position I might take. "Do you favor or oppose legislation to eliminate 'joint and several liability' in medical malpractice suits?" Or "Do you favor or oppose legislation to require corporate excise tax estimated payments be made in four equal quarterly amounts and to eliminate the current accelerated collection of corporate excise taxes?" (I suppose I have a slight tilt against "accelerated collection" of any taxes, but I know nothing about the issue and can't imagine why such a system would ever have been initiated.) This speaks not so much to the campaign as to the possibility of my actually getting elected.

I will call Evan to ask him what I think, just as I probably would do in the event that I join the legislature and have to face such questions and actually cast a vote.

★ ★ ★ The *Globe* piece couldn't have been friendlier. It was, as Jonas warned me, largely about Green and Toomey, but I am in the lead and the kicker:

In the 26th, it's Starbucks vs. Dunkin'

By Michael Jonas, Globe Correspondent

July 11, 2004

While uncontested races are the norm across the local landscape this fall, democracy is flourishing in one corner of Cambridge and Somerville, and Tim Toomey can't be too happy about it. The veteran state representative is up against a hard-charging Democratic primary challenger as well as a Republican poet who knows he's likely to go down in defeat but who plans to freely dispense his punch-packing prose along the way.

Toomey, 51, who also holds a seat on the Cambridge City Council, is facing his most serious State House challenge since he was elected to the 26th Middlesex District seat in 1992. Hard on his heels is 30-year-old Avi Green, who cut his teeth in local politics by heading the state's Young Democrats organization and running Jarrett Barrios's winning campaign for the neighboring Cambridge state representative seat in 1998.

With their tightly packed two- and three-family homes, the East Cambridge and East Somerville neighborhoods that make up the district have long been the working-class anchors of the two cities. But soaring home values and the continued allure of city life have brought lots of fresh faces over the past decade.

The outcome of the Democratic match-up may say as much about how the district has changed as about the strengths and weaknesses of candidates.

Toomey, native of the district and the son of a Cambridge cop, reflects the district's blue-collar roots and plays up his constituent service record, a posture that has served urban pols well for decades.

Green, who came to Cambridge seven years ago to attend Harvard's Kennedy School of Government, says the district needs more than that, and offers himself as a liberal leader with broader vision—and a willingness to go up against House Speaker Thomas Finneran.

Boiled down to coffee culture, it's Starbucks versus Dunkin' Donuts. "I think it's a litmus test for how much the district has changed and is changing," says Glenn Koocher, a former Cambridge School Committee member. "It's going to be a groundbreaking race to see whether Toomey can hold his base or whether someone is going to redefine the East Cambridge/East Somerville district."

"Of course there's some element of old versus new," says Green. "But if this race is only about old versus new, it's not a race that I want to win."

Along with appealing to liberal newcomers, Green says he is picking up lots of support from "old-time Portuguese and Italian and Irish families" as well as from Haitian and Hispanic immigrants.

Green says the race is really a test of whether the district wants a true "progressive Democrat" (himself) or a "pick and choose progressive" who's "just plain conservative" on some issues (Toomey). Toomey is a Finneran loyalist who serves as House chairman of the Public Safety Committee, and he has been a consistent voice against abortion in the Legislature.

"To me it's the Democratic Party period," says Toomey, dismissing efforts to give labels to those within the Democratic fold. Such big-tent talk, of course, is convenient statesmanship from an incumbent facing a primary challenge, which is designed precisely to tease out differences between those running under the same party banner.

What's more, with his support secure among more conservative Democratic voters, Toomey played up his liberal leanings at a June 30 candidate forum in Cambridge. "I vote 94 percent of the time with Alice Wolf," he said of his fellow Cambridge representative. "And I don't know anyone who is going to call her a conservative."

While most eyes are on the Sept. 14 Democratic primary match-up, the victor will then have to get by Republican David Slavitt in the Nov. 2 general election. The wry 69-year-old poet and novelist got off the best lines at the late June forum, but knows it will be a taller task to reel in the most votes in November.

"The fact that you are an underdog does not mean you should not enter the Belmont," he says. "Smarty Jones does not win every race."

My e-mail message to Jonas:

Dear Michael,

A very good piece! I think you have us all accurately. To pursue your metaphor—as poets are wont to do—the coffee I'm drinking at this moment is Peet's Viennese Blend. It figures, doesn't it? Thanks, and all best, David

★ ★ ★ Governor Romney has a counterproposal for the naming of an interim senator in the event that Kerry wins the election in November: he will send a nomination to Senate president Travaglini and Speaker Finneran and one of those would have to approve the appointment within three days. Failing that, the governor would send up a second name, and then, if necessary, a third, after which time he could name anyone at all without their approval. The interim senator would serve until 2006 and then would be eligible to run for election, which would obviously give him or her a considerable advantage. Secretary of State Galvin expressed doubts that this was constitutional, and he suggested that the governor's idea was "gamesmanship" and that Romney might be trying just to run out the clock. If there is no new law, Romney retains the power to name a successor on his own.

I'd guess that the governor knows he can't win and wants to appear cooperative and reasonable to embarrass the Democrats. The trouble is that Travaglini and Finneran are shameless. There is no point in telling a nudist his fly is unbuttoned.

★ ★ ★ Instead of trying to place signs today or even asking some of those who said they would help me to do that, I am sending letters to every Cambridge resident who gave the maximum $500 to Romney's 2002 campaign:

> Dear CONTRIBUTOR:
>
> You were generous in your support of Mitt Romney's campaign two years ago, and I venture to call upon you now to continue and extend your efforts for his success. I am the Republican candidate for State Representative in the 26th Middlesex district (East Cambridge and Somerville) and I am running with Governor Romney's endorsement and support. It is my hope that I can help not only to sustain his vetoes in the State Legislature but also to accomplish his laudable goals of reforming state government, eliminating wasteful spending, and holding the line on taxes.
>
> I shall be running against the winner of the Democratic Party primary (Avi Green or the incumbent, Tim Toomey) and it is an uphill fight—but not a hopeless one. I invite you to look at my website and see the kind of press attention I have been getting, and I ask for your help.
>
> With thanks and all best wishes,

★ ★ ★ It was a good day, yesterday, for sign placement. I went up to Union Square, where I had, I thought, a sign in the window of a coffeehouse that I'd been allowed to put up when I met Doug Holder there for my *Writer to Writer* appearance. But the coffeehouse had gone belly-up, and its windows were covered with newspaper. A couple of restaurants were willing to let me place signs, however, as was Riverside Motor Sports, the motorcycle dealership on the south side of the square. I told the owner of the good reception Evan and I had had collecting signatures at the Revere motorcycle rally a couple of years ago, where many of the bikers were off-duty policemen and Republican. He wasn't surprised. His window is a great location. Even for cautious people like Janet and me, these machines are brightly colored sculptures, all the more attractive because they are so dangerous.

A Chinese grocer was particularly welcoming, not only letting me put my sign in his window but then taking me upstairs to his office, which looks out over the square. "From here," he said, "everyone will be able to see it!" I put one there and thanked him sincerely. A jeweler, an optometrist, and another Chinese restaurant all have Slavitt signs in prominent places. I didn't see a single Toomey placard, and I know that both he and Green have worked the area, because in one of the places that refused my sign, the owner said he didn't want to take sides and that the others had been there asking. He was friendly and said he'd been to the June 30 debate. I gave him a bookmark, which I promised wouldn't alienate anyone. From there I went on up toward Malden to have dinner with Evan, and on the way saw that my sign at Mongo's was gone. It turns out that Mongo's mother took it down. Mongo is a momma's boy?

★ ★ ★ The United States Senate has taken up the question of a constitutional amendment to prohibit same-sex marriage, even though they all know that there are not enough votes for passage. The point is not to legislate but only to embarrass senators who might resist the political benefits of bigotry. It is that "wedge issue" that brings out the hard-core, right-wing faithful. The protection of minorities and their rights? The senators don't worry about that, or, if they do, they think politics trumps it. Those to whom they are appealing are believers and are beyond belief. With God and the Bible, they not only know they are right but think that toleration of an "abomination" is, itself, sinful.

Meanwhile, there is a suit that comes to trial in Suffolk Superior Court where the plaintiffs—eight same-sex couples and some city clerks who object to the constraints on them about issuing licenses—are asking a judge to allow out-of-state gay couples to marry, pending a final ruling on that 1913 law. Attorney General Reilly is arguing that the old antimiscegenation law is, in fact, "an important tool in avoiding a national backlash." Without this law, he says there will be greater pressure for amendments in other states to ban same-sex marriages. So it's a liberal thing! It is protection for the homosexuals, for whose rights he is so much concerned. Michele Granda, of the Gay and Lesbian Advocates & Defenders and the lead lawyer for the same-sex plaintiffs, called Reilly's argument "ironic." Other characterizations come to mind, but it is probably unwise for a practicing lawyer to say to reporters that the attorney general is out of his fucking mind.

★ ★ ★ I'm booked into Temple Beth Shalom on Tremont Street for July 24. I get to go to Sabbath services at nine thirty (egalitarian upstairs, with women on the bimah; traditional downstairs), and then there's a kiddush and a lunch, at which I speak. They are having a series of candidates. Green will talk to them sometime next month. What I plan to do that he cannot match is read a little of my translation of *The Book of Lamentations*—the twenty-fourth is only two days before Tisha b'Av, the fast commemorating the destruction of Solomon's Temple. This is a piece of work of which I am especially proud, and it shows that I am a serious fellow. My only worry is that this is close to what I really do and is therefore risky, as my Out of the Blue gig demonstrated. It is safer not to offer any glimpse into the scholarly and artistic parts of my repertoire, but also cowardly and self-defeating.

★ ★ ★ A letter from Nina Selvaggio, Chair of Mass NOW PAC:

Dear David
    I am writing to thank you for filling out the Mass NOW PAC endorsement questionnaire and to convey in writing the results of our PAC decision for the 26th Middlesex district.
    Our PAC has voted to endorse Avi Green. We considered a variety of factors in making our endorsement decision. While we respect your commitment to public service, we felt that Mr. Green's candidacy was a better match for the Mass NOW PAC's endorsement.
    Please to not hesitate to call us if our educational arm can be of assistance in giving you more information on any public policy issues or on other non-electoral matters. . . .

What arrant nonsense. They are lefties and he's a Democrat. The issues? I'm pro-choice and in favor of same-sex marriage. What more do they want? I sent back a civil reply:

Dear Nina Selvaggio,
Thanks for your note about your decision to endorse Avi Green. May I assume, however, that if Tim Toomey (pro-life!) beats Green in the primary, you might reconsider and endorse me for the general election? I am, after

all, pro-choice, in favor of same-sex marriage, and hold, I think, all those views that you'd want to have expressed and represented on Beacon Hill. Kind regards,

It is like seeing some ham-handed poetaster getting a rich and prestigious poetry prize. In the long run it doesn't matter, and the fact that one is a better poet than the recipient of the honor and money hasn't changed. But in the long run we're all dead.

I really do hope that Toomey beats Green, so that these self-righteous biddies have to come back, swallow their pride, hold their noses, and endorse me after all.

⋆ ⋆ ⋆ You get what you wish for, but not the way you wanted it. Finally, a letter to the editor appears in print—but not in the *Globe*. Instead, I'm in the *Times Literary Supplement*, which is more prestigious and will do me no good whatsoever:

> Sir, — George Perkins' very interesting letter (June 18) about the Supreme Judicial Court decision that ended slavery in Massachusetts gives the name of the Chief Justice as "C. J. Cushing." It was actually William Cushing. He served as Chief Justice from 1777 to 1789 and was then nominated to the United States Supreme Court as an associate justice by George Washington. It is believed that he was the last American jurist to wear a wig.
>   David R. Slavitt

Mr. Perkins's letter was what alerted me to Justice Cushing's decision, and I referred to that in the debate, as I discussed the workings of the courts in a democracy. I Googled Justice Cushing and discovered that Perkins had the name wrong. Hence, my letter, which I figure, even in Cambridge, is unlikely to get me a whole lot of name recognition.

Still, there it is, and even if Cousin Louis laughs at me for it, it feels good.

⋆ ⋆ ⋆ The U.S. Senate voted against closure, which was a procedural way to kill the anti-gay-marriage amendment. I watched on C-Span and am wondering whether my foray into politics may not be a hideous mistake. Once I have considered an issue and come to a conclusion about it, I find it boring to continue to debate it and tedious to explain it to people who can't or won't see the obvious. This is hardly statesmanlike.

★ ★ ★ Lorene Leiter—along with seven thousand other people all over the country—had another Bush/Cheney party last night where Laura Bush spoke by computer hookup, and then the president came on to thank us for our support. It was an opportunity for me to hand out flyswatters and contribution envelopes. It felt good to be in a room full of Republicans. The downside was when I handed an envelope to a former city chairman of the party and asked if he'd contribute. He said that he couldn't give money to someone who supports same-sex marriage. I could have smiled through that, but I watched him folding the envelope again and again so that it was unusable. They cost twenty cents apiece! I didn't mind his not giving, but it was irksome for a Republican to be taking away. I didn't argue, because argument is irrelevant on this subject. I just smiled and said that I hoped he'd vote for me anyway.

On the way home, driving down Cambridge Street, I saw that my sign was gone from that pizza place. But when I came home, Janet pointed out a piece in the *Cambridge Chronicle* that left me feeling a little less bad:

Political sign torched on lawn

Police and fire crews responded early Sunday morning to a flaming campaign sign on a Fayette Street lawn.

The suspected arson occurred at 2:30 a.m. in front of 23 Fayette St. when a campaign sign for Avi Green was ignited. Green is running for state representative for the 26th Middlesex District.

The Cambridge Fire Department extinguished the blazing sign without incident.

Well, it wasn't me. And I can't believe it was Toomey or his people. So it was kids, ruffians out looking to do mischief. The irony, of course, is that Avi's solution would be . . . more educational opportunities and social workers, and maybe midnight basketball.

★ ★ ★ In the *Chronicle*, in the same issue:

Letter: Candidate needs to learn manners

Thursday, July 15, 2004

Recently, Avi Green, who is a candidate for state representative against Rep. Tim Toomey, came to our door as part of his campaigning. After he introduced himself and told me why he had come to my house, I told him nicely that we supported Rep. Toomey. His personality instantly changed and he said rather pointedly, "Well, don't you know that he holds two offices." I told him that I was well aware of that and it was because he represented us so well as city councilor and state representative that we and so many others in the district strongly support him. He then became further agitated and asked why I wouldn't listen to him. At that point, because of his belligerent attitude, I terminated the conversation and closed the door.

I have some advice for Mr. Green. If his campaign strategy is to continually harp on the fact that Tim Toomey is our city councilor and state representative, he has chosen a losing strategy. And on a personal note, if he wants to continue in politics, he has to become less belligerent to voters who don't agree with him and as gracious as Rep. Toomey is to all his constituents. PAULA POPOVICS

The desperate people in Central Square soliciting signatures to get Nader onto the ballot are better trained, always pleasant, never argumentative. The MASSPIRG volunteers in their red jackets trying to fight for the environment never argue. The candidates ought to be at least as disciplined as these street workers. Paula Popovics must have been really pissed off not just to slam the door in Avi's face but to sit down and write a letter. I get Toomey loyalists and buddies, too, and my response always is that he's a decent fellow but he votes with Finneran all the time, and that's maybe not such a good thing for Cambridge and Somerville. That he holds the two jobs just isn't that much of an issue—because while some object to his "double-dipping," there are others who believe the people have a right to elect him to as many jobs as he has time to do, or at least run for.

★ ★ ★ Any listing in the *Globe*'s City Weekly is depressing, because I have to go to these things, shake hands, introduce myself, hand out bookmarks and flyswatters, and be the candidate. In theory these events are to celebrate the Democratic National Convention across the river and gain attention to what the city fathers and mothers are billing as "Destination Cambridge—The Unconventional City." The appellation is correct if one takes "unconventional" as a synonym for weird or queer, but here are the events:

Wednesday—from five to eight, A Taste of Cambridge, with samples of the cuisine of fifty local restaurants. Grazing and handshaking. Then, from seven to ten thirty, a free salsa concert by Willie Colon in Cambridgeport. Local salsa band Kilombo Mambo opens the show at eight. And there will be a competition to break the Guinness record for salsa dancing. (Endurance, I suppose.)

Friday—from noon to six, the Central Square World's Fair Music Festival with multiple stages with jazz, gospel, rock, and Motown. (No klezmer? No clog dancing?)

Sunday—a Citywide Parade from Cambridge Common along Mass. Ave. to Central Square with marching bands, floats, and other such dreckerai.

Monday, July 26, a Rock the Vote rally to register young adults in the CambridgeSide Galleria.

I have to show up, with my paraphernalia and my SLAVITT tag hanging from my neck. I should be grateful for these opportunities rather than burdened by their strenuousness and foolishness. Bread and circuses is what democracy degenerates to.

★ ★ ★ As if there were some guardian angel looking down, ready to intervene when I need encouragement, I got a phone call this morning from Brock Parker of the *Somerville Journal*, who is doing a story about the endorsement by the Progressive Democrats of Avi Green. I explained that it was not surprising that the Progressive Democrats endorsed Avi. Toomey is a loyal Finneran supporter, and the Progressives find Finneran an embarrassment to the party and democracy itself. On the other hand, Toomey would feel aggrieved. He has worked hard all these years and feels that the voters owe him their gratitude and support. This made Parker chuckle, and he invited me to comment further and share my views about the Democrats' primary election, which I said I could not predict. But I shot zingers at both Green and Toomey, the former for his unrealistic notion that social workers can solve Somerville's gang problem, and the latter for his Democratic bias that keeps him from admitting that any of the $700 million surplus ought to be returned to the taxpayers whose money it is or that the referendum in which the voters asked that the tax rate be rolled back to 5 percent might be honored and adopted. I told Parker about Toomey's basic view that—in his words—if the Republicans were in control, there would be no social programs and no public education. I've learned, since that first encounter with Deb Eisner, how to do these interviews.

It is like writing a poem: one has the satisfaction of having performed well. But as with writing poems, the good feeling lasts only an hour or so. That angel of mine ought not to relax his vigil.

★ ★ ★ In today's mail, there is a letter addressed to me on the letterhead of Darrell W. Crate, chairman of the Massachusetts Republican Party. It begins:

Dear David,

This just in . . .

The head of the Massachusetts Democratic Party is vowing to raise $1 million to fend off a looming wave of Republican challengers fueled by Governor Romney's desire to cut into the Democrats' iron fist majority in the legislature.

I am not at all happy about the idea of "cutting into" an "iron fist majority," and wonder if Crate actually read the letter. The breathless fragment at the beginning is also puzzling, because the date on top of the page is July 12, while the enclosed story from the *Boston Herald* has a dateline of May 9, so it isn't "just in" at all.

But let him (or whoever wrote it) continue:

As Chairman of the Massachusetts Republican Party, I will *not* sit by and let all our hard work go by the wayside.

I will *not* allow powerful Beacon Hill interests to bulldoze over us.

Bulldoze *over* us?

I *will*, however, acknowledge the gauntlet thrown down by the Democrats and *step up our fundraising efforts so we can match them dollar for dollar*.

David, that's why I am setting up a special Republican Legislative Campaign Fund and calling upon you to provide the early money today.

From here it gets quite predictable and, without noticeable solecisms, hits me up for money that "will help elect a Republican majority to the state legislature in the November elections"—an impossible goal that ought not to be proposed to serious people.

What upsets me most, though, is the paragraph on the second page, all underlined, that says, "*Your generous contribution will be used to fund the campaigns of Republican challengers in strategic, targeted 'swing races.' In these races, additional campaign dollars will significantly increase the likelihood of a Republican winning the seat.*" That they pick among the likelier contenders and put their money where it can do the most good is reasonable, but what it means is that well before the November election, I will have heard from the state party or not, will have got the money or not, and will know with what enthusiasm or lack of it they are supporting my not inconsiderable efforts.

★ ★ ★ There is a front-page story in the paper this morning about Governor Romney's veto of the moratorium on charter schools, which the state legislature actually sustained. This extraordinary event brings to mind the discussion I had with Minority Leader Jones about how the legislators could be, at least on occasion, collegial. There was a deal here, apparently, but a good deal on both sides. The governor agreed that the formula for funding the charter schools was unfair and took too much money away from the conventional public schools (which were left with the expensive job of educating the special-needs students), and he promised to change the reimbursement level to the actual costs of educating each child. The charter schools have greater freedom than the public schools and can hire and fire teachers and principals and set their own curricula. When they work well, as some of them do, they can be a wonderful alternative to public schools, which too often are playthings of school boards and hostages to the teachers' unions. I am pleased by the news and reassured to know that, in the event that I have to serve for a couple of years, it may not be altogether hopeless and irrelevant, or at least not all the time. There were seventy-eight votes to sustain Romney's veto and only seventy-seven to override.

Tomorrow, in the *Chronicle*, I shall find out how Toomey voted. (One would think the *Globe* might have seen fit to list legislators' votes, but one would be wrong.)

★ ★ ★ I checked with Brad Jones's office, and Toomey voted to override. He needs to have his knuckles rapped. My letter, then, to the *Cambridge Chronicle*:

Representative Tim Toomey's vote last week to override Governor Romney's veto of the moratorium on charter schools is one more demonstration of his abject subjection to the interests of the teachers' unions, even at the expense of the students whom we are supposed to be educating and their parents who want a wider range of choices for their children. The fact that the legislature was able to transcend party divisions last week and sustain the governor's veto in a rare show of collegiality and statesmanship (and compromise, for Governor Romney is changing the formula for the payments to the charter schools to make them more equitable) gives us cause for hope. And it makes Representative Toomey's entrenched resistance all the more deplorable. For the sake of the students of Massachusetts whose parents do not have the option of expensive private schools, we need legislators who care enough to take the risk of offending the vested interests of the unions as 78 legislators did last week. But Tim Toomey was not one of them.

★ ★ ★ Taste of Cambridge could have been worse, I suppose. It was a pleasant enough array of restaurateurs offering goodies, and one could graze in a pleasant MIT courtyard, find seats at tables in the shade, and—in the intervals between the excessively loud songs of an Edith Piaf imitator—even talk a little. I went from group to group asking if anyone lived in East Cambridge or East Somerville and from time to time got answers in the affirmative, to which I would respond with a minispiel and a bookmark. But half an hour of that kind of effort is wearing, and an hour is mind-numbing. From time to time, I'd get some hostility when I identified myself as a Republican ("but a Chris Shays Republican, or a John Chafee Republican!"). Still, there were some self-righteous old-lefties who asked if I could vote for George Bush or if I'd seen *Fahrenheit 9/11.* To the first question, I could say that probably I would. And that would lead to a discussion of the war, in which I pointed out that Kerry's position, so far as it is clear that he has one, is indistinguishable from Bush's. To the other question, I just said, "No, not yet," which is not quite a promise that I would see the movie as soon as I could.

Janet showed up a little after six, and we mostly ate and drank. Then, after Councilman Ken Reeves offered some welcoming remarks and introduced his fellow councilman Brian Murphy and City Manager Healy, we decided to pack it in. We didn't need Salsa at Sunset, Willie Colon, or the attempt to break the Guinness world record. There was still the Dance Party to look forward to on Friday and then the World's Fair on Sunday. And my legs were aching enough for me to wonder about the necessity of the city's spending $100,000 of taxpayers' money for this hoopla to make Cambridge better known (and there's another $140,000 in contributions) and also for me to rethink the efficiency of politicking at these events. I had, in two hours, found eight or ten people who probably live and vote in the district. I'd do almost as well door-to-door.

★ ★ ★ My performance on the telephone with Brock Parker seems to have been almost entirely in vain. I did make him laugh and everything I said was relevant and well put, but none of it made the story in the *Journal* and the *Chronicle.* Still, Parker was entertained. There are three months and a bit to go, and our paths may cross again.

In the same issue of the paper, there is a letter from a Toomey supporter:

Toomey support is clear

Avi Green was right at home with the recent debate sponsored by the Progressive Democrats since he is a member. He gave the answers the audience wanted to hear and, in fact, I agree with his progressive opinions. However, Green's demeanor was arrogant and pompous. You get the feeling that if it came down to a choice between his political ambitions and my needs as his constituent, political ambitions would win out.

David Slavitt, with his acerbic wit, outlined his Republican belief that government is not the solution but the problem. Unfortunately, his wit devolved into nastiness as he ridiculed the Democrats and his opponents. But you've got to hand it to him for going into the lion's den.

Rep. Tim Toomey, the target of both Green and Slavitt, eschewed a confrontational approach. He took Green to task for calling him a conservative Democrat by stating that his voting record is similar to well-regarded Progressives.

However, it was Toomey's closing statement that affected me the most. He supported the principles of the Democratic Party and blasted the Republicans for their insensitivity to the needs of working families. He again took Green to task for distorting his record.

It's clear to me that Toomey deserves re-election.

KENNETH JACKSON

In his closing statement Toomey verged on insanity. But in Cambridge, who would notice?

⋆ ⋆ ⋆ I passed Mongo's again and saw a Toomey sign in the window. I stopped, went in, and learned that it wasn't Mongo's mom who had taken mine down; it was "Mama" as in "Big Mama," a hefty dame who owns this dermatographic salon, and she is a Toomey supporter and a Democrat. Hates Romney, hates Republicans, and thinks the state should keep every nickel of the surplus and spend it on social programs and education. I asked her if she had either of the signs I'd left. One was gone, but the other she extracted from behind a watercooler and returned to me.

⋆ ⋆ ⋆ I have a questionnaire from the National Rifle Association, asking naturally enough about my attitudes about gun control and registration. But the letterhead of their cover letter is a not-so-subtle nudge: National Rifle Association of America Political Victory Fund. We get rated and graded, and this information is used to determine whether there shall be "any involvement in your race in September and/or November" and is in any case distributed to members in a Political Preference Chart. The temptation, therefore, is to tilt as far as I can toward their point of view. And the questions are teaching tools as much as anything else. One of them reads:

> In 1994, President Clinton signed the Omnibus Crime Control Act, which imposed a 10-year ban on the manufacture, for sale to private citizens, of various semi-automatic firearms, redefining them as assault weapons.* The law also prohibited the manufacture, for sale to private citizens, of ammunition magazines capable of holding more than 10 rounds of ammunition. State and local law enforcement agency reports, and two studies conducted for the National Institutes of Justice, have shown that the guns and magazines in question were never used in more than about 1% of violent crime. These federal provisions will sunset in 2004 unless congress reauthorizes them. If Congress does not, it is expected that gun control advocates will push to enact similar bans at the state level. *Would you support state legislation restricting the private possession, ownership, purchase, sale and/or transfer of any semi-automatic firearms?*
> ___a. Yes, I would support such legislation. Please specify:
> ___b. I would oppose such legislation.

> *The term assault weapons has been inappropriately applied to semi-automatic firearms commonly used for hunting, sports, and protection. All semi-automatics fire only one shot each time the trigger is pulled. They are not fully-automatic machine guns, which have been strictly regulated since 1934.

I am not convinced that anybody needs a Glock semiautomatic pistol for "hunting, sports, and protection," but neither am I persuaded that we are much safer if these weapons are prohibited to citizens, in which case only the bad guys can buy them. I am probably more sympathetic than either Green or Toomey to the NRA, but almost certainly insufficiently gung ho for their members: I do think handgun owners ought to be fingerprinted and licensed and can't see why anyone needs to buy more than one gun a month unless he is a dealer. I filled out their questionnaire but didn't feel good about it.

★ ★ ★ The Citywide Dance Party was . . . without me. Janet and I were delayed, because we'd driven up to Everett to adopt a couple of young cats from the Cat Action Team there. We got back to find Fred waiting for us. He said it was unbearably loud (so that one couldn't talk or do any politicking) and that neither Toomey nor Green had shown up. I was tired and relieved not to have to go to Central Square to lose more of my hearing and watch Mayor Sullivan (who is the shape of the Pillsbury Doughboy) try to boogie. We went to dinner with Fred and talked, mercifully, about other things.

⋆ ⋆ ⋆ At Tremont Street shul there was a long service—nine thirty to noon, and all in Hebrew—and I sat or stood through it patiently enough, although with the nagging feeling that my presence there was not quite authentic. I was waiting through it to pitch my candidacy and read from my *Book of Lamentations.* (Even that felt slightly commercial. I wanted them to buy the book or take it out of the library.) At one moment the *gabbai* offered me an aliyah, and I hesitated (Is my Hebrew good enough to do the blessing without practice?) and shook my head, no. It was an honor they were extending to a guest. I should have accepted and felt bad about not having done so.

Afterward there was a sit-down kiddush downstairs, where I got to speak for ten minutes. I told them who I was, why I was running, and what distinguished me from Toomey and Green. And I did read the first half of the first chapter of my version of Lamentations. They were receptive enough, and several people asked for information about the book. One or two also wanted to know if I had any campaign literature, and I gave them bookmarks. One young woman introduced herself to me as a reporter from the *Jewish Advocate.* I gave her a bookmark too. If she follows up and does a piece about me, the morning's efforts will have been worthwhile. But even as I write that, I realize how bizarre it is. I wasn't there as a congregant, following along in the prayer book or the Torah reading and singing at least those songs I knew the melodies to. The young man who led the end of the service has a tradition—his own, I think—of singing "Adon Olam" to different tunes every week. In mid-July, on the Sabbath before Bastille Day, for instance, he does it to "La Marseillaise." And on the Sabbath after the Red Sox have been mathematically eliminated from the playoffs, he does it to taps. Today, to mark the beginning of the Democratic National Convention on Monday, he sang it to "Happy Days Are Here Again." It almost fit, but he had to do a lot of repetitions.

⋆ ⋆ ⋆ There was one awkward moment after that kiddush, when a woman of a certain age and presence asked, in a friendly way, how I was going to vote for president. "You call yourself socially liberal and fiscally conservative. Bush is socially conservative and fiscally reckless. How can you hold the views you do and vote for him?" I had to admit that it would not be easy. Her observation that Bush's positions are quite different from mine and even, in some ways, abhorrent troubles me. Not that it makes much difference. Kerry will carry Massachusetts. Even McGovern did. Even Mondale.

★ ★ ★ In the *Somerville News*, there is a charge of skulduggery that Toomey makes about the videotape of the June 30 debate. It is not quite clear whom he is accusing, but he is unhappy that the tape never got played on Cambridge or Somerville community television stations, which puzzles me, too. The *News* piece goes on to say:

> Toomey said he was told July 14 by a member of the Progressive Democrats of Cambridge that the last ten to fifteen minutes of the June 30 debate co-sponsored by both the PDS and PDC was erased.
>
> The debate was supposed to be a determining factor in deciding the progressive endorsements, but three weeks after it took place it has never aired on Cambridge Community Television or Somerville Community Access Television, Toomey said.
>
> "We have asked for copies of the tapes and nobody will give us a straight answer," he said.
>
> "I was very pleased with my performance at that debate and I thought I made a very powerful closing statement. Later that night, I was having dinner with friends and I told them: 'Mark my words, that tape will never see the light of day.'"
>
> Toomey said that if he ever got a copy of the tape, he would request that an independent video technician ascertain whether the closing statements were deliberately deleted.

I asked Evan whether I should volunteer my audiotape—either to Toomey or the *News*—and he said sure. "Even though it's better for me if Green wins?" I asked. "What would be the right thing to do?" he asked back. And so I sent Toomey an e-mail:

> Dear Tim,
> I hope that it is simply a series of inadvertencies and errors rather than any conspiracy, but it is indeed odd that the debate of the 30th has never run on Community TV either in Somerville or in Cambridge.
>
> I have an audio tape of the concluding remarks that all three of us made, and if you think it is a good idea, I'd be happy to release a copy to the Somerville News (or anywhere else you suggest). We tried to tape the whole thing but it is an auto-reverse machine and it re-recorded over some of the

beginning. The end, though, is on the tape and is of good enough quality to be perfectly audible.

I think both of us sounded good in our last few minutes, and I'd be pleased to cooperate in getting our words out there. These debates are important and it has been good of you to participate.

Kind regards, David

We'll see if we can make some trouble. And I came off well in those closing remarks.

★ ★ ★ The Central Square World's Fair and Unconventional Parade was a big crowd of people with platforms where gospel singers or loud combos blared while along both sides of Massachusetts Avenue vendors sold various kinds of food, Indian, Italian, Caribbean, Tibetan, and whatever cuisine fried dough comes from. There was a parade, too, that started off at the Cambridge Common and wound down Mass. Ave. to end up at a reviewing stand in front of City Hall. That had contingents from Senator Jarrett Barrios and Representatives Alice Wolf and Tim Toomey, as well as one from Kristine Glynn, who is a candidate for the Eighth Suffolk District seat that Paul Demakis gave up. I asked her how she got herself included in the parade and the blunt truth is that she asked, which means that if I'd thought of calling the organizers of the parade, I would have been allowed to have a contingent as well. What I had was three volunteers with Slavitt signs and bookmarks. So there were four of us. Toomey had seven friends carrying his signs and two more carrying a big banner. Avi didn't show.

These herds of people are not congenial to me. Indeed, they are so foreign that I can project myself into a character who asks strangers if they vote in Cambridge or Somerville. I'm picky. Fat girls with tattoos on their backs or in their cleavage are unlikely to be receptive to Republicans. Multiple body piercings are inauspicious. Well-dressed gay guys, though, are good prospects, and my bookmark announces my stand on same-sex marriage. I chatted with maybe a dozen voters in two hours.

★ ★ ★ Paul, one of my volunteers, e-mailed me this morning with news that the contributions page of my website doesn't work. One can't get to it. I've e-mailed the webmaster in North Carolina to ask her whether it can be fixed. It's unlikely that I've missed many contributions, but I'd thought that was all done, and it has come unstuck.

Paul also wants to know whether I shouldn't put up a series of position papers. I might, but then every position I take is likely to alienate those who don't share my views. I already have the broad strokes—socially liberal and fiscally conservative. And the endorsement of same-sex marriages has cost me the slammed doors I remember from the signature-gathering days. So I probably will not do more than I absolutely have to. The positions don't matter so much anyway. As David Brooks points out, voters don't ask themselves what are the five or six or seven important questions of the day, decide what they think, and then look for candidates who agree with them. It's the other way. We inherit our party affiliations from our parents or adopt them early on, and that dictates not only what our views will be on policy questions but even how we see external reality. Democrats thought the rate of inflation was increasing during the Reagan years when in fact it was going down. These are not political parties, then, but religions. And if that is so, my campaign as a Republican in Cambridge is hopeless.

★ ★ ★ Mayor Menino has achieved labor peace, working out contracts with the holdout union in Boston so that there will not be any picketing of the conventioneers' festivities. The *Globe* reports this as a triumph for the mayor. At least it is an evasion of catastrophe. But the costs to the city will be huge and involve no concessions from the unions. At least one city councillor accused the city officials of "caving in," saying, "The pressure of the DNC should not dictate where and when these contracts are resolved."

★ ★ ★ I went down to Evan's office to have lunch with him, and the Fleet Center is only a block away, so I saw all the security arrangements. It was truly weird. I wonder what these people are thinking. For one thing, I'd never seen the Boston Transit Police in all-black uniforms. Why? To look menacing? Are there many potential terrorists who see the black uniforms and decide, "I don't know, Ahmed, maybe we shouldn't try this!"? For another thing, there were lots of soldiers in green camouflage uniforms. This is a city. The green camouflage works in the jungle, but on city streets these guys are quite visible. And finally, there were Coast Guard helicopters overhead, which I thought were mostly used to save people from drowning. Evan quite reasonably supposed that the security people just borrowed them from the Coast Guard. I wondered, though, whether there might not be an actual danger of the DNC delegates drowning in pools of bullshit.

★ ★ ★ I was on Vincent Dixon's community TV show last night, and he asked me about the virulence of the anti-Bush sentiment as it has been expressed with such frequency around here during these convention days. ("Buck Fush" T-shirts were on sale at the Cambridge World's Fair, and "Re-Defeat Bush" and "Defoliate Bush" bumper stickers are on a lot of automobiles.) I surprised myself, answering that the protesters' style of the sixties had a voice in Dean and there was a terrible letdown as the Dean campaign collapsed and Kerry emerged as the nominee. The only way for the party to work up any kind of enthusiasm was to revile the opponents and demonize Bush and Cheney. I hadn't read this anywhere. It just popped into my head. But I find it at least plausible.

★ ★ ★ The *Cambridge Chronicle* ran my letter about Toomey's vote on charter schools. I couldn't have asked for a more favorable conjunction, because in the same issue there was an article in which Toomey's campaign announced that he has received the endorsement of the Massachusetts Teachers Association. "Toomey said that 'Public education is the backbone of our society. As we prepare students to compete in the global economy and train them for high-tech jobs of the 21st century, it is crucial that we provide strong, safe and healthy public schools and colleges in which to learn.'" Toomey went to Suffolk and wouldn't recognize an education if it bit him in the ass. It isn't education he's interested in, but the Massachusetts Teachers Association and its large membership. He is their lackey, and as long as he is useful and obedient, they reward him by voting for him. The listing the *Chronicle* runs under their "Beacon Hill Roll Call" rubric lists Toomey's vote to override Mitt Romney's veto of the Charter School Moratorium, to which my letter refers.

A page-one story, meanwhile, announces: "Toomey-Green race heats up." What it is about is a silly squabble in which Toomey is accusing Green of being . . . "green," an adherent to the "Green-Rainbow principles." Green apparently tried to change the minutes of the Somerville Green-Rainbow Party to excise a phrase that said he was in favor of "radical economic change." For Green—who *is* a radical, the word is allergenic, just as "liberal" is poison to liberals, who these days prefer "progressive."

According to the *Chronicle*, Steve Grossman, a "State Democratic heavyweight," links Toomey's attack to "lingering bitterness about Ralph Nader's 2000 presidential run on the Green ticket." As if Gore hadn't carried Massachusetts! And as if Toomey hadn't won in 2000 and in 2002!

★ ★ ★ My sign disappeared from the window of the Store 24—a terrific location in the corner window where it was visible both from Broadway and from Prospect streets. It had been there for a couple of weeks, I guess, and then, poof, one afternoon it was gone. I went in yesterday to ask about it. The clerk, from India or Bangladesh, called into the refrigerated case, and a fellow employee from the subcontinent appeared and told me to come back in the morning when the manager would be on duty.

Mongo's Mama again? How many desperado businesses can she be involved in? But my reception was entirely friendly. The manager (different one from the one I remembered from a few weeks ago) was perfectly obliging. He had no idea what had happened to the sign. Did I have another? Of course, I said, and went out to my car for a replacement. He even gave me a piece of Scotch tape to affix it properly. To place a sign is satisfactory, but to replace is even better. It's a loss made good. This is magical thinking, but which of us can resist such blandishments? A. J. Liebling wrote that there were some buildings in Manhattan where he had the sense that he'd never make a dollar from anyone in any of their offices. Freelance writers live on the fringes of society as surely as politicians, and it takes more mental balance than most scribblers and most pols can muster not to look for omens and auguries.

There was also an auto body place on Cambridge Street where I'd had a sign that had gone missing and where they let me replace it with a new one. I am a lobsterman, checking my traps as I drive the streets of the district where I've put up my placards.

★ ★ ★ The legislature has concluded its business for this session. Finneran took up the last hours of the session overriding Romney's veto so that, if Kerry wins, we now must hold an election for a new U.S. senator between 145 and 160 days after the vacancy occurs. This keeps Romney from naming a Republican. More important, it prevented other business from coming to the floor, so that no one had to go on record as voting against the rollback of the state tax rate to 5 percent as demanded by the referendum in 2000. The surplus of almost three-quarters of a trillion dollars is theirs to spend and buy votes with. They don't want to give back a dollar, but neither do they want to vote against a rollback. According to the *Globe*, "Hooting and hollering broke out on the usually staid House floor as . . . Finneran pushed through the [special election] bill yesterday afternoon, the final day of formal legislative business."

The posturing is also impressive. "One person, whoever happens to be the governor at this particular time, will not make the decision for you," said

William Straus, Chairman of the Election Laws Committee. On the other side, Republican George Peterson of Grafton said, "I can't understand why anyone would want to leave us unrepresented in the US Senate, at any point in time." Not that Kerry is strenuously and attentively representing us there now!

But the real point of the exercise was to keep that tax bill from coming to the floor, and they did that. The session ran past midnight, and Finneran just waited it out.

The month, week, and day began with mild pangs of guilt. It's August already. I ought to have been out this weekend, trudging the streets (or, to use the *Harvard Crimson*'s cruel word, "limping") and meeting voters. But my daughter and her family stopped by on their way to the Cape. That took up Saturday and much of Sunday. And then I just goofed off and went to a movie with Janet. What galls me is that it doesn't make any difference. If I were working twice as hard, I'd still lose. The only thing that can propel me into the legislature would be some catastrophe befalling Toomey—an Avi Green victory, for starters. And whether that happens or not is entirely beyond my control.

So I come into the study to crank up what spirit and energy I can. I call Shira Schoenberg at the *Jewish Advocate* to ask about that piece she said she was interested in doing about me. She is receptive enough. Her editor was away last week. (This was a sensible thing for any Bostonian to do during the Democratic National Convention.) But he's back today and she will run it by him. Then I get a call from Debbie Miller, also of the shul, to ask me if I'll be available on September 7 or 12 for a candidates' night. (The primary is the fourteenth.) I say I am free both nights.

So there is at least the illusion that things are happening. The weather, meanwhile, is fair and not too hot, so I can go out and canvass this afternoon. It may not get me elected, but it will keep the superego at bay.

★ ★ ★ I had a phone call yesterday afternoon from Tim Toomey, taking me up on that offer I'd made of a copy of the audiotape of the concluding remarks of our debate. I will drop it off at his headquarters this afternoon. I can't help wondering what he is planning to do with it or how it might affect the primary. I'd rather fight Green in the general election for an open seat. I'd get more support and attention from the party, and I'd probably be able to raise money more easily. I'd begin to look plausible.

Toomey may be correct in suspecting the Progressive Democrats of suppressing the video of the debate—it has not played on Cambridge or Somerville community TV. And Avi Green was less than stellar. I asked Eric Weltman, one of the Progressive Democrats, for a copy of the tape, but never heard from him. And I have inquired at the Cambridge Community TV station, and they say they never got it. Very strange!

★ ★ ★ Making the tape for Toomey, I couldn't find the instructions on the reel-to-reel dubbing recorder, so I did it the quick and dirty way, playing the tape and recording the sound from the speaker. It's only talk, so the quality doesn't matter too much. But doing it this way, I realized that I had forgotten, or had blocked out, how bizarre Green's closing remarks were.

> When I was born, my father was in jail, and so he wasn't there on the day that I was born. For the first several years that I was growing up, my mother raised me as a single mom. Throughout his life, my father wrestled with a chronic illness. For most of the time, his doctors, his family, his health insurance comes [sic] together, and he is able to do his trade, which is that he's a massage therapist for people with Parkinson's and MS and other chronic diseases. He literally helps them be able to move a little bit more. When he's ill, however, and he's in the hospital, it means that he can't help his patients. It's not just bad for the family and bad for him, and bad for his doctors. It's bad for everyone. I believe that this is a metaphor for the actual decision that is facing us when we decide whether we want conservative or progressive government. Conservatives believe that you're better off on your own, that it's better for us all not to put in our money or our energy or our efforts to try to make the world better, but rather to concentrate on ourselves. Progressives believe that we are better off together. When we invest in each other as a community, all of our lives are improved. I strongly believe that and I'm proud to be a progressive Democrat—and I'm proud to be the progressive Democrat in this race. I'd like to thank everyone for coming tonight, and I'd like to ask humbly for the endorsement of the Progressive Democrats of Somerville and the Progressive Democrats of Cambridge. And I'd like to ask everyone who came here tonight to be sure to register and, please, vote in the Democratic Primary on September fourteenth and then again in the general election in early November.

No wonder Toomey wants this circulated! It used to be that these shameful secrets were what candidates worried might be used against them; now they invoke them proudly as qualifications for office. When I deliver the tape, I will throw in a transcription of Avi's remarks to save Toomey or his people the trouble of transcribing them.

★ ★ ★ My guess turns out to be correct. Tim wasn't there, but Kate Glidden and Kevin Rogers, his campaign manager and committee treasurer, were in the Toomey-for-rep office (just down the street from his state rep office for constituent services). I was a bit intimidated by the idea that the two of them and another guy working at a desk were all occupied in his campaign and surrounded by bumper stickers, signs, fliers, and sticks for displaying the signs. I have a few signs in the basement and almost no organization. But that is what his advantage as an incumbent translates into. If, as Tip O'Neill said, money is the mother's milk of politics, then people are the cookies.

I gave Kate and Kevin the tape and the transcription. Their view is that Avi tried to bury these remarks just like he tried to take back the "radical economic change" remark and get it expunged from the minutes of the Green Party meeting, even though that is exactly what the note taker remembers him as having said. And if he can try to take back those words, then it is not beyond imagining that he should have thought better of his closing remarks about his jailbird papa and has been more than an innocent bystander as the Progressive Democrats (which endorsed him) "lost" that part of the videotape of the debate. My recording and transcription then become valuable. My hope is that they will embarrass Green but also make Toomey look less than wonderful for having cruelly exploited Green's stupid mistake.

Eliot says in *Murder in the Cathedral* that "the last offense is the greatest treason: / to do the right thing but for the wrong reason," but I have always thought that that was nonsense. I have done the right thing, and only hope it works out badly for both of them.

It also crosses my mind that there is something gratifying about even so tentative a venture into an arena in which words count as they do here. I may say rash things sometimes, but I am willing to stand by them.

★ ★ ★ There was a book signing at the Boston Public Library yesterday, with Governor Romney writing his name in copies of *Turnaround*, his account of his experiences with the Salt Lake City Olympics. The signing was aggressively well organized. Those who attended were all invitees, and there were name badges for each of us. We stood in line and, as we got toward the front, we were asked by an aide how we wanted the book inscribed. I thought it would be nice to get one of these for Evan, and she wrote his name on a Post-it, stuck that onto the half title, and put the front flap into the book so that it would open to that page. After a minute or so I was at the head of the line, where Kerry Healey greeted each of us and then, when the governor had finished with the previous guest, propelled us toward the table where he sat.

The point of my appearance and my purchase of the book (twenty-five dollars) was to get this moment with the lieutenant governor to tell her that I'd heard that Tim O'Brien was arranging her appearance at my fund-raiser and to thank her. She said she was glad to be of help. (I can now take this to Evan to take to O'Brien—that she has agreed!)

When the governor was free, Healey directed me to proceed to his table. Romney may have been indicating friendliness, or a particularly warm welcome, or respect for my age, or perhaps he was just stiff from having been sitting for a while, but he stood up to welcome me and shake my hand. He asked how the campaign was going. I said that it was "strenuous," which was a way of letting him know that I was plugging along, and was going "better than one might have hoped," which is no great claim. With a felt-tipped pen, he inscribed my book. Then I was ushered through a side door to a pretty Italianate courtyard I'd never seen before, an imitation, I'm told, of that in the Palazzo della Cancelleria at the Vatican. There was music, and there were hors d'oeuvres, and a there was a bar—free, for the first time, I believe, in any of these Romney encounters. But then the putative hosts were either Borders, Regnery Publishing, or the library.

★ ★ ★ The Harvard Yard picnic was a success. The flyswatters went like crazy. I took two great sacks full of them (one for me and one for Fred Baker), but people were reaching out and grabbing for them, and there were so many at the picnic that I realized I'd very quickly exhaust my supply if I gave them out indiscriminately. I asked if people were from East Cambridge, where my district is. Cambridgeport and North or West Cambridge residents can't vote for me, after all. I was not too particular, so that if people were willing to lie for a forty-five-cent flyswatter, I handed one over. I was not willing to give more than one to people who asked for a bunch of them, joking that if they needed more than one flyswatter, they should perhaps improve their housecleaning.

I distributed all the flyswatters in the first forty minutes or so, then came back to the apartment to refill my pouches and returned to the Yard, where Fred was waiting. I gave him one of the sacks, and we worked the crowd together—he recognized most of the East Cambridge people and could steer me to the right tables.

Toomey was there, of course, and his people—three of them at least— were handing out little American-flag key chains (which had no imprinting, so that voters would have to remember that these were from him). Alice Wolf was giving out little plastic pens and those dry sponges that swell up when you dip them in water. These were both imprinted with her name. The sponges, in fact, say "Alice Wolf / Dip in Water—See What Happens." I'd guess you'd get a wet Alice Wolf. James DiPaola, who is running for reelection as Middlesex County sheriff, gave out blue rubber jar openers with a white six-pointed-star sheriff's badge and his name in yellow. My flyswatter was the winner, I do believe, in the tchotchke contest.

Ken Reeves greeted me and told me that people who weren't in my district had complained that they couldn't get flyswatters from me. "That's your first political mistake," he said. "Is it?" I asked. "Remember, I'm a Republican. You Democrats give everything to everybody. We Republicans tend to be more careful."

He looked dubious. "It's easy for Tim," I added. "Voters who aren't in his state rep district can vote for him next year for city council. And he's got more money than I do." Reeves grinned and said that, after the election, we must get together.

I did not sit down to eat the unappealing fried chicken lunch, and I didn't wait for the songs. I had spent two hours greeting people, repeating my mantra about two-party government in Massachusetts, giving out flyswatters, and asking people to remember me in November. So Fred and I took off. It was only on the way home that I realized that Green hadn't shown up. Or at the Central Square World's Fair either. Has he given up?

★ ★ ★ The *Somerville News* has this story in the current issue:

PDS June 30 Debate video mishap
by Courtney H. Naliboff

The cameraman who taped the June 30 debate between the state representative candidates for 26th Middlesex District seat, told The Somerville News his errors caused the loss of debate's last 10 minutes.

"Toomey accused Progressive Democrats of withholding the tape [but] that is not the case," said Eric Weltman, a Progressive Democrat involved in filming and producing two debates between David R. Slavitt, R, Avi Green, D, and the incumbent State Rep. Timothy J. Toomey Jr., D-Somerville. The first debate was sponsored by this paper.

Simple errors and lack of preparation caused volunteers to incompletely tape recent debates between the politicians, he said.

"Nothing nefarious was intended by the Progressives' failure to tape Slavitt's opening remarks in one instance, and Toomey's closing remarks in another," he said.

"We're all volunteers. I didn't miss Slavitt's opening remarks because I have anything against Republicans, I missed it because I'd never filmed anything before," said Weltman.

Weltman forgot to turn the camera on, he said.

The second debate, which Weltman said he helped organize, was filmed by another volunteer, he said. "She had only brought one one-hour long tape, that's why the ending wasn't filmed."

"It had nothing to do with Toomey," he said.

Weltman said he thought arrangements to distribute the debate tapes to community access channels had never been made, and said he attributed it to the volunteer-run nature of the Progressive Democrats.

It was unfair to read more into the mistake than there is, he said.

All this is plausible, but alternative explanations—that Green thought better of his weird closing remarks, or that the Progressive Democrats figured that they could be helping him more by messing up the taping—do not recede into absolute impossibility.

It was too charming an opportunity to resist. I sent the transcription of Green's remarks to the *Somerville News* with a cheery prolegomenon:

I am inclined to believe that the Progressive Democrats are more incompetent than malevolent (these are two views between which Republicans often must choose), but what gave the conspiracy theory its legs was that Avi Green's remarks at the June 30th debate were so peculiar.

I also let the *News* have a transcription of what I'd said at the beginning of the debate, with my guess about the reason for Progressive Democrats' lapse:

The fact that they didn't get my opening remarks doesn't surprise me. They were distracted, because I was shocking them with uncomfortable truths.

★ ★ ★ On the same-sex marriage front, 70 percent of the voters in Missouri approved a proposed amendment to that state's constitution to bar gay marriages. The amendment passed in every county except the City of St. Louis. And at least nine other states are expected to vote on similar amendments, four of those being swing states in the presidential race. On the other hand, a Superior Court judge in Seattle ruled that there was no evidence that same-sex marriages threatened children and that barring such marriages served no state interest and violated the constitutional rights of gay couples. My guess is that if the Bill of Rights were on the ballot, it would probably fail.

★ ★ ★ An e-mail this morning from Laura Leichum, the publicist of Northwestern University Press, informs me that bound books have appeared of *The Regrets of Joachim du Bellay*, which is great news, of course, but also worrisome. She asks where she should send review copies for local coverage—reporters who have been writing about my campaign. It was a fundamental tenet of Bernard Geis—an aggressive publisher with whom I did a few books back in the sixties and early seventies—that the best place to have book news was off the book page, where people might actually see it. This was true, perhaps, for big-money novels (like *The Exhibitionist*, which I wrote as Henry Sutton and which he published with some success). But . . . du Bellay? How many literate, well-educated people have ever heard of him? I have gone through the explanation many times, saying that he was a Pléiade poet and a friend of Ronsard. That doesn't get me very far. And adding "in Valois France" doesn't do much either.

Part of the reason I chose to translate du Bellay in the first place was that few Anglophone readers had heard of him, so it would be a useful service to bring this charming body of work to their attention. But my nerve now fails me. I seem not to have recovered altogether from my Out of the Blue experience, and can't help wondering what political reporters will make of this book. (To be candid, the people who cover literature and the arts in Boston are quite dim enough, thanks very much.)

Still, the book is something I've mentioned to the press and I feel obliged to persist, as if I had not had many occasions in my life already, even before this campaign began, to realize how far removed my tastes are from those of the general public. My real audience seems to be a group of a few hundred, only some of whom I know. Still, some reporter may think this exquisite bibelot is wacky enough to write about and may give the book and me a little space and attention. Toomey and Green are unlikely to have anything comparable to offer. I will overcome my hesitations, get up a list for Laura, and see what happens.

★ ★ ★ I had a haircut yesterday, which is generally an encouraging experience. George, at La Flamme, always asks how the campaign is going. And he does a great job, making me look trim but not shorn. But while I was waiting for him, I picked up a copy of *Newsweek* and read an article about John Thune, the Republican challenger to Tom Daschle in South Dakota. Daschle is against same-sex marriages, but not ardently enough, being unenthusiastic about an amendment to the U.S. Constitution to ban them. Thune, a Hard Right evangelical crazy, not only doesn't believe in same-sex marriages but also doesn't believe in evolution. (Neanderthals don't find the theory congenial.)

This is scary! That people like him are in the Republican Party is depressing. Do I want to redo my doorhangers to demonstrate my proper Cambridge enlightenment?

- Supports same-sex marriage
- Pro-choice
- For excellence in education
- Believes in evolution.

It is not altogether a joke. I am going to a breakfast Romney is giving next Thursday at the downtown Harvard Club, a thousand-dollar-a-plate affair ($50 for candidates) to meet big givers. Mickey Edwards, the former congressman who has taught at Harvard and is now on the faculty at Princeton, is the featured speaker. I am planning to bring along my bookmarks and my contribution envelopes, but some of these major donors, I suspect, will be turned off by my support of same-sex marriage.

Come to think of it, I have not heard any expression from Mitt Romney of his views about evolution.

★ ★ ★ A mixed day out on the streets. One young man was delighted to find a Republican in Cambridge, gave me his e-mail address, and said that he wanted to volunteer to work in my campaign. But there were several people who handed back my bookmarks as if they were unclean and told me, in horrified tones, that they'd *never* vote Republican. One woman, just around the corner from me, said in what can only be described as a music-hall German accent, "Ze Republican pahty is ze most dangerous pahty in the verldt." I smiled and did not tell her, no, that would be the Nazi pahty. But my restraint didn't make me feel any better.

★ ★ ★ I took a couple of days off to visit an old friend up in Maine. When I got back, there was an e-mail from the Progressive Democrats, who can't even screw up with any authority. They have now managed, after the adverse publicity in the local papers and the Sunday *Globe,* to put together a CD of the debate. Michael Jonas referred to the "charges of a Watergate-like gap in a videotape at the end of a candidate debate," and *le voilà!* They offer copies to Representative Toomey and to me (but interestingly not to Green, who, presumably, has one already).

My guess is that it is the same kind of incompetence as that which caused Kerry and Edwards to roar past a thousand supporters standing out near the tracks in Lawrence, Kansas, in the middle of the night with signs and flags. Edwards was dispatched back to Lawrence to make nice. But the apology doesn't put Humpty Dumpty together again.

★ ★ ★ That Jonas piece, "Toomey-Green race puts heat and stress on social fault lines," does make a couple of things clear. One is that even though Toomey is presently good on the same-sex marriage issue, he has not always been such a supporter of gay rights and voted, in the early nineties, against extending benefits to same-sex domestic partners. While the Lavender Alliance likes his present pro-gay stance, they are socially liberal (as one might expect) and are therefore unenthusiastic about his pro-life position. The article goes on to contrast Toomey, the "lunch-bucket incumbent," with Green, the "left-leaning challenger who is appealing to better educated, more recent arrivals in the district."

I guess what I am hoping for is that if Toomey wins, some of those better-educated types will be disgusted enough with the old-pol lunch-bucket guy to vote, in desperation, for the Republican poet. On the other hand, if Green wins, some of the old labor types on whom Toomey has relied all these years may not be able to stomach Green and could sit out the election.

★ ★ ★ There is a piece in the *Globe* this morning about another veto by Governor Romney that the legislature did not get around to overriding. I am surprised to learn how many vetoes were *not* overturned (105 out of 222), but this does not mean that Romney is more powerful than we had believed. There was apparently a terrible pressure of time, with the end of the legislative session and the Democratic National Convention taking up a lot of the attention of the majority party. I have been saying that my main duty, if elected, would be to help sustain gubernatorial vetoes, but I am nonetheless distressed about one of these that the article mentions. There had been a provision that would have allowed about four hundred children of undocumented aliens to qualify for in-state tuition rates at state colleges and universities. They would have to have lived in the Commonwealth for three years and to have graduated from a Massachusetts high school, and they would have to have filed an affidavit saying that they were in the process of becoming citizens.

In vetoing that provision, the governor said, "I hate the idea of in any way making it more difficult for kids—even those who are illegal—to afford college in our state," but he also said, "equally, perhaps a little more than equally, I do not want to create an incentive to do something which is illegal."

It's a bothersome business all around. The kids didn't break any laws; it's their parents who brought them here, often when they were very young. And now that they're here, they'll be more valuable members of society if they are educated. But these niceties of economic consequences played only a small part, I think, in the legislature's failure to overturn Romney's decision. The legislators did not want to be vulnerable to a sound bite charging that they wanted to give tuition breaks to illegal aliens.

None of this has much to do with me, except insofar as I allow myself to wonder what I would do if I were elected and had to vote. Would I go along with the governor? Would this be important enough for me to cross him? Would I abstain? Would I thank Speaker Finneran for protecting my ass and keeping the question from the floor?

★ ★ ★ No sooner do I admit to myself these finical qualms about our treatment of illegal aliens than in comes a questionnaire from the Massachusetts Immigrant & Refugee Advocacy Coalition (MIRA) to buck up my xenophobic spirits. It is more than a little disingenuous in the way it asks the questions. "Do you support in-state tuition eligibility for immigrant students?" does not quite make it clear that we are including illegal aliens.

"Do you support an increase in funding for adult basic education and English as a second language programs?" seems less skewed, but I wonder what the current level of support is, what the immigrant groups are doing themselves to help their fellow immigrants, and whether an increase in funding would measurably improve results.

Where they really get to me, though, is in their question about drivers' licenses, which asks, "Would you support access to drivers' licenses for working, tax-paying immigrants residing in Massachusetts who are not permanent lawful residents?" This is too cute by half, implying at least grammatically that there may be impermanent lawful residents. They are knocking themselves out to avoid using the word "illegal," although that is the issue. And if the states start issuing licenses to illegal aliens, then the feds will push for national identity papers, which I strenuously object to. Drivers' licenses are identification. You can get into the country with them from Canada, Mexico, or the Caribbean. And although some of the illegals may need to drive "to get to work, to take their children to school/daycare, or to keep necessary medical appointments," as MIRA puts it, it is also true that these people snuck into the country, breaking the law to get here, and that some of those likely to do so are potential terrorists. So, no.

There is no point in filling out the questionnaire, because they will write me down as a bad guy. Toomey's view may be different. Many of the illegals in Cambridge and Somerville are from Ireland (even though the Irish economy is now robust and the auld sod is no longer poor). But that is not going to come up. MIRA has a problem. Their immigrants and refugees are not a constituency with much influence in our system, because they are not citizens and don't vote. If the coalition were smart, they'd spend less energy and money lobbying and more organizing English classes and car pools.

★ ★ ★ I went to that preconvention breakfast at "The Downtown Harvard Club." You have to show photo ID to get into the building, and with a terrible sinking feeling I discovered that, in my effort to remember bookmarks and contributors' envelopes, I had left my wallet on the bedroom dresser. What to do? But then I realized that my photo is on my bookmarks. I flashed one and the guard let me through.

The breakfast was pleasant enough. Lieutenant Governor Healey now knows me by sight, and she greeted me in a friendly way and asked how the campaign was coming. I did the ten-second version, reporting that Green and Toomey were beating each other up and that my hope was that the supporters of the losing candidate would be angry enough not to bother to vote. "If you win," she said, "you'll be the smartest person on Beacon Hill." I've actually thought that, but it was nice to hear her say it. My reply was, "I've been in that situation before, and it's not altogether pleasant."

I handed out bookmarks and envelopes to Key Club members, reciting the line about the ugly primary fight that gave me a real chance. What they want to hear, after all, is that you are working hard and that you have a chance to win. Mr. Crews, the Paleolithic candidate who is pro-life and wants to defend traditional marriage, said hello and we shook hands. We differ, but we're both Republicans. I wondered exactly how far one is supposed to go with principles and issues. But I wanted to be at least as pleasant as he was, and we wished each other well.

Governor Romney appeared, and we said good morning. I wished him a safe trip. He is on his way this evening to Athens to bask in the dim Olympic glory of the Salt Lake City "turnaround." The boast is essentially Nixon's "I am not a crook," which separates him from the International Olympic Committee and, for that matter, many of the athletes.

There was a decent but hardly lavish spread of coffee, fruit juice, Danish pastries, and bagels and cream cheese (but no lox, not even at a thousand bucks a head). I got coffee and sat down to listen to Kerry Healey introduce Mitt, and Mitt introduce Mickey Edwards. Romney was in fine fettle and spoke about how busy he had been, what with the Democratic National Convention, and the Olympics. As early in the morning as it was, this was his second appointment of the day. He'd been at a photography session for *Newsweek*, which, for whatever reason, had wanted him on horseback, so he'd gone out to a stable in the burbs and climbed up on a horse. He said he had been so busy as sometimes to lose track of where he was. He had taped a television interview and, on Sunday morning, was watching it in his bedroom. His son Tagg had come in and asked, "Is that live?" (It wasn't so weird a question after all: he wanted to know was that playing "live" on television or was this a tape someone had made that he and Ann were watching.)

Then Edwards came to the lectern and made some gracious remarks that hinted that the governorship might not be the pinnacle of Romney's career. With a nice allusion to the title of Romney's book, he talked about turnarounds. When he was elected to Congress in the sixties, he was the first Republican to have served from Oklahoma since the twenties. Now both senators and all the congressmen but one from that state are Republicans, as is the governor. So it could happen here in Massachusetts, which is not, he claimed, a "liberal state." It has repealed rent control and almost repealed the state income tax. It has been a one-party state, but more by tradition than on the issues. It all comes down to grass roots, he said, the door-to-door canvassing, the local organization, the turnout of voters on Election Day. Not really surprising, his tone was somewhere between encouraging and nagging. But he was so optimistic that one could hardly object. Ours is not a Sisyphean task, he said, and we are not rolling that rock endlessly up a hill.

After Edwards was done, Romney returned to the lectern to thank him, and to joke about that reference to Sisyphus, which Romney said he'd translated for himself to Wile E. Coyote. During the course of his remarks, he explained what help candidates who look like they have a chance might expect from the state party. They will, like the incumbents—all of whom are in this category, having already demonstrated their viability—get three thousand dollars each, which is the legal limit of what the party can give to individual campaigns. (That is about what I have on hand now.) And there will be fund-raising events at which he and the lieutenant governor will be appearing. (I've already arranged for that to happen.) There will also be some television ads Romney will make for the Reform Team in which he will talk about the need for a revitalization of the two-party system for the political health of the state. (That could be of real help to me.)

Afterward, I had a chance to ask "Professor Edwards" about David Brooks's theory that people inherit party affiliation and take positions on issues according to that affiliation, rather than the other way around. If this is true, I said, then my efforts are doomed. Edwards said he thinks Brooks is only partly right. It does happen, sometimes, the way Brooks describes. "But that's only the hard core of each party. The majority of voters now are independents, unenrolled in any party, and they can be reached."

I thanked him and told him I hoped he was right.

★ ★ ★ Prompted by Mickey Edwards's speech, I was out with the doorhangers and the bookmarks again, working the area around our condo. It is interesting that even an enclave of wealth and privilege like Cambridge has its pockets of squalor, with great houses chopped into one-room apartments with dark halls where people cower in un-air-conditioned darkness. I ring bells, and sometimes someone acknowledges my presence and sometimes not. Occasionally, someone appears interested in what I have to say, or, just as likely, an old man in his pajamas will tell me, "I'm blind! I don't vote!" and slam the door.

A black man sitting on the steps of a garden apartment on Harvard Street retrieved the day for me. "Are you a voter, sir?" I asked. "Yes, a Democrat." "Well, perhaps you'll want to rethink that. I'm the Republican running against Toomey."

"Against Toomey? That's different. Don't like Toomey. He's a double-dipper."

I agree that that's true. And I say that he's a decent enough fellow but that he always votes with Finneran. . . .

"Finneran! Now there's another one of them!"

The only way to throw the bums out, I tell him, is to have another bunch of bums to put in, at least for a while.

He laughs at that and takes my bookmark, and then, feeling encouraged, I ask if he'd distribute some doorhangers inside, at the doors of those who might be receptive.

"I'd be glad to!"

You can't ask for better than that. I was ahead for the day and ready to quit.

★ ★ ★ Back at the house, I got an e-mail from Fred Baker with three possible dates for our fund-raiser at Ryles in Inman Square. I called the lieutenant governor's State House office to find out which of them might be convenient for her. The aide there said that she couldn't be having this conversation and I'd have to go through the party office on Merrimac Street. Those are the people I'd asked more than a month ago and who never got back to me. I called, and Tim O'Brien wasn't in, and St. Hilaire wasn't in. I called Michelle O'Connor, Kerry Healey's finance director, whom I had met at a candidate's fund-raiser some months ago. She told me I had to go through St. Hilaire but offered to get a message to him and have him call me.

This began to seem . . . difficult. I asked her whether the lieutenant governor was booked on the three dates that Fred had offered me. No. I remembered Healey's remark at breakfast about how she and Governor Romney would be going to fund-raisers all through September and October, and I realized that these had already been scheduled. So my request had not necessarily been ignored, but their silence might be an answer.

Another sudden connection: at a certain point in her remarks, Lieutenant Governor Healy had referred to the great number of candidates the party was putting up this fall, and she had read off a list of names, from which mine was missing. I wasn't pleased but attributed it to inefficiency or inadvertence. Later on, after Edwards's talk, Governor Romney had asked if any candidates had been omitted from Healey's list. Two of us raised our hands, and he invited us to say who we were.

Mistakes happen. But when there is a pattern, then there can be a sense that they are not mistakes after all but significant, as Freud found some lapses could be.

A wave of despair. They think I can't win. I'm not worth half an hour of the lieutenant governor's time! And they are politicians, so they don't want to spell that out for me. They allow me to suppose whatever I like but are not responsible for my assumptions.

But at the governor's book signing, hadn't Healey and I talked about this? What had I said? That I had discussed a fund-raiser with Tim O'Brien at which she would be appearing and that I was grateful for her help. "I'm glad to do it," she had said, which I translated to, "I will appear" but which actually meant,

"If they set it up and I am scheduled to, I will be glad to do it, or at least will say so, because that's my job."

We're back at Versailles, where some poor son-of-a-bitch nobleman from Anjou comes up to get some help with a swamp-draining project and spends a fortune on clothing and wigs and goes to parties where he can meet the Marquis de Quelquechose, who can introduce him to the mistress of the Duc d'Inconnu, whose illegitimate brother is the appropriate minister. Only these days the players are less stylish.

What do I do? Quit? Or at least pull back, stop these strenuous efforts, and be as realistic about my chances as are the party functionaries on Merrimac Street? That would be quitting without announcing it and would be a deceit of my contributors. But then, they are not fools either, and I wonder if any of them have expectations of my winning in November. I'm having fun, they think, and they are indulging me.

So what if Kerry Healy does not come to a fund-raiser? How much would we take in, after all the work of organizing and promoting the event, inviting Cambridge Republicans, and making the up-front investment in hors d'oeuvres and the bartender's fee? Say that it cost the campaign six hundred dollars and that we got a thousand, which would be a lot. It would be a lot of work and worry for four hundred dollars or so.

None of that changes the fact that I feel betrayed. The party asked me to run, knowing I had no chance. The party wanted to be able to say that they had fielded 130 candidates and that Romney was a leader of a great reform movement. I accepted, well aware that the odds were against me. But in return for my time and my efforts, don't they owe me at least the candor of straight answers when I ask for an appearance by the lieutenant governor? Don't they owe me the courtesy of returning my telephone calls?

I have been dealing with publishers for more than forty years, and after such experiences with liars, hypocrites, boors, and crooks, I should be inured to churlishness, but apparently I am not. Should I be proud of these tatters of innocence?

★ ★ ★ An e-mail from Joshua, my younger son, references a page of the online *Harvard Gazette* and says, "Yay, you! See link below." I click and find a picture of myself and Mayor Sullivan at the Harvard Yard picnic. Not quite enough to restore my spirits, it reminds me that, at moments, campaigning is almost fun.

★ ★ ★ No one at the state party office has replied to my phone messages. The nonparanoid take on it would be that they haven't replied to Evan's messages either, and as counsel to the party, he could be calling to tell them that the governor's hair is on fire. Evan says that they are busy with meetings. Still, even though I am not even sure I want a fund-raiser with Healey's appearance, I am annoyed that a Thursday afternoon message isn't answered on Friday and that it will be Monday before anyone gets back to me.

Meanwhile, I have evidence that, despite his absence at the Harvard Yard picnic, Green is still campaigning. A flier in my mailbox invites me to meet Avi Green at the home of Eric Weltman and Sarah Bennett, 97A Inman St. Cambridge. It says:

> Avi green is a progressive Democrat
> running to represent our neighborhood in the legislature.
> He is a strong advocate of mass transit, human rights,
> a woman's right-to-choose, and funding
> for education, health care, & affordable housing.
> He is challenging an ally of Tom Finneran,
> the autocratic House Speaker.

The primary is a month from tomorrow.

★ ★ ★ Whatever my private inclinations, I can't just quit. If I were to do so and make public my complaints about the indifference of the party and their lack of support, it would make a terrible stink. If Romney should quit—either to run for Senator Kerry's seat or to take some Washington job in a second Bush administration—then Kerry Healey would become acting governor, and she and Evan are friendly. I can't embarrass my son.

The other side of that coin is that if I really want Healey to appear at a fund-raiser, Evan can probably arrange it. But I'm not sure that I do. I had lunch on Wednesday with a classmate and a friend of his at the Harvard Square Legal Sea Foods. It was a civilized hour or so, and then each of them sent me a check. I shall deposit their contributions today, and it's a much more agreeable way to get three hundred dollars than to work like crazy to provide a crowd for Kerry Healey, who can then say nice things about me.

Come to think of it, she *has* said nice things about me. When I take newspaper ads in October, I can say: "If you're elected, you'll be the smartest guy on Beacon Hill. —Lieutenant Governor Kerry Healey." She never told me I couldn't use it.

★ ★ ★ I had coffee with Evan, who was reassuring and reliably shrewd. He allayed my worries about the party, the indifference of which is not, he claimed, calculated. They are simply in some disarray. Since Dominick Ianno left as executive director, the party has been struggling, Evan told me, and his evidence for this was the appearance here in Boston of such a stellar figure as former New York City Republican mayor Rudolph Giuliani during the Democratic convention. The event was badly mismanaged. A large number of people showed up to see Giuliani and the room was too small. It was a mess. Even if Healey is booked solid for September, Evan says he can get through and arrange an appearance in October, if I decide I want one. Of course, it is ridiculous to take comfort in the fact that the party organization is . . . disorganized.

It is raining today, so I have an excuse for not going out on a Sunday afternoon. I am like a not-very-bright kid in school rejoicing at a snow day.

★ ★ ★ A letter from the office of the mayor of Cambridge:

Dear David:

I would like to thank you for attending the 29th Annual Harvard Senior Picnic on August 4, 2004.

I would also like to extend my congratulations to you on being one of our raffle prizewinners. Enclosed please find a gift certificate for Dinner for 2 at Frank's Steak House.

I look forward to seeing you next year at this memorable event.

Sincerely,
Michael

Michael A. Sullivan, Mayor

And of course there is the gift certificate. To get the invitation I thought I needed to get into the Harvard Yard picnic, I had gone to the Senior Center on Massachusetts Avenue, where they took my name and address and I was entered for the drawings for the prizes. A cheerful omen. I have written the mayor to thank him.

The Honorable Michael A. Sullivan
Mayor of Cambridge
795 Massachusetts Avenue
Cambridge, MA 02139

Dear Michael:

Many thanks both for the gift certificate to Frank's Steak House, and for your friendliness in posing with me for the photographer from the *Harvard*

Gazette. I am learning to believe a little in omens and auguries, and I am heartened by these extraordinary signs of good fortune.

I know that as a Democrat you cannot endorse me, but you have been doing as much for me as any Republican could ask for, and I am deeply grateful. I admire your leadership of the city, and I shall raise a glass to you (alcoholic beverages are not included in the gift certificate) at Frank's to wish you well.

I look forward, too, to next year's picnics, perhaps even as one of the incumbents.

With kindest regards,
David

★ ★ ★ After all that shtuss, I heard from St. Hilaire this afternoon (Monday, returning Thursday's call), with satisfactory news—that the lieutenant governor will come to my fund-raiser at Ryles on September 27. He also sent the guidelines for events with the governor or lieutenant governor:

The Governor is looking forward to attending a fundraising event for your campaign committee. In order to have the smoothest event possible, these guidelines should help to organize your event.

—Do not publicly advertise your event. Invitations, e-mails and other methods of notification that are distributed to lists are fine. Public notification (newspaper advertisements, fliers, etc.) is not acceptable.

—The event is closed to the press. Please do not notify the press of your event prior to it taking place. Private photographers are welcome so long as they are restricted to candid, non-posed photographs.

—Please provide a podium and amplified sound system for the speakers at your event. If the audience will be standing, please put the podium in an elevated position of some kind so that all guests may see the speakers.

—The Governor will arrive approximately thirty minutes past the start time of your event giving all guests the chance to arrive and get comfortable. The speaking program will begin immediately after the Governor arrives. We suggest having an individual who will introduce you briefly (no more than one minute). As part of your remarks, we suggest you mention other dignitaries and elected officials that you would like to recognize or thank for attending your event. At the close of your remarks, you will introduce the Governor. A very simple, one or two-line introduction would be perfect.

After the Governor speaks, he will spend some time mingling with guests. While he will spend as much time as his calendar will allow, please be aware that the Governor frequently has further commitments at night and may not be able to meet all of your guests.

Please do not make any arrangements for the Governor for parking, building entrances, etc. The logistical aspects of the Governor's visit will be handled by his office.

If you have any questions or concerns, please don't hesitate to give me a call at XXX.

I am glad that it is more than a month away. There is a lot to do organizing Cambridge and Somerville Republicans or those from out of the district, for that matter, and getting them to come out for something like this. It will be interesting to see how many of those precinct captains and volunteers I can get actually to do something, making phone calls and beating the bushes. . . .

13

★ ★

I read this morning that the legislature has advanced that antiloitering bill, acting on the home-rule petition that Somerville presented in order to combat MS-13 and other gangs. It allows the police to order known gang members to disperse and subjects them to fines or imprisonment if they return within three hours to any place within three hundred yards of the area from which the police ordered them away. The ACLU hates it because of its vagueness and because it leaves much to the discretion of the police. Other opponents have objected to it because it might disproportionately affect minority groups. Put in clearer terms, these people are suggesting that because Salvadoran gangs are Hispanic they should be immune to police action, which would inevitably be discriminatory.

The original impetus for this legislation is that MS-13 gangsters committed a couple of rapes in Foss Park in Somerville in October of 2002. And our legislators have been dicking around with this legal language for almost two years! (Do I want to have anything to do with these people?)

Jarrett Barrios, chairman of the Senate's Public Safety Committee, says that he opposes the bill because it does not address the root cause of the problems, and, like Green, he wants more community programs and social workers. But even though he is against the bill, his spokesman said that he will not block its passage.

He makes Senator Kerry look positively decisive.

★ ★ ★ I had an interesting lunch with an old friend who asked, assuming that Toomey beats Green, what are the chances of getting Green to endorse me? Well, Green claims to be a loyal Democrat, but he's as anti-Finneran as I am. And at my age, I'm unlikely to serve for more than a term or two. I'd be holding Green's place for him, or I could promise him that, anyway. Would that be enough to whet his appetite for a Republican?

I can have Fred Baker sound him out after the primary. Who knows what's likely to happen? And there may be things he can do to help, short of endorsing me publicly, that would sway a few votes or raise a few dollars. It is an interesting notion. Just as I'd rather run for an open seat, Green, in 2006 or 2008, would rather run for an open seat, presumably against Toomey, who would have the stigma of having been beaten by me.

★ ★ ★ I discovered, at nine in the morning, that there was a seniors' picnic in Somerville at Powerderhouse Park—in two hours. Janet had the car, so I called MBTA to ask how to get to Powderhouse Square (two buses, changing at Harvard Square, but still, with a transfer and as a senior, it is only a quarter). I filled up a couple of pouches with flyswatters, put on my Romney-Healey hat and my Slavitt for State Rep sticker, and skedaddled. It took a little less than an hour (by car it would have been fifteen minutes). All the oldsters were sitting at long trestle tables waiting for the entertainment and the free lunch. I worked the rows of tables, handing out flyswatters, asking people if they were in Ward One or Ward Two but not pressing too hard if they really wanted one. It took me three-quarters of an hour to hand out 180 or so. I decided to hang around a little longer to meet Mayor Curtatone, to greet Toomey, and to see if Green would show up.

It was only then that I learned from one of Sheriff James DiPaola's people that distribution of fliers and tchotchkes was not permitted. What kind of nut rule is that? I asked the DiPaola worker who was in charge of the picnic and she referred me to Cindy Hickey of the Council on Aging. Ms. Hickey confirmed that distribution of campaign materials was not permitted, because, as she said, "This is a social event."

I asked a cop—there were a good half dozen standing around, lest the elderly of Somerville turn rowdy—whether Mayor Curtatone was present, and one of them pointed out a slender, dark-haired young man not twenty feet from me. He was picking up a two-year-old as I approached him. He confirmed what Ms. Hickey had said but added, as if he were doing me a favor, "But you're welcome to go around and introduce yourself."

I did that for a while, saw Toomey, who was as affable as usual and who had his aide take a couple of photographs of us standing together, but didn't see Green. Then I packed it in, took my empty pouches back to Cambridge, and dashed off a press release:

The David Slavitt Committee
35 West Street, #5
Cambridge, MA 02139

David R. Slavitt, Republican candidate for State Representative in the 16th Middlesex District, made an appearance at the Somerville Senior Citizen's Picnic in Powderhouse Park today (August 18, 2004), to greet voters and hand out the flyswatters he distributed recently at the Cambridge Seniors' Picnic in Harvard Yard.

He passed out 180 of these, targeting the voters in the First and Second Wards in which he is running against either Representative Tim Toomey or his challenger in the Democrats' primary, Avi Green. It was only after he had distributed all the flyswatters that learned that such distribution of political materials is forbidden. Cindy Hickey, Director of the Somerville Council on Aging which sponsored the picnic, told him that this was a "social event, not a political one," and said that while he was invited to introduce himself to the citizens of Somerville, it was not permitted to hand out materials.

As Slavitt said to the *Somerville News*, "This of course was a violation of my free speech rights. If I introduce myself to these people, that is political and not social, and my flyswatters, which say 'Republican Swat Team: David R. Slavitt 26th Middlesex District," are political speech and therefore constitutionally protected and privileged."

Slavitt then introduced himself to Somerville Mayor Joe Curtatone. "He was," Slavitt reports, "actually kissing a baby at the moment I walked up to him, but reality often imitates bad novels." Mayor Curtatone said Ms Hickey was correct. "But in Cambridge, one can hand out such trinkets," Slavitt protested. "Why not in Somerville? Is Somerville cleaner or purer?"

"Better," Mayor Curtatone replied, with a forced smile.

"Not better for civil rights," Slavitt says is what he managed not to say.

"We've been doing it this way for twenty-five years," Mayor Curtatone added.

"This is what Stalin could have claimed, but that doesn't make it right," Slavitt told the *Somerville News*. "If I'd been younger, I would have tried to get myself arrested and dragged off, just so I could make the point in a courtroom that this is outrageous. It violates our rights as Americans—

which extend even to Somerville. The city's politicians ought to be ashamed of themselves."

It wasn't inadvertence. According to Alderman White, with whom I spoke on the phone later that afternoon, there used to be a Somerville ordinance prohibiting political signs. Eventually, some candidate took the city to court and got that thrown out as unconstitutional and, indeed, crazy. This prohibition about distributing materials at the picnics is not a law, though, White explained. "It's just a gentleman's agreement."

Why is it that "gentleman's agreement" is the term for people conspiring to behave illegally and unconstitutionally, whether it has to do with selling property to blacks and Jews or with politicos who want to discourage challengers?

★ ★ ★ An e-mail from Shira Schoenberg of the *Jewish Advocate* informs me that they're doing an issue about political candidates. She wants to interview me and asks that I respond to some questions that she includes. These are the questions and my answers:

From: Community News [mailto:communitynews@thejewishadvocate.com]
Sent: Wednesday, August 18, 2004 12:23 PM
To: David R Slavitt
Subject: Re: greetings

Dear David,

I hope your campaign is progressing well. We just decided to run a political issue next week, and would like to profile you. If it is ok with you, we would like to do a question and answer, then a profile. I am attaching a number of questions to the bottom of this e-mail, which I would ask you to answer in writing, in under 100 words each. I would also like to set up a time, maybe Thursday or Friday, to do a short interview, either in Boston or Cambridge. Let me know what would be most convenient for you. I'm looking forward to speaking with you.

Thank you,
Shira

—Shira Schoenberg
Community News Editor
The Jewish Advocate

1. What will you do to make healthcare and medicine more affordable for senior citizens?

Realistically, there is little a first-term legislator can do to make healthcare more affordable. The present system is set up in such a way that bills must be filed in mid-December, while legislators are not sworn in until early January. My campaign is more strategic than tactical. I believe that a two-party system works better if there are two parties in it. The Democrats are hostages to the nurses' unions and want to enact legislative requirements that look as though they would result in better patient care but do not take into account the realities of life in hospitals, in which a nurse in a burn unit, say, takes care of fewer patients than one on an obstetrical floor. I'd resist such legislative pandering to the demands of the unions. The nursing shortage cannot be solved by legislative fiat anyway. And doctors and administrators share the same goals as nurses and patients have: everyone wants the best possible care delivered in the most economical way.

2. Are you in favor of increasing tax credits to promote building affordable housing?

The best way to provide more affordable housing is to relax some of the regulations that discourage builders and landlords. If rooming house operators had the same privileges as those who run shelters (to throw out disorderly tenants or those who cause damage to the property), we'd have a solution to the homelessness problem. The social engineering of the Democrats works toward a utopia at the expense of those of us who live in the here-and-now.

My answer to your specific question would depend on considerable study (what are the tax credits now available? What would be the requirements for builders to qualify for them?). The devil is in the details, and I'd have to look at these.

3. With a state deficit, what should be done to ensure the safety net for the Commonwealth's most vulnerable, in terms of social services?

Our tax revenues are now running at three-quarters of a billion dollars ahead of projections for 2004. I favor Governor Romney's proposal to return about half of that to the taxpayers. This is particularly important in the light of the referendum of only a few years ago in which the voters asked for a roll-back to 5% in our state tax rate. Speaker Finneran (with 7600 votes in

Mattapan) obstructs the will of the voters and the efforts of the Governor (with 1,100,000 votes state-wide) on our behalf.

Again, the details of your question are vague and require specifics. What social services are you asking about? At what level are they now being provided? I am against suffering and hardship, but I am also against theft from the taxpayers in the name of the needy.

4. Should the state government amend the Constitution for same-sex marriage?

Absolutely not. In 1783, Chief Justice of the Supreme Judicial Court William Cushing ended slavery, finding that the Massachusetts constitution, declaring all men to have been created equal, prohibited it. He was not overreaching but doing the work that the SJC ought to do. Likewise, Chief Justice Margaret Marshall was correct in the Goodridge case, protecting the rights of a minority against the prejudices of the majority. Homosexual acts are no longer illegal in this country, and there is no rational reason for discriminating against a class of citizens only because the religious right finds them worrisome.

5. How would you ensure the success of children's education?

I am in favor of Charter Schools and opposed to the cap on those schools that the Democrats tried to impose. There, again, the Democrats showed themselves to be stooges of the teachers' unions. Having taught at Princeton, Columbia, Penn, and elsewhere, I know how hard it is to educate youngsters. It takes passion and commitment, not a collective resistance to change. Principals should be able to fire incompetent teachers and promote those who show initiative and have success in the classroom. The unions find this unfair. Education is unfair—which is why there are grades. Some are smarter than others, or work harder than others, and some are lazier and duller. But the entire undertaking presumes that merit will be rewarded and promoted. And those who get in the way should get out of the way.

The questions are earnest, boring, and pretty much irrelevant. Perhaps at the interview there will be a more general discussion, in which I can make a coherent pitch. We are to meet at Carberry's this afternoon.

★ ★ ★ The interview went well, I think, although I won't be able to tell until the piece comes out. She is very young, the ink just barely dry on her college degree (from Columbia). This is her first job. I managed gracefully to move from the discussion of "issues" to the realities of the political situation in Massachusetts and the need for a healthy opposition party, if only to keep the majority party honest.

Honesty turns out to be a not at all irrelevant issue. An article in the *Herald*, a couple of days after my interview with Ms. Schoenberg, reported that Speaker Finneran's report to the Office of Campaign and Political Finance shows some astonishing expenditures—and a grand total of $382,484 for last year. "Among the major items was $24,000 for Web site design work, $52,926 on trips to Hawaii, Italy, Las Vegas, Biscayne, Florida, and Washington, DC" (the last seems plausible, but what political business could he have in Italy, Hawaii, or Florida?). He apparently put his car lease ($6,000) and automobile insurance ($4,460) on the campaign's charge card. As the *Herald* article says, "The rules ban spending on items that are 'primarily for the candidate's personal use.'" Finneran's spokesman called the *Herald* story "a hatchet job."

Well, the numbers are the numbers, and Finneran seems to have set them up himself. Some jobs call for a hatchet.

★ ★ ★ A phone call from Temple Beth Shalom on Tremont Street tells me that the candidates' night is canceled. Representative Toomey turns out to be busy on September 7, and the message never got through to him. Given the size of his staff, that's not inconceivable, but it seems likelier to me that he has decided to bail out. Green and Slavitt, two nice Jewish boys, will be on home turf. Toomey, from the Sacred Heart Parish, might feel at a disadvantage. If this is the real reason, then Toomey is worried about Green (the primary is September 14, a week after the date that had been set for our joint appearance).

This is good news. If Green wins and Toomey's party faithful stay home on Election Day, I've got a better shot than I had any right to expect.

★ ★ ★ A postcard came in to Janet, inviting her to a fund-raiser for Green at which Robert Reich will be appearing. Impressive! And I should think, to Toomey, a bit threatening. A big gun, and a real draw for contributions. Former Secretary of Labor Reich wasn't able to get himself the Democratic nomination for governor, but he put up a respectable showing, and his endorsement of Green is likely to be persuasive to leftish voters in the district.

I'd been worrying about Avi, not having seen him at the Harvard Yard or the Powderhouse Park picnics. It may be, though, that he'll win the nomination, and I'll be worrying about him in other ways.

★ ★ ★ And from the Toomey camp, also addressed to Janet (which means that this has gone out to every Democrat and to every unenrolled voter in the district), an expensively produced mail piece in four colors announcing:

Fighting for our Values
State Rep. Tim Toomey is Fighting for us!

Underneath that, he has the four areas in which he has been fighting: public education, women's rights, human rights, and gun control. Women's rights? On the back, his explanation is that "over the last two fiscal years, Tim Toomey led the legislative fight to restore over $6 million in funding for family planning services and rape crisis centers throughout the Commonwealth." This is as much as a pro-life guy can claim, but it requires that the voter be awake to notice what's missing.

The "Fighting for Human Rights" turns out to be Toomey's votes against the constitutional amendment banning gay marriage. But he doesn't want to say that (it would turn away some voters). He doesn't even allude to the issue. All he says is that "Tim Toomey was one of only 12 legislators who voted consistently this year to extend the same rights and benefits under state law to all citizens of the Commonwealth." Who could be against that? (Almost half the voters, so he couches it in these artful terms.)

There are pictures of big shots endorsing him: Congressmen Barney Frank and Mike Capuano, Somerville mayor Joseph Curtatone, Cambridge city councillors Denise Simmons and Ken Reeves, and Cambridge vice mayor Marjorie Decker. Oddly, there is not a picture of Toomey himself, but then he looks a little like a serving of corned beef with hair on the top.

I must work up a mailing for late in October to all the Republican and Unenrolled voters, or even to all the registered voters in the district. Pricey, but after the costs of the newspaper ads, we'll see how much we have left and spend it all. The chances of my being able to go off to Hawaii or Italy on campaign business are not great.

★ ★ ★ In an idle moment, I found myself wondering what kind of nifty website Speaker Finneran must have, after spending $24,000 on it. It's an extravagance for someone running unopposed and should be interesting to see. But "Thomas M. Finneran" found only the official website he gets as a state rep—and it has one speech on it, but nothing special, no bells or whistles. "Finneran Campaign"? Or "Re-elect Finneran"? These turn up only articles from the *Globe*, postings from Common Cause, or a story from the *Weekly Dig* about his abuses of power and dishonest testimony before the federal judges last spring. A fictional website, then? Go know.

★ ★ ★ In fact it is www.tomfinneran.com and is fairly impressive. It has a lot of pulldowns and is available in English, Spanish, Kreyol, and Vietnamese. It has RealAudio interviews—with Finneran's appearance on NPR's the *News-Hour* with Ray Suarez—and all kinds of interactivity. It has a slideshow of the Twelfth Suffolk District. Although it is largely a vanity operation, it is a model of what you can do with a website.

★ ★ ★ It is the last week of August and the tasks ahead are formidable, but at least they are coming clear. I have to arrange for ads in the *Cambridge Chronicle* and the *Somerville Journal*, both of which are owned by the *Boston Herald*. And I'll have to take out an ad in the *Somerville News*, which is a give-away paper but a good one and has been good to me. We'll also have to have at least one mailing to voters in the district. I have only a vague idea of how much each of these efforts will cost. (A quarter page in the *Cambridge Chronicle* is $859, or, if I pay a 25 percent premium for favorable placement—on page 3 or 5—then it's $1,073.) We also have that fund-raiser at Ryles on September 27, about which I have been worrying. Will we get enough people so that the lieutenant governor won't be displeased? Will we make back our $500 investment? We've got about $3,400 in the account now. The three ads and the mailing would wipe that out and even push us into the red. (I can give only $500 to the campaign but can lend it more.)

My visit to the gun nuts down in Braintree on Wednesday looks to be more important as I face these fiscal demands. Having no very strong views either way, I feel uncomfortable about saying sympathetic things to the gun owners in order to get money out of them. But then where is it written that political life ought to be comfortable?

There will also be another debate, or at least I hope so, between me and whichever candidate the Democrats choose in their primary—almost certainly Toomey. And I must start to shake the trees to try to get more media attention. Mr. Jonas of the *Globe* said that he was interested in doing something, but I'll believe it when I read it.

★ ★ ★ According to the papers, there is an organization called Support-Equality.org that is funneling money to candidates against the amendment to limit marriage. The trouble is that both Green and Toomey have positions that are the same as mine, and these gay rights people will put their money into races where they can make a difference. What is interesting, though, is that the report in the *Globe* finds that same-sex marriage is not a huge issue. A number of pollsters report that many candidates are simply avoiding the issue for fear of alienating voters on either side. The parties aren't saying much either. According to a Suffolk University poll taker, only 5 percent of voters say that gay marriage is important in this election, and of those half are in favor and half are opposed.

This does not mean that I have been wrong, though, because the political and ideological topography of Cambridge is farther to the left than most of the Commonwealth. A Republican has to run toward the center to have any chance. Fortunately, my personal views happen to coincide with political expediency here. But as a citizen, I'm happy to read how things are going: I doubt that even our watered-down amendment (defining marriage as male-female but requiring the authorization of same-sex civil unions) has much chance of passing next year.

★ ★ ★ Justin Kaplan and Anne Bernays are going to have a wine and cheese reception for me in September, which is generous of them, inasmuch as they are Democrats. But they are also friends, and friendship trumps politics. What I like about this is that I don't have to do anything or worry about what the turnout is. They'll invite some of their friends, and Janet and I will show up, and I'll be charming and maybe get some donations. If their guests are generous, I can take a half-page ad in the *Somerville News.*

★ ★ ★ An e-mail from the party headquarters:

From: Kelly Sullivan
Sent: Thursday, August 19, 2004 5:42 PM
To: Tim O'Brien; Alex Dunn
Cc: 'victory@matgauvin.com'; Andrew Goodrich; Matt St. Hilaire
Subject: CONFERENCE CALL AUGUST 25th

Hello Everyone—

This e-mail is to inform everyone of an IMPORTANT conference call that will be taking place Wednesday, August 25th, at 8:00 PM. The purpose of this call is to discuss the statewide campaign that we have planned for this fall. CANDIDATES ONLY will be allowed on this call. If you would like other people from your team to be included, they will need to be on the same phone line. To partake in this call, please call 1-888-275-9159, and reference Code # 9607555, and Alex Dunn's name. You will only be let in to the call if you are on a pre-approved list, and the only people on this list are candidates.

This is an extremely important call and Alex Dunn, Tim O'Brien, Matt St. Hilaire, Mat Gauvin and Andrew Goodrich look forward to speaking with you all on Wednesday.

Thank You,

Kelly Sullivan
Massachusetts Republican Party

My first reaction was annoyance, because I am committed to the gun toters for the time they specify. And having participated in one of these conference calls already, I am bothered by their high-tech officiousness. There are no subjects that can't be covered by e-mail. But they feel powerful to have a "pre-approved list" and a reference code.

I call the party offices on Monday morning, just after nine, to speak with Ms. Sullivan to find out whether Evan do the call for me—he's the counsel to the party, after all, and can be privy to whatever secrets they are imparting. She is in a meeting. Is Matt St. Hilaire available then? Or Alex Dunn? They are all in the same meeting, I am told. So I leave a message on Ms. Sullivan's voice mail. And wait. And go about my business. Late in the afternoon, I realize that she hasn't ever called back. I call again, wondering what the hell these people think they're doing. All these meetings and voice-mail machines, and conference calls don't mean a thing if the candidates can't get through to them in a reasonable time.

She can't answer my question about Evan and transfers me to Matt, who says, of course, that it's fine. It shouldn't have taken a whole day to get that information.

★ ★ ★ In front of the house, I found a Toomey doorhanger someone had thrown away. (It's good, I guess, that somebody threw it away! That suggests a lack of enthusiasm.) The doorhanger is impressive for its weasely cleverness. It is large, 15 inches high by 6 wide, and the front of it shows the TOOMEY name on a slight rising slant, not unlike my own signs and labels. He has not done this before, and imitation is a kind of flattery. But the impressive part is the large format, which allows him to turn the bottom 4½ inches into a detachable, self-addressed postcard. You just tear at the perforation, and fill out a questionnaire that asks about extending the Green Line, expanding the recycling program to include liquor and water bottles, and whether cops should be able to stop drivers for not wearing seat belts. Nowhere does it say what Toomey's positions are on these questions. All it suggests is that he cares, or that if you care, he might care.

Only a moron would suppose that these results will be tallied in any scientific way and that Toomey will then take the positions that most of his constituents hold. He has a question about devoting one cent of the sales tax to education, but "One penny for education" is a weighted phrase. Who would be so mean as to begrudge the little children a penny? That it works out to a fifth of the entire take of the state sales tax and turns out to be a very great many pennies indeed is left to those of us who can count beyond ten without taking our shoes off.

But the main message is that he cares, is listening, and wants to know what you think. Even if you don't send back the postcard (which will cost you a stamp), you know you could have done so, and how can you not like the guy for wanting to hear from you?

★ ★ ★ I woke up this morning worried about going down to the Gun Owners' Political Action Committee's "Freedom Tour 2004" meeting in Braintree. My subconscious had translated my ambivalence into simpler, more dramatic terms, so that I was worrying about the traffic on the Southeast Expressway at rush hour. It is, indeed, fearsome, but what I'm worried about is the appearance itself with those bazooka lovers who like to kill things and conceive that that is one of their civil rights. But I need the money. My campaign is facing a lot of necessary expenditures, and I have even thought of another one. We'll need a place to get together on Election Night to watch the returns together—maybe at the bar of the S&S, the deli across the street from Ryles. (They're both owned by the same people.)

I'll have my cell phone and Toomey's number so that I can call him and concede. And I'll thank my supporters for their hard work. What was it that Adlai Stevenson said, quoting Lincoln? "I'm too old to cry but it hurts too much to laugh."

On the other hand, I ought to be mildly encouraged, because yesterday's canvassing was relatively successful. I was deep in the heart of Toomeytown, over on Fulkerson, south of Cambridge Street, within a couple of blocks of his campaign office, his parish church, and his house. My expectations, therefore, were modest. But everyone I talked to was polite and some were actually encouraging. "We need a change. He's been in there too long," was what several of them said. And I found one or two Republicans who thought my appearance was almost miraculous. If that small sample is significant, then he is in trouble in his home precinct, and my efforts are not hopeless.

None of that makes my trip to the gun owners any more appealing. I can amuse myself by telling some of them about a review in this week's *Times Literary Supplement* of *Kandahar Cockney*, a book about a transplanted Afghan who lives in England, working as a security guard and operating a pizza restaurant. James Fergusson, the author, takes Mir, his subject, to visit at Brasenose College at Oxford and invites him to shooting parties in the country. Mir thinks it is unsportsmanlike to shoot ducks with shotguns. Back in Afghanistan, he insists, they use Kalashnikovs, which takes skill. Kalashnikovs, I think, are not legal here. (Or I hope they are not.)

⋆ ⋆ ⋆ Having sent a check for a thousand dollars as a deposit for the ads in the *Chronicle* and the *Journal*, I am now wondering what to put in the space. The basic message is that the two-party system needs two parties in order to function properly. It is tempting to try to say more than will conveniently fit into a quarter-page ad, or more than can be absorbed by a casual reader whose eyes skim across the copy in a matter of seconds before he or she turns the page.

The website home page is at least a place to start. Its design is eye-catching enough to arrest the flighty attention of a newspaper's casual reader (who, on page three, will not yet be fatigued). I can also use something much like that on my mailing. There are probably 3,500 households in my district, and the mailings will cost about fifty-five to sixty cents apiece, so we're looking at another two thousand dollars.

So I will have to be nice to these gun guys, remember that they are not "weapons" but "firearms," and keep quiet about Mir's views on bird shooting.

⋆ ⋆ ⋆ The worst part was getting there. I'd decided to play it ultrasafe and allow myself an hour and a half to get 16¼ miles (which Mapquest told me ought to take twenty-four minutes). But it was stop-and-go driving from the Longfellow Bridge to Storrow Drive, and then through that multibillion-dollar Big Dig tunnel. I felt less in danger than at other times—when people in Beamers come roaring through at sixty—but it was frustrating as my margin dwindled down to what a reasonable person might have allowed, and then, as I crawled along and into Milton and Quincy, I realized I would actually be late.

The Braintree Rifle and Pistol Club is a forbidding enclave that used to be out in the woods in the middle of nowhere but with prosperity now finds itself in the armpit of Liberty Woods, an upscale development. You drive into the Liberty Woods entrance and then, at the rotary, take a sharp right and go until you reach a gate with Private Property! Keep Out! signs, which make sense, after all, if they are firing weapons there. Or firearms. The gate was open, and I found a group of unformidable, mostly elderly men and women eating rigatoni and meatballs and drinking canned sodas at long trestle tables while Mike Jones, the Republican candidate for Bill Delahunt's Tenth District seat in Congress, talked about the shortcomings of his opponent (who is far to the left and doesn't work very hard) and of the Democrats generally. (Jones worked for the Republican National Committee during the Bush-Gore election, was in charge of the absentee votes of the military, and had scandalous stories to tell about Gore's people getting many of those ballots disqualified for lack of postmarks—which APO mail doesn't have—or simply destroying them by emptying watercooler bottles into the mail sacks.)

He was an energetic speaker and had the shootists with him, particularly when he spoke of Delahunt's vote to prevent the application of the death penalty to bin Laden, to placate the French. His audience stopped eating and applauded. Red meat!

So when I was introduced, I knew more or less what to say and how to approach them. No jokes about duck hunting with Kalashnikovs. No jokes at all, in fact. I gestured to the service flags up on the wall behind me and, pointing to that of the U.S. Coast Guard, said it was a particular privilege to be standing beneath it. I told them about Isaac, my grandson, who had just completed swab summer and has begun classes at the Coast Guard Academy. I then told them that I am the Republican candidate for state rep in Cambridge and Somerville and that it is not a joke, because I have a chance of winning if enough of the supporters of whichever Democrat loses the primary are disaffected and don't vote for the man who beat him.

I told them Evan's theory about the guerrilla campaign, and how we can do things more cheaply than would be possible if we were in Leominster or Harwich. But I said I still need money for the ads in the local newspapers and for a mailing just before the election. Jones had mentioned the $4,000 limit on contributions to a congressional campaign. I said that the limit for my campaign is $500, but that $50 would be a great help and that contributions of $25 or even $10 add up. I left a pile of envelopes, and some bookmarks. (I worried about the bookmarks—these did not seem to be a crowd of readers, and the bookmarks have "Supports Same-Sex Marriage" and "Pro-Choice" on them, which are probably not the majority views here. Still, some of these geezers may be grown-ups and understand what it takes to run in Cambridge, never mind win.)

There was one more candidate, but Jones hadn't thought it necessary to hang around to listen to me, so I figured it would not seem rude if I took my leave also. I walked outside into the quiet suburb, taking only the most theoretical reassurance that, if terrorists should threaten Braintree, the members of the Braintree Rifle and Pistol Club would be ready to defend their hearths and homes.

★ ★ ★ There is a disturbing piece by Louis Menand in the new *New Yorker*, "The Unpolitical Animal," which talks about the political theoreticians, who seem to have the same weird relationship to politics as literary theoreticians have to literature. The current thinking, according to a number of books and articles he cites, is that the public's take on political decisions and on candidates is at best impressionistic, and often incoherent. Philip Converse, in "The Nature of Belief Systems in Mass Publics," points out that voters' beliefs display what he calls a "lack of constraint," which is to say that they don't connect a particular opinion (such as wanting lower taxes) with its inevitable consequence (they also want more government programs and entitlements). Their beliefs are also not deeply felt, for when the same question is asked in different ways, poll takers get contradictory answers (only about a quarter of the respondents to a couple of polls in the eighties thought too little was being spent on welfare, while two-thirds thought that too little was being spent on assisting the poor: and it wasn't the math that was wacky but the voters).

I was depressed but not surprised as I read through this account of why the entire system makes no sense, for I have learned these things in my day-to-day encounters with prospective voters. And I have adjusted to the sad truth that I'm not so much talking to voters as I am manipulating their prejudices and appealing to mental shortcuts that would be contemptible in any other area of intellectual life.

Apparently, these shortcuts are called "heuristics," which is a fancy term that gives these kinds of sloppy thinking a seriousness and even a respectability they do not deserve. President Ford, for example, tried to eat a tamale with the corn husk on it, and this gaffe made the papers and probably lost him much of the Mexican-American vote. According to Samuel Popkins's "low-informational rationality" theory, the Mexican-Americans were "justified in concluding that a man who did not know how to eat a tamale was not a man predisposed to put their needs high on his list." As Menand points out, "Ford was not running for chef."

Well, yes, of course, but I am now experienced enough in politics to understand how the simplistic views of high school civics classes don't apply and probably never did. My discomfort, though, is as valuable as my understanding, for when a politician no longer chafes at the stupidity of what he is doing or regrets or resents having to pander to the electorate—as is the case, I suspect, with Finneran—he has lost most of his value as a player in the game. In advertising and mass media, those tatters of refinement are useless baggage, but in politics, they are the valuable cargo, the purpose of the whole enterprise.

★ ★ ★ The substance of the conference call of last night was that there will now be an Issue of the Week posted on the Campaign Portal, and each of us is expected to adapt this to our local needs and send out press releases to the media. The first issue is the embarrassing behavior of some state reps and the failure of the Democratic leadership to take any action. I adapt this and "announce" it as coming from my own campaign:

For Immediate Release
August 25, 2004

Contact: David R. Slavitt
000–000–0000

David Slavitt announced today that he joins with the Republican demands announced by Governor Romney and GOP Chairman Darrell Crate for radical reform of the legislature. Pointing to the recent arrest of State Representative Paul Kujawski and previous arrests of State Representatives Brian Dempsey and Christopher Asselin, along with the unwillingness of the legislature to police itself, Chairman Crate today called on the State Legislature to adopt new ethics reforms that would ensure the voters of the Commonwealth that accountability and standards are indeed a priority on Beacon Hill.

"Tim Toomey is clean as a whistle," Slavitt said, "but he is a member of Speaker Finneran's leadership team, and there are times when guilt by association is reasonable and even inevitable."

In the last nine months three Finneran loyalists in the House have been arrested for, among other things, Racketeering, Bribery, Money Laundering, Extortion, Drunk Driving, Open and Gross Lewdness, and Disorderly Conduct.

When Representative Asselin was charged with Racketeering, Bribery, Money Laundering and Extortion Common Cause requested that the State Ethics Committee launch a full investigation and we hoped that the Leadership would support an honest and transparent investigation in order to restore some confidence in the legislature. Since that time the silence from Speaker Finneran and the Ethics Committee has been deafening.

Representative Toomey must feel a private disgust at the behavior of some of his colleagues and an acute embarrassment at the failure of Speaker Finneran to take action. But he owes more to the voters of Cambridge and Somerville. If he cannot speak out against these grotesque lapses in decency, then the voters should turn to someone who can and will.

What the Republicans propose is similar to the arrangement that obtains in the United States Congress—that the Ethics Committee become a truly bi-partisan committee by assigning five seats to the Democrats and five seats to the Republicans. More disclosure and transparency of committee business including but not limited to public reports of finding, notification of investigations and public committee hearings. Any legislator that has been arrested or indicted for a crime will be removed from any leadership positions including loss of leadership pay pending the resolution of the matter.

Will any of the Cambridge or Summerville papers run it? And if they do, will the voters react? It's worth a shot.

★ ★ ★ What an improvement! I spent an hour and a half yesterday evening making phone calls, and the Campaign Portal with its update is much better than it used to be. Now, instead of half the information about voters in my district being out-of-date, there are only two or three people on a page who have moved or died. And I was nice to myself, calling only Republicans, mindful of Tip O'Neill's dictum that "they'll give you their vote, but you've got to ask for it." So I called people likely to be receptive, and they were.

One interesting bit of information that I heard from a Republican voter was that she'd been called by the Toomey people, who had urged her to change her registration to Unenrolled so she could vote for Toomey in the primary. It makes sense. I'm running unopposed and will win. And Toomey is more conservative than Green, and therefore more palatable to Republican tastes. But it is a low-yield exercise and, unless Toomey has more workers in his campaign than he knows what to do with, it could be a sign of nervousness.

The article on the front page of the *Cambridge Chronicle* also suggests something other than confidence, on both sides:

Toomey, Green spar over $$, debates
By Brock Parker/ CNC Staff
Thursday, August 26, 2004

State Rep. Tim Toomey's campaign this week accused opponent Avi Green of having "something to hide" in his financial records.

But Green's campaign is blasting Toomey back, saying the six-term incumbent "refuses" to square off in a debate.

The barbs between the two campaigns for the 26th Middlesex House of Representative seat began after Toomey, D-Cambridge, challenged Green, also a Democrat, in a letter last week to submit his campaign finance reports by 5 p.m. on Wednesday, Sept. 1, before the state's Sept. 7 deadline.

"We just wanted the public to have the opportunity to see before the election who contributed and the amounts [they contributed to the campaigns]," Toomey said.

Toomey said Monday he challenged Green to submit the records early because the Labor Day holiday on Sept. 6 will delay the normal deadline for submissions. As a result, Toomey said he was concerned the information in the reports would not be available for newspaper reports in time for the primary election on Sept. 14.

But Toomey said he hasn't received any response to the challenge from Green.

"Obviously, they don't want the public to see," Toomey said.

"Apparently they have something to hide and do not want their campaign records scrutinized before the election," said Bob Perry, the treasurer of Toomey's campaign. "We're wondering what they have to hide."

Avi Green spokesman Josh Sugarman refused to directly answer if Green would accept Toomey's challenge to submit financial records on Sept. 1.

"We're going to do the best we can," Sugarman said. "We were kind of surprised, frankly, to see Mr. Toomey so committed to campaign finance reports after voting to gut clean elections for so many years."

Sugarman said Green was not available for comment. Sugarman said Green "wants to talk about the issues" and considered Toomey's campaign records challenge an attempt to divert attention to "insider stuff."

"We think this is once again a diversion from the issues," Sugarman said. "Avi wants to talk about the issues. Mr. Toomey has consistently talked about [campaign finance reports] and endorsements."

Turning the table on Toomey's campaign, Sugarman said Toomey had "pulled out" of two upcoming debates at the East End House community center and the Tremont Street shul, also known as the Temple Beth Shalom.

"Mr. Toomey has refused to debate," Sugarman said.

But Toomey's campaign denied the accusation.

"For the Green campaign to say we pulled out is baloney," Perry said. "This is all a red herring from Green's campaign."

Perry said Toomey's campaign asked the coordinators for both candidate forums to submit the dates to Toomey's office so they the campaign could clear Toomey's schedule. But the dates for the events came into Toomey's office too late, Perry said, and the representative had already committed to other events.

Michael Delia, the director of the East End House, said a meet-the-candidates event at the East End House had been canceled because of scheduling conflicts. When asked if the event was canceled because Toomey pulled out of the event, Delia said: "I don't believe that is accurate."

"Getting everyone to agree to a date was too difficult, so we just nixed the idea," Delia said.

Miriam Klapper, director of the Tremont Street shul, said the temple had planned a Sept. 7 meet-the-candidates event.

But Toomey couldn't make the event, Klapper said, and planning the candidates' night so close to the Jewish holidays became too much work.

"The reason we canceled was not because they pulled out; it's a High Holiday and we couldn't handle it," Klapper said.

My guess is that Toomey is accusing Green of getting money from outside sources—Jews in Brookline, mostly. And he wants to show his Irish, Italian, and Portuguese loyalists that he is being attacked by *Ausländer*s. Wherever Green has been getting his money, though, he has been getting a lot of it. And Toomey is not happy. Green's accusation about Toomey's unwillingness to debate is more reasonable. These events are important enough so that Toomey could have rearranged his schedule. He just didn't want to show up and get clobbered by the two Jews in the Tremont Street shul.

That Toomey has been so friendly and polite to me may turn out simply to be a sign that he doesn't think of me as a threat. Clearly, as the article suggests, he is capable of less than cordial behavior. That I had not been invited to the East End House event is also worrisome, but maybe they never got to the point where they had a date for which they could issue an invitation. (On the other hand, they never even asked me what my availability would be.)

★ ★ ★ A card from the Green campaign announces that "Avi Green is pro-choice. Tim Toomey is anti-choice." There are endorsements from NARAL and NOW. Did they pay for the mailing or did Green? It's a fair postcard—except for the fact that Tim is in eyeglasses and looks old compared to "energetic," unbespectacled Avi.

★ ★ ★ Lieutenant Governor Healey signed a bill yesterday at Foss Park in Somerville that would authorize the police there to disperse gang members. Foss Park is where MS-13 gangsters are alleged to have raped a couple of disabled young girls. Healey, a former public safety consultant, said that the bill is a model for other cities that are troubled by gang violence. (If I had known that she was going to be signing this bill in Somerville, I'd have tried to get myself invited to be a part of the ceremony.) Worries about the misuse of the law seem to have been addressed well enough: Police Chief George McLean said that each police car in the city will be equipped with a list of seventy or so known gang members with their names and photos. And in the past two years, as the bill awaited legislative approval, police have arrested twenty gang members on charges including assault and robbery and have confiscated knives and machetes. As Healey pointed out, they have their regalia (the bandanas) and their tattoos (from Mongo's?), and identifying them "isn't rocket science."

★ ★ ★ Fred and I had breakfast to talk about strategy. Whichever Democrat loses the primary, Toomey or Green, will be angry and looking to recoup in 2006 or 2008. Each might prefer a Slavitt victory in 2004 as a way of guaranteeing an open seat in two or four years, and might therefore be willing to help me in some way. But even if we can't get to the losing candidate, we might be able to get to his supporters. Signs are out there, and we can go to each house where there is, say, a Green sign and ask if the people there want to put up one for Slavitt. Even if they don't, they might listen to our pitch.

★ ★ ★ We spent a couple of hours doing just that, taking down the addresses of all the Green signs. He has been out there working the territory, I must say. Fred still expects that Toomey will win the primary, in which case all those

Green supporters—the ones with the signs out on their lawns are the fervent ones—will be approachable.

Evan thinks I should issue a challenge to Speaker Finneran to debate—either in Mattapan, his home district, or in Cambridge. The chances of his accepting are zero, but if Toomey avoids a debate, I can make political hay, challenging Finneran and saying that he is the ventriloquist and Toomey is the dummy. I can send out releases to the *Globe* and the *Herald* and see how much attention I can get. This kind of mischief is actually fun.

14

★ ★ ★ ★ ★ ★ ★ ★ ★ ★ ★ ★ ★ ★ ★ ★ ★ ★ ★ ★

The *Somerville News* endorses Toomey in the Democrat primary, which is not al-together surprising. It's what I'd have done if I were running the paper. They say:

> In the 26th Middlesex District, we endorse Timothy J. Toomey. This was an easy decision to make. Not because Tim's opponent is a bad guy—he's not—but because in Toomey we have a seven-day-a-week guy fighting tooth and nail every waking minute of every day to better serve the residents of Somerville and Cambridge. Toomey is someone who has always believed in constituent services and has attainted [sic] the Chairmanship of the Joint Committee on Public Safety. Despite Toomey's seniority and his lofty title as Chairman—he remains a regular guy who answers his own phone and will follow up until your problem is resolved. That's commitment to the job.

Well, all that is true. But do we want pothole politicians or do we want a more radical reform of the politics of Massachusetts? (And it is interesting that, while conceding that he is not a bad guy, they do not mention Avi Green by name.)

★ ★ ★ A nasty piece in the *Globe* yesterday by Scott Greenberger and Elise Castelli criticizes Romney for being out of the state so often. During the month of August, he spent fifteen workdays out of the state. He went to the Olympics in Athens and to New York for the Republican National Convention, and he took a couple of other trips to New York and Washington to promote *Turnaround*. (But while he was in Washington he attended a Homeland Security meeting.) He also spent some time in New Hampshire at his summer place on Lake Win-nipesaukee.

But get serious. It's August! He's entitled to some vacation time. And part of the job of governing is to represent the Commonwealth nationally and internationally. To treat him like a shopkeeper who has to sweep out and open the state every morning is absurd, not so much anti-Republican (although it may be partly that) as anti-incumbent.

In any event, we have not been invaded by Connecticut or Rhode Island. And the likelihood is that the governor has a cell phone.

★ ★ ★ Speaking of Romney, I have an invitation to another of those Key Club breakfasts, this one at Locke-Ober on the fifteenth, with him and Rhode Island's governor Donald Carcieri. I don't think I'll go. It's fifty bucks of campaign money, and I didn't get a penny from the Mickey Edwards breakfast.

The other item in the mail was an announcement from Darrell Crate that the "in kind contributions" from the party to my campaign are $9,000. That represents my part of the cost of the Campaign Portal as well as "opposition research and issue briefs, statewide polling . . . the Governor's fellowship program," and other items I do not understand or never benefited from. I certainly have not had any statewide polling results. I have no idea what they are talking about, but we will post the information. The frightening thing is that if you multiply that figure by this year's 130 candidates, you get $1,170,000, a considerable sum. At the least, when the Office of Campaign and Political Finance publishes the September numbers, my campaign will look less anemic than it would without the state party's nine grand.

★ ★ ★ There are some uses to the Campaign Portal, of course. It allows me to quantify my hopes and goals. It tells me, for example, that there are 19,603 registered voters in the Twenty-sixth Middlesex District. Of these 14,888 are "likely" voters. And of this number, 5,356 are Republican or Unenrolled. So to get the 7,500 or so votes I would need to win, I need to hold my base and attract a couple of thousand Democrats (or Greens, or Rainbows). If I can get that number of disaffected Avi Green supporters, I am in like Flynn.

Two years ago, Toomey won with 6,258 votes. This is only approximate, and the turnout will be higher in a presidential year. But 7,500 would still do it, just, and that is not an impossible goal. Of course, the portal offers no polling results by representative district, so I have only the vaguest idea how I'm doing. But the uphill incline is less severe than I might have guessed.

★ ★ ★ Senator Zell Miller's speech in New York last night at the R.N.C. was an old-fashioned political harangue, and that kind of political oratory is all but obsolete. Our campaigns are now waged in sound bites, and we have less sense of the timbre of a candidate's mind. I missed Romney and, of course, Kerry Healey's introduction of the governor. It was an honor for each of them to speak in prime time, even briefly. I wonder, though, about Kerry Healey's job, or at least the part of it that I have been able to observe. She introduces the governor, again and again. How does she keep from letting her boredom show? Is she not tempted to say absurd things now and then, to say that she likes to listen to the governor playing the bassoon in the office next to hers or perhaps throw in some wild-card allusion, if only to keep herself awake? When I was at *Newsweek*, we used to play a game in which we'd think up some arcane or wacky reference and then see which of us could get it into the magazine first: "Fafner and Fasolt," for instance, or "Trotsky's Bar Mitzvah." We had more freedom than she does and were reviewing books and movies and plays, where such assertions of quirky personality were not altogether inappropriate, but the constraints of Kerry Healey's job must tempt her now and then at least a little in that direction.

But she resists. In all lists I have seen of Republicans who might run for president in 2008, Romney's name is included, which means that Kerry Healey has at least a plausible shot at moving her office and dropping the "Lieutenant" from her title. But is such a prospect enough to sustain her, week after week, month after month, as she stands at one lectern after another and winds up once again with "my favorite Republican"?

★ ★ ★ This morning's *Globe* has an outrageous demonstration of partisanship, an article by Frank Phillips masquerading as a news story—the headline being "Democrats Hit Romney on absences." What the *Globe* did was call up various Democrats, ask them about their own story of a couple of days back, and invite them to comment, as, of course, the Democrats did, only too cheerfully. "We are a little bit fed up with the hypocrisy coming out of the governor's office about John Kerry and his record and what he has done for Massachusetts lately," is what Representative Capuano had to say. He is my congressman, a Democrat from Somerville, and he called a press conference to exploit the *Globe*'s reportage and get his mug shot into the paper.

"Capuano," Frank Phillips's piece tells us, "speaking for the state party, pointed to a *Globe* article earlier this week that reported that Romney has only been at the State House seven of the 22 working days in August. The governor's out-of-state jaunts included book-signing events in Utah and Washington, D.C, accepting an award at the Olympic Games in Athens, spending a good part of the day this week appearing with President Bush in Nashua, and vacationing at his estate on Winnipesaukie Lake [sic] in New Hampshire."

Jaunts? How about "trysts," or "caprices" or "escapades"? And what about that "Winnipesaukie Lake"? They can spell it however they please, but do they refer to Lake George as George Lake? The entire exercise is altogether transparent as petty and shameless, but it is not surprising, from either Capuano or the *Globe*.

The fact that the governor and the lieutenant governor of the Commonwealth were speaking at the Republican National Convention might have made the pages of that newspaper, but to read what they said in their speeches, one had to go to online transcripts. There were allusions to Romney's remarks in a *Globe* editorial—they picked up his joke about Senator Kerry's opinions coming in fifty-seven varieties—but there was nothing at all about Healey's introduction. As if it were too small-town to include anything like that. The point of the editorial was to suggest that Romney might have presidential ambitions. (Well, duh!) Or, as they put it, had been "bitten by the presidential bug," as if it were a social disease.

Boston is a small town but with big-town pretensions, the worst of both worlds.

I must remember the *Globe*'s journalistic slovenliness and partiality, so that when they slight me—as, no doubt, they will—I shall have some ground for not taking it personally.

"Anti-Semit?" my father would have asked, stressing the last syllable. Not anymore, but according to a prep school classmate of mine who worked for the *Globe* for most of his life, they used to be. They didn't even have Jews out there selling ads to merchants, who were, more often than not, Jewish.

★ ★ ★ A letter on what looks like Swissôtel stationery, with what looks like Mitt Romney's signature over the envelope's return address. It says, in part:

Dear David,
Greetings from The Big Apple!

I'm thrilled to be here at the Republican National Convention in New York City.

I can't remember the last time I was around so many Republicans. I have become so accustomed to being the lone Republican among all the Democrats on Beacon Hill.

In fact, during the Democratic National Convention in Boston, a reporter asked me what it was like to have so many Democrats in town.

I replied, "I don't notice a difference!"

Being here in New York City talking to fellow Republicans is exciting. It's also a bit disconcerting because it reminds me just how much opposition I face at home.

I'm just so sick of it, David, and that's why I am taking a few minutes to write you from my room at the Drake Hotel. I simply couldn't wait to get back to Boston to be in touch and state my case for help.

As I chat with fellow Republican governors, I marvel at all they've been able to accomplish because they have competitive two-party legislatures made up of representatives from both parties with a common goal: to make their state better.

In Massachusetts, we have Tom Finneran and his gang of old-school lieutenants who like back-room deals and arrogantly do what they want—without thinking of the common good of the Commonwealth.

The arrogant leaders on Beacon Hill fight me at every turn while we try to implement our reform package. Good commonsense ideas like limiting enormous Billy Bulger–style pensions, combining the Turnpike Authority and Highway Department, and implementing the voter approved tax roll-back; all get bottled up in a legislature dominated by status quo Democrats.

But we can make a difference this year.

We have over 130 qualified, reform-minded Republicans on the ballot across the Bay State. Like you, they wholeheartedly support my reform efforts. . . .

Being here at the Republican National Convention only reinforces my determination to elect more Republicans to the state legislature and end the one-party rule that has held back Massachusetts for too long.

Thanks, as always, for taking the time to read this letter and for your continued and generous support.

Sincerely,

[Signature]

Mitt Romney

Governor

Commonwealth of Massachusetts

P.S. We must not allow Democrats to ride Kerry's coattails to victory! Please send a contribution in one of the suggested amounts to the State Party today.

Paid for by The Massachusetts Republican Party.

It is a clever way of capitalizing on Romney's moment of glory at the Republican National Convention, and I hope people do send in their contributions.

★ ★ ★ I went last night to the Hampshire House, across from the Common and upstairs over the famous Cheers bar, for a Bush party. A whole roomful of Republicans! It ought to have been reassuring and encouraging, but they are such flakes and wackos. I went up to one nattily dressed fellow with one of my contributors' envelopes, but it turned out that he was a part of the group trying to get Margaret Marshall removed because of the *Goodrich* decision. And my argument that, whatever our differences, it would surely be better to have more Republicans on Beacon Hill didn't do much for him. He handed back the envelope, which I guess is better than his tearing it up and throwing it away. There were several people like that, who disapproved of my socially moderate views. For them, Giuliani, Schwarzenegger, and Weld were not "real" Republicans either.

It is a persistent and worrisome problem, and I wish I believed more deeply in my usual answer—which is that unless people like me continue to participate in the life of the party, we cede it to the hard-line, right-wing homophobes.

★ ★ ★ The good news is that last night Fred Baker told me that the Toomey campaign has been in touch with him to accept our invitation to a debate in October—time and place to be determined after the primary. I am pleased and relieved. I still think Toomey was ducking the candidates' evening at the Tremont Street shul, but if he has agreed to debate with me, then Avi Green was the one he was avoiding, either because he was worried about Green or more probably because they dislike each other. If Toomey were smarter, he'd avoid debating me, too. He knows that I'm good at this and that he isn't. But he's a decent, honorable guy. And he feels he owes it to the voters.

★ ★ ★ The *Globe*'s nasty anti-Mitt campaign continues. Brian McGrory's column in this morning's paper carries the headline "Hey, Mitt, come home," and his first couple of paragraphs are worth setting down:

> Silly voters. Silly, moronic, naïve little voters. Back in November 2002, you thought you were electing a new governor of Massachusetts. So did I. Instead, what we were electing was a Bush family lackey, a spectacularly coiffed frequent flier who wears his ambitions so far out on his sleeve it's a wonder he can move his wrists.
>
> After seeing his singularly languid performance at the podium of Madison Square Garden this week, I have just one bit of counsel for Mitt Romney:

Come home, our wandering little friend. For your own sake, for our sake, for God's sake, come back to Boston.

The gist of the obviously orchestrated piece is that if Romney has presidential ambitions, he will first have to get himself reelected in 2006, and this time his opponent won't be Shannon O'Brien but Attorney General Tom Reilly, a tougher opponent. McGrory urges Romney to prepare himself by building up a record of achievement.

I have always assumed that the paper is, like the *New York Times* that owns it, leftish. But I hadn't quite realized that it is essentially *Pravda* in English. Except in the business department, of course, where they are union-busting, hardnosed, right-wing guys when dealing with their own workers.

★ ★ ★ The poetry reading at Toast was less terrible than I had feared. There was a reasonable crowd—thirty or so, which is good for a poetry reading. And I shared the microphone with Don Share, with whom I am friendly. He is a good poet, technically accomplished, although still young. He may get better as life teaches him its difficult lessons, but he is off to a good start. He read first, which was appropriate, and then I did my half hour to an audience that was polite and responsive, laughing at the laugh lines and occasionally applauding after a poem. The reading will resonate, because the *Somerville News*, which sponsors the series, will do an article about it. I read what I have been calling my Republican poem, and to do that does not betray the piece:

Stress

Because birdsong is such an intricate behavior, it may be a sensitive indicator of a male's fitness. Producing a song is a difficult task for the brain, and any additional challenge—lack of food, infections, or other types of stress—is likely to take a toll.

—*Clive Catchpole, University of London*

The appeal to nature is dangerous, but we cannot
therefore ignore it altogether. Consider
the sparrows Nowicki and Searcy had fed, as much
as they wanted: they flourished and learned to perform their songs

correctly. But we are not just talking art.
It is procreation, repeating the genes, for the females
demand precision, a sign of health if not
of cultivation and taste. The birds they'd fed less

learned the songs less well, achieving an average
sixteen syllables right of a possible twenty.
(They were also somewhat smaller and often weaker.)
Their twitterings, imperfect and less than accomplished,

won them fewer offers of copulation,
and the females, the theory goes, were right to be picky,
wanting to mate with the best and the strongest. The lesson
for poets? It's what we knew all along, that stress
and deprivation, however melodramatic,
and even appealing—think of those dreadful lives
we read about of Mandelstam, or Célan,
or Rimbaud—cannot compare with classical training,

proper tuition, and uninterrupted practice.
Our hearts may not go out to these creatures of comfort,
children of Mandarin privilege, unacquainted
with the urgent woes of our time. But they've learned how to sing.

If there is any meaning at all to the claim on my bookmarks and door-hangers that I am in favor of "excellence in education," surely it is somewhere in this poem, but what the policy implications are, I am not at all sure. But it identifies me as more committed to "excellence" than to diversity, for instance.

★ ★ ★ This morning on NPR, I heard that the World Health Organization estimates that seventy-eight thousand women a year die of illegal abortions. I must use that in my debate with Toomey. He cannot call his anti-abortion position "pro-life" if it involves the deaths of more than two hundred women every day. Or, annually, twenty-five times as many people as died in the World Trade Center. I will not go so far as to say that the federal government and the Vatican make al-Qaida look like amateurs in the deadly fanaticism game, but the inference is there to be drawn by the more acute members of the audience.

It's a Republican-sponsored debate, and therefore I get to set the rules, which will be more favorable to me than the other two have been. What I want is longer speeches, five minutes rather than two, and more interaction. I have been hearing how Senator Kerry wants less structure and President Bush wants more, which figures, the wolf and the sheep discussing what's for dinner.

★ ★ ★ The polls have Bush ahead of Kerry by 11 percent, which is extraordinary, evidence of not just a postconvention bounce but a real shift in voter attitudes. The Kerry campaign is doing what it always does in times of trouble, which is to switch personnel. The guy they are bringing aboard, though, is John Stasso, a veteran of the Dukakis campaign. This is what Evelyn Waugh would dismiss as being too absurd, even for a comic novel.

The talking heads were encouraging. And this e-mail, from Susan Imrie, was encouraging, too. She offered to write a letter to the *Cambridge Chronicle*, and I encouraged her to do so. We'll see if they print it:

To the Editor,

This is a response to the one-issue, pro-choice voter who recently wrote an endorsement letter for Avi Green, who is running against Tim Toomey for 26th Middlesex State Representative in the Democratic primary.

Aside from supporting abortion rights, based on Green's own statements at debates it is clear that he is a typical Cambridge elitist who has no faith in any individual's rights to make any of his or her own choices.

A good example was Green's support for the moratorium on charter schools, making it clear that "as a former educator" he opposed parents' rights to be able to choose where their own children attend school or the method of being educated. Green also opposed legislation that would allow police to break up public gatherings of gang members, gatherings that restrict the choices of ordinary citizens to be able to walk around safely and freely in their own neighborhoods.

Electing Green would likely diminish our choices of where to work. Green claims to support job creation, yet on his web site he publicly opposes Tim Toomey's votes to extend corporate tax credits. Green claims to be so in touch with his district yet hasn't noticed that the Kendall Square area is ghost town of empty office buildings—and that private companies are closing down or fleeing Taxachusetts. Green seems not to understand that private industry is the ONLY significant generator of jobs, tax revenue and growth.

None of these attitudes of his should come as any surprise. Green is a self-described "progressive", that being the new euphemism for "liberal", a word the left has noticeably backed away from since their co-opting of it transformed it into one connoting a self-righteous and narrow-minded dedication to the promotion of socialist ideology.

If the voters truly want a State Representative that stands for individual freedom and economic growth, as well as a move away from the one-party system that has controlled Massachusetts for way too long, the Republican candidate David Slavitt is the only real choice. David Slavitt supports a woman's right to choose, the right of gays to marry, and the promotion of policies to help, not hinder, the private sector. In every debate so far David Slavitt has blown away both Toomey and Green with his wit, his common sense, and his erudition.

I strongly recommend that all 26th Middlesex voters get to know David Slavitt by viewing one of the debate broadcasts or by checking out his web site at *www.davidslavitt.com*. Most important, I urge Democrats and Independents in the district to open their minds and consider voting for David Slavitt, the true voice of intelligence and reason in this state representative race.

Susan Imrie
East Cambridge

★ ★ ★ In anticipation of the primary, there are ads in the *Somerville Journal* for Toomey and for James DiPaola, the candidate for sheriff. I am looking at these as models, and what I find depressing is that they don't say anything and really can't. Toomey's shows a photograph of him walking somewhere with Mayor Curtatone, and the caption identifying them says, "Working together to fight gang violence in Somerville." Then: "Vote Tuesday Sept. 14 for State Representative Tim Toomey/Democrat." He also says that he is "Endorsed by the Somerville Police Employees' Association" and offers "For a ride to the polls, call 617–492–6565."

Not much to chew on there. Law and order, I guess. And Democrat. And union. And the association with Mayor Curtatone.

What I've got to do, then, is get that endorsement from Bill Weld. And repeat my doorhanger and bookmark line: "Vote Republican for the sake of Democracy." You don't have time or space for anything more than that.

We're back at Versailles, of course, and the question is what color plume to put in my hat to get noticed.

★ ★ ★ It is a pleasant Sunday afternoon with just a hint of the crispness to announce that fall is on its way. There is no evading it, so I grab my satchel with the bookmarks and the doorhangers and drive over to East Cambridge to do another couple of blocks.

I have developed a game plan, which is to canvass until it hurts. Either the pain is physical, and I am made aware by my hip or my knees that I've done enough, or else the trauma is to the psyche as I encounter resistance and hostility. A couple of young girls are playing on a boat in the driveway in back of one of those houses, and I ask if their mommy is home. A woman's voice, alert to the inquiry of a male stranger, asks who it is. I introduce myself as the Republican candidate for state rep. She is, she tells me, a Democrat, as she leans out of the window with a cigarette in her hand. But if Toomey beats Green in the primary, would she be interested in a pro-choice Republican? No, she is for Toomey and doesn't care what his positions are.

One such person is tolerable, I guess. But the second is less affable. We get to the pro-choice part of the discussion, but she is not interested in discussion. She wants confrontation. She is angry, I suspect, at the Democrats' debacle and Kerry's implosion. Where do I stand on the graduated income tax? Do I want to protect the rich and burden the poor with taxes? Where do I stand on Bush's tax cuts? On the war in Iraq?

It is useless to argue. I tell her that Ho Chi Minh, when asked whether he thought the French Revolution was a success, said it was too early to tell. It is an elegant evasion, but she is not in an appreciative mood. I am wasting my wit and my time.

I walk back to the car and drive home.

★ ★ ★ There is a sympathetic story in the *Globe* this morning about how state rep Paul Kujawski, the one arrested for drunken driving and urinating in public, is a good guy. Apparently a couple of candidates willing to oppose him have presented themselves. If they can get 150 write-in votes in the primary, which would be the equivalent of the 150 signatures on a nomination petition, that would get their names onto the November ballot. Mark Dowgiewicz, a Democrat, and Dorothy Mann, a Republican, are write-in candidates. Mann's advantage is that her name is easier to spell. It turns out that hers is a "high interest" candidacy and will get help with advertising, and mailings, from the state party. My candidacy is not "high interest," and if I win, I'll remember that. It will make me a better state rep, not burdened by feelings of obligation to the party or by ambitions for higher office.

★ ★ ★ What strikes me this morning is that the most difficult part of running for office has nothing to do with winning or losing. That kind of uncertainty is a given and, in any event, is off in the middle distance. The more immediate obstacle is one of belief. I collect my rubber stamp, ink pad, and doorhangers and am about to stamp my website address on the white space at the bottom of the card when I find myself pausing to ask myself what I think I'm doing. The entire enterprise seems to be an imposture. Writing a novel, one has the same crisis of faith from time to time, but there one can simply put the manuscript in a filing cabinet or a box in the closet and wait for it to beckon (or not), to insist, one way or another. Or, less fancifully, one can wait out the dip in one's mood. To do certain kinds of conceptual art, the first requirement is arrogance. That Rauschenberg painting at the San Francisco Museum of Modern Art that is just a rectangle of whitewashed canvas doesn't take much talent to do, and it doesn't even require a great deal of wit, but the faith it demanded, in himself and his own authority to do such a thing, the sheer nerve of it, was considerable. That the museum bought it and paid real money for it was only an endorsement of the gesture he had made. Similarly, in the campaign, I can hang my little "Slavitt" sign around my neck—it seems to reassure people that I have some kind of identification—and go out there with my sack full of handouts, but I know that this is not the real me, and that even if they are fooled by my repetition of the little set piece I perform, I am not altogether persuaded, myself.

Now and then, it seems funny, a prank, an impish thing to do. But impishness is difficult to maintain over the course of weeks and months. If I am elected, it will be something of a joke, but the joke may not wear well over the course of two years.

★ ★ ★ I did three floors of the high-rise subsidized-living apartment house at 1221 Cambridge Street, knocking on doors and handing out the bookmarks or hanging the doorhangers. Mostly it went well. This was a welcoming building for me during the signature gathering. Mostly, these are old people who are home and have little else to do. One either hears the muffled sound of the television (in which case one gets out a bookmark) or not, in which case the odds are that nobody is at home. The smells are of stale bodies, sometimes cat urine, sometimes cooked cabbage. It is not a cheerful place except at the ends of the long hallways, where there are nice views to the south of Cambridge and to the north of Somerville. I was feeling good about the number of pieces I'd handed out and the number of people I'd talked to, however briefly, when, on my way out, I noticed the sign announcing a dinner in the community room on September 7, sponsored by the Tim Toomey Campaign.

That's how Toomey will beat Avi Green, I expect. And me, too? Maybe I can arrange for a coffee and donuts evening. I e-mailed Fred to ask whether there is something we can do in October.

★ ★ ★ I had lunch with Cousin Louis, who was up here for a wedding. He thinks Kerry is going to pull off this election, which is what I expected he'd say, considering that he's a staunch Democrat and cannot even imagine a Republican victory. But he had a shrewd suggestion about the debate with Tim Toomey—that I should check the dates of the presidential debates and the vice presidential debate and should consult the Major League Baseball schedules to avoid, if possible, a conflict with the division series, the league championships, and, assuming that the Sox go all the way, the World Series. A good idea, and I thanked him.

★ ★ ★ The pundits are saying that the "real" campaign for the presidency starts today, as if everything up to now has been throat clearing. The intensity does increase for the next eight weeks—or, here in Massachusetts, it will be the seven weeks after next Tuesday's primary. We'll have to start our "standouts," a strange ritual to which I am not looking forward with much eagerness. And I'll have to be more assiduous in my telemarketing efforts.

★ ★ ★ I am assuming that Toomey will win next week. Indeed, having thought of an opening for the debate, I am almost hoping that he wins. (Should Green win, what I have can be adapted.) What I wrote out is engaging:

> It is a pleasure to welcome you all here, and to welcome Representative Toomey, for whom I have a certain admiration. He is a hard-working, sincere man. Indeed, he is probably as good a person as you'll find among Tom Finneran's people. Why, then, am I running against him? And why should you vote for me rather than for him in the election in November?
>
> There are basically two reasons. The first is that the domination by the Democrats of our political life here in Massachusetts is not healthy. It has gone on for so long that the idealism of the Democrat party—although it still flickers occasionally in the hearts of some—has been institutionally extinguished. The speaker and the party ignore referenda expressing the voters' wishes. Speaker Finneran lies to federal judges. He exercises tyrannical control over his colleagues, rewarding fidelity and punishing any independence of thought or spirit. And he is an improvement over the previous speaker, Charlie Flaherty, a felon, convicted of taking bribes and evading taxes.
>
> We deserve better. We deserve representatives more interested in the

education of our children than in the votes they can get from the teachers' unions that feel threatened by the Charter School movement. We deserve a legislature that will heed the will of the electorate when we say we want clean elections or we want a roll-back of our state taxes to 5%, or that under some circumstances we want the possibility of capital punishment. We deserve the reform that Mitt Romney has been urging and that Tom Finneran has been obstructing, because he and his henchmen care more about incumbency than they do about the prosperity of the Commonwealth.

The second reason is larger, rather more vague, but also important. Let me put it to you bluntly. The basic function of the state legislature is quite grand, when you think about it. There are two hundred men and women in the General Court, and what they do is meet and decide about how we should live and what our responses should be to the entire range of problems and opportunities that we face as a community and as a society. These people may be Republicans or Democrats, liberal or conservative, but what they are supposed to do is represent us and provide their collective wisdom for the challenges we face together. We look to them for tough practical judgments in which idealism still plays its part. We depend on them for their richness of life-experience. And what we expect at the very least is that they are honest and trustworthy, that they are dedicated to public service, and that they bring to Beacon Hill an awareness of the nobility of their calling.

Now I ask you if these are the terms in which you think of our state reps, of Speaker Finneran, and of the long tradition of knavery and venality of the Democrat Party of Massachusetts. And if the answer is in the negative, then I offer you another—and, in all humility, I think a better—choice.

★ ★ ★ The last part, about the wisdom of the state representatives, is a bold and mostly unrealistic thought, but it was Fred Wiseman who told me what he thought the institution ought to be, after having spent some time in Idaho shooting his new documentary, *State Legislature*. Fred is very smart, and the gap between the intention and the reality is either hilarious or tragic, depending on your disposition. It is what enlivens all his films. It may be that in Idaho there is at least on occasion some remnant of that aspiration. Here, the discrepancy is so great as to take one's breath away.

With my gray hair and my long bibliography, I can plausibly present myself as having attained to a certain degree of wisdom.

Montaigne for state rep? Why not? He was mayor of Bordeaux.

★ ★ ★ I'm being far too grand here, I'm afraid. This morning's paper has a couple of stories that remind me how sordid this business really is. One is a revelation—from the Office of Campaign and Political Finance reports, I am sure—about Speaker Finneran's expenditures during the past year of $11,175 to a defense lawyer fighting the investigation of his false testimony before the federal judges and of another $13,000 to a media consultant to try to spin the story and make it look as though Finneran was being victimized by the media. These disbursements are not actually illegal, and Pamela Wilmot, executive director of Common Cause, says in the *Globe* story that her organization has filed legislation that would revise the rules so that officeholders could use their campaign money only for legitimate campaign expenses. (That this proposal is unpopular with officeholders is not surprising.) The present regulations say that the money can be spent to promote an officeholder's political career, and even Ms. Wilmot admits that avoiding an indictment would qualify.

★ ★ ★ The report reminded me that the campaign finance figures are also available from the OCPF for Toomey and Green, and I looked them up. Their numbers are dismaying. Green has spent $71,007.25 during the year and has $18,304.89 on hand. Salaries, office rent, even polling! He's a twink, but the operation is legitimate and even heavyweight. Toomey, meanwhile, has laid out $87,678.80 and has $15 dollars and change on hand. My numbers are laughable, in comparison. I have spent a paltry $2,827.50 and have $3,194.50 on hand, which will just about cover the costs of my newspaper ads and, with only a little augmentation from the fund-raiser at Ryles, my mailing. But whom am I kidding? Not all Davids win. And most Goliaths don't lose.

Even if you take Toomey's $87,678 and subtract Green's $71,007, on the weird theory that this was mostly money for the primary and that we start fresh next Tuesday, the balance is $16,671, which is huge compared to what I've spent so far.

★ ★ ★ Evan's take on this is that all the money that Green is spending benefits me. And he asks, wittily enough, what I'd have done if I had had more money. Buy more flyswatters? This is absurd enough to elevate my mood considerably.

Then the mail brought in some interesting stuff, two pieces from Toomey's campaign and one from Green's. The Toomey mailings are elaborate, one large piece in four colors, 11 by 17 inches and folded in thirds, celebrating the rigors of Toomey's day (he is up by 5:30 AM and "staying fit for service," as if to defy Green's challenge that he'd bring more "energy" to the job). The other is a flat piece, 8½ by 11 inches, asking in bold red type, "HAVE YOU SEEN THE TWO FACES OF AVI GREEN?" and it shows, of course, two faces, with the caption "Candidate Avi Green is caught lying . . . again," this last being in a kind of sickly green. Overprinted on a slant is the repeated phrase "DON'T BELIEVE THE LIES," which is, even for Massachusetts, relatively hostile. The other side has a hard-hitting piece of political argument, not unpersuasive to those who are, as yet, undecided. I had not known that Green told the *Somerville News* that he would not guarantee that he would vote against Finneran for Speaker and that he wanted to "keep his options open." This was a regrettable misstep, the kind of thing that would make anti-Finneran voters uneasy.

Green's piece is smaller, in his characteristic light blue (wimpy), and focused on gun control. It reproduces a *Globe* article with Toomey's picture and the headline: "House OKs bill to weaken the state's gun control laws." Someone getting both these mailings on the same day—as Janet and I did—might well think, okay, so they're both liars.

Which is just what I want!

⋆ ⋆ ⋆ I went last night to a clean elections meeting in Somerville. How can one oppose the idea of clean elections, which is to say publicly funded elections? Democracy is not a luxury, and it stands to reason that there must be a way of getting the power of big money out of the political process. The trouble is that these are all instinctual lefties, and that they are attacking the wrong people. The voters passed a clean elections referendum in 1998 by a two-thirds majority. Finneran didn't like it—because it slightly diminished the enormous advantage an incumbent has in any campaign—and he and his cronies blocked its implementation. When the Supreme Judicial Court ordered the legislature to fund the program, they still refused, and the court had to enter a judgment against the Commonwealth in which its cars were auctioned off to pay the campaign expenses of Warren Tolman, the only candidate to qualify for public funding. The villains were Finneran and the Democrats. And the solution to that problem, and to the gerrymandering problem, which the clean elections meeting also discussed, is that more Republicans should be voted in so that we have an active opposition party.

But these people are such ingrained lefties that the bad guys, for them, are the Republicans in the Texas legislature! And the issues are further muddied by other unrelated concerns. The problem of identification for first-time voters came up, and that led to a discussion about documentation for the homeless. And what about people who are incarcerated but haven't been tried or convicted of anything? And what about drivers' licenses for the "undocumented"—the euphemism for illegal aliens?

The public-funding idea is healthy. Gerrymandering is also a serious issue, and Patricia Wilmot of Common Cause was persuasive as she talked about the Iowa systems in which a nonpartisan commission does the redistricting. But the other speakers on the panel were infuriating, not because I disagreed with them but, on the contrary, because I approve of what they say they are trying to do and can see that they don't have a hope in hell until they sort out their priorities.

★ ★ ★ Saints Cosmas and Damian were twins, born in Cilicia, now southern Turkey, and were doctors. They were the first to attempt a transplant of a human limb. They were nice guys and they treated the poor without payment, which caused resentment on the part of some less generous colleagues, who denounced them to the Romans, accusing them of being Christians. They were tried, found guilty, and sentenced to death by torture. The Romans cast them into the sea with their hands and feet bound. Cosmas and Damian freed themselves and swam back to shore. The Romans tried to burn them at the stake, but the flames failed to harm them. They tried whipping, but the lash wouldn't touch their bodies. At this point they were asked to renounce their Christian faith—but their belief had been strengthened by the three odd experiences they had just undergone, and they refused. So the Romans beheaded them. This worked, and they died. On September 27, 287. They became the patron saints of Gaeta in Italy, where their intercession is believed to have prevented an outburst of plague in the eighteenth century.

Why am I reciting these entertaining if bizarre details? Because the Festival of SS Cosmas and Damian is a big thing here in Cambridge every September, and I am supposed to go and hang around, passing out bookmarks, shaking hands, eating sausages, and endearing myself to the voters this weekend. And I am looking forward to it as something a little different from the routine of campaigning.

★ ★ ★ The new issue of the *Cambridge Chronicle* is out, and they endorse Toomey.

On my way back from canvassing, I bumped into Avi Green, who was also out ringing doorbells in the alley behind our condo. We greeted each other in a friendly way, and, after he'd finished talking to the woman at the door, we had a moment to chat. I told him that Evan had figured out that, if he loses on

Tuesday, there might be ways for him to help me so that in 2006 or 2008 he would be running either against a Republican or for an open seat. He seemed interested and said that we should talk again after Tuesday—either about debating each other or perhaps about my suggestion.

★ ★ ★ I watched the Avi Green DVD I'd found at one of the doorsteps on my route, left there, I was sure, by mistake, because the house looked to be unoccupied. It is an extraordinary production, very professional, and . . . long. It's a five-and-a-half-minute movie about what a wonderful guy Avi is and what energy he has, and how he is pro-choice and anti-gun, but mostly it shows him in shirtsleeves, looking earnest, talking to voters who are also looking earnest. There's a lot of earnestness in Cambridge, which is probably what's wrong with it. But this is a slick piece of promotion. I looked up on the Office of Campaign and Political Finance site what Green's expenditures had been to see if I could find out what this had cost him. If I have the right item—photography, $2,500—it was a bargain. Still, next Tuesday, one of them will lose, and my bet now would be that it will be Avi.

★ ★ ★ The *Jewish Advocate* piece is out:

A poet and translator, Slavitt is running in September's primary

By Shira Schoenberg
Advocate Staff

David Slavitt is an intellectual. While he has no political experience, the Republican candidate for State Representative of the 26th Middlesex district will publish his 79th book before the election.

As a poet, novelist, and translator from Latin, Greek and Hebrew, he believes he can be an expert on arts and education in the legislature.

Yet to Slavitt, his greatest qualification is his party affiliation. "Checks and balances are a great idea. And we haven't had them in Massachusetts politics in 50 years. We need to rejigger Massachusetts policy to throw the bums out—whoever they are. We need enough people running against the Democrats that if people are outraged, they can vote in someone else."

Does a Republican have a chance in Cambridge? "If supporters of one Democrat stay home, the other guy in the race is me," he said.

Slavitt calls himself socially liberal and fiscally conservative.

He plans to cut taxes, because he says, "People are sick and tired of being taxed to death. If you cut rates, people will spend or invest. Either is good for the economy."

Socially, he is pro-choice and supports same-sex marriage.

Slavitt is proud of his sharp tongue.

"I can hold people up to the contempt and ridicule they deserve," he said.

He does not hesitate to use it against what he calls a political system that favors incumbents, and Speaker of the House Tom Finneran, who, he said, ignored a voter referendum to return money to taxpayers and disagrees with a program to reward merit in schools with tuition breaks.

Slavitt, 69, graduated from Phillips Academy in 1952, and from Yale University in 1956, magna cum laude. He received his master's degree in English literature from Columbia University, then taught for a year at Georgia Tech.

He then got a job as a movie reviewer at *Newsweek*, which he left after seven years to become a freelance writer, occasionally teaching at Princeton, Penn and Columbia.

He lives in Cambridge with his wife of 26 years, Janet Abrahm.

It may get me a few votes. It certainly can't hurt.

★ ★ ★   The *Boston Phoenix* comes out with an endorsement of Avi Green:

Voters in the 26th Middlesex District, which takes in parts of Cambridge and Somerville, have a . . . difficult dilemma. The race pits a smart, young newcomer against a long-time state representative, Tim Toomey, who opposes abortion rights and has voted in favor of capital punishment, though he says he has since changed his mind. The difference is that Toomey . . . supported gay marriage at the constitutional convention by voting against every amendment aimed at weakening it. Because of that, Toomey has been endorsed by the state's major gay-advocacy organizations, as well as by Congressman Barney Frank and State Representative Liz Malia, both of whom are openly gay.

Nevertheless, the *Phoenix*'s endorsement goes to the newcomer, Avi Green. Unlike Toomey, Green is a multi-issue progressive, supporting not just same-sex marriage but also abortion rights and gun control, and opposing cuts in social-services spending and the death penalty. The two also hold different positions on House Speaker Tom Finneran, a conservative Democrat whose admirable intelligence and fiscal restraint have long since been eclipsed by his dictatorial tendencies. Toomey is part of Finneran's leadership team; Green says he'll vote against re-electing Finneran as Speaker. Those words may come back to haunt him, but Green deserves credit for guts and independence.

Might they come out and endorse me in November, should Toomey win in the primary?

★ ★ ★ What the pollsters learn, crudely and expensively, an alert candidate can discover from conversations with voters. I had been avoiding houses with Toomey or Green signs, but recently, in the hope that I might get some votes from Green supporters if he loses the primary, I began knocking on their doors, leaving doorhangers and, if I could, talking with them for a minute or two about what they might do in the event that Toomey and I are the candidates in November.

The reactions vary, and I have no way of guessing what the numbers are. But the range is clear. There are some who dislike Finneran or are pro-choice and who say to me, "Oh, if that's the choice, I'd already decided I'm voting for you," and they thank me for coming by. Others are more traditionally partisan, allergic to Republicans, or nutty on some particular issue. A woman I talked with yesterday asked me what I thought about the MCAS tests, and I said that I was pleased that the scores were trending upward, and that the most dramatic improvements were among the Hispanics and the African-Americans. The tests, I said, seem to be doing what they were supposed to do—putting the feet of the schools to the fire and insisting on measurable results. But she explained that she was a teacher and she thought it was terrible to put so much emphasis on a single test. What happens to the kids that fail?

I was tempted to say that it is only in Lake Wobegon that all the children are above average. But I didn't want to seem like a smart-ass. I told her that I was a teacher too and have taught at Princeton and Columbia and good places. And I said that one of the few really good things to have happened in American education in the last thirty years is that that youngsters who drop out, for whatever reason, can return. Continuing education welcomes them back, and they do very well. She was impressed enough—or bored enough—to take a bookmark and let me go on my way.

★ ★ ★ The signs are a campaign unto themselves. Some, like the one in my shoemaker's window or the one in my tailor's window, are loyal and faithful and stay where I put them. Others, where I've asked for permission, wander away, sometimes removed by vandals (or too-fervent supporters of Toomey or Green). That is what happened to the one I stapled to the clapboards on the side of Robert Pann's plumbing establishment on Prospect Street. But other signs just vanish, like the one in the window of the Store 24. I replaced that twice and then, when I came with a fourth sign, was told that the district manager had decided he didn't want signs. Or the one in the gas station window across the street. I put that in the window where they told me they wanted it to go, but then they realized that it blocked their view of cars at the pump. So they took it down, which was okay (but they could have saved it: these signs cost three bucks a piece). When I came back, they said it could be taped on the window on the Prospect Street side of the station, and I did that. But it is gone now, and I don't know whether I should bother with a third.

What I need is a volunteer to take on this job, but it is so unpleasant and requires so much assertiveness that I can't really ask anyone else to do it—or trust anyone else to put in the time and the sheer expenditure of nerve that this requires.

★ ★ ★ I begin to see why Toomey has so little money left. His mailings keep coming in, the latest a scary postcard with the headline "FIGHTING CRIME IN CAMBRIDGE!" in bright red and a blurry figure holding a more sharply focused handgun. The pitch is reasonable, but . . . it's a D if I were grading it. The reverse caption is "FIGHTING CRIME EVERYDAY," and surely he means every day. At the bottom, in large red letters, it says "Fight Back!" Back? *Against* Toomey? *With* the criminals? Not what he spent four grand to convey. (That he says in the body text, "Tim lead [sic] the fight to put information about sexual predators on the internet" is just sad.) He is endorsed by the International Brotherhood of Police Officers and the Cambridge Fire Fighters (Local 30 of the Fire Fighters' Union of the AFL/CIO), but that is not reassuring. Boston cops have been double-dipping, calling in sick while working second jobs as guards at construction sites, and an investigation by the *Globe* suggests that this kind of theft (which is what it is) is fairly widespread. The mayor of Boston and the legislators on Beacon Hill are captive to the unions, and nobody has the character to stand up and say that when law enforcement officers are corrupted, it is a serious business. I can hit him with this at the debate, but I can't criticize his grammar, which would be condescending.

★ ★ ★ The festival of SS Cosmas and Damian was depressing in two ways. For one, it was not particularly productive, politically. I went in the early afternoon, and hardly anyone was there—"there" being a small street running north from Cambridge Street, lined on both sides with food vendors, arcade games where you shoot at things or throw darts at balloons for prizes or operate mechanical racing objects, and merchants of tacky souvenirs. I came back later in the day and there were still relatively few people. But it was also depressing because it demonstrated how cut off I am from all this, not because I am not Italian but because I am a victim of my cultivated tastes. I did not mind the amusing folk-art shrine to the sainted martyr physicians; what bothered me was the T-shirt with an "Italian Stallion" blazon and the fake No Parking sign with the message: "You take-a my space / I break-a you face!" Why would that amuse Italians? I handed out bookmarks and went home, too bummed out to have even a sausage or an Italian ice.

★ ★ ★ This morning's *Globe* has a piece about the Toomey-Green primary race, which they are still reading as a class difference, the working-class and ethnic voters of East Cambridge being naturally Toomey supporters and the newer arrivals, many of them intellectuals, being likelier to vote for Green. My take on this is a version of Lewis Black's near-apoplectic observation—that Toomey's Democrats are the party of no ideas and Green's are the party of bad ideas.

★ ★ ★ In the conference call last night Alex Dunn gave a pep talk to the Republican candidates and mentioned "targeted campaigns." I asked how and when the decision will be made as to which campaigns are "targeted," and his answer was that this will be decided right after the primary elections. What that means, Evan tells me, is that if Green wins, I have a good chance of getting real help from the party. Or if Toomey wins but only by a narrow margin, then they might get behind me. But if Toomey blows Green out of the water and wins by a huge margin, they may decide that there is no hope for me.

That they would be right won't make it feel better. And for seven weeks I shall have to go through the motions, knock on doors and make phone calls, as if I had a chance. By coincidence, last night I saw George McGovern explain to Brian Lamb on *Booknotes* how he realized he wasn't going to win in 1972 only on Election Day, when he told his wife, as they were driving back to his hometown to cast their votes, that it would be odd not having the Secret Service to chauffeur them anymore. She had known for days that he wasn't going to make it, but until that moment he'd been in denial. Lamb asked if he ever had a chance, and McGovern answered that George Wallace got ten million votes in 1968 and would have got more in 1972, mostly from Nixon supporters. If Wallace hadn't been shot, McGovern could have been a contender.

Part Three

15

★ ★ ★ ★ ★ ★ ★ ★ ★ ★ ★ ★ ★ ★ ★ ★ ★ ★ ★ ★

A clear, cool morning, but the secretary of state predicts a turnout for the primary of no more than 10 percent—which favors Toomey. The *Globe* endorses him: "The incumbent, Timothy J Toomey, Jr., is facing a brisk challenge but deserves reelection to his East Cambridge–Somerville House seat." No mention of Avi's name. For all his effort, money, and talk of "energy," he got labeled as "brisk." A tepid cup of tea!

★ ★ ★ I filled in the little oval next to my name and then slid the ballot into the machine. My voting lacked movie music, but that ordinariness was the impressive part of it. On the way out, a volunteer for Common Cause handed me a brochure about fair elections, and I said I was already a believer and introduced myself. He, too, is a Republican, and I invited him to the fund-raiser at Ryles. At the corner, keeping their legal distance, were volunteers for Green, Toomey, and DiPaola, holding signs and drinking coffee. It looked . . . neighborly. I went back to the condo for a sign and returned to join them for a while.

Either Green or Toomey will be out of it tomorrow, but I have to continue for another seven weeks. It is like eating ice cream, where most of the pleasure is in the first few spoonfuls. I've already got most of the good out of this experience.

★ ★ ★ Weld has come through handsomely:

I am most happy to endorse the candidacy of David Slavitt for state representative for the 26th Middlesex District. He is exactly the sort of person we need in the legislature to support Governor Romney and principles of sound government. —Bill Weld

He carried Cambridge the first time he ran, and this will be helpful.

★ ★ ★ Evan says I am thinking about the primary the wrong way. If Toomey wins, the party will not make me a "targeted" campaign, which means I can have fun, do what amuses me, give interviews, show up at the debate, and exert myself only as far as is reasonable. If Green wins and they think I have a shot, there will be pressure to perform. And, if I lose, I will torment myself with questions about how, if only I'd done this or that better, I might have won. Still, it is tough to play a game without trying hard to win.

I have asked Janet to vote for Green, which, as an unenrolled voter, she can do.

★ ★ ★ Toomey got 54 percent of the vote (3,161) to Green's 46 percent (2,666). I'd have liked it to be even closer, but while this may not convince the party that Toomey is vulnerable, it does raise the question. What the numbers don't show is the bitterness, the accusations of each that the other was lying. Some Green supporters might turn to me, if I can appeal to them. Green spent about twenty-six dollars per vote, which was pricey, even if he had won.

I have sent a congratulatory e-mail to Toomey. I'll put in a call to Green in the next day or two. It feels vulturish to do it right away. I've also called Melissa Kogut at NARAL. With Avi out, my candidacy will now look attractive to them.

★ ★ ★ There is a report in this morning's paper about a poll by the Center for Economic and Civic Opinion at UMass/Lowell that mostly has to do with Governor Romney's popularity (which has dropped slightly, from 61 percent approval in April to 54 percent now). What interests me is that the survey indicates that same-sex marriage is "not a major issue among voters," who are more concerned about health care, jobs and the economy, and education.

★ ★ ★ I got through at last to Melissa Kogut, who was eager for me to understand that there was no rancor toward me in their endorsement of Green but only the practical consideration that, in a strongly Democrat district, he had a better chance for success and it was to their advantage to support a winner. Now that the contest is between Toomey and me, that will have to be reevaluated.

★ ★ ★ I was checking the *Chronicle* online to see if the Weld endorsement was featured. It had not yet been posted, but a "Slavitt" search produced an item I'd overlooked:

Slavitt publishes new translation
Thursday, August 19, 2004

Cambridge author David Slavitt announces the publication of his latest book, a translation of "The Regrets of Joachim du Bellay."

As a member of the mid-16th-century literary group La Pléiade, Joachim du Bellay (1525 to 1560) sought to elevate his native French to the level of the classical languages - a goal he pursued with great spirit, elegance, irony and wit in the poems that comprise "The Regrets." Considered one of the finest sonnet sequences in French literature, this Renaissance piece echoes the homesickness and longing of Ovid's poetry written in exile as du Bellay finds himself lost in Rome, the very home for which Ovid longed.

In this translation by Slavitt, these performances retain their original formal playfulness as well as their gracefully rendered, but nonetheless moving, melancholy. In decadent Rome, among hypocrites, thieves and snobs, du Bellay uses his poetry as an opportunity for social satire and caustic self-criticism. It becomes a salvation of sorts, an approach peculiarly modern in its blending of the classical, the social and the personal.

Slavitt is the Republican candidate for the 26th Middlesex state representative seat. He is a published poet, novelist, translator and essayist.

It's the catalogue copy. Will it get me votes? Or sell books?

★ ★ ★ I've talked to people with Green signs. None was eager to have a Slavitt sign tacked onto the existing stick, but all were receptive, listened to my pitch, and took a bookmark. At houses where no one was at home, I left a doorhanger on which I'd written, "Now, perhaps, think of me?" It cannot have been Avi's charisma or shrewd analysis of social and economic problems that attracted them, but that he was pro-choice and opposed to Finneran. So these are all likely prospects. On the way home, I had to pass the Board of Elections office, and I went in to ask how many votes I'd got. In Cambridge, in the thirty-three precincts, I got 73 votes out of 89 that were cast. Eleven ballots were blank. One was overvoted. There were four write-ins. Scary. A ballot with only one name on it? A voter had to fill in an oval and stick it into the machine. Twelve out of eighty-nine—13 percent—failed to perform this task, which a clever chimpanzee could manage. I called Somerville to see how I'd done there, and I got 51 votes in the five precincts. (There were three write-ins and ten ballots left blank.) It is not as though they went to vote and, when they got to my name, couldn't decide. I was the only name, the only candidate. They managed to get to the polling place and ask for a Republican ballot. And then, like a deer in the headlights, they froze?

The break-down of the Green-Toomey vote by precincts:

The Tale of Turnout—Precinct by Precinct

	Cambridge precincts							Somerville precincts				
Candidate	1–1	1–2	1–3	2–1	3–1	3–2	6–1	1–1	1–2	1–3	2–1	2–2
Toomey	302	480	484	176	345	177	180	194	258	205	170	190
Green	123	123	113	192	182	255	420	176	271	169	294	348
Toomey − Green =	+179	+357	+371	-16	+163	-78	-240	+18	-13	+36	-124	-158

The working-class voters in East Cambridge and Somerville went for Toomey. The flower children where Green and I live went for Green. This is where I should concentrate.

★ ★ ★ It took me five phone calls to get through to St. Hilaire, my contact at the party. It was busy over there, I'm sure, and they were thinking and scheming as they contemplated the primary results. But that was why I wanted to reach him, to explain that the raw numbers on the Toomey-Green race did not tell the entire story. I almost succeeded in not reading too much into their languid office procedures. It was not, I kept telling myself, an indication that I was being written off. But as the hours passed, it became more and more difficult for me to see this as mere inefficiency, as Evan has counseled me to do. When I did get through, he was friendly enough—but he is, after all, a politician.

The rancor between Toomey and Green, and the expenditures on both sides, were news to Matt, as was my hope of reaching a significant share of the 46 percent of the Democrats who supported Green. "Has Green endorsed Toomey, or is he going to?" is what St. Hilaire asked. I said that once I had talked with Green, I would let him know.

★ ★ ★ Meanwhile, I had an e-mail this morning from Toomey, thanking me for my congratulations and agreeing that the campaign would be friendlier now. Fred has proposed October 18th for the debate, with Ethridge King as moderator. This will be fun.

★ ★ ★ I've talked with David Avella in Arlington, Virginia, about the mailing. We want to get the piece to all the Republicans and all the unenrolled voters in the district. The surprising success Green had in Somerville, which may be a result of that city's having become more artsy lately, means that we should send the mailing to the Democrats of Somerville, and to those in the Cambridge precincts where Green won or came close. This is expensive but worth doing, even if I have to "lend" the campaign money.

★ ★ ★ Richard Griffin, with whom I have lunch sometimes, e-mailed me about the *Chronicle* headline announcing Toomey's victory in the primary that said, "Toomey returned to seat," which he called "a major blunder" in reporting a primary election. He thinks I should demand a retraction. I hadn't noticed it! I e-mailed the editor:

Dear Michele,

I take the strongest possible exception to your misleading headline in today's Chronicle: "Toomey returned to seat."

As you perfectly well know, and as you actually say down in the text on page 8, he has merely won the Democrat primary and is now the Candidate. The general election will decide whether he is "returned to seat" or not.

My notion is that, being a polite young man, he will give the seat to an older gentleman—me!

But for your paper to have misrepresented the news this way is a serious lapse.

To this, Ms. Babineau replied:

Hi David.

Thanks for your note, and I agree the headline was misleading. We will run a clarification next week, and I have asked that the online version of our paper be changed. Thanks, Michele

And indeed on the website, the headline now reads: "Toomey edges Green."

★ ★ ★ Similarly, the Cambridge City Council blundered. I sent the following e-mail to Ken Reeves and to Mayor Sullivan and Vice Mayor Decker:

Dear Ken,

"Congratulations to State Representative Timothy J. Toomey, Jr. on being re-elected to the Massachusetts General Court in the primary election.

Vice Mayor Decker, Councillor Reeves and entire membership."

The above item on today's agenda, Resolution #4, is not quite accurate, is it? Not unless you guys are seers! Mr. Toomey has won the Democratic nomination, and is, indeed, the candidate of that party, but he has not been re-elected to the General Court. The general election, as I rather think you all know, is six weeks away!

I, too, am a citizen of Cambridge, and it would be unfair of the Vice Mayor, of you, and of the entire membership to tilt so unfairly in an official meeting of the Council.

I trust you will correct the resolution this evening.

Kindest regards, David R. Slavitt

We shall see whether they do anything to fix this.

⋆ ⋆ ⋆ A headline in this morning's paper: "Romney targeting legislative races." I had known I was not one of the favored few but had only a vague idea as to what that meant. Those who have been chosen are getting real help. The party has about a million dollars to spend on candidates for the legislature, and the strategists want to focus on twenty to thirty races—with direct mail campaigns, television ads, appearances with the candidates, and financial help. According to the *Globe*, "dozens of candidates have . . . received $3,000 in cash." Not me! As valuable as the dollars are, there is also the investment of Romney's clout, which will be enhanced by victories but is at risk if the candidates he targets lose in November. "How well Romney does could be key to his political future as a candidate for the White House," the article says. He "is putting his prestige on the line."

One paragraph gives me some comfort: "Republican strategists agree that, despite help from the state party and Romney, local issues will help decide the contests, and the individual candidates will be in charge of their races." The local issue is abortion rights, and I have inherited Green's mantle as the pro-choice candidate. And Evan is right, as usual, about how this decision of the party takes pressure off me: they don't expect me to win; I'll be doing what is doable or is amusing. It is, in a way, a luxury. Still, the three thousand dollars would have helped. It could have bought one more mailing or even the use of a professional phone bank the week before the election. But you go with what you've got.

In the body of the story, Alex Dunn says, "Romney will not push two controversial public policy issues that he has championed . . . a fool-proof death penalty law and a constitutional ban on gay marriage." The election must mean a lot to Romney for him to get off these hobbyhorses. And their prediction seems modest to me—they "hope" to win between twenty-four and thirty seats. There are seven Republicans in the Senate and twenty-two in the House now. Do they think going from twenty-nine to twenty-four is something to hope for?

★ ★ ★ Word comes from Fred that negotiations about the debate are not going well. I thought Toomey was a stand-up guy, dim but honest, a man who, having given his word, would keep his promises. But now that the primary is past and he is looking at the general election, there is little advantage to his appearing with me in a debate.

> Toomey says the 18th is no-go. And he wants a Democratic City Committee to co-sponsor and co-moderate it. With Somerville having no committee, this would be difficult. Hard to say if this will get done or not at this point. —Fred

There are other conditions, too. He wants it to be in Somerville, and he wants it cosponsored by the Democrats and the Republicans. As Fred point out, there is no Republican organization in Somerville. And a debate at Ryles would be good for me but also good for the Cambridge Republican City Committee, giving it some visibility.

I've told Fred that I am not particular about who moderates. But I agree that it should be in Cambridge, under CRCC sponsorship or at least cosponsorship. I suggested that Fred ask Toomey to suggest a couple of dates and let us pick one. He said he would, but he is not confident that they will reply promptly.

Is Toomey starting to take me seriously? Is he worried?

★ ★ ★ There is a soft feature in today's paper—the Saturday paper, when there are fewer readers—about the Republican intern program for recent college graduates. Only now do I see what they do, how much help they are, and how deprived I am, not having had one. There are twenty-three of these "governor's fellows," who work twelve hours a day and get a stipend of two thousand dollars for the entire campaign, plus free housing. They go through a six-week training period and then run errands, organize volunteers, raise money, make phone calls, and do the donkeywork that I have been doing alone for months now, and they get some experience and can then put that rather grandiose title on their CVs. Kyle Plotkin, for instance, is working for Jane McLaughlin down in Bridgewater: he operates a phone bank four nights a week and all day on weekends and has been in touch with four thousand voters so far. Annie Donaldson, assigned to Judith Judson up in Danvers, says that she is "the only full-time person on the entire campaign."

I am the only full-time person on my campaign.

★ ★ ★ I have been working on what will be the mail piece and the newspaper ad, with "Pro-Reform! Pro-choice!! Anti-Finneran!!!" up on the top, in red and blue, and then the picture of Mitt and me under the line "Tom Finneran is the poster child for patronage, waste, and blocking my reforms at every turn. —Governor Mitt Romney." Below the photograph is my name and my tag "Vote Republican for the sake of Democracy," and then the Massachusetts Republican elephant logo. On the verso is the Weld endorsement, then an informal picture of me that Evan took down at the Coast Guard Academy at Isaac's swearing in. There is a blurry crowd behind me, and I'm smiling. Then the text reads:

> Poet, novelist, essayist, teacher, David Slavitt is the socially moderate, fiscally conservative voice the people of Cambridge and Somerville should have to speak for us on Beacon Hill.
>
> The elected officials of the Commonwealth derive their powers from the consent of the governed and, when our representatives betray our trust, they deserve to be booted out. The only way we can do that is by turning to a healthy, robust opposition party.
>
> The wishes of the voters—as expressed in our referenda—are clear:
>> Tax rollback to 5%
>> Clean elections
>> Death Penalty for heinous crimes
>
> Speaker Finneran's Democrats ignore us at their peril.
>
> Over the past two legislative sessions Tim Toomey has voted with Tom Finneran 97.8% of the time.
>
> THROW THE BUMS OUT!
> LET 'EM HAVE IT! VOTE FOR SLAVITT!
> WWW.DAVIDSLAVITT.COM

The work isn't quite writing but more layout and message delivery, involving decisions about fonts and colors and the order things should go in. It is embarrassing, but this is the end result of a half dozen drafts. It is a low-grade poetry, the art of clubbing people over the head.

When Evan looked at my printout of the copy for the mailing, he laughed at the last line and told me there was a candidate somewhere whose campaign slogan was "William Boyce! The People's Candidate." I hope it's true.

★ ★ ★ I worry about the turnout for next Monday's fund-raiser where the lieutenant governor will appear. I'm also upset about Toomey's apparent reluctance to debate. I've been telephoning his campaign office this morning. Nobody answers the phone. I guess that is good news, but it doesn't make me feel any better.

I finally got through to Kate Glidden, who was friendly as usual. We consulted calendars for a couple of minutes and set October 13 as the debate date. Tim had wanted it to be cosponsored by the Cambridge and Somerville Democratic committees. There isn't a Somerville Republican committee, and that would show us up as being rather improvisational. I explained that to Kate and said that I relied on Tim, as a decent fellow, not to embarrass us. She was agreeable. I said I was not particular about the moderator but I wanted longer times for statements and replies, and the opportunity for more interchange between the debaters, a format that would enable rather than inhibit our addressing the issues and each other. She said that was no problem. So I have something to look forward to. And we can have our own people videotaping it to be sure of the entire thing getting to the Cambridge and Somerville Community TV stations.

★ ★ ★ Avi Green does not return phone messages. Of course, he could be on a beach somewhere, recovering or simply rejoicing in not having to campaign anymore. But I can't wait for him to surface. I have written him an open letter I'll send the local papers:

Dear Avi,

I congratulate you on an energetic and hard-fought primary campaign in which you came within a few hundred votes of dislodging an entrenched incumbent.

Now that it is over and Tim Toomey is the Democrats' nominee, I call upon you to make good on those things you were saying so eloquently in our debates, in your mail pieces, and in your conversations with voters. If you truly believe—as I am sure you do—in a woman's right to choose, and if you are deeply convinced—as I know you are—that Tom Finneran's control of the state legislature is unhealthy for the Commonwealth, then I call upon you to direct your supporters to vote their consciences and to be true to those principles that motivated you to spend so much time and money in this laudable effort.

We differ on a number of issues. Our approaches to social problems are not always the same. But on these two important questions—the speakership and women's reproductive rights—we are entirely in agreement. We are presently only five House votes away from a pro-choice majority and this is, as you are well aware, a critical year. My hope is that in two years you will run again, but that I will be the incumbent you are then looking to unseat.

With kind regards,

David R. Slavitt

★ ★ ★ The Kerry Healey appearance yesterday for Richard Babson, who is running in the Eighth Suffolk District, was interesting. I now know what to expect on Monday. Fred will introduce the lieutenant governor, who will talk for a few minutes and introduce me, and then I'll speak. That's it. If we're lucky, we'll have enough bodies. Whether it produces the cash I need is another question, but even if we come up short, Lieutenant Governor Healey won't know. Chances are that I can get through the event without chagrin. But I have to prepare my remarks. Mostly I'll crib from what I got up for the debate. Toomey won't be there, and Healey may be impressed. With that appeal at the end to the nobility of the calling, it has loft! Also it's the right length. And already written.

★ ★ ★ My admiration for the lieutenant governor is only increased by the news I've received that, on the twenty-seventh, she has not only my event to attend but also one for George Field out at Wellesley and then another for Greer Tan Swiston in Chestnut Hill. She will deliver slightly different versions of the same speech, I'm sure, with the same attentive smile and the appearance of intense interest in what each candidate has to say. Grim!

★ ★ ★ An odd column in yesterday's *Globe* talks about Governor Romney's attacks on Finneran and quotes Romney as saying that he didn't read the actual words that were going out over his signature—such as the line in his fundraising letter from the Drake Hotel that I am using in my mailer and in my newspaper ads. There was also a line in another release from the party that said, "Tom Finneran represents all that is bad about politics. As the Democrats' most feared, controlling, and vindictive party boss, Finneran has made it his personal business to co-opt any reform efforts I put forth." But according to Scott Leigh's column, the governor telephoned the Speaker with a "halfway apology," saying that he hadn't been "personally involved" in writing those words. According to the Speaker, Romney "apologized for the language that was contained in these letters, the words that were used, and the like." (The mushiness of that locution is deplorable but convincing: it sounds just like what Finneran would say.) The columnist then suggests that it would have been more "manly" of Romney to have issued a public apology, and he gets Finneran to agree with him, or at least to go far enough to say that "if he didn't say this, somebody did, and he's the head of the team."

What's going on? The next day's paper makes it clearer. The two of them met at the Ashmont T stop on the Red Line, where Finneran actually got down on bended knee before the governor, who in turn announced that the station would get the $44 million for renovation that had been promised by the legislature but had been spent on work at the Savin Hill, Fields Corner, and Shawmut stops. Finneran told the reporters that people had come to his office to ask that the work on their station be done, too, and he had told them that, "notwithstanding the news stories in the paper about sometimes tension between the Legislature and the governor, I was prepared to get on my knees and plead for the funding of this program." And there's a picture of Finneran, in shirtsleeves, kneeling before the governor, and everyone is smiling.

There is no question about the station needing the renovation. It was built in 1927 as a hub for bus and trolley routes and as a stop on the Red Line. The Mattapan trolley turnaround breaks down and blocks the busses. The T station roof leaks for days after a rainfall. The site is isolated from the neighborhood and is dangerous, so that in 2001 and 2002 there were several kidnappings and rapes, which prompted the MBTA to shuttle passengers to their homes. But the clarity of the dislike these men have for each other is compromised. You go along to get along, but it is rarely admirable.

✳ ✳ ✳ The NARAL Pro-Choice Massachusetts Political Action Committee has endorsed me, which is not astonishing, considering that Timmy Toomey is pro-life. We have a Catholic Democratic majority, and contraception in Massachusetts for married couples became legal only in the midsixties. We are five votes shy of a pro-choice majority in the legislature. The Red Sox, the Democrats, and the Vatican! What we have here is a small Balkan country that is attached to the United States and devoted to lost causes.

I went to a NARAL meeting last night to thank them for the endorsement and, mostly, put in an appearance. Senator Barrios was there, and Marty Waltz, who is running against Babson in the Eighth Suffolk District. It was in a terrific apartment with impressive art—a Frank Stella, a Hockney, a very good Picasso, a Lichtenstein, a set of four de Koonings, and a Mary Cassatt to die for were looking down from the walls on a collection of women (almost all were women), most of whom could be played without any fundamental miscasting by Bea Arthur. I said the brilliantly wrong thing, of course, to Melissa Kogut, the political director. It was intentional: I wanted to tease her a little. I told her I felt just a little like the first runner-up for the Miss America title who, if Miss America cannot serve, will be asked to serve in her place. She glared at me for a half second, but I was smiling and so she smiled back.

I get to announce that I'm endorsed—by these people, by Citizens for Limited Taxation, and by the poor Log Cabin Republicans. I have to put all that on the mailing.

★ ★ ★ There is, on October 2, a Cambridge Senior Town Meeting at the citywide Senior Center across the street from City Hall, and one of the events is "Meet the Councilors," which gives Toomey a platform (as a city councillor) but not me or Marty Waltz or Richard Babson, all candidates. So I call the senior center, and they tell me that it is up to City Hall. So I call Mayor Sullivan. He's on the phone, but I'm invited to wait and, eventually, he takes my call. He tells me Denise Simmons is the one I have to talk to.

I tell him that I want to come, but that it might be better to stay away if Toomey is up there and I'm excluded from the proceedings. He gives me some campaigning advice, straight talk and, I'm sure, well meant: if there are four people anywhere in a phone booth, you want to be the fifth.

So I call Denise Simmons and get an answering machine. She does not return the call. And I call the senior center again to arrange for a registration form.

★ ★ ★ The big news this morning is that Speaker Finneran may step down. Lighting out, now that he smells the tar and feathers and sees the rail the feds have been preparing for him? Or just taking that as a nudge to sell out, as he'd been planning to do all along?

He has been in discussions with the Biotechnology Council, an advocacy group for the pharmaceutical industry, which is to say a lobbying organization. They are hiring Finneran's muscle to keep the Massachusetts legislature from allowing the importation of cheaper drugs from Canada. James Mullen, chief executive of Biogen Idec, was candid: "Advocacy groups are for advocacy, and they have to have political muscle. Few people in Massachusetts have more political muscle than Finneran."

There are three Democrats jockeying to replace him. These include John Rogers, the Ways and Means chairman; Salvatore Di Masi, who is more liberal socially (supports gay rights) but who has been the majority leader, whose job, therefore, has been to enforce Finneran's discipline; and William Straus, chairman of the Elections Committee, whose main appeal is that he has not been a Finneran henchman. Within the last couple of years, the *Globe* reports, Di Masi has spent seventeen thousand dollars on dinners, lunches, and golf outings, campaigning for Finneran's job. And Rogers has spent ten grand on such things as moonlight cruises for his committee members and their spouses—even Republicans.

★ ★ ★ I shall have to change my ads. It will be the same message, but I won't have the convenient poster boy for arrogance and deception. It's the Democratic Party I shall have to attack, and that, in Massachusetts, is a harder sell. The best I can do is to take out the "Anti-Finneran" line and replace it with "fiscal conservative." And the tag line over the picture of Mitt and me isn't the attack on Finneran anymore (Mitt didn't actually write those words anyway) but a more general "This is the year to bring change to Beacon Hill," which he probably didn't write either. But it was in the press release I was authorized to send out. On the verso, though, I think I can still attack Toomey for having voted with Finneran 97.8 percent of the time. A new ventriloquist doesn't much change the career of the dummy.

★ ★ ★ A friend of mine got a fund-raising letter from the Toomey people. It suggests that Tim is worried and says in part:

September 24, 2004

Dear Neighbor:

The headline in the September 17, 2004 *Boston Globe* says it all—"Romney targeting legislative races" As the Democratic candidate for State Representative in the 26 Middlesex District and for my tough opposition to Governor Romney's agenda, I have been targeted for defeat by the Romney Republican machine and I need your help. From protecting much needed social service programs for our most vulnerable citizens to defending the civil rights of our gay and lesbian neighbors, I am a voice for Democratic values on Beacon Hill.

Governor Romney has raised more than $2 million to oust Democratic legislators and he, Lieutenant Governor Kerry Healy, the Republican State Committee and many other Republicans have already contributed to my opponent. After a rigorous primary campaign, I was pleased that Avi Green said on election night, "We are all Democrats. I will be the first to say I am proud that on November 2, I will be the first to cast my vote for Tim Toomey." Avi understands how important it is to defeat Governor Romney's hand picked candidates to ensure our Democratic agenda is not destroyed.

After the primary, I do not have the campaign funds to compete with my Republican opponent. To defeat the Romney Republican machine, I ask for your financial support. I have enclosed an envelope to return any assistance you can provide. Please make checks payable to the Toomey Committee.

What he doesn't know is that I have not been "targeted." I only wish I had been. But it's nice to know he's broke. And worried enough not to refer to me by name!

★ ★ ★ I am, of course, also struck by the news that Avi has endorsed Tim. It isn't so much a surprise as a disappointment. I'd thought he might be smart enough to see that his principles and his interest would both be served by his remaining neutral, but evidently not. He and Toomey have had a fairly bitter fight, and it couldn't have been pleasant for him to say these awful things about how he will be "proud" to vote for Tim. I delight in the discomfort of his self-abasement.

On further reflection, I am depressed to realize that what it means is that Avi doesn't think I have a prayer. He's being a realist. Cambridge and Somerville are Democratic towns.

The negotiations over on Beacon Hill have been quick and brutal, and there is no deal, but there is a deal. Di Masi will be the next Speaker. Without actually agreeing to it, Di Masi, who is fifty-nine, allowed Rogers, who is thirty-nine, to understand that if he gets the speakership, he will reinstate the rule limiting possession of that office to four terms (eight years). Finneran had managed to get that rescinded, which was a way of being emperor for life. Rogers also got—or thinks he got—a commitment that he will at least have a say in the appointment of a new chairman of Ways and Means. The *Globe* story quotes a "senior legislative source" who maintains that Di Masi did not agree "specifically" to any of Rogers's "suggestions."

So Di Masi is less of a social Neanderthal than Finneran, but he has been Finneran's Rottweiler for the past few years and is not, presumably, a nice guy. But even if he is a Daniel come to judgment, what kind of way is this for our leaders to come to power? It is as democratic as what goes on in the People's Republic of China.

★ ★ ★ The Sunday night conference call was all about Sal Di Masi (rhymes with Daisy), who he is, and what his voting record has been. It will be posted on the Campaign Portal tomorrow. One candidate asked what the criteria were for being a "targeted" campaign. Alex Dunn's answer was that you need to be within ten percentage points of your opponent and have to demonstrate that with numbers from an impartial poll. I can't afford a poll. What is irksome is that, with Avi having done so well in the district, I could be within ten percentage points of Toomey. I'll call Dunn tomorrow, but that's a Monday and they are all in a meeting on Monday morning, which means I won't get through until the afternoon or even Tuesday. My hope is to schnorr them into doing the poll themselves. I shall have to work hard not to let my annoyance show through.

★ ★ ★ I talked this morning to David Avella at the mailing house. The mailing I need will cost more than the three thousand dollars I have on hand. Maybe another thousand? And that is cutting it fine, sending the piece to all the Republicans and Unenrolleds in the district and to all the Democrats in precincts Green carried. At least, I'd want to send it to all the *female* Democrats in those precincts, who are likelier to support women's rights. I can give myself five hundred dollars and lend myself the rest. I realize how much I need the fundraiser this evening to be a success—not just for Kerry Healey but for the money.

★ ★ ★ This morning's paper has a slightly different version of the weekend's negotiations between Di Masi and Rogers. Now the claim is that while Rogers asked for a commitment from Di Masi that he would serve only for a limited term as Speaker, Di Masi had enough votes already so that he didn't have to promise anything. And as majority leader, he surely would have been able to do the vote count accurately. What Di Masi put out to the press yesterday was that he was "humbled by my colleagues' expressions of confidence in my judgment, leadership skills, and experience." The translation is that he is not "humbled" at all, but delighted that his years of scut work have finally paid off. "I want to thank my colleague, Representative John Rogers, for recognizing that a leadership fight would have been counterproductive for House members and for the state as a whole. He deserves credit for helping to unify the House during this critical time." Or, in other words, na-na, na-na boo-boo!

★ ★ ★ Finneran's legal situation is unclear. The Biotech Council is apparently prepared to hire him even though the FBI investigation is still underway. We "presume" innocence, of course, but we also assume that the FBI and the U.S. Attorney's office are not morons and do not waste their time and the public moneys investigating nothing at all. The question is what they can prove in court. In 1989, after an investigation that lasted for two and a half years, the U.S. Attorney announced that there was not sufficient evidence to indict the then Senate president William Bulger—not that he was innocent.

★ ★ ★ The fund-raiser at Ryles was scary. At a quarter of six, there were nine people in a large room, and the state cop assigned to security and in charge of crowd control came in, looked around, and was too polite to laugh. I was certain that my worst fears would be realized and that Healy would be embarrassed and convinced that she had wasted her time. But by ones and twos people trickled in, and by the time she arrived there were twenty-one in the room. Twenty-two, if you count the bartender.

She greeted people and was poised and charming. But she asked me if I wanted to do any "formal remarks," which suggested that maybe there weren't enough bodies in the room to warrant that. I thought we should go ahead. At a certain point, Fred called us to order and introduced her, and then she introduced me. She was tactful. She began by saying that this was the largest number of Republicans she'd ever seen in one room in Cambridge, and recalled her days at Harvard when, as a young Republican, they never managed to have more than a dozen at any meeting. She did her bit of the week—explaining how the administration had cut back on the Department of Environmental Protection staff by 30 percent but was using the personnel better so that the number of citations to violators was actually up, and how they are saving money by moving the homeless out of expensive and inconvenient units in motels to better accommodations, and that the money they save is being put right back into the program to help the homeless in other ways. She got the polite applause she was expecting. Then she turned to me and acknowledged that there are some differences between the administration and me, but said we are on the same page about basic issues and our desire for reform. She was very good.

The only thing that might have made it better would have been if she could have waited another three or four minutes to hear what I had to say, but she did have three other stops to make, and she did apologize. She accepted one of my flyswatters, invited photographs, and then left me up there to decide whether to wing it, as she'd done, or read from my two-and-a-half-page text, which I decided to do because I liked the text. And twenty people is not so puny an audience for a poet, after all.

The decision turned out to have been the right one, because Mike Jonas from the *Globe* and Neil McCabe from the *Somerville News* both showed up after I finished speaking. I was able to give Jonas a copy of what I'd said and could e-mail the text to McCabe, so they were covered, and there were fair prospects that I might be, too.

There were chafing dishes with four kinds of hot food—chicken wings and odd nibblies—and cheeses and canapés. It was competitive with what they serve at the expensive shindigs the state party runs at flossier places. I hung around, talking to Jonas, McCabe, and the guests. As I left, I took the contribution envelopes from Fred so I could report the donations to Evan and deposit the money. We took in $735, which meant that the net was $235—slightly less than the $250 check from Richard Babson, who was good enough to show up and to make this contribution. He is running in the Eighth Suffolk District and is a millionaire—as Marty Waltz, his opponent, keeps pointing out, as if she were accusing him of something bad. But this was generous, I thought.

What I remember is that moment when there were only eight or nine people in the room. Evan was sitting at a table and reading. I told him that this didn't look good. "It is what it is," he said. Meaning? That it was too late to do anything about it. That whatever it was, I'd have to buck up and get through it. That whatever it was, it would be over soon. It was reassuring. And whatever he meant, it was hard to argue with.

16

I appeared this afternoon on the *Connie Murphy Show* on WROL, a weird AM radio station operated by the Salem Broadcasting Company, a Far Right religious outfit that leavens its programming with Spanish-language broadcasts of the Red Sox games. Connie—short for Cornelius—is an old operator who knows politicians and union guys and for years made a living putting them together for meetings and conferences. Then he decided it would be fun to be a talk show host. I had some worries about being Right enough for him, but he was civilized and generally a good guy, even though his mouth doesn't always do what his brain tells it to do. He kept referring to Finneran as Finnegan, and as an Irishman he ought to be able to distinguish between the two.

I came home to find an invitation to the Cambridge Lavender Alliance meeting next Monday. There was also a stiffy, a nicely done cardboard invitation to a Mike Motzkin event at the Palm at which the governor will make an appearance. (But that is on October 13, which is when I am supposed to be debating Tim Toomey.) In other words, there is a kind of ratcheting up of interest in the election. Now that the primary is over, I am, at the very least, Toomey's opponent.

A letter from Mayor Sullivan came in that more or less acknowledged this change in my status:

Dear Mr. Slavitt: [but then that's crossed out in ink and "David" is written over it]

I wish to thank you for taking the time to email me relative to your concern about Resolution #4 on Monday's City Council agenda. I have confirmed with the City Clerk's Office that the appropriate wording changes have been made to this resolution to ensure its accuracy.

Again, thank you for the time to bring your concerns to my attention. As always, if there is ever anything that I can do to be of assistance, please do not hesitate to call me.

Sincerely,
Michael.

A decent guy. (On the other hand, this didn't cost him anything, and I was right: Vice Mayor Decker's resolution to congratulate Toomey on being "relected" was way out of line.)

★ ★ ★ Sheets of rain, and I was soaked when I came back from the radio station. I thought for a while that I might not even go to the reception for Lieutenant Governor Healey at which former governor Bill Weld would be making an appearance, but then I decided that I owed her, and him, too. But it also crossed my mind that Alex Dunn might be there—and I wanted to confront him and let him know that it was insufferably rude for him to take two days to return a telephone call. So I changed my clothes, put on dry socks, and went back downtown to the Harvard Club. Five hundred bucks to get in, but fifty to the candidates. And while my campaign committee's check would have been legal, all that would have meant was that I'd have to "lend" the committee the fifty. So I just paid with my own check. It was worth the fifty to thank Kerry Healey and to ask her the question that I was in fact able to put to her—whether my fund-raiser last night was the smallest audience she'd had this year. It was. I told her that my gratitude was proportionately greater, and that we did well financially. (I didn't actually define "well.") She is always poised and pleasant. As is Bill Weld. He told me that he didn't even feel obliged to look me up and check me out. The fact that I was Evan's father had been enough for him to trust and endorse.

Dunn wasn't there, as it turned out. But I saw Darrell Crate, the chairman of the Massachusetts GOP, and I let him know how angry I was that this rude young man had taken two days to return a telephone call to me. And I told him that if this had been the first time, I might have been able to invent excuses, but it wasn't and I couldn't. Crate promised that Dunn would get back to me. And then Mark Rowe, who is listed as "liaison to Darrell Crate" (this is, I guess, a fancy word for assistant), came up to me and promised he would have Dunn call me.

Nonsense, of course. It is now ten in the morning. No word from Dunn. And Crate and Rowe are not in yet. Nor is Tim O'Brien, the acting executive director. What I want to tell them, of course, is that this could be a winnable district, but if they don't take or return calls, communication becomes difficult.

Janet has a medical meeting in New Orleans on October 9 and 10. It is a weekend, and I probably ought to be here campaigning. We could do standouts, or I could be going door-to-door with a greater likelihood of catching voters at home. But if the party is so unresponsive and indifferent (or convinced that I'm going to lose, or just inept enough so that I can't get any help from them and cannot win), there is no point in my staying here and knocking myself out. I could go down to the Big Easy with her, have dinner at Galatoire's, maybe with a Yale classmate who lives down there, walk around the French Quarter, look at antiques, and have a good time. So a part of me hopes I never hear from these guys or that, if I do, they will be unimpressed by the information that I have, in fact, already given to Matt St. Hilaire (but without any confidence that he passed it on, or that they would have listened to anything he had to say).

★ ★ ★ Dunn called, at ten thirty, and asked for "Evan Slavitt." It is not difficult to imagine that the message he got was "Call Evan Slavitt's father," which also shows where I am with the party. But once I'd explained who I was, I was able to make my case to him, and he agreed that the situation was interesting enough to warrant an "automated" poll—which isn't quite so accurate but is a lot cheaper than the conventional kind. And he will, of course, let me know the results. I pretended to be entirely mollified. He pretended to believe me.

★ ★ ★ An annoying e-mail this morning from Planned Parenthood:

Dear Mr. Slavitt,

I'm sorry to be late getting back to you. The Planned Parenthood Advocacy Fund has decided not to make an endorsement in your race against Representative Tim Toomey. Our endorsements were released this past Wednesday. As a non-incumbent, our guidelines would require us to schedule an interview with you before making a decision, and with the election so close, it was decided that there just wasn't enough time. We thank you for your support of reproductive health care and certainly wish you the best of luck in your campaign.

Sincerely,
Colin Moore

Colin Moore

Government Relations Manager

Planned Parenthood League of Massachusetts

Take Action and Make a Difference—Join the Planned Parenthood Action Network at http://www.pplm.org

To this, I replied:

Dear Colin Moore,

I wish I could understand your thinking. Representative Toomey is firmly committed to the pro-life position. I am pro-choice and have been endorsed by Naral. What's the hard part? Had you wanted to interview me, I could have popped over to your offices at any time.

This is a tight race. Avi Green, who is also pro-choice, lost by only a few hundred votes and got 46% of the Democrat votes in the district. If I can attract some of his supporters, reach out to the unenrolled, and can count on the Republicans in the district, I could win, and that would bring the legislature one vote closer to a pro-choice majority. The morning-after contraception pill bill that passed in the senate failed in the house. Your policies are getting in the way of good sense. Are you committed to them or to women's rights?

Sincerely, David R. Slavitt

★ ★ ★ Meanwhile, in this morning's *Cambridge Chronicle* there is another nice letter from Susan Imrie, who mentioned to me at the fund-raiser that she had sent it in:

Letter: Chronicle off-base with Toomey headline
Thursday, September 30, 2004

Is the Cambridge Chronicle trying to pull a "Dan Rather" on us? The post-primary front-page headline last week mistakenly announced that the Chronicle-endorsed incumbent Tim Toomey had won the 26th Middlesex seat, when in fact, all he won was the right to run again as the Democratic Party nominee. This week a letter appeared lamenting that another anti-gay marriage representative would be going to Beacon Hill, with no editor's footnote that the election hasn't even happened yet!

Toomey's libertarian-minded opponent, David Slavitt, is pro-choice, supports gay marriage and has a deep respect for the principle of checks and balances that should guide our government. Are the staff of the Chronicle so mortified that Slavitt is running as a Republican that they dare not mention him?

Would it really be so awful to elect a socially liberal representative who may occasionally vote no to a spending bill—a rarity in Massachusetts—and that a glimmer of independent (i.e. anti-Finneran) opposition might see the light of day here?

I subscribe to get local news, yet except for the announcement of Bill Weld's endorsement of David Slavitt, the Chronicle simply does not want voters to know that there is a real race with a real challenger in the district that spans East Cambridge and part of Somerville. Now I can't help but wonder what else is being ignored or misreported.

SUSAN IMRIE

East Cambridge

They also have my open letter to Avi Green. And they have a piece about my kickoff, so it is a big Slavitt day in the paper.

Slavitt kicks off election campaign

David R. Slavitt, Republican candidate for state representative in the 26th Middlesex District, kicked off his election campaign at Ryles Jazz Club last week, at a party at which Lt. Gov. Kerry Healey made an appearance. Healey introduced Slavitt to his friends and supporters and welcomed him as one of the members of Gov. Mitt Romney's Reform Team.

Slavitt thanked her for her support and the governor's, and praised them for their vision of public service.

"There are 200 men and women in the General Court," he said, "and what they do is meet and decide about how we should live and what our responses should be to the entire range of problems and opportunities that we face as a community and as a society. These people may be Republicans or Democrats, liberal or conservative, but what they are supposed to do is represent us and provide their collective wisdom for the challenges we face together.

It is a noble calling, and many of the incumbents seem never to have understood this, or, worse, to have known it once but then to have forgotten it."

Slavitt is a novelist, poet, translator, essayist, and teacher. He is married, the father of three, and the grandfather of nine. This is his first campaign for public office.

★ ★ ★ It's ten minutes to seven, and the phone rings. I pick up and hear an automated voice ask me if it can ask me a few questions.

Is this it? Are they polling me? Yes!

"Are you a registered voter living at this address? Press one for yes, two for no."

I press one.

"If the election were being held tomorrow, would you vote for David Slavitt or Tim Toomey? Press one for Slavitt and two for Toomey."

I press one.

"Are you registered as a Republican, a Democrat, or an Unenrolled voter? Press one for Republican, two for Democrat, and three for Unenrolled."

I hesitate. Should I pretend to be a Democrat to make those numbers better? No, I'll do it straight. I press one.

The voice thanks me and disconnects.

I am delighted, even excited. They did what they said they would do. If the results are no good, it will be based at least on some evidence, rather than just the prejudice that Cambridge is a hopelessly one-party town. On the other hand, if what I have been thinking, calculating, speculating, hoping, and sometimes hearing has any truth, we may find out that I'm competitive. If I am within ten points of Toomey, they will help me. I am lucky to have made it this far. I am also a little bit proud.

★ ★ ★ I spent the morning at the Cambridge Citywide Senior Center on Massachusetts Avenue. The event was billed as a Senior Town Meeting, and there must have been a couple of hundred seniors who showed up to meet the mayor and members of the city council, and to speak about issues that were troubling them. Also for the free lunch, a sandwich from the S&S deli, a bag of chips, a cookie, a soft drink, and coffee. I got there a little after ten o'clock, and the proceedings were already underway. Congressman Michael Capuano was talking. I grabbed a cup of coffee and a bagel and sat down to listen.

It was increasingly outrageous. Capuano is an unprepossessing fellow with a high, grating voice. He was wearing a short-sleeved sports shirt and looked more like the proprietor of a cigar store than a member of the House of Representatives. But it was what he was saying that was annoying. Here was a public meeting to which seniors had been invited to meet the members of their local government, and Capuano was turning it into a political rally. He was a slightly more articulate version of Tim Toomey. "I have had the easiest life in

the history of mankind," he announced, "because *you* fought to give it to me."
And if the Republicans were left to their own devices, they would, he suggested, destroy the Social Security system, abolish the forty-hour week, and
return us all to the breadlines of the thirties. More articulate—but not much
more—than Toomey, he admitted about Social Security, "Yes, they've got
problems, but we're not going to get rid of them." (Them? The problems? The
system? The administrators?) His version of Toomey's rallying cry was "You
either believe we're all in it together or you don't." No hint what "it" is, but the
implication is clear that he is a collectivist and that he wants to continue government handouts because handouts make it clear to the voters that they are
beholden to the city, state, and federal government and should demonstrate
their gratitude on Election Day. If it were up to Republicans, he said, "my
mother would not have Social Security, Medicare, or senior housing." Are we
against his mother? Are we going to throw his poor mom out onto the street?

After Capuano spoke the mayor made a few remarks. And then Emmett
Schmarsow, program manager for Councils on Aging and Senior Centers in
the Executive Office of Elder Affairs, got up and gave us numbers, because he
is a numbers wonk. He talked about how the population is aging—without
making the obvious connection to the way that imperils the Social Security
system. You just can't have more and more beneficiaries living longer and
longer with fewer and fewer workers paying into the system. But the senior
center is hardly a venue for sophisticated economic thinking. It is more of a
playgroup for second childhood, with classes in pottery, painting, creative
writing, line dancing, English as a second language, and movies, and God
knows what else. And it's all so politically correct that you could puke. The
woman who teaches the ESL classes described how she uses the classes to explain what programs are available to seniors, like flu shots, which she does not
necessarily endorse. "There's no right or wrong answer. Some people believe
in Chinese medicine after all."

There were workshops, and then they served the box lunch. Then the seniors could get up and complain about the lights at the crosswalks, the lack of a
senior center in East Cambridge, the fact that the new MBTA buses don't have
places to hold onto at the front of the bus, the light on Bishop Allen Way and
Inman Street that flickers. . . . Mayor Sullivan, with saintly patience, wrote
these things down. As the microphone came near me, I got up, said who I was,
and praised the work of the center, but suggested that in the future events like
this should be less blatantly political and that Representative Capuano had
been out of line. Like Elvis, Capuano had left the building. So had Toomey.

★ ★ ★ More politicking, this time on a pleasant, cool, clear day in Danehy Park in North Cambridge. Rides, free hot dogs, free T-shirts (for kids, and you had to have the kids with you). Janet decorated a plastic sun visor so that it said: "Slavitt / 26th Middlesex" across the front and then, at the sides, in bright green, "Vote." I went around asking people if they were from East Cambridge or Somerville, talking to those who were in the district, giving them bookmarks, and doing the short version of my spiel. I got the usual range of responses, but for those who were confirmed Democrats or friends of Toomey, I now had another maneuver. I could invite them to Ryles on the thirteenth for the debate: "Tim and I will both be there. Come and hear us both and decide for yourself." That was so reasonable they could not dismiss it, or me. I got a couple of Toomey partisans even to the point where they were willing to shake hands with me and wish me good luck.

I did this for two or two and a half hours and am exhausted. My impulse now is that, unless I'm actually ahead in that automated poll, I will go down to New Orleans with Janet next weekend. I deserve a breather. Then will be the debate and four weeks of exertion, after which I expect to return to private life.

★ ★ ★ The Slavitt-Toomey debate is the same night as the last of the Bush-Kerry debates. Kerry's debating coach at Yale was Rollin Osterweis, who also coached Bill Buckley and me. And President Bush took Osterweis's course in the history of American oratory. I saw the first of the Bush-Kerry debates, thought it was too long, recognized Kerry's gestures as typical Osterweis moves, but didn't see it as such a clear-cut victory for Kerry as the polls suggest. Kerry doesn't have any plan for withdrawing from Iraq, and the only difference between him and the president seems to be that Kerry would try to involve more of the international community. They would be no more likely to volunteer for service with his administration than they have been with Bush's. And Bush's answer—that they would not be likely to join an undertaking that, in Kerry's own words, is either a "diversion" or "the wrong war in the wrong place at the wrong time" seems convincing to me. Stylistically, Kerry looked smoother, but that doesn't always win voters' hearts or minds.

I think what lost it for Bush, if he lost it, was that he seemed annoyed and unhappy to be there. American life is so relentlessly affable. Any departure from perfect affability is unlikely to be overlooked or forgiven.

Evan has been telling me that I should be more low-key and upbeat, but I think righteous indignation is the right note, and it's one I can sound naturally and well.

★ ★ ★ I went to the Old Baptist Church yesterday evening to meet with the board of the Lavender Alliance of Cambridge and try to get their endorsement. I arrived a minute or two late, having wandered around the large building trying door after door until I found the correct entrance. Tim Toomey and Kate Glidden were just leaving. We greeted each other in a friendly way and then I sat down at the table, answered questions, and did my number. I conceded that Tim was a supporter of gay rights and had voted properly in the constitutional convention, but I pointed out that he is much less good on other social questions, particularly abortion rights, and if the Lavender Alliance endorsed Green in the Democrats' primary, then they might want to think about me for the same reasons, and also because the two-party system would work better with two actual parties. I talked about Tim's animus against Harvard and praised Harvard for its ability to use its vast wealth to undertake projects in sciences, medicine, and the humanities that would, at least in the short term, lose money but may be valuable in the future. I conceded that Harvard occasionally does unattractive things, outsourcing whenever it can to save money, but they are driven to this by economic realities.

The panelists—some of them, anyway—work for Harvard and are members of various unions. I tried to be sympathetic but realistic, mentioned my own experience as the unit chairman of the Newspaper Guild at *Newsweek*, and alluded to the demise of the *New York Mirror*. But more than anything I said, I think it was my witty sallies that won them over—if, indeed, they were won over. I said that labor negotiations with Yale and Harvard were perhaps complicated by the fact that both Larry Summers and Rick Levin are economists, so that the unions are not merely negotiating but also questioning the academic authority of these gentlemen, who do not take it well and, at least in Levin's case, dig in their heels.

As I was leaving, Carolina Johnston came in. She is the Green Party candidate running against Alice Wolf, and so far as I can see doesn't have a chance. I renewed my offer of a debate—after the election—and she smiled but made no promises.

We shall see how the Lavenders decide. In a community in which most of the members of the Cambridge City Council are gay, their endorsement is likely to weigh more heavily than it might in more conventional districts. Toomey thinks he deserves it because he voted right and because he is, for God's sake, gay, albeit not openly. But maybe the fact that he has never come out will be irksome to some of the panelists. And his pro-life position is less liberal than they are likely to be.

★ ★ ★ It is Tuesday morning, and I have yet to hear the results of that poll the GOP took last Thursday night. I'm sure they have the numbers, but the only person I can get through to is Jane Hirsh, a low-level volunteer. She tells me that Tim O'Brien is the only one who has the information, but he has never taken a call from me and has never returned any of my calls. It is infuriating, even though Evan keeps telling me it isn't personal. It's just incompetence, he insists.

★ ★ ★ Sue Hyde has called from the Cambridge Lavender Alliance to say that they've decided to endorse Toomey. Apparently I impressed them a lot, but I talked too much about Cambridge issues rather than statewide issues. (They could have asked me questions about statewide issues but didn't.) She said that they liked me and hoped I'd run for city council sometime.

Not in a million years.

She thanked me for coming by and wished me good luck. I almost believed her and thanked her for calling. On reflection, I decided that it isn't that they are lavender so much as that they are lefties. Toomey is a Democrat, and so are they. It's that simple.

★ ★ ★ A fund-raising letter from the state Republican Party arrived today over Darrel Crate's signature, and it explains at least a part of what "targeted" means. The chosen candidates get from two to six districtwide mailings, at a cost of about five thousand dollars apiece, and as far as I can tell, that's mostly it. Would that make the decisive difference? Well, it might help. But so would it help if there were an actual Republican organization here in Cambridge. I don't have enough volunteers to do the telephoning on Election Day or on the day or two before that. I don't have enough money to buy cupcakes for the senior citizens in the assisted living and low-rent housing units the way Toomey will be doing.

On the other hand, if I got two or three mailings from some candidate, and a cupcake, would that change my vote?

★ ★ ★ O'Brien finally called with the dismal news that the poll numbers are 51 percent for Toomey, 40 percent undecided, and 9 percent for Slavitt. So I don't have to knock myself out anymore. I'll do what Evan said to do—have fun, do the things I feel like doing, and work on a graceful concession speech.

★ ★ ★ Fred thinks this is less catastrophic than it might appear. For Cambridge? For a six-term incumbent Democrat to have only 51 percent in a poll a month before Election Day? He thinks I should keep plugging and see how much I can get of that 40 percent undecided. The debate hasn't happened yet, and it will play on Cambridge and Somerville community television. The mailer hasn't gone out, and the ads haven't run. Keep at it, he says. But the e-mail this morning from David Avella is worse than what I had expected:

David—

Here is the pricing for the "Bio" mailing.

Quantity—9,512
6 x 11, full color, 100# cover
Production—$3,329.20
Postage—$1,807.28
TOTAL—$5,136.48

Payment in full is required once artwork is approved and before production begins.

Mailing to arrive in mailboxes the week of Oct 25th.

Thanks,
David

It's more than what is in my campaign committee's account. I can write a committee check for $3636.48 and throw in my own check for $2,500.00, $500 of which can be a contribution and the rest a "loan." Chances of the committee ever being able to repay me are zero, but I'm not Babson, throwing tens of thousands of dollars into this quixotic enterprise.

Still, thousands.

★ ★ ★   How do I think of such an expenditure? An extravagant dinner for a few friends in a great restaurant? A New York weekend with the theater, hotel, dinners, and the air fare? An expensive indulgence, but one that I can afford. It is not so dismaying, I suppose. I only wish I weren't depressed by the poll numbers or that they hadn't come in the day before this bill from the mailing house. The conjunction is menacing in itself.

My present expectation is that I may wind up doing about as well as Paul Lachelier when he ran against Toomey two years ago on the Green Party ticket and got 37 percent of the vote. That was thought to have been respectable.

It also crosses my mind that the anti-Bush sentiment, which is so strong these days, may be hurting me simply because I am running as a Republican. I don't share the president's social views, think he is wrong and even dangerous in his views on stem-cell research, and am uncomfortable about Attorney General Ashcroft's excesses. I am uncertain about the war in Iraq—as Kerry seems to be, too. But as I have been saying to those who are not so filled with hatred of the president that they can listen, the party is not all Bush and Ashcroft. And unless moderates like me continue to be active, the evangelicals will take it over entirely, which would be worse.

The poll was taken a couple of nights after the first Bush-Kerry debate, and Kerry did well, and Massachusetts voters—Somerville and Cambridge voters— were roused. Or am I simply trying to blame something else, when the truth of it is that if I'd been out there more, knocking on doors, or making more phone calls, or doing what I'm doing but more vigorously, I'd be in better shape? There is no way to know.

★ ★ ★ One of the odd consequences of the poll is that I find I have turned into a liar. Candor, transparency, honesty . . . these are qualities we look for in our politicians, but the system militates against these virtues. It would be not only ruinous but also embarrassing for me to admit that I have attracted the support of 9 percent of the voters in the district. So I omit that interesting bit of information and continue to talk as I did last week and the week before about how Green got 46 percent of the Democrats' votes and if I can connect with those supporters, hold my Republican base of 13 or 14 percent, and some-how reach out to a fair share of the Unenrolled, I can win. I don't believe this anymore, but the chances are nil of my raising money or even of getting people to listen to what I say if I announce that I am a fringe candidate, less popular than even the Green Party loser of two years ago.

It is stressful to be foisting fictions on friends and acquaintances. And the psyche tries to find ways of reducing stress, so that, as I hear myself saying these things that I know to be untrue, I learn by the mere repetition to gener-ate some notional belief that if the debate is a great success, and if the ads are as eye-catching as I believe them to be, and if the mailer works as well as one could hope, then they might turn out not to be barefaced lies after all. I almost believe what I am saying—as all politicians must, telling reporters, support-ers, and voters that they are in good shape and are going to win.

Bravery? Pluck? Or delusion and mendacity? It depends on how you slice it.

★ ★ ★ A message from Fred about the debate next Wednesday outlines a format, which seems fine to me:

(I) INTRO: F. Baker [5 minutes or less]

Thank everyone for coming, thanks Ryles for hosting, remind people that bar is open throughout debate but try to keep noise to a minimum. State that both candidates have agreed to the time, date, location, moderator, and format of the debate. Quickly outline format of debate. Make a quick plug for the Republican City Committee: contact info, web site etc. Introduce candidates and then introduce moderator.

(II) DEBATE: E. King [1 hour max.]

(1) Candidate opening statements: 3 minutes max. each.
(2) 5 questions from moderator, 2 minute response from each candidate.
(3) 2 questions from each candidate for the other, 2 minute response to each.
(4) 3 questions chosen by moderator from audience submissions: 2 minute response to each.
(5) Closing statements by candidates: 2 minutes each.

(III) ADJOURNMENT: F. Baker [2–3 minutes]

Remind audience of free food, compliments of Republican City Committee, thank candidates, audience and moderator for participating. Take quick vote on a small City Committee administrative matter. Ask audience to consider small donation to help defray costs of event. Remind audience that contributions are used for activity costs and that the CRCC does not give money to candidates or PACs.

I find that I am rather more cheerful about this event. It is a part of the campaign, but it has its own dynamic, and just as a game it is fun to play, whatever the poll numbers may be. Toomey doesn't know how bad they are for me, and neither does anyone in the audience.

★ ★ ★ The announcement of my endorsement by Citizens for Limited Taxation is in today's *Chronicle:*

Endorsements: Slavitt endorsed by CLT group

Thursday, October 7, 2004

David R. Slavitt has won the endorsement of CLT's 2½Political Action Committee in his election bid for state representative from the 26th Middlesex District.

CLT's 2½ PAC, the political arm of Citizens for Limited Taxation, was originally created to support candidates who would defend Proposition 2½ in the state Legislature. It now endorses candidates who support taxpayers on a variety of issues, and uses the CLT Legislative Rating to identify pro-taxpayer legislators.

Francis J. Faulkner, executive director of the PAC, said the group endorsed Slavitt based on his support for limiting taxes and government. "Taxpayers need people like Dave Slavitt in the state Legislature to support the voters mandate on the income tax rollback and to fight any attempt to impose new taxes. Dave has taken the taxpayer protection pledge which asks candidates to 'oppose any and all efforts to increase taxes.' Signing the pledge means he is serious about not raising taxes and will change the focus on Beacon Hill from tax hikes to better management of state revenues. In contrast, his opponent, Rep. Toomey, received a low 14 percent in CLT's most recent taxpayer rating, and voted for more than a billion dollars in tax increases."

In serving the taxpayers and the economy, the CLT's 2½ PAC urges voters of the 26th Middlesex District to vote for Slavitt Nov. 2.

There is also an announcement of the Slavitt/Toomey debate next Wednesday. This is good for us because this week's issue of the paper has extra push. Sponsored by the Ten O'Clock News on Channel 56, seven thousand free issues of the paper have been distributed to Cambridge residents. So a lot of people will know about my endorsement and about the debate.

Meanwhile, with the paper still spread out on my desk, I had a phone call from Michele Babineau, the editor, who wants me to show up at their offices next Thursday to be interviewed by the editorial board, which will be determining which candidate they—the Chronicle and the Somerville Journal—will endorse.

★ ★ ★ The page-one story in this issue of the Chronicle is of Richard Babson's campaign finances. The headline is "Babson fills own coffers," and the numbers are even more painful than mine, as I had suspected they would be. As of the reporting date, he had $32,325 in his war chest, but of that, $30,000 was his own money. The story is slanted to be as unflattering as possible, suggesting that "only seven actual supporters—including four who live out of state—donated to Babson's campaign over the summer," but that obscures the fact that his kickoff was only a month or so ago and was well attended and, I'm sure, took in more than seven contributions. Even I sent him a small check, as a friendly gesture.

Marty Waltz, his Democratic opponent, had raised $65,000 and change. But what the story does not report is that she spent much of that in the primary, running against Kristine Glynn.

★ ★ ★ From the *Somerville Journal*:

Slavitt fails to raise a dime in Somerville
By Auditi Guha/ Journal Staff
Thursday, October 7, 2004

Zip, zero, zilch.

That's how much money one state representative candidate has collected in Somerville, despite the eastern part of city comprising nearly half the district.

"This doesn't mean I am hopeless in Somerville," said David Slavitt, Republican challenging state Rep. Tim Toomey for his seat in East Somerville and East Cambridge.

Between Jan. 1 and Aug. 30, Slavitt raised $5,147, according to reports filed with the state Office of Campaign and Political Finance. He also received a $9,000 in-kind donation from the Massachusetts State Republican Party, which is supporting several dozen Republican candidates around the state. "It's quite a large investment allocated out to each of us," he said.

Toomey's campaign finance report indicates receipts worth $77,145 and total expenditures of $87,663. He received $6,438 in contributions from Somerville, $23,909 from Cambridge.

Ward 1 School Committee member Maureen Bastardi and Tony Lafuente contributed to his campaign, among Somerville notables.

Slavitt points to the lack of organized Republican groups in the city as the reason he did not receive any money from Somerville. But he still said he expects to win voters in Somerville with the campaigning he has done here in areas where Avi Green beat Toomey in September's Democratic primary.

Slavitt said he plans to use the fact that he is pro-choice and an artist to leverage the support of Green's base. Toomey is pro-life.

"I am optimistic simply because Avi [Green] did so well," Slavitt said. "All I need is 13–14 percent of the Republicans, Avi's supporters, a fair share of the Unenrolled and I could surprise everyone—me too."

After edging out challenger Avi Green in the Democratic Primary, Rep. Tim Toomey will face Slavitt in the general election on Nov. 2.

Toomey could not be reached for comment.

I called Ms. Guha to complain that she never asked me about contributions from Somerville, and that the figures from the Office of Campaign and Political Finance are from early September, which was the reporting date. This was what the *Chronicle* had done with Babson, whose fund-raiser didn't show up in the OCPF figures, as mine in Cambridge hadn't either. I've had contributions from residents of Somerville, I insisted.

She asked me how much and from how many people, and I promised I'd try to find out from my committee treasurer. It won't be a robust number, but it is better than "zip, zero, zilch."

There is also a condescending editorial in the same issue of the *Journal*:

Editorial: Money makes the world go round
Thursday, October 7, 2004

If dollars translate into votes, both of Somerville's Republican candidates for state representative are in trouble.

Neither Dane Baird nor David Slavitt made a good showing in collecting donations from Somervillians. Of the $6,399 Baird raised, a paltry $379 came from the city he seeks to represent. And Slavitt fared even worse: Not a signal [sic] Somerville address appears on his campaign finance report.

Both of candidates waved off questions about whether this will hurt them. Baird said he will get to know people in the city better if he is elected. And Slavitt blamed the lack of Republican organizations for his poor showing. Well, we've got news for you, boys: Politicians are expected to know people in the community before they seek office, and voters do not need to belong to a group to give money.

You can't write off either candidate for failing to collect Somerville money, but as politicians they should realize there is a connection between contributions and support. People who are passionate about a candidate use their checkbooks to show their love. If you can't get a single person in our city to show you that love, how can you expect us to believe you are the right choice for us?

Along with this disagreeable piece of prose, there is an inept and malapropos cartoon by Frank Bernard, the point of which seems to be that without local funding from constituents, Dane Baird and I are creations of Mitt Romney and beholden to him.

★ ★ ★ My letter to the editor:

To the editor:

Your condescending (you ought not address a senior citizen as "boy") and misspelled ("single" and signal" are two different words) editorial is also bizarre in its inferences and nutty in its conclusions. You suggest that "People who are passionate about a candidate use their checkbooks to show their love." Do you seriously suppose that the union PACs of the Boston and Cambridge police, firemen, and carmen (all of which contributed as generously as the law allows to the Timothy Toomey campaign fund) are expressions of love? Or are these groups unsentimental enough—and practical enough—to expect favors from the chairman of the legislature's public safety committee?

Your partiality—in the news report, in the editorial, and in the inept cartoon—is transparent. I am not a Romney puppet. The governor and I have differed on a number of issues that are important to him, but we agree that the GOP is a big tent and we make allowances for each other.

The only opacity is why you would want to protect and maintain the one-party system that has been the bane of our political life in the Commonwealth for longer than you, young lady, have been alive.

David R. Slavitt

★ ★ ★ The *Somerville News* was friendlier, with a nice piece about the Ryles fund-raiser:

Lt. Gov. Healy Ryles-up Slavitt campaign
by Neil W. McCabe

Supporters of the Republican challenger for the 26th Middlesex seat in the state legislature, including Lt. Gov. Kerry Healy gathered at Ryles in Inman Square to gear up for his final push before the November election.

"I really go out every day as if I can win," said David R. Slavitt, who is running against State Rep. Timothy J. Toomey Jr., a Democrat. The seat represents parts of East Somerville and East Cambridge.

Slavitt, who was born in 1935, said he goes door-to-door until his knees give out, then he returns home and works the phones, making calls until he is ready to go out again.

In her remarks, Healy said it was refreshing to see such a crowd of Republicans in Cambridge.

When she was with the College Republicans at Harvard, she said it was rare to get a crowd larger than a dozen at a meeting.

Healy said she and Gov. W. Mitt Romney were aware of philosophical differences between Slavitt and themselves. But, she and the governor welcomed the idea of an intellectual like Slavitt in the legislature.

Slavitt was the film critic for Newsweek in the 1960s, and in addition to books of poetry, he has published novels and translations of poetry.

"For her to fit me into her schedule at all is outrageous," Slavitt said. The event was the first of four she attended that night.

Before Healy left, Slavitt said he handed her a campaign fly swatter. "She seemed a little confused until I explained it was for the Republican SWAT team."

Beyond his knocking on doors and making phone calls, Slavitt said he is reaching out to the supporters of Avi Green. Green lost the Sept. 14 Democratic Primary to Toomey.

Toomey has agreed to debate Slavitt Oct. 13 at Ryles, he said.

Although Green endorsed Toomey the night he lost the primary, Slavitt said he has called Green and sent him e-mails.

Slavitt said he believes that because he supports abortion rights and other socially progressive positions, Green's voters have more in common with him than they do with Toomey.

Slavitt wrote an open letter to Green's voters making the case that issues are more important than party, he said.

In addition to the social issues, Slavitt said he and Green both agreed that the leadership of the General Court must change.

Despite the resignation of former House Speaker Thomas M. Finneran, Slavitt said the new speaker, Salvatore F. Di Masi, D-Boston, is just as bad. "Only the faces have changed."

"Di Masi was Finneran's Rottweiler, who was in-charge of rewards and punishments for him," he said.

Slavitt said the way the leadership change was handled by the House Democratic leadership was evidence enough that nothing is different. "The process had all the transparency of the Chinese Communist Party."

★ ★ ★ Evan was, as usual, more cheerful than I about the *Journal* coverage. He congratulated me on my first political cartoon. I guess it is a kind of half-assed achievement.

Janet doesn't like the "young lady" phrase in my letter to the editor, but then I didn't like their "boy," and this is tit for tat.

"You should be bigger than that," she said. "I should be," I agreed. "But I'm not."

★ ★ ★ ★ ★ ★ ★ ★ ★ ★ ★ ★ ★ ★ ★ ★ ★ ★ ★

17

The trip to New Orleans was probably a mistake. The weather was foul, and I spent much of the weekend worrying about whether the planes would get me back to Boston on Monday. I have an interview with the *Somerville Journal* on Tuesday, a poetry reading on Tuesday evening, and then the debate on Wednesday. And on Sunday there was an e-mail to Fred Baker and me from Toomey that was quite unsettling.

> Fred:
>
> I'm sure David would agree with me that debates today, including the two in which we have participated, are not really debates and actually boring, therefore I propose the following format:
>
> > 5 minutes opening statements
> > Questions only from David and me to each other, with 2 minutes for a response and 1 1/2 minutes for rebuttal, with the moderator, at his option, allowing another 30 seconds each for surrebuttals.
> > 2 minutes for closing statements.
>
> This format will provide an informative and lively discussion for the voters.
>
> I look forward to David's earliest agreement to this proposal so we can both begin preparing for this debate.
>
> Tim

I agreed to this immediately, figuring that the less constrained the debate was, the better off I'd be. But once I'd sent my acceptance, I began to wonder what had prompted him to offer this change. All I have been able to think of is that he plans to ask me wonky questions that he thinks may embarrass me as they reveal how little I know about, say, the crime figures in Cambridge and in the Commonwealth for the last four years, or the MCAS scores, or the overtime pay for firemen. . . .

He has mastered a vast amount of data about which he can demonstrate my ignorance. What I have to do, then, is figure out a strategy by which I can extricate myself from such awkwardnesses and turn my ignorance into an advantage. In the middle of the night, with the sound of the rain beating on the windows from the tropical storm that was passing through, I realized that I can dismiss such demands for detail as irrelevant. For members of the state House of Representatives, there is no particular advantage in knowledge or competence when long, complicated bills are worked out behind the closed doors of the leadership offices and then dropped on the desks of the legislators who have to cast their votes that day on two or three hundred pages of impenetrable text. It is all they can do to read the instructions on how to vote.

Toomey cannot attack me on my record: I don't have one. All I have to do is implicate him in the Beacon Hill mess. His complicity with the speaker has been rewarded with a committee chairmanship, and his success is a badge of dishonor. Better to be independent—and an outcast—like Pat Jehlen of Somerville than a team player like Toomey. My preparation will be much like that involved in studying for an essay exam. You learn a few facts and memorize a quotation or two so that you can give the illusion of mastery, implying that you have much more of this kind of thing available but are constrained only by time.

The only other motive for Toomey's offer I have been able to imagine is that he too has taken a poll and is distressed to find that, after serving six terms, he has the support of only 51 percent of the electorate. This could worry him, or anger him, or in some way prompt him to take risks. I am still worried, however, because Toomey is giving me exactly the kind of debate I've always wanted, and I can't believe that there isn't a catch somewhere. He may not be an intellectual giant, but he's shrewd and has managed to survive and prosper for some years now. I should not underestimate him.

★ ★ ★ Another way he could appeal to the audience is on the basis of his twelve years of experience in the House: he has clout over there and knows everyone, which makes him a more effective representative of his constituents in Somerville and Cambridge. My answer could be that we already have people with connections to the Democratic leadership. We are in the district of Senate president Travaglini, after all. I'd have more clout with the executive branch and might be better able to intercede with the governor's office on behalf of constituents. (Is this true or not? It sounds reasonable.)

I can also attack Toomey for his coziness with the unions representing the police and the firefighters and the detectives and the carmen (MBTA workers). He looks out for them on Beacon Hill, and they contribute to his campaign chest every year, but who looks out for us when these public safety workers rip us off?

★ ★ ★ Five minutes each for opening remarks and two each for closing statements means that we've got about forty-five minutes for the questions. Figuring that each question will take about four minutes (the answer, the rebuttal, and perhaps a second exchange if the moderator thinks that such further talk is necessary or warranted), we have time for eleven questions, which means I need six or, just to be safe, seven. The first two are about capital punishment and Toomey's idea about taxing Harvard and MIT. The rest:

(3) The *Globe* reported last month that significant numbers of policemen in Boston are taking sick pay and reporting for duty at construction sites, which is unethical and illegal. You are the cochair of the Joint Committee on Public Safety. How can we expect you to investigate these abuses and to find legislative ways to prevent their recurrence when your campaigns are the recipient every year of the maximum contributions that the law allows from the detective's union PAC, the Boston Patrolmen's PAC, the Boston Carmen's Union PAC, and the fire-fighters' union PAC? You are supposed to be our representative, but after six terms in office, you seem to be representing the police and firemen against the interests of the public. Are you not at least embarrassed by this apparent conflict of interest?

(4) You describe yourself as "pro-life" when you mean that you are against women's right to choose what happens to their own bodies. When the WHO estimates that 78,000 women a year die from botched abortions in places where they are illegal or otherwise unavailable—that's more than 200 every day—should you not at least use less misleading language to characterize your views?

(5) In 2000, the people of the Commonwealth voted 60 percent to 40 percent for a rollback of our state income tax to 5 percent. You have said in these debates that you are against such a rollback—even with a surplus of $700 million over predicted revenues. We have the fourth-highest tax rate of all the fifty states. The money that Massachusetts citizens earn is theirs, and they can spend it and invest it more sensibly than Beacon Hill. Lower tax rates would

attract business. Have you been following the dictates of Speaker Finneran on these issues or are you in economic error entirely on your own?

(6) Cambridge library renovations, budgeted in 1994 at $30 million, are now estimated at something like $63 million and not a shovelful of earth has been turned. Assembly Mall in Somerville has been dragging on for almost as long, and that city, which is in precarious shape financially, has missed out on just under $2 million a year in tax revenues that could have been generated there. Is there nothing that you could have done as a Cambridge city councillor and as a state rep for Cambridge and Somerville to reduce these inefficiencies and prevent the hemorrhage of taxpayers' money?

(7) When I was interviewed by Deborah Eisner for the *Cambridge Chronicle*, we were at Carberry's and I offered to pay for her coffee. She refused because of journalistic ethics. She didn't want to accept my hospitality and then feel beholden. You held a dinner at 1221 Cambridge Street for the residents of that building, and I am sure that there have been other such events at other venues, and you paid for these out of your campaign funds. Is there not the same appearance of impropriety? Isn't this close to vote buying? And should that kind of thing be permitted under Massachusetts law?

These should be enough to keep him occupied. What I have to do is to plan out my answers to what he is likely to ask.

★ ★ ★ A distressing call came in from Justin Kaplan that informed me that he and Anne Bernays sent out twenty invitations to the wine and cheese fundraiser for my campaign and have not had a single acceptance. I thanked them for trying, promised that we'd get together after the election, and hung up feeling terrible, not for my sake (the chances of my recovering any of that money I lent the campaign are now nil) but theirs.

★ ★ ★ I was interviewed yesterday by Auditi Guha, a young woman on the staff of the *Somerville Journal*, and we were at a table at Carberry's—where Deb Eisner interviewed me months ago. I was somewhat unbuttoned, as I can afford to be because I am not burdened by any expectations of winning.

An e-mail from the Massachusetts GOP invites me and my staff to the Wyndham Westborough at seven on October 19 to hear one of their strategists talk about getting out the vote. Whatever their strategies, I don't have a staff! If I get three or four people making phone calls on the weekend before the election, that'll be a huge achievement.

On the other hand, Janet and I were having dinner with a Yale classmate and his wife last night, and I mentioned Greer Swiston, whose campaign in their district in Newton I've been following with some envy. She seemed really to be getting it together. But my classmate's wife had never heard of her. And Kay Kahn, her five-term incumbent Democrat opponent? "Oh, she'll win easily," my classmate's wife said.

✴ ✴ ✴ My NARAL endorsement is in the *Cambridge Chronicle*. The key passage is: "'We are only five votes away from a pro-choice majority in the Massachusetts House, and Mr. Slavitt's election would bring us that much closer to a Legislature that recognized and respected women's rights,' said Melissa Kogut, executive director of NARAL Pro-Choice Massachusetts. 'Pro-choice voters have one choice in this election, and that choice is David Slavitt. He trusts women to make their own reproductive health decisions,' said Kogut."

✴ ✴ ✴ I had an e-mail this morning from one of my fellow candidates:

Hello fellow reform candidates,
I just want you all to know that I have a company doing my broadcast calling for only 3.9 cents per call! If anyone wants the info about this company, e-mail me and I'll let you know. I've signed up for two rounds of calls. Their server can do 25,000 calls per hour.

Good luck to everyone,
Marc Lombardo
Candidate for 22nd District State Representative, Billerica

This is salt in my wounds. My committee's cash balance is $372.00, and I have to kick in a hundred bucks as my half of the payment for the videotaping of the debate last night.

✴ ✴ ✴ The debate was a success, I guess, but it accomplished little. I was disappointed that Evan couldn't be there. (He had to go to Texas to take a deposition.) He'll see it on the videotape, but that isn't the same thing.

There were maybe forty people upstairs at Ryles, which was considerably fewer than showed up at the Filarmonica on Cambridge Street when Green, Toomey, and I were on the panel together. I told myself that the primary audience would be the people who saw it on television, but I'd have preferred a larger crowd. (The second play-off game between the Yankees and the Red Sox was scheduled for the same evening—what Cousin Louis warned me about—

but that didn't start until an hour after we were done. There was also the presidential debate between Bush and Kerry at nine.)

Toomey was cordial, as usual. And his opening remarks were more or less what I'd heard before, including the little zinger about how, "whether you have lived here all your life or have only moved into our community recently, you know that for me representing Somerville and Cambridge is not merely an academic exercise but rather a commitment to the community." In other words, I am a newcomer and an egghead but he's the real deal, the lifelong Cantabrigian who went to Matignon High School and Suffolk University and is, therefore, a guy you can trust.

"You have come to know me and my commitment to the people of the Twenty-sixth Middlesex District," he said. "My commitment can be seen in my attention to constituent services, my leadership in directing state resources to the district, and my hard work to improve the quality of life that makes us want to live and work here." There followed a litany of his concerns and achievements, modest in scope but real. His first reference to me was amiable enough: "My opponent is a decent person, a great wit, and a superb debater, yet he has one serious flaw. He represents a Republican Party that, both nationally and statewide, doesn't understand or represent the needs or the ideals of the people of the Twenty-sixth Middlesex District. He rails against the Democratic majority in the legislature, but under governors Weld, Celucci, Swift, and Romney, the Republicans have controlled the executive branch for sixteen years—sixteen years that have included the biggest boondoggle in the history of the United States, the Big Dig, the poster child for government waste and mismanagement."

He then went off the rails a little, referring to the *Somerville Journal* cartoon that showed me as Romney's puppet and suggesting that the bulk of my campaign had been funded by Governor Romney—a misreading of the OCPF numbers, with that nine-thousand-dollar in-kind contribution merely representing my 130th portion of the capital expenses of the party's statewide effort. My reaction, at that moment, was that I could correct him easily enough but that he and his people had done their homework, even if they were wrong about this particular item. He had a sheaf of papers with him, an inch-thick pile of notes and sources in various folders, and I was flattered to have been taken so seriously.

As it turned out, my fears that he was going to wonk me to death with arcane legislative details I couldn't possibly have at my fingertips were unfounded. He believes in himself, in the rightness of what he has been doing, and in the hard work he has put in. He was convinced that in the most open and free-form debate, his qualities would somehow emerge. The worst I can suppose about his motives is that he wanted to give me enough rope and see if I'd hang myself with some smart-ass remark I'd regret later.

"This is the most important legislative election in decades," he said toward the end of his opening remarks. "The goal of the Romney Republican machine is to elect enough Republican representatives to uphold vetoes based on his right-wing agenda."

So the terms of the debate would be friendly enough, each of us attacking the other's party rather than the other's character. I could go after him from time to time on his record, but having no record myself, the chances were not great that he could do much damage to me, except by demonstrating my ignorance here and there.

★ ★ ★ His first question to me was about the Big Dig and how it had been mismanaged by "Republican administrations that are supposedly financially prudent and claim strong backgrounds in business administration."

"An interesting question," I said, thinking fast, because I have almost no idea who was responsible for that mess. "What it assumes is that there is in the General Court at least a contingent through whom and by whom the governor can exercise any kind of power over anything. What we have is a weak governor whose main power seems to be that he can open the window and yell, or call a press conference and get people to come and listen to him when the abuses of the legislature are far too great. The attorney general is a Democrat. The treasurer is a Democrat. There are only the governor and the lieutenant governor, and it would take fifty-four votes in the legislature, as you perfectly well know, to sustain a gubernatorial veto. The Democrats can do anything they want. And their habit is to do that and then blame the governor, because, what the hell, he's the governor."

Toomey came back, insisting that the governor and the lieutenant governor have "enormous power" in Massachusetts, that they have been exercising it for the past fourteen years, and that it is their duty to work with the legislature. The Big Dig project, he said, is out of control and over budget, and that is simply not acceptable.

"I'm not sure that the governor's powers are anywhere near what you claim they are. If the governor were as powerful a figure in our state politics as you have suggested, he could have put an end to the Turnpike Authority like that," I said, snapping my fingers. "He wanted to reduce the size of the Alcoholic

Beverages Control Commission, but the Democrats not only said, 'No, you can't,' but voted to take it away from him and put it under the control of the treasurer—who's a Democrat."

My question to him was about capital punishment, to which he replied as I expected, except that he referred to how, "during the past couple of years, evidence of DNA has exonerated individuals around the country." I was able to turn that around and point out that, with DNA evidence, it is now possible to have a greater degree of certainty about who did what to whom, and that the chances of miscarriages of justice are diminished. But the part of the question that related to Joseph Druce, who had killed Father Geoghan in prison, was one he never answered and couldn't answer.

Toomey's next question to me was about my A rating from the Gun Owners' League. Do I support the ban on assault weapons in Massachusetts? I said that the difference between legal and illegal weapons under this law is largely cosmetic. More to the point, the present situation allows Massachusetts criminals to get hold of guns just by driving down to Virginia or Florida, while law-abiding citizens are prevented from having weapons. "We have a society in which the criminals are armed and the good guys aren't, and no western with that kind of setup is going to do well at the box office."

For my turn, I asked about his proposal to tax Harvard. The surprise in his answer was that the constitution of the Commonwealth has a clause written into it protecting Harvard's tax-exempt status. I hadn't known that, but it became clear to me at once that Toomey's proposal had never been serious and was only demagoguery playing on the envy and resentment of working-class Cambridge residents against this enclave of wealth and privilege. His answer was lame. He thinks that Harvard should be paying more than "a paltry $1.5 million to the City of Cambridge," which is a reasonable position for him to take, but the answer has to be negotiation with the university, not an attempt to change the constitution and impose his Looney Tunes tax of one day's increase in the endowment, which he estimated at about $17 million. I dismissed his proposal as silly and actually used the word "demagoguery," but his response was graceful and disarming. He said that he is a Red Sox fan and that he thinks anything is possible. I countered by saying that the Red Sox have been losing and the Democrats have been in control since 1913, and maybe this will be the year when the Red Sox will take it all and the Republicans will make a comeback as well. I got a laugh and then a round of applause. The moment had been defused and the sting was gone, but the point, I think, had been made.

Toomey then asked me the trickiest question of the evening. "Speaking of

Harvard and MIT," he said, "in an article in the *Harvard Crimson* of April 28, 2004, you were quoted as saying, "Without Harvard and MIT, Cambridge is basically Everett or Somerville. I'd like you to explain what you meant by that."

"I am grateful to you for the question, and I invite you to take a walk sometime in Kendall Square, which is in our district. And you'll see all of the wonderful economic growth which is the result of our scientific expertise and biotech savvy. Somerville is a suburb of it. Everett is a suburb of Somerville. Harvard and MIT are driving this economic engine, and this is what is keeping the residential property tax rates lower in Cambridge than they are, say, in Arlington or Lexington." Toomey then said that he is proud that the city council has been able to keep residential tax rates low. He got a chuckle. I got another, saying that I want to keep him on the city council, as it says on my doorhangers.

The ball was back in my court, and I asked about the police corruption with the double-dipping and the abuses of the Quinn benefits, which give cops automatic raises for taking courses that are often too easy and which I connected to his receiving those campaign contributions from the detectives and the patrolmen and the firefighters.

This was the only moment when I was close to losing patience with him as he resorted to his choirboy sanctity, which may be hypocritical but is difficult to attack: "Certainly I think our police and firemen and emergency personnel are heroes, people we should look up to, and I know that you do, too. They put their lives on the line for us every day." Otherwise, all he had to say was that the Quinn benefits have been reformed and that double-dipping is already illegal.

He then asked me whether I support the extension of the Green Line into Somerville. "Sure," I said. And let that hang there. The silence got a laugh.

But Toomey forged ahead: "At our first debate, you did oppose it. You thought it would cause gentrification of Union Square. . . . I'm glad we're in agreement now."

"I said it would cause gentrification," I answered, "but you misunderstood. I think gentrification is generally a good thing. Property values go up. Businesses that were failing succeed. I mean, I think capitalism works. I think we should try it here in Massachusetts!" This got a big hand and actual cheers.

"It sounds like there are a few successful capitalists in the audience," Toomey remarked. "Successful capitalists," I replied, "or would-be successful capitalists. The basic difference between us is that you tend to be collective and think we should look out for each other, and Republicans are for self-reliance and individual achievement. Those are differences in emphasis. The question is where you draw the balance."

And here Toomey agreed with me. "The Democratic Party looks to take care of all classes of people," and at that he got cheers from his supporters in the audience.

My question about the appropriateness of the "pro-life" label for Toomey's anti-abortion position turned out to be too tricky, and too easy for him to dodge. Instead of replying to my niggle about whether or not "pro-life" is an appropriate label, he came back with a rationale for his "seamless garment" position, which he shares with Father Drinan and Father Berrigan, and which is protective of life and against the death penalty. I conceded that he and Drinan and Berrigan and, indeed, the entire hierarchy can take whatever positions they like, but for them to legislate and impose these views on the general public is overreaching.

His next question to me quoted my campaign literature about how the two-party system depends on there being two parties, and "considering how both houses of Congress and the White House are controlled by Republicans, will you be supporting Senator John Kerry for the 'vital health of democratic government' in Washington?"

To this I had my best answer of the evening. "Well, I was for him before I was against him," I said, and that got a big laugh. Then I tap-danced a little and said that "all three of us, after all, are Yalies, and the question is how does the old-boy network slice. I have real differences with George Bush on social issues," I said, and then I remembered that there was a way of getting back to his opening remarks. "But I also have real differences with Mitt Romney on some social issues. That cartoon to which you alluded before seemed to me unfair and silly." I explained how the big contribution to my campaign was merely an artifact of the system, that I wasn't beholden to the governor, and that the lieutenant governor had acknowledged our differences here at Ryles not long ago. I then returned to Toomey's question about which presidential candidate I was supporting, saying that "if I believed that Kerry had a plan rather than merely a plan to have a plan, I would be willing to listen to what it was. But so far as I am able to tell, his plan is to do almost exactly what President Bush has been doing. It's above our pay grade, but I happen to think the incursion into Iraq was correct. And I'll vote for Bush."

I then asked Toomey about the tax rollback, as I'm sure he expected me to do, and he answered as I expected him to do, except that the House voted to keep the tax rate at 5.3 percent and he voted to increase it to 5.95 percent. He was impressive, talking about the cutbacks in government services and their effects on the disadvantaged, but my guess is that there is not a lot of enthusiasm for a proposal to raise taxes, particularly at a time when the revenues have been coming into the state coffers at more than $700 million ahead of projections. In my rebuttal, I said that the way to do this is through fiscal restraint, matching the expenditures to the revenues, which is what every one of us in this room has learned how to do. The reality is that there are things most of us would like to buy that we just can't afford. That's a reality that the state can face also.

The last question was Toomey's, and it was a good one—for both of us, I think. He said that Governor Romney had vetoed medical and educational benefits for legal immigrants. He asked whether I'd vote to uphold the governor's veto and whether I would, for example, support the right of legal aliens to the lower in-state tuition rates at Massachusetts public colleges and universities, which would save a young person ten thousand dollars a year in educational expenses. And I said that it seemed like a good thing to me, and if that were a freestanding, separate question, I would indeed vote to override the governor's veto.

We'd used up most of the hour and went on to our closing remarks. I gave mine, and then he thanked the Republican City Committee for hosting the debate and said, in conclusion: "People say that there are no differences between the Democrats and the Republicans. There is a great, great difference between the Democrats and Republicans, and I do get excited when people say there isn't. I appreciate the issues that David has raised in a great and spirited campaign, both in the Democratic primary and now with David. I strongly believe in the democratic process and I'm glad that we are able to sit here at Ryles in Inman Square and hold this debate in a free and open society, and I think that's fantastic. . . . I do believe that government serves a purpose, and that is to help people when they need help. And I do firmly believe that if it wasn't for the Democratic Party and the unions, we would still be having the seven-day workweek in this country. There's no question about that. That's one of the major differences between us. The Democratic Party stands for our working people, stands for immigrants, stands for our seniors, stands for our young people, and for those who have no voice in society. We have a moral obligation to stand up for all those individuals, and when people are in need, need assistance, there is a role for government to play. It's very simple. Government is not the enemy; government serves a very valuable purpose. And the Democratic Party, much more so than the Republican Party, stands for the working-class people, families, and our seniors, and that has been borne out by the raft of vetoes that Governor Romney has done to a lot of the social service programs, public education, early intervention, substance abuse programs. . . . All these programs serve a purpose: to help people. I am a public servant, and I believe in that very deeply—that I am there to serve the public to the best of my ability. And I hope that I have been doing that for the past twelve years, and I hope to do it for the next two years, and I ask for your vote on November 2."

That was it, verbatim, and if it wasn't pretty or original, it had an earnestness to it that was impossible to dismiss. I thought I did well enough, better in ways than he did. But he did well too. It wasn't an empty show when we shook hands at the end.

★ ★ ★ From the next day's *Harvard Crimson:*

Thursday, October 14, 2004

Harvard Affiliate Debates in Local Race

By Michael M. Grynbaum, Crimson Staff Writer

Democratic State Rep. Timothy D. Toomey faced off against long-shot Republican challenger and Leverett Senior Common Room member David R. Slavitt in a lively and wide-ranging debate last night, trading barbs over taxing Harvard, abortion rights and capital punishment.

The debate, held before a small crowd at the Ryles jazz club in Inman Square, was the third and last meeting between the candidates for state representative from the 26th Middlesex District, which includes parts of Cambridge and Somerville.

Toomey—a six-term incumbent who has held the office since 1993—emphasized his legislative experience and local ties while Slavitt—a writer, critic and translator running his first political campaign—lashed out at his opponent's pro-life views and the inertia of a State House that he said has been dominated by Democrats for too long.

The two clashed early when Toomey dug into Slavitt in his opening remarks, painting his opponent as representing a party that veered too far to the right.

"My opponent is a decent person, a great wit and a superb debater," said Toomey, who wore a plain blue, collared shirt. "Yet he has one serious flaw. He represents a Republican Party that both nationally and statewide doesn't understand or represent the needs or ideals of the people."

Slavitt responded with a searing critique of Democratic state leadership, whose idealism he said has been "institutionally extinguished."

"The domination by the Democrats of our political life here in Massachusetts is unhealthy," Slavitt said. "Their only concerns are incumbency and power, which they abuse."

Slavitt dominated the proceedings rhetorically, drawing on his debating days at Yale under the tutelage of legendary coach Rollin Osterweis, whose other pupils included William F. Buckley and presidential candidate Sen. John F. Kerry, D-Mass.

But Toomey, seated only a few feet from his opponent, held his own on substance.

Looking to appeal to the socially liberal electorate of Cambridge and Somerville, Slavitt questioned Toomey on his pro-life stance.

The incumbent responded that he has never misled voters on his views on the subject.

"I do believe . . . that all life should be protected . . . It's a deeply felt conviction I have," Toomey said.

"One is entitled to any position you want," Slavitt snapped back, "but to attempt to force these views on other people is governmental overreach."

While social issues dominated most of the proceedings, a clash over town-gown relations produced one of the night's most heated exchanges.

"I don't think Harvard would be financially deprived by increasing the amount of money they pay to the city of Cambridge," Toomey said.

Slavitt ridiculed this plan, noting that Harvard's tax-exempt status is written into the Massachusetts State Constitution.

"Taking a public position that you want to tax Harvard and its endowment is simply demagoguery," Slavitt said. Later he loudly chastised Toomey: "It's not going to happen! You're perfectly aware it's not going to happen."

Toomey casually responded, "I'm a loyal Red Sox fan, so I do believe everything is possible," drawing cheers from the audience.

While the debate appeared to end in a draw, the election may not be as closely contested. Toomey has strong ties in heavily Democratic Cambridge, and he already overcame a strong primary challenge from fellow Democrat Avi E. Green. And Republicans—even centrists like Slavitt—rarely have a chance in the "People's Republic of Cambridge."

Though Slavitt remains a long-shot, his campaign manager Fred Baker remained upbeat about Slavitt's candidacy.

"It's an uphill battle. Even if we don't win, we're going to turn some heads trying," Baker said.

And from the *Somerville Journal* of that same day:

Congenial Toomey, Slavitt disagree on the issues

By Auditi Guha/ aguh@cnc.com

Thursday, October 14, 2004

He hasn't had a Republican challenger in 12 years, and his opponent thinks it's about time.

Rep. Tim Toomey, D-Cambridge, will be facing off newcomer David Slavitt on Nov. 2 for the 26th Middlesex District.

Both are busy going door-to-door, but one seems to do it purely for the joy of it, if not to win.

"I am running for the fun of it and because I can afford to," said Slavitt this week. "I have twice as good a chance in a presidential year than not."

Pro-choice and a supporter of women rights (his wife and daughter are both doctors, he pointed out), Slavitt has been endorsed by NARAL, Citizens for Lower Taxation, the Log Cabin Republicans and former Governor Bill Weld.

Toomey has been endorsed by a long list of local groups and officials, including Congressman Mike Capuano, gay and lesbian, state and national organizations, unions and more. "Most important are the voters who elect me on election day," he said.

Slavitt believes that many groups have not endorsed him because they are scared of offending Toomey and because his Republican alliance bothers them though he is pro-choice.

"They endorsed Avi because he is pro-choice, but the fact that I am pro-choice, too, didn't cut it with them," he said.

Toomey narrowly beat challenger Avi Green in the 26th Middlesex House of Representative Primary race, and Slavitt hopes to harness at least those who voted for Green.

"If I can pick up a substantial number of Avi's 46 percent, 14–15 percent Republican votes and a fair share of the Unenrolled, I could win," said Slavitt.

Toomey clearly thinks he has the edge over Slavitt, though he has named a full-time campaign manager for the first time. "I take the elections very seriously," he said. "Constituents know me, and every day is an election day."

With a strong presence in Cambridge and an office on Cambridge Street, Toomey said he has been trying to get space in Somerville for constituents to visit him at least a couple of days in the week. So is Slavitt.

The candidates respect one another and seem to be comfortable with their differences.

"Clearly there are major differences in how we view government," Toomey said. "I've met Mr. Slavitt a couple of times, and he seems to be an engaging individual and a decent person."

"I think Toomey is likeable—very earnest and very hardworking," Slavitt said. But he also said Toomey has a 1930s trade-unions-corporations-bad, working-man-good kind of mindset that can be "irrelevant but harmful." Moreover, he believes, "The idealism that Democrats once had is almost extinct . . . Anyone with half a brain can see that a two-party system works better with two parties in it."

Slavitt believes the district is an interesting mix of blue-collar and ethnic voters on one end and white-collar intellectuals on the other. A poet and writer soon coming out with his 80th book, he wonders why they cannot see the value of having a Republican fighting for them at the State House and said he is sick of how much the Democrats dilly-dally over issues instead of tackling them head-on.

"I am a freshman, minority representative. I'd be good on community and constituent services," he said. "You got a problem the governor can solve, you call me. You may or may not agree with him—and I have differences with him—but he'll listen to me."

But at the end of the day, his biggest disadvantage is being a Republican in the area.

"The very word 'Republican' produces hives in Cambridge. There's a lot of anti-Brahmin sentiment from people who feel badly used—we are the good guys," he said. "They pride themselves on what an intellectual place this is, well, I am an intellectual."

Toomey is not fazed, as Slavitt looks forward to debates and his particular brand of humor to cut Toomey down in debates this week.

"I am gaining the trust of people and am hoping to be re-elected by Democrats everywhere," Toomey said.

★ ★ ★ I saw this up at their offices in Davis Square, where I went the next day to meet with the editors. Toomey had been invited, too. So we sat there together in their conference room and had another minidebate, answering the editors' questions. It was a friendly, relaxed encounter, and I allowed myself a few wild-man remarks, such as the observation that entirely too much money and manpower are being put into the war against drugs, and what we need to do instead, post-9/11, is to put those resources into the war on terror so that containers in cargo ships are inspected. I said the war on drugs is mostly a failure, and while I would keep the recovery centers open and maintain and even increase funding for programs for addicts who want to quit, a lot of the law enforcement effort seems to be a waste of time and a distraction from the more important threat. If I had any real expectation of winning, I probably would not have volunteered such a view, even though I think it is correct.

18

★ ★ ★ ★ ★ ★ ★ ★ ★ ★ ★ ★ ★ ★ ★ ★ ★

There is a piece in the *Globe* this morning about the Republican legislative races that are "targeted." Mostly the Republican candidates who were chosen to re-cieve extra help are incumbents, or those running for open seats, or special cases such as Larry Wheatley down on the Cape, who lost last time around to Matthew Patrick by only seventeen votes. I'm not on the list. Neither is Greer Tan Swiston, or Richard Babson, or Mike Motzkin, or any of the people I've met and with whom I have become friendly. The GOP is willing to accept mir-acles, but, according to the Raphael Lewis story, they expect to pick up very few seats. I asked Evan what his take was on this report, and he said the state party just wanted to field an opposition so that, in two and four years, it wouldn't be absurd on its face for a Republican to be running. They're spend-ing two or three million now so that in 2006 and 2008 they'll have a real chance of making some gains. From the beginning, then, I have been a sacrificial pawn, having fun maybe but with no actual prospects of getting elected. But then, I knew that. Or ought to have known it.

★ ★ ★ I spent the morning at my first stand-out, up at Inman Square, near Ryles. There are seven streets that come together, and there's a good deal of traffic, so Fred Baker, Susan Imrie, Karen Hunter, Henry Irving, and I could position ourselves with Slavitt signs and wave them as cars passed by. I also stopped pedestrians, asking if they were registered to vote and if they lived around here. I did my pitch and handed those who would accept one a doorhanger. The weather was fine, the sky a bright clean blue after a heavy rainstorm last night. I was in a good enough mood not to worry about the fu-tility of what we were doing. None of the other sign holders was unaware that the odds were against us. But they'd come to stand on the corner and hold signs with my name on them, for me or the Republican cause, or for the sheer orneriness of it.

After the stand-out, I drove up to deliver a copy of the debate tape to the Somerville Community Access Television station. When I got home, I found a mail piece from the party—sent, I'm sure, to all registered Republicans in districts where they have a candidate. It is a request for an absentee ballot and has a picture of Romney and below, my name. This is actual help. Name recognition is where you start.

The Sunday *Globe* did not have that piece about me that Jonas has been promising. Maybe next week? (Or mid-November?) But there is a story about how Governor Romney will not be doing any TV blitz. The party coffers are much reduced (where has the money gone?) and there is only half a million on hand. The governor's estimates for Republican results next month are modest indeed. He says that there were four Republican resignations and that without this huge effort we'd have lost these seats. As it stands, we have a chance of holding on to them and maybe even picking up one.

★ ★ ★ Monday morning, the start of the penultimate week, I sit down at my desk realizing that some things have clarified for me. The first has to do with my website, which I checked over the weekend. Patty Ayers of Carolina Web Solutions took down the debate announcement, as I had asked. If I were still engaged and hopeful in this campaign, I'd almost certainly have sent her the Grynbaum piece from the *Harvard Crimson* and the Guha piece from the *Somerville Journal* to put on the Press page. But that would cost the campaign another seventy dollars, and I can't persuade myself that the expenditure makes sense. How many more votes would I get? A dozen? I doubt it.

On the other hand, I have to do something to keep dejection at bay, and the Campaign Portal beckons. I can spend three or four hours a day making phone calls. The election is now close enough so that it makes sense for me to leave messages on answering machines. The script that has evolved is straightforward and brief, as these things must be: "Hello, this is David Slavitt, the Republican candidate for state rep here in the Twenty-sixth Middlesex District. I am the pro-choice Republican, running against Tim Toomey, a pro-life Democrat. He wants to raise your taxes; I want to lower them. Take a look at my website, www.davidslavitt.com, and, if you like what you see there, I ask for your vote on November 2. Thanks for your time and, I hope too, for your vote."

This is the spiel that has emerged from my conversations with live people on the telephone. My mention of Toomey's name sometimes gets a friendly response. There are a fair number of Cambridge voters who are tired of him and looking for a change. That 51 percent of the voters support him suggests that he's vulnerable. The phone calls are a way of persuading myself that I am doing what I can. I reach more people this way than I do trudging from house to house. But it is mindless and sometimes disagreeable. People can be rude and sometimes hang up on me. I try not to take it personally. They don't know me, after all. And I'm unlikely ever to meet them out there in the world. But no amount of ratiocination can make it feel good.

If Romney is playing the game of lowered expectations, so am I. My hope is that I can lose respectably, beating Paul Lachelier's vote count of two years ago. Each friendly reception I get on the phone is one vote closer to the four thousand I need to accomplish that.

⋆ ⋆ ⋆ Yesterday's calls were a blur of almost unrelieved drudgery. The Campaign Portal is much improved from what was originally available. On a screen of fifty names and phone numbers, no more than eight or ten of those people are likely to have moved, died, or discontinued telephone service. A lot of the voters in Ward Two, Precinct One, don't have phones at all or, if they have phones, they don't have answering machines. But on the other hand, that's where the projects are, and those people are likely to be home. Whether or not they speak English is another question, but that is a precinct where Green did well, and it makes sense for me to prospect there.

Once I have done my telephoning of Republicans and Unenrolleds, I will go to Democrat women under thirty-five, who are likely to be receptive to a pro-choice message. Older women, especially those with Irish names, might share Toomey's pro-life views. With a limited amount of time and virtually no help, I have to focus my efforts.

⋆ ⋆ ⋆ No team has ever come back from a three-zip deficit to win a seven-game series, and the players know this, but the Sox hunker down and slog on, living as much as possible in the moment and, almost miraculously, succeeding in the next two games. The odds are that they will lose one of the two final games in New York, but their determination is impressive. I am also struck by the "We Believe" signs the fans at Fenway have been holding up, as if it were a religious test of some kind. The bodily assumption of the Virgin Mary? Sure! The chances of the Red Sox to win the league championship and play in the series? Why not?

★ ★ ★ A piece in the *Globe* clarifies one of the questions that Toomey asked me at the debate—that business of in-state tuitions for legal aliens. He was wrong. I took the opportunity to try to correct the record and get some space in the *Cambridge Chronicle:*

> At our recent debate at Ryles, one of Representative Toomey's questions to me—whether I would vote to override a gubernatorial veto of in-state tuition rates for *legal* aliens—was either disingenuous or misinformed. (I said I would do so, unable to imagine any reason for discrimination against those who are here legitimately, whether they are citizens or not.) The question our Representative ought to have been posing, however, and one that would have had relevance in the real world, was whether I would vote to override Governor Romney's actual veto—of in-state tuition rates for *illegal* aliens. Governor Romney announced this veto last June, saying, "I hate the idea of in any way making it more difficult for kids, even those who are illegal aliens, to afford college in our state. [But] equally, perhaps a little more than equally, I do not want to create an incentive to do something which is illegal." And that one, I'd have voted to sustain.
>
> Representative Toomey is, I believe, a straight-shooter. I cannot think he intended his question as a trick. He was merely misinformed—but that is not altogether reassuring in a State Representative with so many years of experience on Beacon Hill.
>
> David R. Slavitt
> Republican Candidate for State Rep, 26th Middlesex

★ ★ ★ There was a Getting Out the Vote session at the Westborough Wyndham, a mostly boring presentation, that offered a couple of useful bits of information. I can go to the Election Board on Monday, see who asked for absentee ballots, see which of them have not yet been returned, and then call the Republicans on the list to make sure they get their votes into the mail. I wouldn't have thought of that on my own. The other interesting tidbit was that this is as early as Election Day can come. The first Tuesday after the first Monday can't be the first of November, but it can be—and is, this year—the second. Which means that the agony is shortened a little. And that the Sunday night get-out-the-vote calls have to be truncated because we don't want to interfere with Halloween. The rest, however, was mostly obvious or irrelevant. Phone banks? I don't have a phone bank. No volunteers, no office, no phones. I guess I could ask Evan if I can use his offices the weekend before the election, and Fred and

I might corral six or eight people to sit and make calls for two or three hours. But would it make a difference? Anyway, there was nothing that couldn't have been posted on the portal or explained in one of those ridiculous Sunday night conference calls.

★ ★ ★ The reply from the *Chronicle*:

Hi David,

No election letters in next week's paper . . . it's our endorsement edition and we don't run anything election related the week before the election. Thanks, Michele

Swell, but they could have told me this in advance. In the new issue of the paper:

Slavitt: Sacrifice 'stupid kids' for worthy prescription drugs
By Auditi Guha/ CNC Staff Writer
Thursday, October 21, 2004

While Republican challenger David Slavitt and incumbent Democrat Tim Toomey agree on many things, drugs are not one of them.

"Kids know drugs are terrible," said Slavitt, who noted his wife and daughter are doctors. "It is impossible for us to be responsible for the mistakes of everyone in the world . . . Every kid who is an addict once started [taking drugs]." Asked about the kids who die addicted, Slavitt said, "It is OK to sacrifice 50 stupid kids every year."

Toomey and Slavitt, who are vying for the 26th Middlesex District seat on Nov. 2, met in debates last week. Slavitt is Toomey's first Republican challenger for his seat in East Somerville and East Cambridge in 12 years. Toomey won a narrow victory against Democrat Avi Green in September.

They faced off at a community debate where they asked questions of one another at Ryles in Cambridge, and were quizzed by Cambridge Chronicle and Somerville Journal editors and reporters at an endorsement meeting last week.

Perhaps the biggest point of contention was in the area of drug abuse. Slavitt noted the great medical uses of OxyContin, the drug linked to several recent deaths in the city. Instead of banning the drug to get rid of the drug problem, he said those kids "stupid enough" to take the drug could be sacrificed.

Toomey said he supports more programs and support in schools, while Slavitt placed the onus of the burden on the decision of kids who decide to do drugs despite knowing about the dangers, and said that too much money and manpower is spent on "absurd drug laws." However, Slavitt does support detox centers and said he would never cut funding to centers.

It went on from there, recapping what we'd said the evening before at Ryles.

Should I have make the crack about my willingness to sacrifice fifty stupid kids (nationwide) for the benefits that OxyContin can bring to cancer patients? Ms. Guha might have reported my remark a little more accurately and in context. My next sentence was to the effect that the cancer patients hadn't chosen their disease but the high-school druggies had a choice and had chosen wrong. (Some days later, I heard that Toomey thought the story and the headline had been "unfair.")

Still, having said what I did, and believing it as I do, I was content. I was like one of those hockey teams in the last minutes of play, so desperate to score that I leave my goal unattended to have another man on offense. This piece is on the first page and is wacko enough to attract the attention of the *Globe*, the *Herald*, or the radio talk shows, where I can expand on what I said and defend the position reasonably well.

Kids drink and drive and get killed, and we "sacrifice" a number of them every year, but no one argues that we should take automobiles off the road. The pharmaceutical company bears some responsibility, having marketed OxyContin too aggressively to family docs rather than to pain specialists and oncologists whose patients are likeliest to need it. But the calls to take the drug off the market are excessive and cruel.

★ ★ ★ I went to the Sacred Heart Church yesterday afternoon to hand out bookmarks and introduce myself to the bingo players, almost all of whom were from the district. I was supposed to meet Fred at five o'clock but got there a little early, and it seemed silly just to sit in the car and wait, so I went inside and chatted with the geezers and geezerettes at the tables with their Dab-o-Ink bottles at the ready and their lucky toys spread out before them. I was friendly, jocular, and only a little uncomfortable to be in Toomey's parish church, but not everyone here loves him. Almost all of the players took a bookmark.

Fred showed up just after five and told me that I couldn't do this in the parish hall. The custom is to stand outside and greet the people as they are coming in. "You don't want to violate the sanctity of the bingo games?" I asked. "They're not my rules," he said. Which is how it is with the Church, in a more general way. But I followed him outside, and we stood there in the chilly evening, handing out bookmarks, chatting up the voter/players, and making our presence known. It was like the stand-outs, not something that wins votes, but a custom which our failure to observe could cost us votes. After an hour or so, we packed it in. I was cold and tired, but I had the satisfaction of knowing that I'd done my duty.

★ ★ ★ I am less confident this morning about the *Chronicle* piece. Most people will not read past the headline. There is a kind of truth telling that is all but excluded by the political process. I think of Mitt Romney's father, whose presidential aspirations were ruined by the "brainwashed" phrase. He had, indeed, been brainwashed about Viet Nam by the generals and the DOD, but to say so was beyond the pale of acceptable political discourse. You just can't call kids "stupid." Particularly dead ones. Any kid that is shot or run over, as Tom Wolfe demonstrates in *Bonfire of the Vanities*, becomes an honor-roll student. It is a piety no one dares violate.

Meanwhile, the *Somerville News* is on the stand, the issue in which my six-hundred-dollar ad is running. And my hope is that in the next issue—the one that comes out just before Election Day—they will endorse me, which is better than an ad.

I shall spend a mind-numbing day on the telephone, calling voters. I realized yesterday that I prefer it when the person I am calling is not home. I can leave my message on the machine and go on to the next name on the list. My aim is making progress down the page, getting through the fifty names on each screen, at the end of which I can give myself a treat, a fresh cup of coffee or a game of solitaire. It is ridiculous to be so reduced, but one can't deny the truth of the experience. To perform a stupid task, for whatever lofty reason, is to become, at least for the time it takes, stupid.

That word again.

★ ★ ★ We had another stand-out this morning, over on Cambridge and Third streets. Four or five people standing in the chilly gray morning, holding up signs with my name on them, and I was almost embarrassed for them. Yes, it looked as though I have friends enthusiastic enough to come out and do this for me and for my campaign, but how demeaning! Who ever figured out that this is a reasonable thing to do in politics?

At noon, we broke up, and I went up to Somerville to pick up a copy of the *News* with my ad in it—half of page 9. It looks good, and I am satisfied I've come this far. These ads almost wiped me out, but not to run them would be to admit defeat.

Then back to the house to have a grim afternoon, slogging through another couple of pages of telephone numbers. I have further refined the message so that, for Republicans, I talk about the two-party system needing two parties and the fact that I want to lower taxes while Toomey wants to raise them. These things are both true, but what I leave out is the statement that I am the pro-choice Republican. A fair number of Republicans, after all, are right-wing loonies, and I don't want to lose their votes. Mostly, I recite into the machines, which is safe. Live people, even Republicans, can say that they're not interested, or that they can't talk now, or they can just hang up on me, which feels terrible.

As Evan said, "It is what it is," a phrase that a friend of mine tells me was originated by a McKenzie executive, from whom it filtered out into the business world.

★ ★ ★ I was disappointed—no, dismayed—not to find anything in today's *Globe* about my campaign. There is only the one Sunday left before the election. And the indifference the media have shown to my campaign is more than irksome. I sent Michael Jonas an e-mail, notable mostly for its restraint:

> Dear Michael,
>
> Nothing in today's paper. I assume the Globe will be waiting for . . . the last possible moment? Or after the election?
>
> I am truly mystified by the indifference of the Boston press to what I'd think might be the most unusual candidacy of this election cycle.
>
> Do let me know whether to expect anything in next weekend's paper.
>
> Kind regards,
>
> David

I am also aware that there are 130 races and that they can't cover all of them. On the other hand, how many of the candidates are poets? There is one guy running who is a funeral director, which is unusual and newsworthy. But writers used to play a part in the cultural life of the country. It is not impossible that we still do but that the *Globe* has no way of noticing this. Their "Ideas" section, which includes books, is a disgrace. I look at it only to check the "Bookings" listings to see who is reading where. And that's not reliable, either.

★ ★ ★ I had an inquiry from Josh Stern, a Harvard undergraduate doing a senior thesis on state rep races, who wanted to follow me around as I did my campaigning. I figured that at the least it would be less lonely this way and perhaps he might have interesting questions. So I invited him to come along while I went door-to-door. He could carry my signs, in case I found anyone eager enough to want one.

It turned out to be a fine couple of hours. We walked up Beacon Street in Somerville, and the reception we got was better than anything I had previously encountered. A manager of one apartment house listened to my short spiel and not only took a bookmark but asked for twenty more so that she could distribute them to the apartments in the building. We found several people who were Republicans. We found several who were Democrats but pro-choice and said they would vote for me. And when we got to the parking lot of Johnny's Foodmaster, we met one voter after another who took the bookmarks or the doorhangers, agreed that we need two parties, and said that they'd vote for me, and one who asked for a bumper sticker to put on her car.

A part of me knows that I am going to lose, but from what he saw yesterday afternoon Stern would have had no reason to think so, or at least no grounds for certainty. We came back to the apartment, and I gave him tea. We talked a little longer—he's from northern New Jersey, went to a public high school, and wants to go to law school. Then I went up to have dinner with Evan and the gang in Malden.

I got back from Malden to find a message on the machine from one of the people in whose mailbox I'd left a doorhanger. I returned her call. She'd never heard of me, but she was interested in my pro-choice position. I explained that this was one of the big differences between Toomey and me. "But you're a Republican," she said. I explained that I was a liberal Republican, a Weld Republican. We weren't all evangelicals. She thanked me for returning her call, said she would vote for me, and promised that she would tell her friends about me. It's too little and too late, but it's nice.

On the other hand, my ads run this week in the *Chronicle* and the *Journal*. My mailing goes out this week. It will either happen this week or it won't. This campaign, which seems to stretch back into the mists of antiquity, is, for most voters, just now starting.

★ ★ ★ As if it were a law of physics, for every up there is a down, and my attempts to follow through on the party's suggestions about maximizing the absentee ballot results have been a catastrophe. I went to the Boards of Elections in Cambridge and Somerville to ask for the absentee ballot reports—who had requested such ballots and which of these had been returned. The

Cambridge Elections Board provided me with a sheaf of fifty pages that covered my seven precincts in this city. It is all efficient, clear, and easy to work with. You look at the names and see the party affiliation. You check for the R and see if the ballot has been returned. But in all those names, only fifteen are Republicans. Four have sent the ballots back. So there are eleven possible votes I can chase down. Out of fifty pages? And of those fifteen Republicans, there are several names that do not appear on the Campaign Portal lists, which is unsettling. Some of those voters don't have listed telephone numbers at all, which may be why the portal doesn't have them. I made three phone calls. One couple is on an extended trip, but an employee said that they had mailed their ballots yesterday. The second couple had requested two ballots because the husband has had a heart attack. The wife's ballot had arrived at their home but the husband's hadn't. The wife wanted to know whether she could give him her ballot and then go and vote, in person, herself. I gave her the Election Board's phone number to let them sort it out. As for the last couple, the wife is a Republican and the husband a Democrat, but they are both friends of Toomey and are both pro-life. They seemed vague about the election, and the chances are that my call may have prompted them to hunt up the absentee ballot and send it in—for Tim.

Somerville was even more dismal. They were going to charge me twenty cents a page for the names, but when I asked why Cambridge gives them out for free and Somerville charges, they decided "not to argue about it" and did not charge me. So I saved $2.20. They handed me eleven legal-size pages, photocopied on both sides, with as many as twenty-four names to the side. But they are not distinguished by party, so I have to look each name up on the portal, going to the correct ward and precinct and then finding the street on which the voter lives. If the name shows there, it will have an R, a D, or a U. I looked up a dozen of those who had not yet returned ballots and found four names, but three were Democrats and one was Unenrolled. It would have been better if I'd been phoning Republicans and Unenrolleds on the portal lists. Indeed, it would have made more sense if I'd skipped that Westborough get-out-the-vote meeting and put in those three hours on the phone.

★ ★ ★ The script continues to evolve. At the suggestion of a friend of mine who is in sales, I now mention the name of the person I'm calling, if only to make it clear that it is not an automated call and that a live person is on the telephone.

★ ★ ★ Deb Eisner calls from the *Somerville Journal* and tells me she's doing a story about campaign finances. Have I filed my campaign finance report that was due yesterday? No, I tell her. Evan tried to file it electronically, as we are required to do, but there was some sort of computer glitch and it didn't register. He is trying to do that today. I ask her why she is interested, and she tells me that she's doing this story . . . the point of which, obviously, is to be as embarrassing as possible, which the *Chronicle* and the *Journal* confuse with high-minded journalism. I tell her that there is nothing scandalous or even interesting in my report. Have I been following Toomey's reports? she asks. No, I tell her, I think he's an honest guy. He's an incumbent, and he gets money from a lot of the public safety unions, but we know that. You don't think he's a crook, do you? She can't answer, because of her journalistic high-mindedness.

When will my report be filed? she asks. I tell her I have no idea. Maybe today or tomorrow. Or, if not, then when Evan gets back from Texas, where he has a trial this week that is more important than this stuff. The penalty is only ten bucks a day, and we can pay that, if necessary. He'll get to it when he can.

She asks if I know how many contributions I got from Somerville. I tell her there have been only a few, and that as she knows there is no Republican organization there, but I'd rather have their votes than their money. I hear computer keyboard noises, so she's taking some of this down. Most of Green's money was from outside Somerville, I tell her, and he carried all five of the Somerville precincts of our district. Clickety-clickety-click. She's typing like a house afire. The opportunity to be knowledgeable and snide is just delicious, and she is making the best of it. She thanks me and I tell her, without much warmth, that she is quite welcome.

One more goddamn week of this.

★ ★ ★ Curious, now that I'd been made aware of the OCPF reports, I looked up Toomey's and found that he has spent almost $33,000 since the primary, running against me. And that he has lent his campaign $15,000, which makes me feel less bad about having lent mine the $2,000. He is apparently paying Kate Glidden, his campaign manager, $5,000 dollars a month. This is about what he makes himself as a state rep who is chairman of a committee. He is taking this seriously.

(As it turned out, the OCPF filing for January was even more impressive. The Twenty-sixth Middlesex race cost nearly a quarter of a million dollars: Toomey spent $144,299, of which he lent himself $17,000; Green spent $97,369. And Richard Babson? He lent himself $40,000, in addition to the $30,000 he'd put into his campaign before the primary. This is the maximum that a candidate is allowed to kick into his campaign, and he failed to win a single precinct. Jeesh!)

★ ★ ★ My friend Richard Griffin, with whom I have lunch at Leverett House at Harvard most Fridays, has a column that runs in a number of small-town papers, including the *Cambridge Chronicle* and the *Somerville Journal*. He gave me his week before Election Day space:

Senior candidate enjoys the risk of a political campaign
Wednesday, October 27, 2004

You have to admire a guy who, nearing age 70, decides to run for public office for the first time.

Even when you know he has zero chance of getting elected and you do not agree with most of his positions, his taking the plunge demands respect.

That's what I feel for my friend David Slavitt, Republican nominee for the 26th Middlesex District of the Massachusetts House of Representatives.

Before tossing his beret into the bullring, David consulted with me about the wisdom of running. Yes, do run, I advised him, but only if you keep two principles firmly in mind.

First, remember that you have absolutely no chance of winning. And second, you owe it to yourself to have fun while running.

I must report that, as to my first counsel, David has proved inconstant. Like almost every other candidate I have ever known, he sometimes allows himself to fantasize about sitting among the elected representatives of the people. He lapses into the impossible dream that he can upset a Democratic incumbent of 11 years' standing.

Admittedly, that incumbent, Tim Toomey, eked out a surprisingly narrow victory in last month's primary over a novice challenger who was not nearly so well known in the district. Clearly Slavitt has allowed this near miss to encourage fantasies of knocking off the Democratic nominee. But he is also clearly having fun.

Out for entertainment, I attended a debate last week between Toomey and Slavitt. Not being a resident of their district, I felt no personal stake in their contest and could be present in a lighthearted spirit. But I did look forward to hearing some of what I have come to call Slavittisms. David did not disappoint.

As a nonbeliever in political correctness, he can always be relied on to favor wit over tact.

Until recently, this political nouveau venue would have been lambasting Tom Finneran, the erstwhile Speaker of the House. Even now, however, he takes a swipe at the man. Of the former Speaker, Slavitt does not shrink from charging that he "lied to a panel of federal judges."

By now, however, the position of speaker has devolved to Sal DiMasi whose policies may be similar to Finneran's. So Slavitt has turned his rhetorical guns on the new speaker, calling him "Finneran's Rottweiler."

Like others, I laughed at this characterization. But as a non-dog person I had to look up the term. I learned that these pets are named for a German city. Tall and powerful and mean looking, they often serve as guard dogs. They bite.

Asked what he thinks of the presidential race, David does not hide his own educational pedigree. Speaking of the candidates and himself, he acknowledged: "All three of us are Yalies." Of Kerry, he says: "I was for him before I was against him."

Is he in favor of extending the MBTA Green Line into Somerville at the risk of furthering gentrification? To this question from Toomey, his challenger replies: "I think gentrification is generally a good thing." He also makes fun of the station at Lechmere, which has been "temporary for the last 80 years."

Toomey went after my friend for calling Somerville a suburb of Cambridge. David holds to this position, one that seems hardly attractive to voters from the part of Somerville that falls within the 26th district. Without Harvard and MIT, he claims, Cambridge would offer little more than its neighboring city.

One of Slavitt's favorite issues is the abuse that he perceives happening under the so-called Quinn Bill. That 1970 legislation provides promotions and other benefits for police officers and firefighters who take courses in public colleges and universities. David complains that "the cops are taking worthless courses." Worse still is the double dipping he believes they practice: "The cops become crooks," he charges.

About Toomey's opposition to rolling back the state income tax, David asks the incumbent: "Are you going along with your leadership or are you in economic error entirely on your own?"

Even Rep. Toomey smiles at thrusts like this one. He knows his opponent is enjoying himself and so, no doubt, is he. But the incumbent does not appear to underestimate the perils of being challenged by the author of some 80 books.

In a fine frenzy of rhetoric, Slavitt concludes the debate by characterizing what he calls the Democrat party as "corrupt, complacent, self-congratu-

latory and overbearing in its stranglehold on public life in the commonwealth."

Early in his campaign, Slavitt attended a Republican rally where Gov.
Mitt Romney addressed his party's aspirants for state office. David took inspiration from Romney's reflections on the meaning behind electoral politics. "You are all going to die," Romney said, much to David's astonishment.

With this quixotic saying, Romney was suggesting that one should take
risks in a lifetime that does not last forever. Sticking your neck out is worth
doing, even when you end up tilting at windmills.

Can't hurt. Might even help. But, as he says, I am lapsing from time to time
into hope.

★ ★ ★ The *Chronicle's* endorsement went to Toomey, although they treated me
respectfully:

In the 26th Middlesex District, we support Rep. Tim Toomey. Toomey's victory over Avi Green appears to have refocused the longtime rep, and we
hope he brings this renewed vigor back to the State House. Republican David
Slavitt injected some wry humor into the race, and we'd encourage him to
seek city office. His voice would add depth to any city board.

I can live without their encouragement, but I'm content with "depth,"
which is, for them, a compliment. Elsewhere in the paper, there is that piece
about the OCPF reports that Deb Eisner was working on. I come out of that
well enough too, I think:

House—26th Middlesex: Rep. Tim Toomey raised more than 10 times the
dollars garnered by his GOP foe, David Slavitt. The writer and poet took the
differential in stride. "I know Tim and I like him," said Slavitt. "I think he's
an honest guy. I think he's [been] in power for a long time, and therefore it's
easy for him to raise money."
     Toomey accepted $100 from the (former) Speaker Finneran Victory Fund.
Although the controversial Finneran has stepped down, some Democrats
returned donations from his fund.
     Slavitt, unlike his fellow Republican Babson, received $250 each from
Gov. Mitt Romney and Lt. Gov. Kerry Healey. Slavitt filed his report one day
late and will be fined $10 by the Office of Campaign and Political Finance.

And then, in that same issue, there is my ad.

★ ★ ★ The *Somerville Journal* was less friendly, and their endorsement of Toomey was almost ringing:

Editorial: We endorse
Thursday, October 28, 2004

For state rep of East Somerville, we endorse Tim Toomey in the 26th Middlesex. He's got a record of thoughtful decisions at the State House, and as chairman of the public safety committee, he's got some pull as to what we can do to improve the safety of our fair city. He's also shown that he can learn from his primary race, promising to spend much more time in Somerville than he has in the past. We fear we can no longer call him the Cambridge city councilor who represents East Somerville at the State House.

While a headline writer's dream is to have a flame-thrower like David Slavitt, some of his ideas are too far-flung for us to even give him a nod. Sacrifice kids for the worth of a drug? Surely there is a better way to start the debate on what to do with the problem of addicted teens.

You can't make jokes with people who are too earnest or too stupid for them.
Their version of the finance story is more elaborate:

Toomey hauls in $32G for election effort after primary
By Deborah Eisner/ Journal Staff
Thursday, October 28, 2004

In the last six weeks, Tim Toomey has raised nearly twice the combined contribution totals of the other state representative candidates facing opponents next week.

Toomey logged $32,803 in contributions between Aug. 30 and Oct. 15, according to reports filed with the Office of Campaign and Political Finance. Only $595 of it was from Somerville, and $15,000 of it was a loan from himself.

Toomey said he did not "step up" fund-raising efforts in Somerville, even after losing the city to his primary opponent.

"Clearly I have to do more outreach for fund raising, but I just want to get through this campaign," Toomey said Tuesday. "I've never been one to do the aggressive fund raising. I certainly hope more people from Somerville will contribute, and we'll go from there."

The Democratic incumbent, Toomey will face off against Republican David Slavitt in Tuesday's general election. Toomey beat Avi Green, 54–46 percent, in September to win the Democratic nomination. Toomey had $28,345 in liabilities at the end of the primary campaign, finance reports show.

Slavitt reported $4,335 in contributions, including $2,500 from himself. None of the itemized contributions were from Somerville residents, although Slavitt said he did get "three or four" donations from the city.

"The difficulty is that there is basically no organized Republican Party in Somerville, so there's no people to do this kind of thing," Slavitt said. "If Somerville gives me zero dollars and a lot of votes, that's fine."

He said he does not equate contributions with community support. . . .

I am glad my ad in their paper is only half the size of the one in the *Chronicle*. Perhaps tomorrow the *Somerville News* will break ranks and come out with an endorsement for me. But will that make a difference?

★ ★ ★ Making my phone calls this morning, trying for women in Somerville registered as either Democrats or Unenrolled, I reached a household where an elderly man answered the phone and told me that they had already cast absentee ballots. On a whim, I asked if either of them voted for me. He told me his wife had voted for Toomey but he had voted for me. So much for my theorizing about reaching out to women because I'm pro-choice. On the other hand, it was impressive to find myself talking to someone who had cast a vote for me. It's real. Or it would be, if there were enough such people.

More typical of those with whom I manage to speak viva voce (rather than to their machines) are voters who have no questions, listen to my spiel, promise to think about it, and then leave me wondering whether I haven't wasted my time as well as theirs. Or, slightly worse than that, there are those who don't understand that the Toomey-Green election was a primary, and that this is the general election. Or there are those who want to vote for me but are voting for Kerry—and I have to explain to them that it is possible to split their ticket, voting for Kerry and Edwards on the presidential line, and then for a Republican farther down. Possible and legal. "Oh, really? That's good to know."

I say I am glad to have been able to help, but what I am is appalled.

★ ★ ★ As I went through the papers to retrieve my ads and cut them out for the album I am keeping, I noticed that there were no ads for Tim Toomey, which was odd. I checked on the Office of Campaign and Political Finance reports, and there are no expenditures to Community Newspapers or Prospect Hill Publishing. Has he decided not to bother with print ads? Is his experience that ads in these local papers don't reach enough people to be worth their cost? Or is he so annoyed with these people that he refuses to do business with them? Either way, it is curious that their editors, all tetchy liberated women, should be endorsing him—a pro-life guy who doesn't advertise in their pages—rather than me, a sympathetic pro-choice candidate who does.

Or are the editors so lofty—I remember Deb Eisner's refusal to let me pay for her coffee—that they feel compromised by any advertising and like to demonstrate editorial independence by supporting people who have not bought space in the paper? That's absurd, which does not, of course, make it untrue.

Toomey has spent substantial sums on mailings, but none of these has appeared in our mailbox, which is surprising. Janet is on the voters' lists as "Unenrolled," after all, which makes her a target of any mass mailing.

No ads and no mailings? Dare I think about winning?

★ ★ ★ Less relevant to my race but interesting nonetheless is the odd surge in the stock market during the past week. The Dow has come up a couple of hundred points and has broken back through the ten thousand mark, which, if my tea-leaf reading is correct, is good for President Bush. It is just barely over that mark I set for him some months ago—that he'd win if the Dow were above ten thousand on Election Day. The World Series victory of the Sox over the Cardinals is harder to read in terms of electioneering except as a demonstration that anything is possible.

★ ★ ★ There are four more days of telephoning. It is a terrible job. I can appreciate what a soft life I have that does not oblige me, most of the time, to do such disagreeable chores. In the time that remains, I should be able to get through the precincts that I have yet to do. I keep at it, not because I expect it to make the difference between losing and winning, but as a part of the exercise and to improve my numbers   Or, more candidly, it is less burdensome to do this than to admit that the entire effort has been lunacy and that I should give it up now, walk out of the study, sprawl out on the couch, and read a book, which is how the real me mostly spends his time.

★ ★ ★ The *Jewish Advocate* is heard from:

Slavitt, Toomey battle for State Rep. seat
The race pits newcomer Slavitt against Toomey, a 12-year incumbent
By Shira Schoenberg
Advocate staff

In Middlesex District 26, which includes Cambridge and parts of Somerville, Republican David Slavitt is fighting an uphill battle against Democratic 12-year incumbent Tim Toomey in the race for State Representative.

Both candidates agree that the big issues are financial. Slavitt wants to roll back income taxes from 5.35 percent to 5 percent.

"This is what the governor is trying to get done and what the people said they wanted," Slavitt said.

Toomey countered, "I don't think the state can afford to roll back the personal income tax right now. It will mean major cutbacks in programs of health care, prescriptions, public education and jobs, because of the fiscal situation on a national and state level. These programs serve the needs of my constituents."

Although the district is highly Democratic, neither side is taking the outcome for granted.

"David's campaigning very hard, so we're out there campaigning, too. There's no lock on anything," said Toomey.

Despite the odds, Slavitt maintains hope for victory. "If the Red Sox, who haven't won the World Series since 1918, come and win, can the Republicans be far behind?"

He added, "Even in Cambridge/Somerville, a Republican with the positions I have would look good. Avi Green got 46 percent of the Democratic vote (in the primary). Toomey's not invulnerable."

Both expect high voter turnout due to the presidential election. Toomey, who prides himself on his constituent services, sees high turnout working in his favor: "I have years of experience, people know me on a personal basis, see me in the district."

Slavitt counters that the "amateur" voters may well swing his way. "New voters, people who are not the party faithful and union guys who come out in snowstorms to vote Toomey are very significant."

Although Slavitt knows he is the underdog, he said: "It's healthier for Cambridge/Somerville, for the entire Commonwealth, if the two-party system has two parties."

★ ★ ★ I drove up to Somerville to pick up a *News*, but the new issue is not out until Monday, November 1. The good news is that my ad remains in the current paper over the weekend. The bad news is that I'm hoping that they will endorse me, but if they do, it will come only one day before the voters cast their ballots.

★ ★ ★ I am at the end of my tether. I am just sick and tired of being hung up on by self-righteous twerps who, when they hear me say, "I am David Slavitt, the Republican candidate for state rep . . ." snap back, "I'm not interested," and slam the phone down. Presumably, they are Democrats, full of love for their fellow creatures, earth-hugging, antiwar, gentle souls who, because of their deep humanitarian commitments, can behave like savages and thugs and feel good about it. Women, who ought to be well mannered enough to listen to my next sentence about my being pro-choice and running against a pro-life Democrat, don't even hear me get that far or explain that I am not a scary Ashcroft or Rumsfeld Republican but one of the civilized Massachusetts variety.

Once or twice, I guess, I could be a big boy and take it. But five times in an hour? I am just sick of it. Let them have Tim Toomey and the archbishop and the Vatican and that whole seamless fabric of life. Let them have the mediocrity they deserve. Fuck 'em!

★ ★ ★ A man of character would have just quit at that point, but I didn't. I re-jiggered the spiel to get their attention sooner. "Hello, this is David Slavitt, the pro-choice Republican running for state rep against Tim Toomey, the pro-life Democrat." This put the "pro-choice" in front of the poison party label. It didn't always work, but it got fewer hang ups. And at the end of the call, I suggested that if they liked what they saw on the website or in the ads, they could split their ticket and "vote for me, David Slavitt, for state rep next Tuesday."

I didn't get any solid commitments, but I did get five or six women who said that these were important issues for them and that they would look at my website. It also helps that I have five people making these phone calls for me, each of them supplied with a three- or four-page list and a script, and that what they do I don't have to do myself.

★ ★ ★ Michael Jonas of the *Globe* comes through with a friendly couple of paragraphs:

The Political Trial
By Michael Jonas
October 31, 2004

Finishing with fun
He says the odds against his victory are perhaps 15–1. But Cambridge Republican David Slavitt, who is challenging veteran Democratic state Repre-

sentative Tim Toomey, doesn't seem bothered by that. In fact, the 69-year-old poet and literary translator thinks his odds have improved since the summer, when he considered himself an even longer long shot.

A libertarian-leaning Republican who supports abortion rights and gay marriage, Slavitt has tagged Toomey as an obedient functionary of the Democratic establishment on Beacon Hill. Toomey points to his votes against a constitutional amendment banning gay marriage and support for a hike in the state income tax as evidence of his independence from former House Speaker Tom Finneran.

Toomey opposes abortion, and Slavitt is hoping to pick up votes from some liberal, pro-choice voters who supported Toomey's Democratic primary challenger. With a huge turnout expected for the presidential contest, Slavitt is also looking for support from more independent-minded "amateur voters" who show up for big elections.

Though Lieutenant Governor Kerry Healey made a brief appearance at a recent Slavitt fund-raiser, he has hardly been on a money-raising tear, putting his total take for the campaign in "the upper four figures."

Instead, Slavitt says he's been waging an old-fashioned shoe leather campaign, going door to door in the district.

"I'm learning how to do it," says the professorial political newcomer, who seems like he'd be more comfortable discussing French literature over a glass of wine than water and sewer bills on an East Cambridge doorstep.

"And if I don't get elected I can always sell aluminum siding."

★ ★ ★ Meanwhile, the *Boston Phoenix* endorses Toomey:

Two conservative Democratic legislators who took unexpectedly strong stands in favor of gay marriage have earned the Phoenix's endorsement. In the 26th Middlesex District (parts of Cambridge and Somerville), Representative Tim Toomey should be re-elected over Republican challenger David Slavitt. In the Suffolk and Norfolk District, which includes Dorchester, Senator Marian Walsh is a social conservative who put her career at risk by supporting the right of same-sex couples to wed. She should prevail over her independent challenger, Robert Joyce.

The *Phoenix* is a gay paper, and while Toomey and I have the same position on gay marriage, he's more attractive because he is (a) an incumbent and (b) one of their own.

★ ★ ★ We had our last conference call last night, with candidates asking questions of Alex Dunn and other party functionaries. The most upsetting issue was Linda Fosburg's in the Ninth Middlesex, whose signs have been disappearing out in Lexington and Waltham. She has been informed that there is a five-dollar bounty being paid to high school kids for each of her signs—they tear them down and turn them in to whatever Democrat malefactor or prankster is behind the operation. Petty and nasty, and the worst of it was that Dunn was not surprised. A few of my signs have been knocked down or stolen, but Fred has not suspected anything organized. It is just casual vandalism, which is not exactly comforting but neither is it grounds for paranoia.

19

★ ★ ★ ★ ★ ★ ★ ★ ★ ★ ★ ★ ★ ★ ★ ★ ★ ★ ★

I was up at six, before the alarm went off, and it was as though I was going to the hospital for an operation. But I managed to shave, dress, and march myself off to the polling place with my doorhangers—I have a couple of hundred left, and they won't be any good to anyone tomorrow—and a big Slavitt sign. As I opened the door to the apartment, I saw the *Times* and the *Globe*, and I looked at the editorial page of the latter to see what they had done to me. Surprise! Nothing! Not a word, which is to say that Tim Toomey is not endorsed or mentioned. A triumph? (I was also pleased to see what a mess the writing was. The last paragraph of the editorial said, "Massachusetts polls are open from 7 a.m. to 8 p.m. We look forward to a heavy turnout so no one regrets not voting tomorrow." What they conceivably mean is that there will be a heavy turnout and people should show up early so that no one, tomorrow, will regret not voting. Nobody can vote tomorrow. The election will be over.)

In a better frame of mind, I went out to the City Hall Annex to hand out doorhangers and repeat my mantra about how I am the pro-choice Republican.

★ ★ ★ It felt good out there, at least some of the time. I stood there under my sign, getting what I thought were favorable reactions. Sometimes people would look at the information on the card and ask how I could be a pro-choice Republican, and I'd mention Chris Shays or Weld or Schwarzenegger, and they would go off to vote. As they are leaving, you can tell who voted for you. The ones who didn't avoided eye contact. Those who did gave me a thumbs-up, or wished me luck, or sometimes said, "You got my vote," and there were enough of those so that I figured I had a good chance of carrying at least my home precinct. For part of the morning and then, later in the afternoon, Henry Irving was with me. Janet, when she got back from work, stood out there for a couple of hours. Another young man, Gautam Mukunda, a graduate student at MIT, joined us. It was companionable, if strenuous. Standing, for thirteen hours, is taxing for me, and I had to go back to the apartment in the afternoon for a couple of Advils and a brief lie-down. But I forced myself to get up again because I had the sense that I was making progress and was getting through at least to some of the voters. Now and then, one would say that she'd heard my phone message or we'd talked on the phone, and she was giving me her vote—although it was the first time in her life that she'd voted for a Republican.

Just before eight, it started to drizzle. I was exhausted and didn't have a hat and didn't want my hearing aid to get wet. So I decided to pack it in and go up to the S&S, where we could have a drink, get something to eat, and watch the returns on television.

We stayed until about ten, but I was exhausted and bade everyone good night. Janet and I went home to watch the same results lying down. There was a call from the *Somerville Journal*, from Brock Parker, with numbers that gave Toomey just under 11,000 votes and me 1,680. He wanted a comment. I couldn't believe his numbers. Could I have done that badly? I told him that I'd been watching the returns on television and that I'd rather wait until there was some confirmation from some other source. I fell asleep before eleven, then woke sometime between one and two, turned on the television set, and saw that, yes, he had been right. Toomey had 87 percent of the votes and I had 13 percent.

Catastrophic. I had the worst results of any Republican state rep candidate in Massachusetts. There was a Socialist Workers' Party candidate who did better. There were a couple of Green Party candidates who did better.

What had happened? According to Governor Romney, as reported on television last night and then in the *Globe* this morning, there was a pro-Kerry tidal wave that was too strong for Republicans to swim in, and this was why the Republicans lost a seat in the Senate and two in the House, so that they are now more clearly a splinter party. This is true and not true. The animus against Bush was not a subject Romney could comfortably raise. Exit polling of the Kerry voters showed that 70 percent were anti-Bush and only 30 percent pro-Kerry. A curious phenomenon. More curious—and not discussed in anything I have seen—is the fact that against Gore, Bush got 32 percent of the vote in Massachusetts but against Kerry, 37 percent, so that the tidal wave was running the other way.

Bush's victory nationally takes much of the sting out of my local loss. The voters are supposed to be unimpeachably wise and always right, but it appears from the results of the presidential race that the Democrats are hardly a national party anymore. They are the blue enclaves on the coasts that have nothing to do with the red heartland. I may be out of step with the voters of Cambridge and Somerville, but they are out of step with America and perhaps the solar system. Bush's popular-vote total is the highest in the nation's history. I think of that woman who showed up a little after six last night having spent the day mobilizing Kerry voters in New Hampshire. She had come back to Cambridge to cast her vote in her home precinct. I handed her a brochure and told her that I was the pro-choice guy. She looked at the elephant. A Republican?

Yes, I said, but a liberal, a sane Republican. Surely she believed in women's rights? Surely she was distressed when the bill to allow the over-the-counter sale of morning-after contraceptive pills failed to pass in the House? She could split her ticket. She said she'd never voted for a Republican before. I told her that for some women, the first time is memorable and wonderful. (Late in the day, one takes risks.) She smiled and accepted the doorhanger. But ten minutes later, she came back out having cast her vote, and, apparently, not for me. She returned the doorhanger (No littering! These people are ecologically responsible!) and said that while she was in line, it occurred to her that I had probably voted for George Bush. She couldn't vote for anyone who had voted for Bush.

Maybe my 13 percent is a badge of honor. It is a fraction of a point better than what Bush got in Cambridge. And 1,680 is not a bad number for sales of a book of poems.

★ ★ ★ Tim Toomey returned my call. I congratulated him and said he must be feeling on top of the world. He was gracious—he always is—and said he was glad it was over. I told him that his was more than a victory; it was a triumph. He had the highest percentage of any member of the General Court, and it was a resounding vote of confidence. I told him that I appreciated his civility and decency during the campaign and I wished him well for the next two years—or, as far as I was concerned, the next twenty. I was glad to have met him and I hoped we would continue as friends.

"There are a few friends of mine who get together for dinner on Thursdays. Maybe you'll join us one evening," he said. I said I'd like that.

★ ★ ★ Evan called to console me, and he asked if I'd had fun. I told him yes, but I was glad it was over. Then he said that he was proud of me, the way he was proud of Isaac at the Coast Guard Academy. Both of us were doing things that were good for the country.

Do I believe this? Sometimes.

Epilogue

It is mid-May of 2005. I had a call from Joel Robbins, deputy director of gubernatorial appointments, or from his secretary, actually. We set up an appointment. And I went over to the State House where, in an odd architectural quirk, halfway between the second and third floor, there is a part of the governor's offices tucked into the building—like that floor in *Being John Malkovich*. Robbins is an earnest if guarded young fellow, perhaps in his early thirties. He had my CV—from Amy Speer, I guess, back when I was trying to get myself appointed to some board or other to look sober and responsible and not altogether an outsider. We talked for a while about education, and I was able to say that I supported the governor's views—in particular, those about breaking the power of the teachers' unions and recognizing merit in such programs as the Adams Scholarships. Either as a reward for my yeoman service in the political wars or because we agree about these things and he wants his views represented there, Governor Romney wants me to serve as a member of the Board of Trustees of Bunker Hill Community College.

It isn't a payoff, because the position doesn't pay anything. And it was flattering to hear that I would be part of the governor's "legacy." (Will he run for reelection in 2006? Or will he focus his attentions, as he sometimes seems to be doing, on a run for the White House in 2008?) But it could certainly happen that he is either defeated or doesn't run again, and Robbins said that the trusteeship is a five-year term.

Bunker Hill Community College? It is one of the Massachusetts Community Colleges, two-year institutions that feed into the UMass system and that provide opportunities to those who didn't get terrific secondary schooling, or didn't do well, or didn't test well, and want to come back and try again, demonstrating that they can do college-level work. Education is meritocratic, but there ought to be a variety of ways of demonstrating merit. The school even has a fairly extensive program for ex-convicts who are trying to make themselves more attractive to employers. There are some seven thousand students, and there's a budget of just under $50 million a year.

And I can get there by the subway. So, why not? It's an honor, and it might be interesting.

Of course it is exactly the opposite of what I'd had in mind. The appointment, I had hoped, would make me look plausible to the voters; as it turns out, it was the campaign that made me look plausible to the governor and his appointments staff.

When the official word comes through, I'll go over there and buy myself a Bunker Hill Community College T-shirt.

INDEX

David R. Slavitt is abbreviated as "DS" throughout the index.

amendment to federal constitution banning same-sex marriage: Daschle as unenthusiastic about, 201; point as to embarrass not legislate, 176; Romney supports, 147–48, 150, 265; vote against closure on, 178

amendment to state constitution banning same-sex marriage: all representative candidates opposing, 151; Constitutional Convention passes, 65–66; as cumbersome process, 47; DS opposes, 218; Finneran proposes, 50–51; "leadership compromise" amendment, 59–60; legislators holding back on, 14; public opinion opposed to, 10; as reaction to state supreme court decision, 7; slipping in other amendments along with, 49–50; SupportEquality.org opposing, 221–22; Toomey opposing, 14, 220, 221–22, 284, 330; as unlikely to pass, 150, 223

American Heritage Foundation, 127

antigang legislation, 95–96, 109, 116, 118, 213, 232

antimiscegenation law of 1913, 66, 85, 113–14, 141–42, 176–77

anti-Semitism, 87–88, 237

Antonioni, Robert, 103

Ashcroft, John, 71, 287, 329

assault weapons, 152, 186, 302

Asselin, Christopher, 228, 229

Auden, W. H., 89

Avalon, Frankie, 88

Avella, David, 262, 273, 286

Ayers, Patty, 312

Babineau, Michele, 263, 289, 315

Babson, Richard, 268, 270, 275, 286, 289–90, 291, 311, 321, 324

Baird, Dane, 27, 28, 83, 43–44, 94, 291, 292

Baker, Fred: becomes campaign manager for DS, 49; as Cambridge Republican City Committee chairman, 73,

74, 135; at campaign strategy breakfast, 232; on campaign tchotchkes, 156; and City Wide Dance Party, 186, 187; at coffee for DS, 151; collecting signatures for DS, 49, 68; draft fundraising letter of, 143–45; DS asks about event at subsidized-living apartments, 245; and DS fund-raiser with Healey, 207, 268, 274, 275; on DS getting signs in windows, 158; on DS going to Republican caucus, 92; DS reminded about Patriot's Day by, 75, 81; on DS's candidacy as turning some heads, 307; on DS-Toomey poll result, 285–86; Fourth of July picnic held by, 163; and Gay Pride parade, 134; and getting-out-the-vote calls, 314–15; at Harvard Yard picnic, 197, 198; helping with DS's mailing, 156; on Mid-Cambridge Neighborhood Association function, 159; on Paine Park Neighborhood Association meeting, 95, 96, 106; and possible endorsement of DS by Green, 214; at Sacred Heart Church bingo game, 316–17; on signs disappearing, 331; at stand-out, 311; on thanking larger donors, 166; and Toomey debate with DS, 161, 239, 262, 265, 288, 295

Barnicle, Mike, 66

Barrios, Jarrett: antigang bill opposed by, 213; and antimiscegenation law of 1913, 114; and Central Square World's Fair, 189; district redrawn, 69; Green as campaign manager for, 5, 25, 173; Green breaking with, 25, 100; at NARAL meeting, 270; as openly gay, 15; thank-you cards used by, 38

Bastardi, Maureen, 290

Bayne, Ian, 120

belief: as most difficult obstacle to running for office, 244–45

Belluck, Pam, 11

benefits for same-sex partners, 48, 202

Bush, George W., (*continued*)
Kerry in polls, 242; Leiter hosts
Bush/Cheney party, 179; Log Cabin
Republicans and, 66; and Marshall
appointment at Yale, 143; national
convention delegates and, 92; national
victory of, 333–34; party for Bush/
Cheney campaign, 90, 91; Romney
appearing with, 236; and Rove, 15;
same-sex marriage opposed by, 7, 85;
South Carolina as likely to vote for, 43;
stock market surge helping, 327; tax
cuts of, 244; virulence of sentiment
against, 191, 287, 333; and Whitman
at EPA, 141
Bush, Jeb, 149
Bush, Laura, 179

Cambridge: as anti-Harvard, 4; death
penalty opposed in, 26; and Democratic National Convention, 180; disparity between Democrats and Republicans in, 20; earnestness in, 251;
Festival of SS Cosmas and Damian
in, 250, 254–55; gay city council
members in, 9, 284; habitual liberalism of, 37; Kerry nomination hurting
DS in, 42, 52, 56; as left of most of
the Commonwealth, 223; library, 43,
298; licenses for same-sex couples
issued in, 9, 112; Patriot's Day in, 81;
as "People's Republic," 87, 307; pockets of squalor in, 206; redistricting in,
68; rising real estate prices in, 30;
same-sex marriage supported in, 66;
Toomey as giving to poor of, 15; and
transient population, 44
Cambridge Chronicle: article on torching
of Green sign, 179; on Babson campaign finances, 289–90, 291; on Citizens for Limited Taxation endorsement of DS, 287–88; at debate between
three candidates, 160, 168–71; DS
announces filing of his petitions, 75;
on DS announcing candidacy, 34,
48; DS asked views on redistricting,
68, 72; DS kickoff piece in, 280; DS
letter on Toomey's charter school veto
vote, 183, 191; DS letter on Toomey's
debate claim, 314, 315; on DS on drug
abuse, 315–16, 317; DS sends press
release about Reform slate, 123, 132;
DS takes out ad in, 130, 221, 319,
324; Eisner interviews DS, 8, 21–22,
24, 298; Eisner's campaign finance
story, 320–21, 324; embarrassment
as goal of, 321; on Green-Toomey
campaign accusations, 230–32;
Griffin column on DS in, 322–24;
headline announcing Toomey primary
victory, 263, 279–80; Imrie letter to,
242–43; interviews to determine endorsement of, 289; letter on Green's
manners, 179–80; media kit sent to,
11; on NARAL endorsement of DS,
299; on nurses' endorsement of
Toomey, 132–33, 143; on Peixoto
candidacy, 59; press release about
DS's grandson, 159–60, 166; on *The
Regrets of Joachim du Bellay*, 261–62;
Toomey campaign material quoting,
121; Toomey endorsed in general
election by, 324; Toomey endorsed
in primary by, 250
Cambridge Citywide Senior Center,
281–82
Cambridge Community Television, 32,
35–37, 160, 164, 188–89, 195, 267, 286
Cambridge Republican City Committee,
20–21, 45, 73–74, 163, 265, 287, 305
Cambridge Senior Town Meeting, 270
campaign finance: Eisner story on,
320–21, 324, 325–26; Finance Plan,
130, 135–36, 139–40; financial disclosure forms, 76–77; in kind contributions, 235, 290, 300; of Toomey and
Green versus DS, 248. *See also* fund-
raising

venality of, 247; voter registration in Somerville, 9; voters express dissatisfaction with, 46. *See also* Progressive Democrats

Dempsey, Brian, 228

de Sponde, Jean, 93

DiCara, Lawrence, 114

Di Masi, Salvatore, 271, 272–73, 273–74, 293, 323

DiPaola, James V., 198, 214, 243, 259

Disraeli, Benjamin, 27

diversity, 89, 122

Dixon, Vincent, 191

DNA evidence, 302

Dole, Robert, 140

Donaldson, Annie, 266

doorhangers: of DS, 37, 45, 91, 112, 113, 133, 201, 319, 332, 334; of Toomey, 223–24

door-to-door canvassing, 133, 206, 243–44, 245, 293, 318–19

double-dipping, 3–4, 16, 180, 206, 254, 297, 303

Dow, Jody, 133

Dowgiewicz, Mark, 244

Dreiser, Theodore, 57

Drinan, Robert, 304

drivers' licenses for illegal aliens, 203–4, 250

Druce, Joseph, 25, 26, 302

drugs and alcohol, 21, 27, 309–10, 315–16, 325

Dryden, John, 89

du Bellay, Joachim, 13, 75, 200, 261

Dukakis, Michael, 19, 33, 42, 242

Dumbing Down: Essays on the Strip-Mining of American Culture (Slavitt), 58–59

Dunn, Alex: automated poll for DS-Toomey race approved by, 278; and Campaign Portal, 155, 156, 162, 165; conference call with candidates, 222, 223, 255; as not returning DS's phone calls, 277; on signs disappearing, 331; on targeted campaigns, 264–65, 273

Eagleton, Thomas, 20

East End House, 231, 232

Edmunds, Lowell, 9

education: Adams Scholarships, 57, 94, 335; charter schools, 103, 170, 182–83, 191, 218, 242, 247; DS named Bunker Hill Community College trustee, 335–36; DS supporting "excellence" in, 8, 39, 201, 241; DS's views on as unpopular, 56–58; DS wanting to get on Education Committee, 94; elitism in competitive, 39; equalization of funding for, 109; grade inflation, 58–59; instate tuition for children of undocumented aliens, 202–3, 305, 314; "Legacy of Learning" program, 38–39; MCAS tests, 38–39, 57, 128, 253; as occurring in the home, 32–33; prayer in public schools, 71, 74; preschool programs, 32–33; as privilege not right, 8; in Somerville and Cambridge, 30; teachers colleges, 57; teachers' unions, 33, 39, 183, 191, 218, 247, 335; Toomey on "a penny for education," 224; Toomey on public, 191; as unfair, 218; universal literacy, 7

Edwards, John, 40, 41, 56, 202, 326

Edwards, Mickey, 201, 205, 206, 207, 235

Eisner, Deborah: campaign finance story by, 320–21, 324, 325–26; DS asked about redistricting by, 68, 69, 72; DS asked about views on same-sex marriage by, 8; DS interviewed by, 21–22, 24, 181, 298; on Peixoto candidacy, 59; refuses to let DS buy coffee, 21, 327

Eliot, T. S., 196

English language immersion, 12, 137

environmentalism, 62–63, 180

Environmental Protection Agency, 141

Estrich, Susan, 19

Ethics Commission, 76, 77

evolution, 201

Exhibitionist, The (Sutton), 23, 200

tenant governor appearing at events, 206, 207; Healey at fund-raiser for DS, 197, 206, 207–8, 209, 210, 211, 221, 267, 268, 273, 274–75, 277, 280, 292–93, 330; Kaplan and Bernays wine and cheese reception, 222, 298; *Somerville Journal* on DS's, 290–92
Funnell, David, 125–26
Fussell, Paul, 41

Gabor, Zsa-Zsa, 36
Galluccio, Anthony, 38, 69
Galvin, William, 52, 72, 76, 175
gangs, 95–96; antigang legislation, 95–96, 109, 116, 118, 213, 232; DS on, 99, 109; Green on, 99, 109, 116, 118, 181, 213, 232; MS-13 gang, 96, 99, 109, 213, 232; Toomey on, 109, 116, 243
Gantt, Harvey, 24–25
Gauvin, Mat, 223
Gay, Dorothy Kelly, 27
Gay and Lesbian Advocates and Defenders, 141, 176
gay marriage. *See* same-sex marriage
Gay Pride parade, 117, 129, 134–35
gays. *See* homosexuality
Gays and Lesbians Against Discrimination (GLAD), 7, 66
Geis, Bernard, 200
genetically engineered food, 62–63
gentrification, 303
Geoghan, John, 25, 302
Gephardt, Richard, 16, 40
Geraigery, Richard, 113
gerrymandering, 249, 250
Getting Out the Vote session, 314
Gillespie, Edward, 122
Giuliani, Rudy, 20, 210, 239
Gleason, Jackie, 55
Glidden, Kate, 196, 267, 284, 321
Glynn, Kristine, 189, 290
Goodrich, Andrew, 222, 223

Gordon, Louis, 4, 5, 56, 93–94, 178, 246, 299
Gore, Albert, 16, 19, 42, 191, 226, 333
grade inflation, 58–59
Granda, Michele, 176–77
Gray, Winifred, 149
Greater Boston (television program), 11, 28, 85
Green, Avi: alleged to be gay, 15; amendment banning same-sex marriage opposed by, 221–22; asks to meet with DS, 22–23; as awkward about meeting people, 159; as Barrios campaign manager, 5, 25, 173; *Boston Phoenix* endorses, 252–53; breaks with Barrios, 25, 100; campaign finances of, 248, 321; and Central Square World's Fair, 189; on charter schools moratorium, 170, 242; and City Wide Dance Party, 186; at "Cleaning Day at East End House," 143; on corporate tax credits, 242; debates with Toomey and DS, 84, 151, 152, 157, 160, 168–71, 184–85, 299; on Democrats in power, 25; DS asks for general election support from, 213–14, 232, 250–51, 267–68; DS expecting to be defeated by, 73; DS on Toomey avoiding debating, 239; DS preferring to run against, 188; DS seeks primary supporters of, 202, 232–33, 235, 253, 260, 261, 273, 287, 290, 291, 308, 313, 330; and DS's literary career, 200; DS's open letter to, 267–68, 280; DS's wife in mailings of, 219, 249; DVD of, 251; Finneran opposed by, 25, 173, 209, 213, 252–53, 261, 267–68; flier sent to DS by, 209; on gangs, 99, 109, 116, 181, 213; gun control supported by, 249, 251, 252; and Harvard Yard picnic, 198, 209, 219; Imrie's criticism of, 242–43; Jonas articles on Toomey and, 167, 172–74, 202; Lavender Alliance

Green, Avi (*continued*)
endorsing, 284; letter on manners of, 179–80; loses primary, 260, 262; meets with DS, 24–25; meets with *Somerville News* editors, 99–100; at Mid-Cambridge Neighborhood Association function, 159; NARAL endorses, 232, 260; and National Rifle Association, 186; and nominating petitions, 45; NOW endorses, 177, 232; primary race against Toomey, 5, 21, 24, 25, 64, 72, 90, 120, 135, 172–74, 178, 179–80, 191, 194, 204, 219, 229, 230–32, 244, 245, 246, 248–49, 255, 259, 260, 307, 324, 328; as pro-choice, 171, 209, 232, 242, 251, 252, 261, 264, 267, 268, 279, 293, 308; Progressive Democrats endorse, 181, 196; "radical economic change" remark of, 191, 196; signs of, 165, 176, 179; at Somerville debate, 83; at *Somerville News* candidates' forum, 74, 108–10, 115–16; *Somerville News* endorses Toomey in primary, 234; and *Somerville News* party at Toast, 102; and Somerville Senior Citizen's Picnic, 214, 219; and Springfield financial crisis, 128; as subject to Finneran's leadership, 94; success in Somerville, 262–63; and tape of Progressive Democrats debate, 188, 194–96, 198–99, 202; tax cuts opposed by, 108–9; at Temple Beth Shalom, 177; and Temple Beth Shalom candidates' night, 219, 231; Toomey endorsed by, 272, 293
Greenberger, Scott, 33, 234
Green line extension, 100, 116, 160, 168, 169, 224, 303, 323
Green Party: DS filtering out of electoral lists, 20; DS offers to debate Johnston, 284; DS polling behind some candidates of, 333; Green at meeting of, 191, 196; Lachelier candidacy, 5, 286, 287; as promising not to field candi-

date, 5, 25; in Somerville voter registration drive, 9
Griffin, Richard, 263, 322
Grossman, Steve, 191
Grynbaum, Michael Mendel, 61, 86, 90, 306, 312
Guha, Auditi, 290, 298, 308, 312, 315, 316
Gumbel, Bryant, 36
gun control: assault weapons, 152, 186, 302; DS on, 113, 152, 167, 302; Green supports, 249, 251, 252; libertarians on, 146; National Rifle Association questionnaire on, 185–86; Toomey supports, 220
Gun Owners' Political Action Committee, 221, 222, 224, 225–28

Hamilton, Alexander, 148
Harshbarger, Scott, 99
Harvard Crimson, 61, 86–90, 194, 303, 306, 312
Harvard University: Cambridge as anti-, 4; DS on significance to Cambridge of, 4, 303, 323; high cost of student housing at, 101; Leverett House, 33, 61, 306; low-cost housing development of, 22; one-party government exploited by, 35–36; Toomey as robbing, 4, 15, 22, 90, 137, 138, 143, 171, 284; Toomey's plan to tax, 302, 307; Yale defeated by, 9
Harvard Yard senior citizens' picnic, 197–98, 208, 209, 210, 219
Havel, Vaclav, 42
H-Block gang, 96, 109
Head Start, 33
Healey, Kerry: antigang bill signed by, 232; campaign contribution to DS, 24, 272, 324; at DS fund-raiser, 197, 206, 207–8, 209, 210, 211, 221, 267, 268, 273, 274–75, 277, 280, 292–93, 330; DS speculates about her job, 235; at

Huckabee reception, 149; Kerry called on to resign from Senate by, 140, 149; philosophical differences with DS, 274, 293, 304; at preconvention breakfast, 204, 205; reception for Whitman and, 140–41; at Reform slate roll-out, 121, 122, 123, 124; at Republican National Convention, 236, 237; Republican Party gets signatures for, 3

Healey, Sean, 24

healthcare, 217

Healy, Robert W., 184

Hees, William, 145, 146

Helms, Chris, 168

Helms, Jesse, 25

Hemingway, Ernest, 89, 101, 118

Henry Sutton novels, 36, 200

Heritage Foundation, 150

Hickey, Cindy, 214, 215

Higgins, Karen, 132

"high interest" candidacies, 244

Hilton, Paris, 23

Hirsh, Jane, 285

Hitler, Adolph, 51

Ho Chi Minh, 244

Holder, Doug, 100, 101, 129, 131–32, 175

homelessness, 153, 217, 274

home rule, 95, 96, 97, 109, 116, 213

homosexuality: benefits for same-sex partners, 48, 202; Gay Pride parade, 117, 129, 134–35; Gays and Lesbians Against Discrimination, 7, 66; Lavender Alliance, 202, 276, 284, 285; Log Cabin Republicans, 7, 60, 66–67, 116–17, 134, 270, 308; U.S. Supreme Court decision decriminalizes, 6, 7, 218. See also same-sex marriage

House Bill 1282, 104, 132–33

housing: affordable, 153, 160, 168–69, 209, 217; homelessness, 153, 217, 274; rent control, 30, 84; rooming houses, 153, 217; student, 101

Howell, Carla, 166

Huckabee, Mike, 147, 148, 149–50, 153

Huckabee, Sarah, 149–50

Hunter, Benjamin, 156

Hunter, Karen, 311

Hussein, Saddam, 9, 23

Hyde, Susan, 285

Ianno, Dominick, 24, 210

illegal aliens, 202–4, 250, 305, 314

Imrie, Susan, 242–43, 279–80, 311

incumbents: Democratic Party as party of incumbency, 37, 71, 92, 247, 307; elections rigged in favor of, 6, 252; as loyal only to incumbency and power, 31; number of signatures on nominating petitions set by, 50

independents, 37, 44–45, 46

initiative referenda. *See* referenda

in kind contributions, 235, 290, 300

interns, 140, 265–66

Iowa caucuses, 40–41

Iraq war, 9–10, 102–3, 112, 184, 244, 283, 287, 304

Irish, 3, 71, 82, 111, 120, 204, 231

Irving, Henry, 311, 332

Italians, 71, 82, 111, 231, 255

Jackson, Kenneth, 185

Jacob, Max, 93

Jacome, Juan, 156, 164, 165

Jefferson, Thomas, 15

Jehlen, Patricia, 27, 28, 83, 296

Jenkins, Shawn, 92, 136

Jewish Advocate, 194, 216–19, 251–52, 327–28

Jewish Community Advocacy Day, 60

Jews, 60, 87–88, 111, 187, 231

Johnson, Philip W., 123

Johnson, Samuel, 36

Johnston, Carolina, 284

Jonas, Michael: article on DS-Toomey race, 329–30; articles on Green and Toomey, 167, 172, 173, 174; at debate

polls, 273, 278, 281, 285–86, 287
Ponge, Francis, 90, 93
Pope, Alexander, 69
Popkins, Samuel, 227–28
Popovics, Paula, 180
position papers, 190
Powell, Colin, 20, 41
prayer in public schools, 71, 74
preschool programs, 32–33
press release, 11–13, 19, 28, 31, 34
primary election results, 260, 261–62
pro-choice position. See abortion
Progressive Democrats: CD of debate of,
201–2; debate sponsored by, 151–53,
168, 184–85; Green endorsed by, 181,
196; tape of debate of, 194–96, 198–99
pro-life position. See abortion
Proust, Marcel, 75
publicly-funded elections, 249–50
push cards, 11
Pushkin, Aleksandr, 13

Quinn benefits, 303, 323

Rather, Dan, 279
Rauschenberg, Robert, 245
Reagan, Nancy, 21
Reagan, Ronald, 17, 129, 149, 190
recycling, 63
redistricting, 68–69, 72, 76, 108, 250
Reeves, Kenneth: and announcement of
Toomey's primary victory, 263; debate
between three candidates moderated
by, 151, 157, 160, 168; at Harvard Yard
picnic, 198; and MIT senior citizens'
picnic, 107; at Taste of Cambridge,
184; Toomey endorsed by, 220
referenda: on Clean Election Law, 12, 50,
69, 93, 137, 247, 249; on death penalty,
26, 50, 93, 137, 247; Finneran and
Democrats ignoring, 50, 93, 108, 137,
144, 148, 246, 247, 252; on tax rate,
93, 108, 181, 192, 217–18, 247, 252,
297

Regrets of Joachim du Bellay, The (Slavitt),
13, 75, 200, 261
regulation, 101
Reich, Robert, 219
Reilly, Thomas: and antimiscegenation
law of 1913, 66, 85, 141, 142, 176, 177;
education of, 67; as possible Romney
opponent, 240; same-sex marriage
opposed by, 10, 66; as unbeatable
incumbent, 3
rent control, 30, 84
representatives: extending term of, 50,
93
Republican Legislative Campaign Fund,
182
Republican Party: Cambridge Republican City Committee, 20–21, 45,
73–74, 163, 265, 287, 305; caucus to
select national convention delegates,
91–92; disparity between Democrats
and Republicans in Cambridge, 20;
DS as too liberal for, 7; Finance Plan
required of candidates by, 130, 135–36,
139–40; Log Cabin Republicans, 7, 60,
66–67, 116–17, 134, 270, 308; Massachusetts versus far-right, 37, 71; Massachusetts voters electing governors
from, 12; moderates not ceding to
right-wing homophobes, 239, 287;
national resurgence of, 205; pro-Kerry
tide defeating Massachusetts, 333;
recruiting candidates to run against
incumbents, 91, 124; in Somerville,
9, 27, 120, 290, 291, 326; Toomey on
difference between Democrats and,
161, 305–6; women in, 141
Revere, Paul, 82
revival meeting, 125–27
Rimbaud, Arthur, 241
Robbins, Joel S., 335
Rogers, John, 271, 272–73, 274
Rogers, Kevin, 196
Roman Catholic Church. See Catholic
Church

Romney, Ann, 24, 26–27, 149, 205

Romney, George, 317

Romney, Mitt: Adams Scholarships proposal of, 57, 94, 335; antimiscegenation law of 1913 enforced by, 66, 85, 113–14, 141, 142; appointing successor to Kerry, 52–53, 134, 174–75, 192–93; Belmont carried by, 74; *Boston Globe* criticizes for being out of state too much, 234–35, 236–37, 239–40; boyish charm of, 17; campaign contribution to DS, 23, 24, 272, 324; campaign letter from New York from, 237–38; campaign to elect more Republicans to Senate, 37; and Carcieri breakfast, 235; on charter schools, 103, 182–83, 191; and civil unions, 51; at conference of mayors, 158; death penalty supported by, 25, 26, 264–65; and debate between three candidates, 169; difficult job of, 18; disavows remarks about Finneran, 268–69; DS and Baird depicted as creatures of, 292, 300, 304; DS appointed Trustee of Bunker Hill Community College by, 335; DS endorsed by, 143; DS invited to holiday dinner by, 13, 16–17; in DS's campaign material, 266, 271; DS seeks commission appointment from, 5, 56; DS soliciting from donors to, 82, 175; federal amendment banning same-sex marriage supported by, 147–48, 150, 265; Finneran as having more power than, 137; Finneran meets at Ashmont T stop, 269; Green as running against, 25; Harvard Club breakfast given by, 201; Healey as possible Senate nomination by, 140; Healey chosen as running mate by, 3; at Heritage Foundation, 150; at Huckabee reception, 147, 149; instate tuition for undocumented aliens vetoed by, 202–3, 305, 314; justification for running for office of, 17, 52, 110, 324; kosher food in nursing homes vetoed by, 60–61; "Legacy of Learning" program of, 38–39; as listening to DS, 309; Log Cabin Republicans and, 66; lowered expectations of, 312, 313; as Massachusetts-type Republican, 37, 71; morning-after pill opposed by, 162; and opposition candidates for General Court, 33, 124, 182, 208; Parker Omni rally for, 38–39; philosophical differences with DS, 274, 293, 304; popularity rating of, 260; as possibly quitting as governor, 209; at preconvention breakfast, 205–6; presidential ambitions of, 235, 237, 240, 335; on pro-Kerry tide defeating Republicans, 333; reform of legislature demanded by, 228, 247; Reform slate of, 121–22, 123, 280; at Republican National Convention, 236, 237; same-sex marriage opposed by, 7, 8, 10, 47, 51, 60, 150; on state party support for candidates, 205–6; supplemental budget of, 128; as sworn to uphold state constitution, 8, 51; as targeting legislative races, 264–65, 271–72; tax cuts proposed by, 108, 128, 217–18; Toomey criticizes, 271–72, 300, 301, 305–6; on Travaglini-Lees amendment, 65, 66; *Turnaround* signing, 196–97

Romney, Tagg, 205

Ronsard, Pierre de, 200

rooming houses, 153, 217

Rooney, Andy, 28

Rooney, Emily, 11, 28–29, 85

Roosevelt, James, 85, 86

Rorty, Richard, 37

Rosenberg, Stanley, 114

Rove, Karl, 15

Rowe, Mark, 277

Rumsfeld, Donald, 9, 102, 103, 329

Rushing, Byron, 152

Russo, Joseph, 7

Sacred Heart Church bingo game,
316–17
salary of state representatives, 54
Salem Broadcasting Company, 276
same-sex marriage: and antimiscegenation law of 1913, 66, 85, 113–14, 141–42,
176–77; Cambridge issues licenses
for, 9, 112; Cambridge Republicans
oppose, 74; Catholic Church opposes,
14, 35; DS supports, 12, 48, 71, 89,
107, 112, 113, 116, 126, 127, 143, 177,
178, 179, 189, 190, 201, 228, 252, 330;
Green supports, 252; Kerry opposes,
148; Massachusetts Supreme Court
ruling on, 7–8, 47, 218, 239; as not
huge issue, 223; public opinion polls
on, 10; Republican Right opposes,
239; Romney opposes, 7, 8, 10, 47,
51, 60, 150; Evan Slavitt urges DS to
make issue of, 8; some gays oppose,
11, 14; state constitutional amendments against, 200; Thune opposes,
201; Toomey supports, 48, 202, 252,
330. See also amendment to federal
constitution banning same-sex
marriage; amendment to state constitution banning same-sex marriage;
civil unions
Sampson, Gary Lee, 25, 26, 152
Sanchez, Ken, 66, 67, 134
Sanchez, Nicolas, 125
Santorum, Rick, 148
Schmarsow, Emmett, 282
Schoenberg, Shira, 194, 216, 218–19, 251,
327
Schwarzenegger, Arnold, 4, 12, 19, 39,
239, 332
Searcy, William A., 240
self-esteem, cult of, 58–59
Selvaggio, Nina, 177
Sergeant, Francis, 37
Seuss, Dr. (Theodore Geisel), 23
Severin, Jay, 11, 28
Share, Don, 240

Shays, Christopher, 184, 332
Sheinfeld, Peter, 156
signatures on nominating petitions:
challenging, 63–64, 136; collecting,
13–14, 43, 46, 48–49, 51, 61–62,
67–68, 73, 83, 86–87, 245; DS files,
75–76; going through voter rolls for
names, 44–45; Harvard Crimson observ-
ing collection of, 61, 86–87; number
required set by incumbents, 50; redistricting and validity of, 69, 76; Republican Party offering contribution for
turning in by April 22, 74; validated,
55, 83–84
signs: cost of, 113, 254; disappearance of,
331; DS canvassing houses with Green
signs, 232–33; DS picks up, 124; at
Gay Pride parade, 117; getting people
to put in windows, 127, 146–47, 158,
165, 166, 171–72, 175–76, 185, 192,
253–54; mounting on sticks, 129–30;
Somerville former ban on, 216; torching of Green sign, 179; at Writer to
Writer appearance, 131
Simmons, Denise, 220, 270
Slavitt, Evan: asks whether DS is having
fun, 52; attorney general campaign of,
3, 71, 88–89; and Campaign Portal
problem, 165; collecting signatures
for DS, 49, 62, 175; and conference
call with candidates, 223; consoles DS
on his defeat, 334; on debate between
three candidates, 160; and Democratic
National Convention security, 190;
DS as "Evan Slavitt's father," 278;
on DS being more low-key, 283; DS
campaign finance report filing by,
321; on DS campaigning on same-sex
marriage issue, 8; on DS challenging
Finneran to debate, 233; DS collects
signatures for, 13; DS dines with, 319;
on DS doing what's entertaining, 124,
285; DS encouraged to run by, 3, 71,
89, 102; at DS fund-raiser with Healey,

teachers' unions, 33, 39, 183, 191, 218, 247, 335

telephoning, 113, 312–13, 314–15, 317, 318, 327

television: violence in children attributed to, 32

Temple Beth Shalom (Temple Street shul), 177, 187, 219, 231, 239

Tennant, George, 128

term limits, 152, 272

Thune, John, 201

Tierney, John, 69

Times Literary Supplement, 178, 225

Toast poetry reading, 240–41

Tolman, Warren, 103, 249

Toomey, Tim, 3–4; advantages as incumbent and city council member, 20; amendment banning same-sex marriage opposed by, 14, 220, 221–22, 284, 330; antigang ordinance supported by, 109, 116; on "a penny for education," 224; attempting to get Republicans to vote in Democratic primary, 229–30; *Boston Globe* endorses in primary, 259; *Boston Globe* not endorsing in general election, 332; *Boston Phoenix* endorses, 330; on Cambridge buying Catholic properties, 55; *Cambridge Chronicle* endorses, 250, 324; *Cambridge Chronicle* headline announcing primary victory of, 263, 279–80; Cambridge City Council on primary victory of, 264–65, 276–77; at Cambridge Citywide Senior Center, 282; at Cambridge Senior Town Meeting, 270; campaign expenditures from last election, 124, 135; campaign finances of, 144, 248, 290, 321, 324, 325–26; campaign manager named by, 308; and Central Square World's Fair, 189; challenging DS's nominating petitions, 63–64; on charter school veto, 183, 191; Citizens for Limited Taxation on, 289; and City Wide Dance

Party, 186; as "confirmed bachelor," 15; on corporate tax credits, 242; and corrupt legislators, 228, 229; and death penalty, 159, 170, 252; debates with Green and DS, 84–85, 137–38, 142, 151, 152, 157, 160–61, 168–71, 184–85, 299; debate with DS, 161, 239, 241, 246, 262, 265, 267, 268, 276, 283, 286, 289, 295–98, 299–310, 322, 323; as decent man, 96, 115, 117, 138, 143, 246; dinner sponsored at subsidized housing by, 245; as doing nothing for Cambridge or Somerville, 30; doorhanger of, 223–24; as "double dipper," 3–4, 180, 206; on drug programs, 315–16; DS announces candidacy opposing, 12; DS as poet opponent for, 6–7; DS at parish church of, 316; DS campaigns in neighborhood of, 224–25; DS conceding to, 151, 224, 285, 334; DS concerned about debating, 43; DS congratulates on primary win, 260, 262; DS defeated by, 333, 334; DS expecting to be defeated by, 73; DS meets, 96, 97; DS needing to be within ten points to get party aid, 273, 278, 281, 285; DS seen as having a chance against, 37, 72; and DS's literary career, 200; DS speculates whether he would support DS if he loses, 232; DS's wife in mailings of, 120, 157, 220; DS trying to place signs near office of, 147; as Finneran's henchman, 4, 74, 83, 89, 115, 117, 137, 152, 174, 180, 206, 233, 252–53, 271, 296, 330; fund-raising letter of, 271–72; as gay, 15, 284; Green endorses, 272, 293; Green preferring to DS, 100; at Harvard Yard picnic, 198; on high turnout as favoring him, 328; and illegal aliens, 204, 305, 314; Jonas articles on Green and, 167, 172–74, 202; Lachelier race, 5, 286; Lavender Alliance endorses, 284, 285; local

unions: Democrats taxing to buy votes from, 128, 138, 171; Kerry refuses to cross picket line, 157–59, 169; Lavender Alliance members belonging to, 284; mayor reaches accord with, 190; nurses', 105, 217; PACs, 292; teachers', 33, 39, 183, 191, 218, 247, 335; Toomey and, 110, 132, 243, 292, 297, 305, 309

Vennochi, Joan, 148
vetoes: of bill for instate tuition for children of undocumented aliens, 202–3; of bill for special election to fill Kerry's seat, 52–53; of moratorium on charter schools, 183, 191; number not overturned, 202; votes needed for sustaining, 12, 31, 83, 92, 93, 118, 153, 301
Vidal, Gore, 129
vote buying, 298

Wagner, Richard, 102
Walker, Thomas, 125
Wallace, George, 255
Walsh, Marian, 330
Waltz, Marty, 270, 275, 290
Warner, John, 148
"War on Drugs," 21, 309–10
war on terror, 310
Washington, George, 9, 178
Waugh, Evelyn, 242

websites, 104, 172, 189–90, 220–21, 225, 312
Weiss, Paul, 32
Weld, William: DS as Weld Republican, 319, 332; DS endorsed by, 243, 259, 260, 266, 277, 280, 308; at Huckabee reception, 147, 149; as Massachusetts-type Republican, 37, 71; as not "real" Republican to right wingers, 239; and Papalimberis, 33; Toomey criticizes, 300
welfare-to-work programs, 33–34
Weltman, Eric, 168, 195, 199, 209
Wheatley, Larry, 311
White, William, Jr., 95, 99, 102, 109, 118, 120, 151, 216
Whitman, Christine Todd, 140–41
Whitman, Walt, 89
Wilmot, Pamela, 58, 69, 248, 250
Wilson, Edmund, 7
Winters, Robert, 90
Wiseman, Frederick, 247
Wolf, Alice, 174, 189, 198, 284
Wolfe, Tom, 317
Wolfowitz, Paul, 9
World Health Organization, 241
Writer to Writer (television program), 100, 129, 131–32, 175

Yeats, William Butler, 34–35, 129
yellow press, 7

ABOUT THE AUTHOR

David R. Slavitt was born in White Plains, New York, in 1935 and educated at Andover, Yale, and Columbia University. A poet, translator, novelist, critic, and journalist, he is the author of more than eighty works of fiction, poetry, and poetry and drama in translation. He is also coeditor of the Johns Hopkins *Complete Roman Drama in Translation* series and *Penn Greek Drama* series. He lives in Cambridge, Massachusetts.